Binding Theory

Binding Theory seeks to explain how different kinds of nominal expressions such as names, noun phrases, and pronouns have anaphoric relations among one another, and how they come to have reference to things in the world. This textbook provides a thorough and comprehensive introduction to modern Binding Theory. Starting at a very basic level, it introduces the reader to a huge variety of nominal and especially pronominal expressions from the world's languages, the ways they can be used, and current theorizing about their grammatical properties and their interpretation. Daniel Büring discusses a wide range of cross-linguistic data and theoretical approaches, and, unlike in existing introductions, pairs the discussion of syntactic facts with a detailed introduction to the semantic interpretation of binding structures. Written in a clear and accessible style, and with numerous exercises and examples, this textbook will be invaluable to graduate and advanced undergraduate students of syntax and semantics.

DANIEL BÜRING teaches linguistics at the University of California, Los Angeles. He has published various influential articles in formal semantics, syntax, and pragmatics, in particular on intonational meaning, focus, and binding theory. He has previously published *The Meaning of Topic of Focus: The 59th Bridge Street Accent* (1997).

CAMBRIDGE TEXTBOOKS IN LINGUISTICS

General editors: P. AUSTIN, J. BRESNAN, B. COMRIE,
S. CRAIN, W. DRESSLER, C. J. EWEN, R. LASS, D. W.
LIGHTFOOT, K. RICE, S. ROMAINE, N. V. SMITH

Binding Theory

Binding Theory

DANIEL BÜRING

University of California, Los Angeles

PUBLISHED BY THE PRESS SYNDICATE OF THE UNIVERSITY OF CAMBRIDGE
The Pitt Building, Trumpington Street, Cambridge, United Kingdom

CAMBRIDGE UNIVERSITY PRESS
The Edinburgh Building, Cambridge, CB2 2RU, UK
40 West 20th Street, New York, NY 10011–4211, USA
477 Williamstown Road, Port Melbourne, VIC 3207, Australia
Ruiz de Alarcón 13, 28014 Madrid, Spain
Dock House, The Waterfront, Cape Town 8001, South Africa

http://www.cambridge.org

First published 2005

Printed in the United Kingdom at the University Press, Cambridge

Typeface Times 10.5/13 pt. and Formata   *System* LATEX 2_ε [TB]

A catalogue record for this book is available from the British Library

ISBN 0 521 81280 1 hardback
ISBN 0 521 01222 8 paperback

Contents

Preface

This book presents a comprehensive treatment of the syntax and semantics of binding. It is meant to fill the gap between existing introductory texts, both semantic and syntactic, and the rich primary research literature on the topic. If you work your way through this book, you should be able to read and understand almost any of the works mentioned in the references.

There are at least two reasons why I thought such a book may be useful. First, Binding Theory figures prominently in a vast amount of works, either as the main research topic, or, perhaps even more frequently, as a diagnostic for constituency, derivational history, and other abstract aspects of grammatical analysis. I felt that an accessible survey of some of the more recent insights into the nature of binding would benefit both those who read those studies, as well as those who want to undertake them in the future.

Second, by its very nature, Binding Theory involves an equal amount of syntax and semantics. As such, it recommends itself as the topic for an advanced level textbook. There is, I believe, no insightful syntactic analysis without a solid semantics to access its adequacy; in any event, there certainly can't be any insightful analysis of the syntax of binding without a semantics to accompany it. The present book, therefore, is an introduction to doing syntactic and semantic analysis side by side. It attempts to show you how to do semantically realistic (or responsible) analysis; it will also show you how, at least in some cases, figuring in the semantics carefully may solve some problems that would seem recalcitrant from a purely syntactic point of view. It's good old *divide et impera*.

The book is organized as follows: the first six chapters develop, in incremental steps, the basic system of NP classification, indexing, and interpretation. They each crucially build and expand on the content of the preceding ones, and should be tackled in that order. Chapters seven through twelve then extend the basic system in various, sometimes opposite, directions, and can be accessed mostly independently of each other; this structure is schematized in the chart below.

Within chapters, certain sections are marked as ⓔ, for "extension"; these often contain more advanced and demanding material, and can be skipped without loss of coherence for later chapters (except possibly the ⓔ-parts therein).

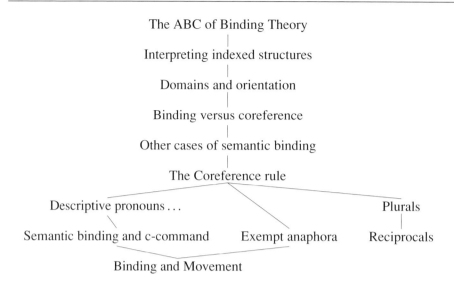

I have attempted to introduce explicitly every piece of machinery used in the analysis, and make all assumptions explicit. I have also included a fair number of exercises, especially in the earlier chapters, that should help to master the material, but also to discover problems and open ends. Despite that, I think that a certain familiarity with linguistic argumentation, as well as with formal syntactic and semantic analysis is required to read this book. Most introductory textbooks should provide the necessary background.

When Cambridge University Press invited me to write this book, I had taught 'The Syntax and Semantics of Binding Theory' at a couple of summer schools, and the plan was essentially to flesh out the existing course materials. In the process of writing the book, more and more literature made its way into these materials, and the scope of the book extended considerably. Still, this book is not a natural history of binding phenomena, especially not cross-linguistically, and makes no claim to do justice to the vast theoretical and especially descriptive literature, of which only a fraction is taken into consideration here. While I tried to use examples from many different languages, where I had sufficient sources, the primary language analyzed is English. And even there, I found that the reported judgments are often very subtle and highly controversial. I sincerely believe now that much more systematic primary work on establishing a firm data base needs to be done; as it is, I mostly report the data as given in the literature, pointing out points of controversy, and occasionally supplementing native speaker judgments I elicited.

There are also some areas that are omitted altogether in this book, mostly for reasons of space, among them the diachronic changes in anaphoric systems (van Gelderen [2000]; Keenan [2002]), as well as their acquisition in young children (Wexler and Manzini [1987], a.o.). Furthermore, older theoretical approaches to Binding Theory are not discussed, though they might often facilitate understanding more recent approaches (I recommend the first chapters of Kuno [1987] for an excellent overview).

More people than I can mention here have helped me in the process of writing this book. I'd like to thank in particular Ed Keenan and Philippe Schlenker, my colleagues here at ULCA, for their input, and Daniel Hole and Chris Potts for their extremely detailed comments and suggestions; thanks also to Christina Kim for helping with the final proofs. Special thanks go to Summer Kern, my *Herzallerliebste*, for her support, encouragement, and patience, and for always (perhaps reluctantly) being willing to double-check yet another sentence or two.

1 The ABC of Binding Theory

1.1 Preliminaries

1.1.1 Reference, coreference, and indexing

What is Binding Theory (BT) about? To a first approximation, BT restricts the distribution of NPs (or DPs, if you prefer) that have the same *referent* (starting with chapter 4, we will add non-referential NPs to the picture, which will be ignored until then). We will indicate sameness of reference, *coreference* for short, by *coindexing*; that is, coreferent NPs carry the same *index*, for which we use integers throughout. Thus in (1.1), the NP *the baroness* and the NP *she* are coindexed, which signals that they are coreferent, which in turn means that they have the same referent – they refer to the same person or thing – namely the actual baroness in flesh and blood:

(1.1)   After $[_{NP}$ the baroness$]_1$ had visited the lord, $[_{NP}$ she$]_1$ left the house.

Note that on this understanding, BT is relevant for nominal categories only, and only for the maximal projections, i.e. NPs.[1] As a convention we assume that two NPs corefer if *and only if* (iff) they are coindexed. Contra-indexing (or lack of an index on either NP) indicates non-coreference. This is illustrated in (1.2):

(1.2)   (a)   After $[_{NP}$ the baroness$]_2$ had visited the lord, she$_2$ left the house.
         (she=the baroness)
         (b)   After $[_{NP}$ the baroness$]_1$ had visited the lord, $[_{NP}$ she$]_2$ left the house.
         (she≠the baroness)

It should be noted that the actual choice of integer is irrelevant; (1.1) expresses the same *coreference pattern* as (1.2a) (as would any sentence in which both occurrences of the index are replaced by the *same* integer). An NP marked 1 is in no sense prior, higher, or superior to one marked 2. All that matters is which NPs have the same index, and which do not.

---

[1] The latter aspect I consider a genuine fact about Binding Theory. On the view pursued here, indexing on non-maximal projections (e.g. signalling specifier-head agreement or head-movement dependencies) simply is not subject to Binding Theory and should be kept separate from it. As for the former aspects, though there are sentential and adverbial (i.e. PP-) anaphors, little work on their distribution has been done, and we will ignore them here (see e.g. Hegarty *et al.* [2001] and the references therein).

In traditional grammars, the NP *the baroness* in (1.1) is referred to as the *antecedent* of the pronoun *she*. We adopt the following:

(1.3)   Definition: Antecedent
             A is the *antecedent* of B iff (if and only if) (i) A precedes B, and (ii) A and
             B corefer.

By our convention, an NP will be coindexed with its antecedent (if it has one). This holds for coreferring NPs within a single sentence, and across sentences. The latter, however, are usually not subject to Binding Conditions of the sort discussed here.[2]

1.1.2   The basic data

Restricting our attention to singular NPs for the time being, two NPs in a given sentence will show one of three logically possible coreference relations (Reinhart, 1983a: 29):

(1.4)   (a)   *obligatory coreference:*   Zelda bores herself.
             (b)   *obligatory non-coreference:*   She adores Zelda's teachers.
             (c)   *optional coreference:*   Zelda adores her teachers.

Given what was said before, grammatical representations for these will look like in (1.5):

(1.5)   (a) $Zelda_1$ bores $herself_1$.
             (b) She_8 adores $Zelda_{15}$'s teachers.
             (c) $Zelda_4$ adores her_4 teachers.   *or*
                   $Zelda_4$ adores her_7 teachers.

Ungrammatical representations for (1.4a) and (1.4b) are given in (1.6):

(1.6)   (a)   *$Zelda_1$ bores $herself_2$.
             (b)   *She_8 adores $Zelda_8$'s teachers.

It will be convenient to summarize patterns as in (1.5) and (1.6) as shown in (1.7), whose logic should be transparent:

(1.7)   (a) $Zelda_1$ bores $herself_{1/*2}$.
             (b) She_8 adores $Zelda_{15/*8}$'s teachers.
             (c) $Zelda_4$ adores $her_{4/7}$ teachers.

The key insight captured in BT is that the (un)availability of coreference between two NPs crucially depends on two factors:

[2] See e.g. Grosz *et al.* (1995); Gundel *et al.* (1993); Walker *et al.* (1998) and the references therein for some discussion of trans-sentential anaphora.

- the morphological shape of the NPs
- the structural relation between the NPs

This is not meant to exclude the possibility of additional factors that influence coreference options (which will be discussed especially in chapters 3 and 11). First, however, we will introduce the relevant NP-types of English and then, in turn, explore and characterize the syntactic configurations in which they require, allow, or disallow coreference.

1.1.3   Three types of NPs

Virtually all approaches to BT in English distinguish three types of NPs by (mostly) morphosyntactic criteria. These are illustrated in (1.8a–1.8c):

(1.8)   (a)   reflexives and reciprocals ('anaphors'):
                  himself, herself, itself, themselves, myself, yourself, ourselves, your-
                  selves
                  each other, one another
           (b)   non-reflexive pronouns ('pronominals'):
                  he, she, it, him, her, I, us, you, me, his, your, my, our
           (c)   full NPs including names ('r-expressions'):
                  the baroness, Peter, this, a disinherited Russian countess . . .

In parentheses I have given the terms for these categories as used in the influential work of Chomsky (e.g. 1981) and his school: anaphor, pronominal, and r-expression (with *r* reminiscent of 'referential'). For the first two, a cautionary remark is in order, because they unfortunately provide potential for confusion: traditionally the term *anaphor* (often with the plural *anaphors* rather than *anaphora*) is used for any NP, reflexive or not, that has an antecedent. Likewise, the term *pronominal* invites confusion with the traditional notion of *pronoun*, which applies to reflexive and non-reflexive pronouns alike. We will thus stick to the terms 'reflexive/reciprocal', 'non-reflexive pronoun', and 'full NP' in the remainder of this book.

We will now motivate this tripartition, starting with reflexives versus the rest (reciprocals, being necessarily plural, will not be discussed until chapter 10). Consider the sentences in (1.9):

(1.9)   (a)   That it rains bothers Peter.
           (b)   That it rains bothers her/him.
           (c)   *That it rains bothers himself/herself.

All these sentences contain but one referential NP (the expletive *it* is of no interest to BT, since it lacks a referent – and perhaps semantic content in general). We can thus omit the indexing for expository convenience, given that no coreference is involved. We simply observe that reflexives cannot occur in this configuration, while both non-reflexive pronouns and full NPs can.

Table 1.1 *Distribution of the three NP-types*

configuration	ex.	reflexive	non-reflexive	full NP
no antecedent	(1.9)	*	ok	ok
non-local antecedent	(1.11)	*	ok	*
local antecedent	(1.10)	ok	*	*

Inversely, only reflexives, but neither non-reflexives nor full NPs, are permitted in (1.10):

(1.10)   (a) *Peter$_3$ watches Peter$_3$ in the mirror.
          (b) *Peter$_3$ watches him$_3$ in the mirror.
          (c)   Peter$_3$ watches himself$_3$ in the mirror.

(Note that the two occurrences of *Peter* in [1.10a] are coindexed, indicating that we speak about the same Peter. The sentence is presumably acceptable if I point at a different Peter upon using the names, just as [1.10b] is of course grammatical if the pronoun is not coindexed with the name.)

Let us finally turn to the difference between non-reflexive pronouns and the rest, illustrated by way of the sentences in (1.11):

(1.11)   (a) *Carla$_4$ thinks that I hate Carla$_4$.
          (b)   Carla$_4$ thinks that I hate her$_4$.
          (c) *Carla$_4$ thinks that I hate herself$_4$.

Here, reflexives pattern with full NPs, and in contradistinction to non-reflexive pronouns. Note that the difference between (1.10) and (1.11) is not the absence versus presence of an antecedent (there is one in each), but seems to be one of syntactic *locality*: the antecedent NP is within the same clause as the anaphor in (1.10), but in a higher clause in (1.11). We summarize these (preliminary) results in table 1.1. What is clear from this table is that at least this three-way distinction needs to be recognized to distinguish correctly the coreference options of NPs in English. Notice also that reflexive and non-reflexive pronouns seem to be in complementary distribution. We will now characterize the conditions for coreference for the three types of NPs in turn.

1.2   Binding

1.2.1   Reflexive and non-reflexive pronouns

We observed above that reflexive pronouns require an antecedent, and an antecedent within their local clause at that. This is illustrated in more detail in (1.12):

(1.12)　　(a)　∗That it rains bothers himself/herself.　　　　　　(no antecedent)

　　　　　(b)　∗Carla$_4$ thinks that I hate herself$_4$.　　　　　　(non-local antecedent)

　　　　　(c)　Peter$_2$ watches himself$_2$ in the mirror.　　　　　(local antecedent)

Turning now to non-reflexive pronouns, recall that they can occur with or without a sentence-internal antecedent, cf. (1.13), as long as the antecedent is not in the same local clause, cf. (1.13c):

(1.13)　　(a)　That it rains bothers him/her.　　　　　　　　　(no antecedent)

　　　　　(b)　Carla$_4$ thinks that I hate her$_4$.　　　　　　　　(non-local antecedent)

　　　　　(c)　∗Peter$_3$ watches him$_3$ in the mirror.　　　　　　(local antecedent)

Based on these data we formulate our first version of the *Binding Conditions*:

(1.14)　　Binding Conditions (preliminary)

　　　　　(A)　A reflexive pronoun must have an antecedent within its local clause.

　　　　　(B)　A non-reflexive pronoun must not have an antecedent within its local clause.

(1.15)　　Ancillary definition:

　　　　　α is within ϕ's *local clause* if α and ϕ are dominated by the same set of clausal nodes (S, $\bar{\text{S}}$, IP, CP, TP, AgrP . . .).

Exercise 1.1

　　　　In the following sentences, Φ designates an NP with the index given. For each sentence, determine by intuition what Φ can/must be (there may be more than one option in some cases). Then give the local clause and the antecedent for Φ and demonstrate that the Binding Conditions in (1.14) are met (example: Φ_3 in [1.16a] must be *himself*, its local clause is the matrix S/IP, and its antecedent is *Peter*, which is, correctly, in the same local clause):

(1.16)　　(a)　Peter$_3$ watches Φ_3 in the mirror.

　　　　　(b)　Masha$_5$ believes that the swamp elks admire Φ_5.

　　　　　(c)　Masha$_5$ believes that [the swamp elks]$_{16}$ admire Φ_{16}.

　　　　　(d)　Masha$_5$ introduced Φ_5 to the swamp elks.

　　　　　(e)　Hermann$_8$ tried to be nice, and Gallia quite liked Φ_8. Now Φ_8 and Gallia go out to see a mud wrestling show.

　　　　　(f)　Masha$_5$ mentioned a swamp elk that was important to Φ_5.

　　　　　(g)　Φ_1's manager takes care of Cecilia$_1$'s business.

　　　　　(h)　Φ_1 takes care of Cecilia$_1$'s business.

1.2.2　　Binding and binder

　　　　Before going on, we need to refine our previous treatment in one small but significant way. To see why, consider (1.17):

(1.17)　　(a)　Carlotta$_{11}$'s dog accompanies her$_{11/6}$ to kindergarten.

　　　　　(b)　∗Carlotta$_{11}$'s dog accompanies herself$_{11/6}$ to kindergarten.

The judgments in (1.17) are the reverse of what the Binding Conditions lead us to expect: *Carlotta* is clearly in the same local clause as *her/herself*, yet we have to choose a non-reflexive pronoun to express coreference. This is in marked contrast to our earlier example (1.10), repeated here, which led to the formulation of the Binding Conditions above:

(1.18)   Peter$_3$ watches himself$_3$/*him$_3$ in the mirror.

One difference is that *Peter* and *himself* in (1.18) are *clausemates*, whereas *Carlotta* and *her(self)* in (1.17) are not – *Carlotta* is the possessor to the subject, but only the subject and *her(self)* are clausemates. We can flesh out the notion 'clausemate' in various ways, e.g. as 'be arguments to the same predicate' (here: *watch*), or 'be immediate constituents of the same clause,' with subtly different results, as we will discuss immediately in sections 1.2.4 and 1.3.

Postponing a precise definition of clausemate, let us say that only an antecedent which is a clausemate to an NP can be a *binder* for that NP:

(1.19)   Binding (preliminary): NP$_1$ binds NP$_2$ if and only if (iff)
           (a)   NP$_1$ and NP$_2$ are coindexed
           (b)   NP$_1$ precedes NP$_2$
           (c)   NP$_1$ and NP$_2$ are clausemates.
           Then NP$_1$ is the *binder* of NP$_2$, and NP$_2$ is *bound* (by NP$_1$).

(1.19a) and (1.19b) are the same as in the definition of antecedent in (1.3) above, but clause (1.19c) is added. A binder, then, is simply an antecedent that is a clausemate of the bindee. We now replace the notion of 'have an antecedent' with the notion of 'be bound' in the Binding Conditions:

(1.20)   Binding Conditions (still preliminary):
           (A)   A reflexive pronoun must have a binder within its local clause.
           (B)   A non-reflexive pronoun must not have a binder within its local clause.

In (1.18), repeated in (1.21a) below, *Peter* qualifies as a binder with respect to the pronoun in the object position of *watch* – it is coindexed with it, precedes it, and, being the subject of *watch*, is a clausemate. Hence Binding Condition A licenses a reflexive in object position, and Binding Condition B prohibits a non-reflexive. All's well:

(1.21)   (a)   Peter$_3$ watches himself$_3$/*him$_3$ in the mirror.
           (b)   Carlotta$_{11}$'s dog accompanies her$_{11}$//*herself$_{11}$ to kindergarten.

In the formerly problematic example (1.17), repeated in (1.21b) above, *Carlotta* is not a binder to the pronoun in the object position of *accompany* (though it is an antecedent); it is coindexed with it, and precedes it, but, being a modifier to *dog* rather than an argument to *accompany*, it fails on the clausemate condition in the definition of binder (1.19c). Binding Condition A thus prohibits a reflexive, and Binding Condition B allows a non-reflexive.

1.2.3   Full NPs

Turning now to full NPs, we observed that they cannot occur with a sentence internal antecedent at all, regardless of whether the antecedent occurs within the same local clause or not. The relevant data are repeated here:

(1.22)   (a)   That it rains bothers Peter.   (no antecedent)
            (b)   *Carla$_4$/she$_4$ thinks that I hate Carla$_4$.   (non-local antecedent)
            (c)   *Peter$_3$/he$_4$ watches Peter$_3$ in the mirror.   (local antecedent)

The question that comes up is whether full NPs are allergic to antecedents, or just binders. To decide that question we have to look again at a case in which an NP antecedes a full NP without actually binding it, for example (1.23):

(1.23)   (a)   Her$_{11}$ dog accompanies Carlotta$_{11}$ to kindergarten.
            (b)   ?Carlotta's$_{11}$ dog accompanies Carlotta$_{11}$ to kindergarten.
            (c)   Carlotta's$_{11}$ dog accompanies the little darling$_{11}$ to kindergarten.

The pronoun in (1.23a) antecedes the full NP with no loss in acceptability. And even another full NP can, as in (1.23b), which is slightly degraded due to the repetition of the name, but head and shoulders above (1.22b); and (1.23c), which features an *epithet*, i.e. a definite NP which is coreferential with, though different in descriptive content from, its antecedent, is impeccable.

We conclude that, just as in the principles governing the coreference options of pronouns, the principle responsible for full NPs must make reference to the notion of binding, rather than antecedence:

(1.24)   Binding Condition C: A full NP must not be bound.

I should like to point out here that the judgments in (1.23), while widely accepted, are not uncontroversial. Generally, name–name cases (*Peter$_3$ ... Peter$_3$*) seem more acceptable than pronoun–name cases (*he$_3$ ... Peter$_3$*) and for many speakers approach the degree of acceptability found in examples like (1.23b) (cf. e.g. Bach and Partee [1980], note 11; Evans [1980]:356 a.o.). This can be seen as a phenomenon outside of grammar (after all, in the double name cases, the coreferential reading is the only way to interpret the sentence at all, while in the pronoun–name cases, there is a host of grammatical non-coreferent readings) or as a fact about BT proper, suggesting that Binding Condition C should only ban full NPs from being bound by a *pronoun* Bach and Partee [1980]; Keenan [1974]; for further discussion see also Bresnan [2000], Lasnik [1986], as well as chapter 6. We will, for the time being, assume these cases to be unequivocally bad.

1.2.4   C-command

Before closing, we need to generalize the notion of binding slightly. As it stands, Binding Condition C does not exclude (1.22b), repeated here:

(1.25)   *Carla$_4$/she$_4$ thinks that I hate Carla$_4$.

The reason is that (the first occurrence of) *Carla/she* in (1.25) doesn't *bind* the second in the technical sense defined in (1.19), because they are not clausemates:

they are not immediate constituents of the same clause, nor are they arguments to the same verb (*think* versus *hate*). We therefore replace the notion of clausemate by a more general, asymmetric, notion, that of *c(onstituent)-command* [Reinhart, 1976]:

(1.26)   Node A *c-commands* node B in a phrase marker iff
          (a)   neither dominates the other, and
          (b)   every (branching) node that dominates A also dominates B[3]

(1.27)   Binding (revised, still preliminary): NP_1 binds NP_2 iff
          (a) NP_1 and NP_2 are coindexed
          (b) NP_1 precedes NP_2
          (c) NP_1 c-commands NP_2
          Then NP_1 is the *binder* of NP_2, and NP_2 is *bound* (by NP_1).

Let us first verify how these new definitions subsume the old ones. Take (1.21a), repeated here; a phrase structure tree for this sentence will have the essential constituency shown in (1.28):

(1.28) $Peter_3$ watches $himself_3$/*him_3 in the mirror.

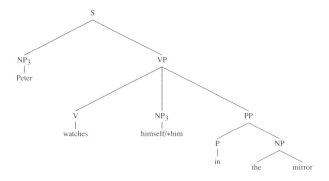

The only (branching) node dominating $[_{NP}Peter]_3$ is S, which means that $[_{NP}Peter]_3$ c-commands VP and everything dominated by VP, including $[_{NP}himself/him]_3$. Thus $[_{NP}Peter]_3$ is a binder for $[_{NP}himself/him]_3$, and, given that it is in the same local clause, it is correctly predicted that the latter has to be a reflexive, rather than a full NP or a non-reflexive pronoun.

Contrast this with (1.21b) repeated here along with a simple tree diagram:

(1.29) $Carlotta_{11}$'s dog accompanies her_{11}//*$herself_{11}$ to kindergarten.

---

[3] Definitions in the literature usually include the qualification 'branching', even though, as Barker and Pullum [1990] and Pullum [1986] note, this is rarely argued for, nor required, by the data in any obvious way. The cases discussed in this book provide no exceptions to that; indeed the notion of semantic binding to be introduced in chapter 4 directly embodies Pullum's stricter and arguably more natural notion of IDV-command, according to which a constituent's c-command domain simply consists of its sister constituent(s).

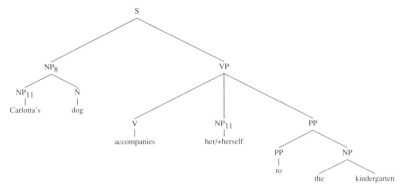

Here, NP$_{11}$, *Carlotta*, does not c-command VP or anything therein: nodes dominating NP$_{11}$ are NP$_8$ and S, which means that NP$_{11}$ merely c-commands the N̄ *dog*; VP, and the pronominal NP$_{11}$ within it, though dominated by S, are not dominated by NP$_8$, which means they are not dominated by *every* branching node dominating NP$_{11}$, *Carlotta*, as is required for binding due to (1.26b). Accordingly, [$_{NP}$ *her(self)*]$_{11}$ is not bound by [$_{NP}$ *Carlotta*]$_{11}$ by the new definition of binding, especially (1.27c), so that the Binding Conditions correctly predict a non-reflexive (or a name) in that position.

Crucially, the new definition of binding is 'downward unlimited', because an NP that c-commands a node A also c-commands every node dominated by A. This is the key to handling the Binding Condition C cases. Consider again (1.22b), repeated here:

(1.30)   *Carla$_4$/she$_4$ thinks that I hate Carla$_4$.

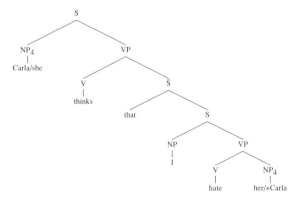

Similar to (1.21a), the matrix subject NP$_4$, *Carla*, c-commands the matrix VP, *and everything dominated by the matrix VP*, including the object NP$_4$. Since the subject NP$_4$ is also coindexed with the object NP$_4$ and precedes it, it qualifies as a binder. Binding Condition C then excludes a name as the object NP$_4$, while Binding Condition B allows a non-reflexive pronoun in that position.

This completes our introduction to the ABC of Binding Theory for English. It should be stressed that the Binding Conditions as stated above are no longer about the traditional, intuitive concept of antecedence, but about a more abstract concept, binding. Binding Theory, so construed, is then a theory only about a subset of anaphoric relations, excluding non-c-command anaphora, both across and within sentences. This embodies a strong and non-obvious hypothesis, namely that c-command, or some other command notion (more about which is discussed in section 1.3), is of utmost significance for BT, and that, accordingly, the data fall into two broad natural classes – binding versus non-c-command anaphora. We will continue to reflect upon the validity of these hypotheses in the course of this book.

On the other hand, if Binding Conditions are indeed based on the notion of c-command, they can serve as a probe into the phrase structure of a sentence: if an NP blocks the occurrence of a coindexed pronoun or full NP', NP must c-command NP'. Binding Condition C in particular will be useful in this regard, since it applies across clause boundaries. It has been suggested, for example, that the pairs in (1.31) and (1.32) show that object clauses, but not temporal adverbial clauses, are c-commanded by the object, while both are c-commanded by the subject:

(1.31)   (a) *The dog told him_1 [that the $horse_1$ would fall].
           (b) The dog hit him_1 [while the $horse_1$ ate lunch].
(1.32)   (a) *She_8'll talk to me [when $Sheila_8$ gets back from lunch].
           (b) I'll talk to $Sheila_8$ [when she_8 gets back from lunch].

While this method can be useful, it should be applied with care, for at least two reasons: first, as pointed out in section 1.2.3 above, the unacceptability of bound full NPs is itself not uncontroversial, and judgments seem to vary between speakers, but also in response to prosodic, stylistic, and discourse-pragmatic factors (see e.g. Carden and Dieterich [1981]; and Gerken and Bever [1986] for experimental results). Second, subordinated clauses are often found in displaced positions (e.g. through topicalization or extraposition), or at least could be for all we know, so that our conclusions from such examples rely in turn on our conclusions about the interaction of Binding Conditions with displacement (more on which in chapter 12). We will suggest that the phenomenon of *semantic binding*, to be introduced in chapter 4, may provide a more reliable diagnostic for c-command. Since we are presently concerned with demarcating the conditions on binding themselves (rather than presupposing them to figure out constituency), we will for the most part ignore constructions whose constituent structure is itself subject to debate.

1.2.5   Taking stock

It will be useful to separate several parts or components of the theory, as these will be subject to criticism, revision, or modification later, independent of each other:

- The **classification** of NPs according to their coreference and binding options. Here: three classes, reflexives and reciprocals ('anaphors'), non-reflexive pronouns ('pronominals'), non-pronominal or full NPs ('r-expressions').

- The identification of one or more **domain(s)** within which binding requirements apply. Here: the minimal clause.

- The formulation of a proper notion of **command** or *accessibility* as prerequisite for, and source of, asymmetry in binding. Here: precedence and c-command.

The general format of a Binding Condition can then be schematized as in (1.33):

(1.33)   An NP of **class** must **(not)** be coindexed with a **commanding** NP within its **domain**.

Developing a general theory of binding is to formulate conditions of the general form in (1.33) for several languages, and in the process, to determine which exact values for the variables **class**, **command**, and **domain** are empirically most adequate, within a language, and cross-linguistically, and which are systematically irrelevant. In this book, we will be concerned with the notion of domain in chapter 3, the issue of classification in chapters 3 and 11, and the concept of command in section 1.3 of this chapter, as well as in chapter 12. Hopefully, the tripartition of the ingredients to the BT will prove useful in keeping track of the discussion.[4]

We have set up our system in such a way that each class of NPs may have (a) positive and/or negative Binding Condition(s) associated with it. Complementary distribution between two classes results if the negative binding domain for one element happens to be the same as the positive binding domain for the other. There is nothing in the formal system that accounts for the intuition one might have that one class of NPs is used *because* of the unavailability of the other, and vice versa. Intuitions of this kind have motivated so-called *blocking* approaches to Binding Theory, in which one form is used if (and perhaps only if) the other is excluded; examples of such approaches include Dowty (1980); Farmer and Harnish (1987); Huang (2000); and Levinson (1987, 1991, 2000); in light of the fact that non-complementary distribution between different pronoun classes is common across languages, including English (see chapters 3 and 11), we will not review these approaches further in this book; but see Burzio (1996, 1998); Kiparsky (2002) for refined, hybrid blocking approaches.

Exercise 1.2

A naïve approach to binding would be that the use of a pronoun is necessary to avoid repetition of full NPs, especially within a single sentence.

---

[4] Most authors appear to assume, implicitly, that the notion of command, once defined properly, is invariant across all Binding Conditions across all languages (but see the remarks at the end of section 1.3); if so, the variable **command** shouldn't be treated on a par with the others; we will leave this issue open in this book.

Use the distinction between antecedence and binding established above to make an argument against this view. Construct and provide crucial examples.

Exercise 1.3

Both sentences in (1.34) below could be used to illustrate that reflexives in English cannot be bound across a clause boundary. Explain how each does it. Can you think of reasons to prefer one mode of presentation over the other?

(1.34)   (a) $John_1$ thinks that $Bill_2$ likes $himself_{2/*1}$.
            (b) *John thinks that I like himself.

Exercise 1.4

Consider the English possessive form *his/her/its own* (pretend that it is a single form). What requirements, if any, does it impose on its binder or antecedent? Formulate an appropriate Binding Condition for it, and adduce (acceptable and unacceptable) examples to support your proposal.

1.3   Command and precedence©

As discussed in 1.2.5 above, the notion of *command* is one key ingredient in the formulation of Binding Conditions. We have used c-command plus precedence in our definition of binding above, hence as our relevant notion of **command** in (1.33). In this section we will critically reexamine these two notions, suggesting that they should perhaps be replaced with an altogether different command notion.

1.3.1   Against precedence

In our final definition of binding in (1.19) we have used two relations that give us an asymmetrical ordering among the NPs in a sentence, c-command and precedence. Is this necessary, or even tolerable? Consider the abstract phrase markers in (1.35):

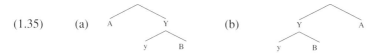

(1.35)   (a)   A   Y   (b)   Y   A
                        y   B   y   B

In (1.35a), the standard kind of case we have been looking at in English, A could bind B because A c-commands and precedes B; and B could not bind A, because it neither c-commands nor precedes A. In other words, according to our present definition of binding, (1.27), there are two different reasons why A can bind B, but not the other way around; the account is thus somewhat redundant, though perhaps harmlessly so.

In (1.35b), on the other hand, A c-commands B asymmetrically, but B precedes A. If both factors are relevant, binding between A and B should be *ineffable*, i.e. impossible either way around, and regardless of the morphological shape of either NP. While English lacks clear instantiations of this configuration, other languages arguably provide them. Reinhart (1983a: 47) provides the following data from Malagasy (attributed to E. Keenan, p.c.), an Austronesian language spoken in Madagascar (for convenience, I have set the pronouns in boldface and the antecedents in italics):

(1.36) (a) namono **azy** ny anadahin- d- *Rakoto*   (Malagasy)
            hit/killed him the sister-   of- Rakoto
            'Rakoto's sister killed him.'
        (b) *namono ny anadahin- d- *Rakoto* **izy**
            hit/killed the sister-   of- Rakoto he
            'He killed Rakoto's sister.'

Malagasy is a VOS language, but, as the translations make clear, behaves rather like English with respect to the BT. In particular, (1.36b) appears to be a Binding Condition C violation, with the subject pronoun *izy*, 'he', illicitly binding the full NP *Rakoto* within the object NP. No such effect is found in (1.36a), in which the full NP is the subject, and the pronoun is in the object.

The data then suggest that the subject can bind the object, but not vice versa. Given that the object precedes the subject, this pattern straightforwardly prohibits a treatment in terms of precedence. C-command alone, however, would seem to provide the correct asymmetry, provided we assume that the basic clause structure of Malagasy is essentially as in (1.37) (cf. [1.35b] above):

(1.37)

We thus conclude that the inclusion of precedence in the definition of binding, while perhaps merely redundant for English, is actually harmful if we want to apply the notion cross-linguistically, and should be dropped.[5]

1.3.2   Limitations of C-command

Unfortunately, c-command is not unproblematic either. Languages that display flexible constituent ordering abound with examples in which a bound element precedes and c-commands its binder. Japanese, Korean, and German provide three examples. They are strictly or mostly left-branching languages with

---

[5] I found exactly one case in the literature in which precedence does seem to play a role, namely Samoan, as discussed in Chapin (1970); and Keenan and Stabler (1995). Whether this requires inclusion of precedence in the BT for Samoan, or can be captured in any other way, will be left as an open question here.

free word order, in all of which we find, for example, (reflexive-like) pronouns preceding coreferring full NPs:[6]

(1.38)   **Zibun** -o   *Hanako* -ga   utagatte iru   (Japanese)
          self   -ACC *Hanako* -NOM *doubts*
          'Hanako doubts herself.'

(1.39)   **Caki casin** -eke   *Kim* -ŭn   silmanghaŏssta   (Korean)
          self   -DAT *Kim* -TOP *disappointed*
          'Kim was disappointed in himself.'

(1.40)   Oft   hat **sich** *der Mann* im   Spiegel betrachtet.   (German)
          often has self the man   in the mirror watched
          'Often the man watched himself in the mirror.'

These data are problematic for our definition of binding, because, unlike in the case of Malagasy discussed above, there is agreement that none of Japanese, Korean, or German has a constituent structure in which the reflexive objects in these examples are c-commanded by their subject antecedents.

It should be noted, however, that in all these examples, what could be called the 'logical subject' binds the 'logical object', regardless of order or c-command. In other words, one could conjecture that some more abstract level of representation displays an asymmetric ordering among constituents, at which all of the examples discussed in this section show the relative ordering in (1.41):

(1.41)   'subject' > 'indirect object' > 'direct object' > 'prepositional object'

I have scare-quoted the notions 'subject', 'object', etc. because these are merely place-holders for whatever theoretical constructs a particular theory regards as relevant here. We will inspect several instantiations of such a hierarchy in turn.

Before that, I want to bring up another set of data on which the c-command condition, even if it doesn't fail as spectacularly as on those in (1.38–1.40), seems deficient, namely so-called non-configurational or 'flat' structures. It is, for example, generally accepted that the objects in double object constructions in English show asymmetries in binding behavior:[7]

(1.42)   (a)   I showed John himself (in the mirror).
          (b) *I showed himself John (in the mirror).

(1.43)   (a)   I showed Mary to herself.
          (b) *I showed herself to Mary.

Suppose that the structure of the VP in double object constructions is as in (1.44):

(1.44)   (a)   (b)

[6] Korean data from Keenan (1988):131.
[7] Reflexive examples from Barrs and Lasnik (1986):347 and Larson (1988):338.

Given this structure, no asymmetries in binding are expected, contrary to fact, since the two objects mutually c-command each other, at least in the double NP case. Similar remarks apply, for example, to nouns with more than one post-nominal attribute:[8]

(1.45)   (Ja čital) stat'ju   *Tolstoja* o   **sebe**.   (Russian)
          I   read   article-ACC *T.*-GEN   *about himself*-LOC
          '(I read) an article of Tolstoj about himself.'

Again, the immediately post-nominal phrase can bind the second one, but not vice versa. But, as in the case of verbal double-object constructions, the constituent structure appears to be flat.[9]

Both these examples would be treated correctly if we assumed c-command *and* precedence as prerequisites for binding, but, in the light of the problems with precedence encountered earlier, it is worth while to look for alternative treatments. A hierarchy along the lines of (1.41) above can provide such a treatment, as it provides a total ordering even among NPs that mutually c-command each other.

To be sure, there have been attempts to reconcile the data in (1.42–1.43) with a c-command approach to binding, notably Larson (1988), which argues that the asymmetries rather show that these structures are more complex than (1.44) and have the essential properties of those in (1.46):

(1.46)   (a)   (b)

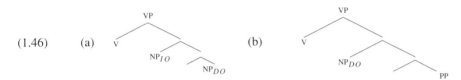

We do not have to elaborate on the details of this analysis (like the identity of the unlabelled nodes in [1.46]). The important thing is that a structure like (1.46) predicts the binding asymmetries as a function of asymmetrical c-command, without reference to anything else.

On the other hand, we saw the need to reconsider the c-command condition anyway in the light of the Japanese/Korean/German cases, and the two alternatives to c-command presented below are intended to capture those and 'flat structure' cases by the same mechanism, namely an independent, non-phrase-structural hierarchy.

This is obviously not the place to rule a final verdict on the (non-)existence of flat structures, but it bears mentioning that the binding facts alone can be treated by a refined command notion, which is presumably required independently, and that structures like in (1.46) are not necessitated by them. We will look at two such notions in what follows.

---

[8] Data based on Rappaport (1986):106.
[9] Note that the simplest binary branching structure would actually be *[[V/N XP₁] XP₂]*, which would yield the opposite asymmetries in c-command from what we find with the binding data.

1.3.3   Θ-command

Let us start with the perhaps most attractive version of a non-phrase-structural ordering among the NPs, namely the idea that this ordering is essentially semantic in nature, more precisely that it is based on the semantics of the *thematic relations* involved. An early and representative example of this approach is Jackendoff (1972):148, where it is proposed that the relevant asymmetric ordering among elements is derived from the hierarchy of *thematic roles* (or Θ-roles for short) in (1.47):

(1.47)   Agent ≻ Location, Source, Goal ≻ Theme

The fact that *der Mann* can bind *sich* in the German example (1.40) above is then due to the fact that *der Mann* bears the Θ-role 'Agent,' which outranks the role of *sich*, 'Theme' on the Θ-hierarchy in (1.47). Likewise, *Rakoto* must not be coreferent with *izy* in the ungrammatical Malagasy example in (1.36), due to the fact that *izy* has the 'Agent' role in that sentence, which is higher than any other role in the Θ-hierarchy. The initial appearance that binding asymmetries correlate with a hierarchy among phrase-structure positions (as established by c-command) is merely an epiphenomenon of the dependence of phrase structure upon this same thematic hierarchy.

There are two more immediate advantages of Θ-command over c-command. First, as it is defined over thematic roles, it captures certain parallelisms between NPs and PPs. Not only can binding proceed 'into' PPs – a fact captured by c-command and Θ-command alike – sometimes it can also proceed 'out of' PPs, if the pertinent thematic command obtains:

(1.48)   (a)   We talked to John about himself.
          (b) *We talked to himself about John.
          (c) *We talked about John to himself.

These examples (from Wilkins [1988b]:208) show that Goal (as realized by a complement of *to*) Θ-commands Theme (as realized by a complement of *about*) and can therefore bind it, regardless of the fact that *John* doesn't c-command *himself*, because the first node dominating it is the PP.

Second, Θ-command allows a straightforward account of binding with so-called *psych-verbs*. With these verbs, a phrase-structurally lower argument appears to bind into a higher argument:[10]

(1.49)   (a)   Stories about herself generally please Mary.
          (b)   Each other's health worried the students.

While obviously unexpected from a phrase-structure point of view, these examples can be captured under the assumption that the role borne by the subject of

---

[10] Examples from Pesetsky (1987):127.

these verbs, Theme, is lower on the Θ-hierarchy than that of the object, Experiencer.[11]

Attractive though the Θ-command notion is for the purpose of BT, it also faces some serious problems. First, verbs that allow alternative realizations of their arguments, such as English double-object constructions, show alternations in binding possibilities as well, as discussed at length above, cf. the examples in (1.42) and (1.43) above; (1.50) reiterates the point:[12]

(1.50) (a) I sold the slave himself.   (Goal binds Theme)
        (b) I sold the slave to himself.   (Theme binds Goal)
        (c) *I sold himself the slave.   (Goal cannot bind Theme)

A Θ-command approach has to grab the bull by the horns and claim that, say, *John* bears a different Θ-role in *I sold the cabbage to John* than in *I sold John the cabbage*, as is done in Wilkins (1988b):208ff., who claims that a Theme, when verb-adjacent, as in (1.50b), is also a *Patient*, which is a higher role than Goal, whereas it is only a Theme if it follows another object, as in (1.50a) and (1.50c), which makes it lower than Goal (a similar strategy is implemented in Jackendoff [1990]'s *action tier*).

This strategy, while technically feasible, highlights a more general weak spot of Θ-based approaches, namely the question of how to determine the role of a given argument in a given structure. For example, according to its proponents, the Theme/Patient distinction *explains* what is behind the dative alternation in English. According to the critics, it merely gives a semantically loaded name to what by all appearances is a purely syntactic distinction, namely that between direct and oblique object (alleged semantic distinctions between the two are indeed subtle, but see Krifka [2004]). According to critics, then, a sufficiently elaborated Θ-command account is just a somewhat misleadingly labelled instantiation of an argument-structure based account, to be discussed in the next subsection.

Before closing this section, let us briefly consider two other areas in which the Θ-command idea has been argued to encounter difficulties. In certain cases of *raising*, reflexivization involves NPs that do not receive their thematic role from the same lexical element. Consider (1.51):[13]

(1.51)   Max strikes himself as qualified for the job.

It would appear that the Θ-role of *himself* (Goal or Experiencer of *strike*) is higher than that of *Max* (Theme of *qualified*) as well as that of the clause *Max* has raised from (which is presumably the Theme of *strike*). Yet, binding can only proceed from the subject to the object position, in violation of the Θ-command condition.

---

[11] The facts are more complicated, as must therefore be the account; see, among many others, Belletti and Rizzi (1988).

[12] From Pollard and Sag (1992:298); in contradistinction to Pollard and Sag, Larson (1988), and others, Jackendoff (1972:157) and Postal (1971:ch. 15) judge both variants of binding in double object constructions as ungrammatical.

[13] cf. Pollard and Sag (1992:299).

The second argument asserts that morphological processes that change grammatical functions also change binding options. Similar to the case of verbs with alternating argument structures, no obvious change in thematic roles goes along with it:[14]

(1.52)   (a)   John shaved himself.   (Agent binds Theme)
          (b)   John was shaved by himself.   (Theme binds Agent)
          (c)   *We expect himself to be shaved by John   (Agent cannot bind
                                                                 Theme)

This argument has to be taken with a grain of salt, though. Many speakers find examples like (1.52b) rather marginal. Cross-linguistically, the diagnosis is actually much less clear, perhaps non-uniform. Toba Batak (Malayo-Polynesian; Sumatra) is a verb-initial language with no morphological case distinctions.[15] Depending on the choice of verbal prefix, *mang* versus *di*, a sentence of the form *V NP$_1$ NP$_2$* is interpreted with NP$_1$ as Theme (or Patient) and NP$_2$ as Agent (*mang*-prefix), or with NP$_1$ as Agent and NP$_2$ as Theme (*di*-prefix). In other words, *mang-* and *di-* determine different mappings between thematic roles and phrase-structure positions and are, as such, comparable to grammatical function-changing operations like passive in other languages. Strikingly, however, the binding always goes from Agent to Theme, regardless of prefix choice and, accordingly, linear order:[16]

(1.53)   (a)   Mang -ida si Ria si Torus   (a')   Di -ida si Torus si Ria
                 MANG *see the R. the T.*   DI *see the T.   the R.*
                 'Torus saw Ria.'   'Torus saw Ria.'

          (b) * Mang -ida si Torus dirina   (b') Di -ida si Torus dirina
                 MANG *see the Torus self*   DI *see the Torus self*
                 'Self saw Torus.'   'Torus saw self.'

          (c)   Mang -ida dirina si Torus   (c')* Di -ida dirina si Torus
                 MANG *see self   the Torus*   DI *see self   the Torus*
                 'Torus saw self.'   'Self saw Torus.'

It appears that neither the change in linear order (and the change in c-command relations presumably accompanying it) nor the change in grammatical function indicated by the verbal prefixes affects the binding options between the two NPs. A good candidate for what remains invariant in all structures are the Θ-relations: *Torus* is the Agent and *Ria* is the Theme. We conclude that grammatical function-changing operations do not provide clear evidence for or against a Θ-command approach to Binding Theory.

---

[14] Examples from Pollard and Sag (1992):298.
[15] See Keenan (1988) and Schachter (1974); Schachter argues that the basic phrase structure is [[V NP] NP], which would make it a VOS language, but nothing hinges on that, cf. also Sternefeld (1992).
[16] Data from Keenan (1988):129f. and Keenan and Stabler (1995):4; very similar data are reported for Balinese in Wechsler and Arka (1998):406ff.

1.3.4   Obliqueness-command

The last command relation to be discussed in this chapter is that of *obliqueness command*, or *o-command* for short (sometimes also called a(rgument)-command for reasons to become clear shortly). O-command occupies a middle ground in between c-command and Θ-command in that it claims that there is a non-thematic, syntactic ordering between the NPs in a sentence, but denies that that ordering is directly encoded in the phrase structure as c-command (or any other phrase-structure relation for that matter). I illustrate the idea using an argument-list notation;[17] a verb like *watch*, for example, will have an a(rgument)-list like in (1.54):

(1.54)   a-list of *watch*: $\langle$ NP, NP$_{acc}$ $\rangle$

The order of elements on the a-list signals *obliqueness*. Thus the first NP on the a-list in (1.54) is less oblique than the second, NP$_{acc}$. Obliqueness does not necessarily correspond to linear order; if, for example, a language allows different linearizations of arguments, the obliqueness relations encoded on the a-list still remain the same. Thus the a-list associated with *betrachten*, 'watch,' in the German example (1.40) above is the same as in (1.54), despite the fact that the accusative NP, the reflexive *sich*, linearly precedes the subject NP (and presumably also c-commands it). Similarly for the Japanese and Korean examples discussed.

Likewise, a flat constituent structure like in (1.44) is perfectly compatible with a total ordering in terms of obliqueness (in fact, by its very nature an a-list is always totally ordered), as, for example, in (1.55):

(1.55)   a-lists for ditransitive verbs like *give*:
         (a) $\langle$ NP, NP$_{acc}$, PP$_{to}$[P-OBJ]$\rangle$
         (b) $\langle$ NP, NP$_{acc}$, NP$_{acc}$ $\rangle$

Using argument-lists, we can now define an alternative notion to c-command, *o(bliqueness)-command*, and use that relation to define the Binding Conditions (cf. Pollard and Sag [1992]:287):[18]

(1.56)   (a)   A *locally o-commands* B iff A is less oblique than B on some a-list
         (b)   A (locally) o-binds B iff A and B are coindexed and A (locally) o-commands B.

---

[17] This is similar to the SUBCAT or ARG-ST list of *Head Driven Phrase Structure Grammar* as presented in Pollard and Sag (1994); Sag and Wasow (1999) or the a-structure of *Lexical Functional Grammar* (Bresnan, 2000, and the references therein). In current HPSG, the ARG-ST list is split up into separate lists, which between them capture what is traditionally called the valency and subcategorization, partly in recognition of the problems languages like Toba Batak and Balinese, as mentioned on page 18 pose for theories that equate argument structure with grammatical relations (Manning and Sag, 1999; Wechsler and Arka, 1998).

[18] These definitions, as well as that of o-command below, assume that the elements on the a-list are the actual syntactic objects, as they in fact are in HPSG, not just category names. For details, see Pollard and Sag (1994). Otherwise we would have to say that A locally o-commands B (in S) if A' is less oblique on some element's a-list in C than B', where A' and B' are the elements on the a-list corresponding to A and B.

(1.57)   Binding Conditions:
   (A) A reflexive pronoun must be o-bound within its local domain.
   (B) A non-reflexive pronoun must not be o-bound within its local domain.

To define Binding Condition C we must generalize the notion of local o-command to o-command *simpliciter*. The idea is clear enough: if A locally o-commands B, and C is dominated by B, then A should o-command C:

(1.58)   O-Command: A o-commands B iff
   (a) A locally o-commands B, or
   (b) A locally o-commands a C which dominates B[19]

(1.59)   Binding Condition C: A full NP must not be o-bound.

To give an example, (1.60a) will be ruled out as a Binding Condition C violation, as it should be, given the a-list of *tell* in (1.60b):

(1.60)   (a) ∗The red-haired baroness told him$_1$ that Casimir$_1$ is nice.
   (b) a-list for *tell*: ⟨ NP, NP$_{acc}$, S̄ ⟩

NP *him* locally o-commands S̄, *that Casimir is nice*, which in turn dominates the NP *Casimir*. Therefore, *Casimir* is o-commanded by *him* and, since they are coindexed, also o-bound by it. This binding violates Binding Condition C in (1.59), hence coreference is impossible.

 O-command based approaches to Binding Theory are presumably the most successful, since they allow for a certain leeway relative to the thematic relations, and relative to the constituent structure. But then this is also a point of potential criticism, which would insinuate that a-lists can simply be written so as to match the binding facts. Put differently, the ordering of elements on a-lists should ideally have other functions than just encoding binding asymmetries, and there should be a tight correspondence between a-lists and thematic relations, on the one hand, and a-lists and constituent structure, on the other, to account for the sort of facts that motivate Θ- and c-command based approaches.

 Arguably, most approaches within the *Principles and Parameters* framework are in essence (equivalent to) o-command approaches. While they assume that the relevant command notion is c-command, Binding Conditions make reference not to the level of surface constituency but to a more abstract level at which c-command and binding go hand in hand. This level, then, encodes in a phrase-structural manner the same ordering that is encoded non-configurationally on a-lists under the o-command approach. Not surprisingly, this level is one which, overall, reflects grammatical-function changes such as passive, raising, and dative shift, and ignores or undoes more 'superficial' movements such as topicalization, *wh*-movement, and 'scrambling' as found in Japanese, Korean, and German (cf. chapter 12). And, as with the o-command approaches discussed above, the more it can be shown that the pertinent level serves other purposes as well,

---

[19] Cf. Pollard and Sag (1992):300; see also the remarks in Bouma *et al.* (2001):8f., 44.

and is linked to surface constituency and thematic information by a rather constrained inventory of transformations, the more such an approach recommends itself.

With these remarks we leave the issue of command. Of course, none of the above possibilities is exclusive, and there exist approaches in which different command relations coexist (e.g. É. Kiss [1992]), just as there exist approaches on which Binding Conditions must apply at more than one syntactic level (e.g. Belletti and Rizzi [1988]). With the exception of chapter 12, which is exclusively devoted to this issue, we will concentrate on cases in which any one of the command notions yields the same ordering among NPs in what follows, which, at least for English, is easily done. That this is possible reflects the fact that all approaches discussed above converge on their core finding. In particular, they all agree that there *is* an asymmetric and transitive command ordering among the NPs in a given structure which determines their binding potential.

Exercise 1.5

Consider the following data from Albanian, taken from K. Williams (1988). Describe the pattern of reflexive binding in terms of grammatical function (subject, accusative object, dative object) first. Then try to put it in terms of one of the command hierarchies above. Argue why you chose the hierarchy you did.

(1.61)   (a)   Artisti$_1$ ia   tregoi veten$_{1/2}$ Dritës$_2$.
                artist   CLITIC *show self*-ACC *Drita*-DAT

         (b)   Artisti$_1$ ia   tregoi Dritës$_2$ veten$_{1/2}$.
                artist   CLITIC *show Drita*-DAT *self*-ACC

         (c)   Artisti$_1$ ia   tregoi Dritën$_2$ vetes$_{1/*2}$.
                artist   CLITIC *show Drita*-ACC *self*-DAT
                'The artist showed Drita herself.'

Exercise 1.6

Consider the following data from Hungarian, from É. Kiss (1992):247. What can you say about the relevant command notion in Hungarian?

(1.62)   (a)   A lányokat megmutattam egymásnak.   (Hungarian)
                the girls-ACC *showed-I   each other*-DAT
                'I showed the girls to each other.'

         (b)   A lányoknak megmutattam egymást.
                the girls-DAT *showed-I   each other*-ACC
                'I showed each other to the girls.'

1.4   Reflexive verbs and reflexive phraseologisms ©

Let me close by adding some observations about reflexive pronouns and their functions. Compare the following sentences:

(1.63)   (a)   Spencer behaved himself.
          (b)   Spencer despised himself.

Himself in (1.63b) functions as a semantic argument (to *despise*), but *himself* in (1.63a) does not. We can conclude this from the syntax, because we can't replace the reflexive in (1.63a) with a full NP, say *Carmen*, the way we can in (1.63b);[20] similarly, we have a semantic intuition that despising is a two-place relation, whereas behaving is a one-place property (though it turns out to be hard to substantiate this intuition further). Verbs like *behave (oneself)* are called *inherently reflexive verbs*; they are semantically intransitive, but syntactically transitive, and show a – presumably uninterpreted – reflexive as the semantically 'inert' argument. Examples of this class are few in English (including *disgrace/betake/vaunt oneself*), but are found in great numbers in other languages, among them the rest of Germanic and Romance.

It is open to speculation why languages have inherently reflexive verbs (instead of proper intransitives), though it seems no coincidence that such verbs are often historically related to transitives. In some cases, we can see this relationship even synchronically, as is the case for the causative/inchoative alternation in German, as found in *etwas schließen – sich schließen, etwas aufhellen – sich aufhellen* ('to close [something]', 'to lighten [something] up').[21]

The opposite of verbs like *behave*, if you will, are verbs like *shave* and *wash*, which can be syntactically intransitive but are clearly semantically transitive (*Quinn shaves* and *Quinn shaves himself* both express that Quinn is the Agent and the Theme of the shaving). *Shave*-type verbs, in English and crosslinguistically, very often describe typically self-directed actions such as acts of grooming (cf. English *wash, shave*); typically other-directed actions such as seeing, beating, or killing are unlikely candidates to be expressed by (optionally) intransitive verbs, and require a transitive construction with a reflexive pronoun when used to describe a self-directed event.

A strikingly parallel distinction is found in many languages that have complex as well as simple reflexive pronouns (like the continental Germanic languages discussed in chapter 3, section 3.5.1): typically self-directed verbs occur with a simple reflexive, while typically other-directed verbs require the complex form. Descriptively, we thus find the following scale of transitive constructions:[22]

---

[20] Other diagnostics for semantically inert reflexives include their inability to be stressed or fronted, to be coordinated, or right-node-raised in conjunctions with non-inherent reflexive verbs.

[21] Note that the reflexive alternants do not entail any implicit agent, as, say, passives do; *sich aufhellen* is thus the proper translation of *to lighten up* in *The sky lightened up*. Another formally similar construction is the middle construction, which is realized without an object in English, but with a simple reflexive object in many other languages, but I do not want to speculate about the question whether middle constructions are semantically transitive or not here (see Kemmer [1993]; Steinbach [2002], and the references therein).

[22] Hellan (1988) argues that self-directed verbs are really ambiguous between an inherently reflexive and a true transitive variant, but see Kiparsky (2002): section 3.8 for convincing arguments against this analysis.

(1.64)   (a)   semantically intransitive (inherently reflexive): *behave oneself*, Dutch *zich gedragen* ('behave'); German *sich schließen* ('to close')

   (b)   typically self-directed verbs: *shave (oneself), hide (oneself)*, Swedish *tvätta sig* ('shave'), *gömma sig* ('hide')

   (c)   typically other-directed verbs: *hate oneself, prefer oneself*, Swedish *hata sig själf* ('hate oneself'), *föreda sig själf* ('prefer oneself')

At least historically, the choice of forms in these constructions is likely to be related to the fact that complex reflexives like German *sich selbst* or Swedish *sig själf* are composed of a simple reflexive pronoun and the emphatic marker akin to *self* (the English situation is more complicated, but note that modern English uses the form *himself, herself*, etc. as an emphatic marker, as in *The director himself opposed the plan.*; see Eckardt (2002) for a formal semantic analysis). The idea is that hating or preferring oneself (rather than someone else) is the unusual case and deserves special emphasis, but shaving or washing oneself is the norm and doesn't require emphasis (see Haiman [1985, 1995]; König and Siemund [2000]; König and Vezzosi [2002] for cross-linguistic data; note that complex reflexives with verbs of grooming *are* acceptable if, for example, shaving oneself is juxtaposed with shaving someone else first, i.e. if there is contrastive emphasis).

Unsurprisingly, semantically inert arguments, as found with inherently reflexive verbs, cannot bear emphasis (Dutch speakers, for example, find **Hij gedraagt zichzelf*, rather than *zich*, as bizarre as English speakers do **He behaved Carmen*). The fact that a language like English, which lacks a simple reflexive, has extremely few reflexive verbs, and never uses a reflexive in inchoative constructions,[23] may well be related to the emphatic heritage of the reflexive form. In the same vein, note that what are arguably semantically inert NPs (note the oddity of full NPs) in positions other than direct objects occur more frequently in English, in the form of non-reflexive pronouns:

(1.65)   (a)   Mary brought her lunch with *her/*herself/*Colin*.
   (b)   Bertrand has many friends around *him/*himself/*Cindy*.
   (c)   Francesca lost *her/*her own/*Ibrahim's* way.

This suggests that Binding Conditions are relevant for the choice of semantically inert NP forms as well: non-reflexive pronouns cannot occur if they are locally syntactically bound (regardless of whether they are semantically interpreted at all); in addition, (complex) reflexives must not be (or at least abhor being) semantically inert. For more discussion, the reader is referred to Kiparsky (2002) and the references therein.

---

[23] Or middles, cf. n. 21.

Exercise 1.7

Try to use reflexives, non-reflexives, and full NPs in the blank positions in the examples below. For each, decide whether that position is semantically inert or active; argue carefully!

(1.66)   (a)   Mr Mitchum wouldn't perjure _____.

(b)   The tactic is to draw speculators' fangs by making them commit _____ to buying put options.

(c)   Carmen has a Spanish look about _____.

(d)   The general looked around _____.

2   Interpreting indexed structures

In the previous chapter we introduced indexing conventions that expressed our intuitions about the (im)possibility of coreference between two NPs in a given structure. In this chapter I am going to provide a semantic interpretation that cashes out this indexing in semantic terms. It is against this formal, precise interpretation of syntactic indexing that we are going to check the predictions of our theory and its possible modifications later on.

2.1   Basics of interpretation

The kind of semantic interpretation we assume here is a truth-conditional one. Linguistic expressions are associated with non-linguistic entities, i.e. things in the world (e.g. my left thumb and the Cologne Cathedral), and set-theoretic constructs made out of these (e.g. the set of all my fingers, or the set of all sets that contain that set). The task of the semanticist is to devise basic meanings for the words of the language and systematic ways of combining them so as to arrive at intuitively correct truth conditions for entire sentences.

Since this book is not an introduction to semantics, I will keep the technical apparatus to a minimum. Also, common semantic concepts and techniques will be introduced only very briefly. The formalism introduced and used starting with section 2.3 is for the most part compatible with that laid out in great detail in Heim and Kratzer (1998). Readers with a desire for more background are referred to this excellent introduction (other introductory textbooks to formal semantics will for the most part provide the same information, though technical details may differ).

We assume an *interpretation function* $[\![\ ]\!]$, which assigns an appropriate meaning or *denotation* to every syntactic object. We say that α *denotes* $[\![\alpha]\!]$. What are meanings? I just give some examples:

(2.1)   (a) $[\![Caroline]\!]$ = the real Caroline in flesh and blood
         (b) $[\![Caroline\ and\ Fritz]\!]$ = the plurality consisting of the real Caroline and the real Fritz (we'll come back to what a plurality is in chapter 9)
         (c) $[\![smile]\!]$ = the set of all those who smiled
         (d) $[\![Caroline\ smiled]\!]$ = 1 iff ('if and only if') Caroline smiled, 0 otherwise

⟦ ⟧ must consist of two blocks: a *lexicon*, from which we get meanings for words/terminal nodes such as (2.1a) and (2.1c); and a set of *composition rules* that tell us how to derive the meaning of a non-terminal node from the meaning(s) of its daughter(s), for example:

(2.2)   ⟦NP VP⟧ $= 1$ iff ⟦NP⟧ is in (an element of) ⟦VP⟧, 0 otherwise

The numbers 0 and 1 used in (2.1d) and (2.2) are *truth values*. We can think of ⟦S⟧ $= 1$ as saying 'S is true', and ⟦S⟧ $= 0$ as 'S is false'. A statement of the form in (2.1d) (⟦S⟧ $= 1$ iff . . .), which is an instantiation of (2.2) with NP $=$ *Caroline* and VP $=$ *smiled*, is a description of a sentence's *truth conditions*. Also, we speak of the meta-language statement following the *iff* (e.g. 'Caroline smiled' in [2.1d]) as the *proposition* expressed by the sentence.

What is most important for our purposes is that the denotation of a singular referring NP – its contribution to the meaning of a sentence – is a thing out there in the world, a person, thing, or place, or as is common to say in semantic jargon, an *individual* or *entity* (as remarked, we will postpone discussion of the denotation of non-referential NPs until chapter 4, and of plural NPs until chapter 9). We will say that an NP *refers* to that individual.

Exercise 2.1
Give denotations for the words *Carl* and *sleeps*. Then derive the truth conditions for *Carl sleeps* along the lines of (2.1) above.

2.2   Enter indexing

2.2.1   Reference and assignments

In section 2.1 we saw that the interpretation function ⟦ ⟧ determines *the* proposition expressed by a sentence, e.g. that Caroline smiles for the sentence *Caroline smiles*. For a sentence with a pronoun in it, say *She smiles*, however, we can't assign *the* proposition it expresses, because it can express as many different propositions as there are individuals that can be referred to using the pronoun *she* (e.g. that Caroline smiled, that the queen smiled, that the *Titanic* smiled . . .). The best we can do is to say which propositions such a sentence *can* express (and thereby indirectly say which propositions it can*not* express).

We therefore augment the interpretation function ⟦ ⟧ with an *assignment function*, or assignment, for short, written as g. The assignment determines which individual a pronoun refers to.

An assignment is a function from the set of natural numbers to individuals. Since indices are natural numbers, an assignment assigns an individual to each index. You can think of an assignment g as a sequence of individuals; $g(n)$ then is the n-th element in that sequence. (2.3) through (2.5) are three different assignments:

(2.3)   1   2   3   4   5   6   7   ...

             ↓   ↓   ↓   ↓   ↓   ↓   ↓

             Bo   Sven   Kim   Ana   Kurt   Eszter Tanya

(2.4)   1   2   3   4   5   6   7   ...

             ↓   ↓   ↓   ↓   ↓   ↓   ↓

             Bo   Kim   Sue   Marge Kurt   Eszter Tanya

(2.5)   1   2   3   4   5   6   7   ...

             ↓   ↓   ↓   ↓   ↓   ↓   ↓

             Ana   Kim   Marge Sven   Kurt   Kim   Tanya

As a first stab, we can now interpret third person singular pronouns as the n-th member of the assignment g, where n is the index on the pronoun. Thus $[\![\text{she}_3]\!]^g$ denotes, or refers to, $g(3)$, which is an individual, just like $[\![\text{Caroline}]\!]^g$. Relative to the assignments in (2.3)–(2.5), it refers to Kim, Sue, and Marge, respectively. The sentence *She$_3$ smiled*, then, can express the propositions that Kim smiled, that Sue smiled, that Marge smiled, etc.

A different way to think of an assignment is as providing the (relevant aspects of the) *context*. *She$_3$ smiled* expresses that Sue smiled in the context/ assignment (2.4), but that Marge smiled in the context/assignment (2.5). This view assumes that the assignment somehow reflects properties of a context, for example that Ana, Kim, Marge, etc. have been introduced in context (2.5), perhaps that they have different degrees of salience, etc. In this book we will usually speak of assignments as contexts, though we will have little to say about just how the assignment comes to reflect an actual context (cf. section 2.4.1). In a narrower technical sense, assignments are simply a device to arrive at the set of propositions a sentence can express (cf. section 2.3.2).

A full representation of the context will include more than just an assignment. It has to include, for example, the speaker s and the utterance situation u. That way, we can define lexical meanings such as:

(2.6)   (a) $[\![\text{I/me/myself/my}]\!]^{g,s,u} = s$
          (b) $[\![\text{you/yourself/your}]\!]^{g,s,u} =$ the single person s addresses in u
          (c) $[\![\text{you}_{pl}/\text{you guys}]\!]^{g,s,u} =$ the plurality of people s addresses in u

We will henceforth write $[\![\alpha]\!]^{g,s,u}$ to mean 'the denotation of α relative to assignment g, speaker s, and utterance situation u'. $[\![\ ]\!]$ in its unadorned form (i.e. without g etc.) doesn't play a role anymore; we will, however, omit s and u where these are of no concern, using $[\![\ ]\!]^g$.

The use of an assignment function to interpret pronouns is borrowed from predicate logic, where assignments are used to assign values to *variables*. It is therefore common to speak of pronouns functioning as variables (or being interpreted as variables – though strictly speaking this should be 'interpreted like variables').[1] Elements that do not depend on the assignment for their meaning – which in natural language include verbs, prepositions, articles, common nouns, etc. – are accordingly called *constants*.

2.2.2   Binding Theory

We begin by making explicit some of the assumptions from the previous chapter, e.g. that (referring) NPs bear indices:

(2.7)   NP Indexing (preliminary):
Every name, pronoun, and definite NP bears an index. Nothing else bears an index.[2]

How do we interpret this indexing? Essentially, as said above, we want an NP with index n to refer to $g(n)$ under a given assignment g. NPs, however, have some lexical content which is independent of the particular context. Even pronouns do: the pronoun *she* for example can only refer to a singular female individual. How can we capture this? By representing those context-independent meaning parts as *presuppositions*:[3]

(2.8)   (a) $[\![he_1]\!]^g = g(1)$ if $g(1)$ is male, undefined otherwise
(b) $[\![her_5]\!]^g = g(5)$ if $g(5)$ is female, undefined otherwise

Relative to an assignment g, sentence S (with a pronoun) will have a denotation only if g happens to meet the presuppositions of the pronoun (e.g. if $g(5)$ is in fact female); otherwise, $[\![S]\!]^g$ is undefined. If $[\![S]\!]^g$ *is* defined, we get one of the meanings S can have.

That the gender (and number) information is a presupposition rather than part of the meaning proper (e.g. something along the lines of '$[\![he_1]\!]^g = g(1)$ and $g(1)$ is male') can be seen by looking at a sentence like (2.9):

(2.9)   Alfred$_5$ thinks that she$_5$ missed the bus.

If the 'is female' bit were part of the literal meaning of *she*, (2.9) should mean something like 'Alfred thinks that he is female and that he missed the bus', given that *Alfred* and *she* are coindexed. But, obviously, there is no such reading. On the

---

[1] Note that this semantic notion of 'variable' does not coincide with the notion of variable as used in the Government and Binding framework (Chomsky, 1981) where the term variable is used to mean 'trace of *wh*-movement'.

[2] In transformationalist terms, we assume that an NP starts out with an index (rather than being indexed in the course of the derivation), although nothing essential hinges on this assumption. This means that indexing takes place at d-structure (or at Merge, or whatever fashion calls it).

[3] Additional complications arise in languages such as Italian and German which have *grammatical gender*. For example, the word for moon is feminine in Italian (*la luna*) and masculine in German (*der Mond*). Consequentially, Italian speakers refer to the moon with a feminine pronoun, Germans with a masculine one. The presupposition of the pronoun therefore cannot make reference to the sex of the referent but to the gender of the expression used to designate it. More complications arise in cases where different words of different gender can be used to refer to the same thing, e.g. *der Zug* (masc.) vs. *die Bahn* (fem.) for 'train' in German. We will not attempt to represent grammatical gender systems in this book.

presupposition treatment, on the other hand, the sentence means 'Alfred thinks that Alfred missed the bus' and presupposes that Alfred is female, which seems intuitively correct (the sentence is thus unacceptable to the extent that we take *Alfred* to be an exclusively male name).

As for proper names and definite NPs, we assume, too, that it is the index which determines the reference, whereas the lexical content of the NP adds an (identity) presupposition. This is achieved by the schema (2.10), which, as an illustration, is instantiated in (2.10a) and (2.10b):

(2.10)   For all names, definite NPs, and 1st/2nd person pronouns $[\![NP_n]\!]^g = g(n)$ if $g(n) = [\![NP]\!]^g$, undefined otherwise.
    (a) $[\![Sarah_8]\!]^g = g(8)$ if $g(8)$ is Sarah, undefined otherwise
    (b) $[\![[the\ fugitive]_4]\!]^g = g(4)$ if $g(4)$ is the only fugitive (in the context), undefined otherwise

Note that rule (2.10) applies to first and second person pronouns, too, so that applying it to, say, a first person pronoun (cf. [2.6a] above) we get (2.11):

(2.11) $[\![I/me/my/myself_n]\!]^{g,s,u} = g(n)$ if $g(n) = s$, undefined otherwise

It is worth noting that, as far as interpretation goes, we wouldn't have to index names, first and second person pronouns, and full NPs for their referent is fixed by their inherent meaning (plus the contextual parameters s and u; see section 2.2.1) anyway. That is, as mentioned above, we assume that – at least in a given context/utterance situation – an NP like *Peter Stuyvesandt, the founder of New York* and even *the waiter* have a unique referent, regardless of their indexing. The need to index full NPs comes from our desire to implement BT. If we were to assign their referents without looking at the index, how could we formalize facts about coreference by indexing? (A possible answer to this question will be discussed in chapter 6.)

The simple indexing and interpretation procedure just introduced ensures that coindexing of two NPs results in coreference, just as desired. Thus it is clear that (2.12) will get an interpretation in which her_6 and $Sarah_6$ corefer, and cannot get one in which they won't, even though (2.13), of course, can:

(2.12)   In her_6 office, $Sarah_6$ introduced him_2 to   the $director_8$.
            ↓   ↓   ↓   ↓
          Sarah   Sarah   Steve   Caroline

          NOT: Tatjana   Sarah   Steve   Caroline

(2.13)   In her_3 office, $Sarah_6$ introduced him_2 to the $director_8$.
            ↓   ↓   ↓   ↓
        Tatjana   Sarah   Steve   Caroline

There is a loophole, though, that we haven't explicitly closed yet. Could a sentence like (2.13), whose indexing meets all Binding Conditions, get an interpretation as in (2.14), where *him₂* and *the director₈* corefer, despite being contra-indexed?

(2.14)   In   her₃   office, Sarah₆   introduced   him₂   to the   director₈.

Tatjana   Sarah   Steve   Steve

For (2.14) to work, g must be an assignment in which the same individual – Steve – occurs twice. Intuitively this is unwanted (and it also clashes with the idea that an assignment is a sequence of individuals, for the same physical individual can occupy at most one place in a sequence, it would seem). Formally, however, an assignment is just a function from numbers to individuals, and nothing is wrong with a function that assigns the same value (individual) to two different arguments (numbers) (in fact, [2.5] above was just such an assignment).

Our intuition when doing the indexing, however, has been that non-coindexing means non-coreference (not just 'possible non-coreference'). That is, we are interested only in a subclass of assignments, namely those which don't assign the same individual to two different numbers. In other words, we want to exclude the possibility that two NPs that are not coindexed accidentally refer to the same individual. This is done through (2.15):

(2.15)   Prohibition against Accidental Coreference (PACO):
            $[\![S]\!]^g$ is a possible interpretation of sentence S only if $g(n) \neq g(m)$ if $m \neq n$, for any natural numbers n, m.

Functions which meet this additional condition are called *one-to-one*. Another way, then, of thinking of the effect of (2.15) is that it requires that any contextual assignment be one-to-one.[4]

Exercise 2.2
Show in detail how (2.15) successfully blocks (2.14)!

Exercise 2.3
The sentence *She thinks Liv is a spy* does not have a reading on which *she* and *Liv* corefer. Discuss in detail which principle(s) exclude(s) each of the following representations, all of which express the incriminated reading, and which don't:

(2.16)   (a)   She₃ thinks Liv₃ is a spy.   (with $g(3) =$ Liv)
            (b)   She₃ thinks Liv₂ is a spy.   (with $g(3) = g(2) =$ Liv)
            (c)   She₃ thinks that Liv is a spy.   (with $g(3) =$ Liv)

---

[4] It should be noted that assignment functions that aren't one-to-one can still be used *in the process* of calculating an interpretation; this will be necessary, for example, to interpret a sentence like *Baszon₃ believes that everyone₉ should get a raise*, which entails that Baszon believes that he himself should get a raise, which, as we will see below, requires an assignment under which both $g(3)$ and $g(9)$ are Baszon. Such an assignment, however, could never be used as a *contextual* assignment by PACO.

Exercise 2.4

It was remarked in section 2.2.2 that indexing first and second person pronouns is necessary to exclude certain BT violations. Provide an example and discuss it!

Exercise 2.5

Is (2.17) a well-formed representation? Should it be? Argue!

(2.17)   Latifa$_6$'s fans admire her$_{14}$.   (with $g(6) = g(14) = $ Latifa)

Exercise 2.6

Above it was said that relative to a context/assignment a sentence containing a pronoun expresses exactly one proposition. But it often happens that you don't quite know which proposition a sentence expresses, precisely because you're not sure who the pronoun refers to. Was the earlier statement wrong, or just sloppy? Clarify!

2.3   Compositional interpretation

In this section, we will provide the formal basis for compositionally interpreting syntactic trees. While all relevant concepts are formally introduced, this section cannot replace a complete introduction to compositional interpretation, for which the interested reader is referred to semantics textbooks (e.g. Heim and Kratzer [1998]:chs. 1–2).

2.3.1   Basics

Types and functions

Above we said that names and NPs in general denote individuals and that sentences denote truth values (both relative to a given assignment). We call those the *denotation domains* of NPs and Ss. Just as expressions belong to syntactic categories, they belong to *semantic types*, according to what kind of denotation domain they denote in. Thus the denotation domain of an NP is the set of individuals (in the technical sense alluded to in section 2.1, including all sorts of objects); we call this set E and we will say that an NP's semantic type is $\langle e \rangle$ (reminiscent of 'entity'). The denotation domain of sentences is the set of truth values, $\{0, 1\}$, and its semantic type shall be $\langle t \rangle$ ('truth value'). Other semantic types and their respective domains can be defined recursively:

(2.18)   Semantic types:
              (a) $\langle e \rangle$ and $\langle t \rangle$ are types
              (b)   if τ_1 and τ_2 are types, then $\langle \tau_1, \tau_2 \rangle$ is a type

(2.19)   Denotation domains:

      (a)   E (the set of individuals) is the interpretation domain of type $\langle e \rangle$, D_e for short

      (b) $\{0,1\}$ is the interpretation domain of type $\langle t \rangle$, D_t for short

      (c)   for any complex type $\langle \tau_1, \tau_2 \rangle$, its interpretation domain D_{τ_1, τ_2} is $D_{\tau_2}^{D_{\tau_1}}$, the set of all functions from D_{τ_1} to D_{τ_2}

Clause (2.19c) introduces the notion of a *function*. What is a function? Take an example: an intransitive verb is of type $\langle e,t \rangle$, i.e. it is a function from individuals to truth values. It 'takes' an individual as its *argument*, and 'gives' 0 or 1 as its *value*, or, as is usually said, it *maps* an individual onto a truth value. For concreteness take (2.20) (where $f : D_1 \to D_2$ stands for 'f is a function from D_1 to D_2):

(2.20) $[\![\text{smiled}]\!]^g = $ that function $f : D_e \to D_t$ such that for all x in D_e, $f(x) = 1$ iff x smiled

According to this, $f([\![Caroline]\!]^g)$ equals 1 if Caroline smiled, 0 otherwise (since there are only two truth values, we can abbreviate this as '... 1 iff Caroline smiled', where 'iff' stands for 'if and only if'); and so on for every other individual. We can now introduce our most important semantic composition rule for non-terminal nodes, *function application* (V^n stands for any verb or projection thereof):

(2.21)   Function Application (FA):

      $[\![V^n \ NP]\!]^g = [\![NP \ V^n]\!]^g = [\![V^n]\!]^g([\![NP]\!]^g)$

According to this rule, whenever we encounter an NP and a verb or verbal projection, which denotes a function, we *apply* that function to the denotation of the NP. Using lexical meanings and function application, we thus get:

(2.22)   (a) $[\![\text{Caroline}]\!]^g = $ Caroline (in flesh and blood)

      (b) $[\![\text{smiled}]\!]^g = $ the function f as defined in (2.20) above

      (c) $[\![\text{Caroline smiled}]\!]^g = [\![\text{smiled}]\!]^g([\![\text{Caroline}]\!]^g)$ (FA)

                   $= f(Caroline) = 1$ iff Caroline smiled (0 otherwise)

Functions, as in (2.20), are rather cumbersome to write, so it will be useful to introduce some abbreviatory conventions. To name a function like f in (2.20), we will alternatively write (2.23a), or (2.23b):

(2.23)   (a) $\lambda x \in D_e.x$ smiled

      (b) $\lambda x_e.x$ smiled

(2.23a) and (2.23b) use the λ *(lambda)-prefix*, borrowed again from formal logic. We employ the following convention (cf. Heim and Kratzer [1998]:37):

(2.24) λ-Convention: Read $\lambda \alpha.[_\phi \ldots \alpha \ldots (\alpha) \ldots]$ as

      (a)   'that function which maps every a to 1 iff $[_\phi \ldots a \ldots (a) \ldots]$', if ϕ is a sentence,

      (b)   'that function which maps every a to $[_\phi \ldots a \ldots (a) \ldots]$' otherwise

We will return to clause (2.24b) below. Since 'x smiled' in (2.23) is a sentence, clause (2.24a) applies: [$\lambda x_e.x$ smiled] is that function which maps every x in D_e to 1 iff x smiled (brackets added for perspicuity). Note that the type of a λ-expression can be read off it straightforwardly: (2.23a)/(2.23b) for example has a λ binding a variable of type $\langle e \rangle$, followed by a sentence, 'x smiled'. English sentences represent meanings in D_t, which means that the whole expression is of type $\langle e,t \rangle$.[5]

Transitive verbs

A typical transitive verb denotation is given in (2.25):

(2.25) $[\![likes]\!]^g = \lambda x \in D_e.\lambda y \in D_e.y$ likes x

Here the sentence y *likes* x has two λs in front of it, each binding an individual variable. Its semantic type is thus $\langle e,\langle e,t \rangle \rangle$, or for short: $\langle e,et \rangle$. To disentangle this, we first apply (2.24b) with $\alpha = x$ and $\phi = [\lambda y \in D_e.y$ likes $x]$, whereby (2.25) is a function which maps every individual x onto $[\lambda y \in D_e.y$ likes $x]$. The latter in turn, according to (2.24a), is a function that maps an individual y to 1 iff y likes x. (2.25) as a whole, then, is a function from individuals to functions from individuals to truth values. Such a function subsequently takes two individuals and maps them onto a truth value:

(2.26)   (a) $[\![Chris\ likes\ Caroline]\!]^g =$
            (b) $[\![likes\ Caroline]\!]^g([\![Chris]\!]^g) =$
            (c) $[\![likes\ Caroline]\!]^g(Chris) =$
            (d) $[\![likes]\!]^g([\![Caroline]\!]^g)(Chris) =$
            (e) $[\![likes]\!]^g(Caroline)(Chris) =$
            (f) $[\lambda x \in D_e\ \lambda y \in D_e.y$ likes $x]$ (Caroline) (Chris) $= 1$ iff Chris likes Caroline

Functions and the sets they characterize

At the beginning of this section we said that an intransitive verb denotes a function from individuals to truth values (type $\langle et \rangle$). In section 2.1, however, it was said that an intransitive verb denotes a set of individuals. While only the former is literally true, the latter almost is, because any function of type $\langle \tau,t \rangle$ uniquely characterizes a set (namely a subset of D_τ), and vice versa. The function $[\lambda x_e.x$ smiled] – call it f_{smiled} – for example, characterizes the set of all individuals x which that function maps to 1, formally: $\{x \in D_e \mid f_{smiled}(x) = 1\}$; informally: the set of all those who smiled.

In the remainder of this book, I will often make use of this equivalence, which is rendered again in (2.27):

---

[5] Note that individuals and functions *are* the meanings of object language expressions. We use names, English sentences, and λ-expressions to *name* those denotations in our meta-language; accordingly, no italics are used here. I will, however, sometimes include expressions used to name a denotation in quotation marks to facilitate reading.

(2.27)   Set/function equivalence and convention:
'$[\lambda x \in D_\tau \ldots x \ldots](y)'$ is equivalent to 'y is in $\{x \in D_\tau \mid \ldots x \ldots\}$'; we
will often write the latter instead of the former

For example, '$[\lambda x \in D_e.x$ smiled]$(Caroline) = 1$' is equivalent to 'Caroline is in
$\{x \in D_e \mid x$ smiled$\}$'. The latter form is sometimes more convenient and more
transparent, which is why I will use it. Also, I find it more intuitive to think of
an intransitive verb denotation as a set of individuals, and of a sentence containing it as true if the denotation of the subject is in that set, than to think of an
intransitive verb denotation as a function from individuals to truth values, and of
a sentence containing it as true if that function applied to the subject denotation
is 1 – though, as stated, both are equivalent.

So, to reiterate, I will regularly describe a denotation by saying 'so-and-so is
in set-x' where our official semantics assign it the denotation 'function-x applied
to so-and-so = 1'.

The reason why we still officially use 'function talk' rather than 'set talk'
is that the former is more general. Recall that, for example, a sentence with a
transitive verb can be interpreted by repeated function application, as in (2.26),
because a transitive verb denotes a function whose values are again functions.
While, alternatively, we could think of a transitive verb as denoting pairs of individuals – those pairs $\langle x,y \rangle$ in which x loves, hates, knows, calls, etc. y – such
a meaning would require an extra rule for combining transitive verb meanings
with object NP meanings.

Compositionality

A theory of interpretation should be *compositional*, meaning: denotations of complex expressions should be composed of the denotations of the
simpler expressions that make them up. For concreteness, let us adopt the following two conditions on interpretations:

(2.28)   (a)   Every syntactic constituent $\mathcal{C}$ has an interpretation.
          (b)   In interpreting a constituent $\mathcal{C}$, no other information can be used for
                 computing $[\![\mathcal{C}]\!]^g$ than that associated with $\mathcal{C}$'s daughters.

The Function Application rule used so far is strictly compositional in this sense.
Consider, for illustration, a different rule:

(2.29)   Non-Compositional S-rule:

$$\left[\!\!\left[\begin{array}{c} S \\ \diagup \diagdown \\ NP_S \quad VP \\ \diagup \diagdown \\ V \quad NP_O \end{array} \right]\!\!\right]^g = [\![V]\!]^g([\![NP_O]\!]^g)([\![NP_S]\!]^g)$$

This rule will assign the same denotations to a transitive sentence as the repeated
application of FA. It is, however, non-compositional. For one thing, VP doesn't

Table 2.1 *Types and their names*

Type	Name	Variable	Categories
e	individual	x, y, z	names, pronouns
t	truth value	p	sentences
et	properties	P	VPs, Ns, APs
e,et	relations	R	transitive Vs and Ns
et,t	generalized quantifier	q	quantified NPs

receive an interpretation, *contra* (2.28a). And, for another, the meaning rule for S directly uses the meanings of V and NP$_O$, which are not daughters of S, in violation of (2.28b). We will continuously check that all our interpretation rules to follow are compositional in nature.

A first inventory of categories and types

Different semantic types have common names in the semantic literature, which are summarized in table 2.1 (not all of them will look familiar to you yet).

In table 2.1 I also indicate the typical variables I use for the different semantic types. This is, of course, just a notational convention, but it will allow us to abbreviate the function notation further by leaving out the explicit domain specification. Instead of (2.25) we can now write (2.30), because it is understood that x and y are variables over D_e (upon demand, variables will be numbered, e.g. $p_1, p_2, \ldots$):

(2.30) $[\![likes]\!]^g = \lambda x \lambda y . y$ likes x

Exercise 2.7

Why must the denotation for, say, *likes* be as in (2.25), rather than $[\lambda y \in D_e . \lambda x \in D_e . y$ likes $x]$? What is the difference? Argue!

Exercise 2.8

Give the denotation for the verb *danced* both in set notation and λ-notation.

Exercise 2.9

Give the denotation for the verb *introduced*.

Exercise 2.10

Give denotations for all lexical elements in the following sentences, and provide derivations of their truth conditions à la (2.26); add indices where necessary:

(2.31)   (a)   Sam danced.
          (b)   Kim likes Jo.
          (c)   She slept.
          (d)   He admires him.
          (e)   He admires himself.

2.3.2   Truth, truth conditions, and meanings

The denotation of a sentence is a truth value, 1 or 0. What is closer to the intuitive meaning of a sentence, however, is not its truth value, but the *truth conditions* the interpretation procedure assigns to it, for example a statement of the form '$[\![S]\!] = 1$ iff . . . '. The goal of semantic theory, after all, cannot be to determine if a sentence is true or false (unless it happens to be a tautologous or contradictory sentence), but to assign systematically to every sentence a description (in English or something resembling English) of the kind of situation in which it would be true.

A slightly different way to think of the general meaning of a sentence involves the situations a sentence correctly describes. Generally, the following holds:

(2.32)   Given truth conditions of the form '$[\![S]\!] = 1$ iff ϕ,' we can say that S is true in a situation s iff ϕ holds in s.

Thus from the truth conditions '$[\![\text{Caroline smiled}]\!]^g = 1$ iff Caroline smiled' we can go to '*Caroline smiled* is true in a situation s if Caroline smiled in s.' The set of situations in which a sentence S is true is often called *the proposition expressed by S*. Instead of saying that a sentence denotes 1 iff ϕ, we will sometimes just say that it denotes the proposition that ϕ; thus *Caroline smiled* denotes the proposition that Caroline smiled.

But sentences contain NPs, and NPs depend on the assignment function, so we have to refine this. Recall that the denotation of an NP_n is defined relative to an assignment g, if $g(n)$ meets the presuppositions of the denotation of NP (e.g. that it be a female individual, or that it be called John, etc.); otherwise $[\![NP_n]\!]^g$ is *undefined*. We can thus say the following:

(2.33)   Given truth conditions of the form '$[\![S]\!]^g = 1$ iff ϕ,' we can say that S is true in a situation s relative to assignment g if $[\![S]\!]^g$ is defined and ϕ holds in s (it is false if $[\![S]\!]^g$ is defined and ϕ doesn't hold in s).

Whether or not $[\![S]\!]^g$ is defined for a given S thus depends on what assignment g we choose. The *proposition expressed by S relative to assignment g* is the set of situations in which S is true relative to g. A given sentence can thus express different propositions relative to different assignments.

This is plausible if, again, we think of an assignment as (part of) a context. Take as a concrete example the sentence *She$_6$ smiled*. We derive the truth conditions $[\![\text{she}_6 \text{ smiled}]\!]^g = 1$ iff ($g(6)$ is a female individual and) $g(6)$ smiled. By (2.33), it then holds that: for any assignment g, $[\![\text{she}_6 \text{ smiled}]\!]^g$ is defined iff $g(6)$ is a single female individual; if defined, it denotes the proposition that

$g(6)$ smiled. Take a g such that $g(6) =$ Caroline; then that means that 'Caroline smiled' is a possible meaning of she_6 *smiled*. But given that there are other assignments g' such that $g'(6) =$ Susan, 'Susan smiled' is also a possible meaning of she_6 *smiled*, and so on and so forth, for all and only those assignments according to which $g(6)$ is single and female.

Obviously, we haven't said anything about how g relates to the actual linguistic context, in other words: about the question which individual a given pronoun will, or is likely to, denote in a given linguistic context (see subsection 2.4.1 for a few remarks). Yet, by virtue of universally quantifying over all technically possible g, we can define the context-independent notion of a possible meaning:

(2.34) ϕ is a *possible meaning* of a sentence S iff there is an assignment function g such that $[\![S]\!]^g = 1$ iff ϕ

For example, 'Caroline smiled' is a possible meaning of *She_6 smiled*, as is 'Susan smiled'. 'Bill smiled' or 'Lake Balaton smiled' are not, assuming that neither Bill nor the popular Hungarian lake are female individuals. More interestingly, given PACO in (2.15), we derive for example that 'Caroline likes Susan' is a possible meaning of *Caroline_2 likes her_3*, but 'Caroline likes Caroline' is not.

Note that the possible meanings for a sentence are independent of the actual choice of indices. Two sentences S1 and S2 that only differ in indexing have the same set of possible meanings, provided all and only those NPs in S2 are coindexed that are coindexed in S1. For example, the set of possible meanings of *She_n smiled* is the same for any choice of index n.[6]

As a consequence, we can go one step further and define the notion *possible meaning of an expression E*, where an expression is a sentence (or rather: tree) without indices: if ϕ is a possible meaning of E, that means that there is some indexing E^1 of E which is grammatical (i.e. obeys the Binding Conditions A–C and whatever other syntactic conditions we'll impose on indexing), and ϕ is a possible meaning of that indexed version E^1 of E.

For example, let E be the expression *She likes her*, which has an infinite number of possible indexings E^1. By Binding Condition B, all of these indexings must assign different integers to *she* and *her*. By the PACO, such an indexing prohibits an interpretation by which *she* and *her* wind up coreferential. Thus the set of possible meanings for *She saw her* (without indices) is the set of all propositions 'x saw y' where x and y are two different female individuals.

The expression *She says Kim likes her*, on the other hand, has infinitely many indexings on which *she* and *her* are coindexed, and infinitely many on which they are not (and all of those have *Kim* counter-indexed with both pronouns). The former all get interpretations of the form *x says Kim likes x*, the latter of the

---

[6] This is not to say that there couldn't be *syntactic* rules or constraints that distinguish S1 and S2, as argued recently in e.g. Heim (1997), or Sauerland (2000); we will discuss some relevant cases in sections 5.5.2 of chapter 5, and 6.5.1 of chapter 6.

Table 2.2 *Semantic objects related to sentences*

truth value	0 or 1
truth conditions	$[\![S]\!]^g = 1$ iff ϕ
proposition expressed by S	ϕ/ the set of situations s in which
(relative to g)	ϕ holds (assuming that $[\![S]\!]^g = 1$ iff ϕ)
possible meanings of indexed S	the set of propositions S can express relative to any g (respecting PACO)
possible meaning of unindexed S	the set of propositions any grammatical indexing of S can express relative to any g (respecting PACO)

form x *says Kim likes* y, with $x \neq y \neq Kim$. Hence all instances of these are possible meanings for the expression *She says Kim likes her*.

In conclusion, the various semantic objects corresponding roughly to whole sentences introduced in this subsection are summarized in table 2.2. Since natural language doesn't come with indices, possible meanings of expressions/unindexed sentences are what our semantic interpretation procedure, in tandem with Binding Theory, should ultimately predict.

Exercise 2.11

Give truth conditions, the proposition expressed, and, where you can, the possible meanings (regardless of indexing) for the sentences in (2.31) (again, add indices where necessary).

Appendix: Meaning relations

Given the above, we define, for the sake of completeness, some essential semantic notions for indexed sentences:

(2.35)   (a)   S1 *entails* S2 iff for any assignment g, every situation in which S1 is true relative to g is one in which S2 is true relative to g.

(b)   S is a *tautology* iff it is true in any situation relative to any assignment (for which it is defined).

(c)   S1 and S2 are *incompatible* if for any assignment g, there is no situation in which S1 and S2 are both true relative to g.

(d)   S1 and S2 are *synonymous* if each entails the other.

2.3.3   More composition rules ^ℰ

Type-driven interpretation

In (2.26) above we used Function Application twice, once to combine the object meaning with the transitive-verb meaning, and then again to combine that VP meaning with the subject meaning. Note that in each case, FA is well defined, since the type of the argument, $\langle e \rangle$, 'matches' the type of the function,

$\langle e, \ldots \rangle$. This is so because any element of type $\langle e, \ldots \rangle$ denotes a function from individuals, i.e. elements of D_e, to something else (depending on what ... is). In a case like that we say that the argument, here an individual in D_e, is in the *domain* of the function.[7]

Among two given meanings M_1 and M_2, exactly one of three possible situations will obtain:

- M_1 is in the domain of M_2, i.e. $M_2(M_1)$ is defined
  (e.g. M_1 is in D_e and M_2 is in $D_{e,t}$ or $D_{e,et}$)
- M_2 is in the domain of M_1, i.e. $M_1(M_2)$ is defined
  (e.g. M_2 is in D_e and M_1 is in $D_{e,t}$ or $D_{e,et}$)
- neither is in the domain of the other, i.e. neither $M_1(M_2)$ nor $M_2(M_1)$ are defined
  (e.g. both M_1 and M_2 are in D_{et})

Given this, we can generalize our interpretation rule as follows:

(2.36)   Function Application, revised and final:
$[\![A\ B]\!]^g = [\![A]\!]^g([\![B]\!]^g)$ or $[\![B]\!]^g([\![A]\!]^g)$, whichever is defined

The reader may verify that this rule subsumes our earlier (2.21). An interpretation procedure along these lines, where the semantic type of the sister constituents (rather than their syntactic category and/or linear order) determines the mode of semantic composition, is called *type-driven interpretation* or, less respectfully, 'shake-and-bake semantics'; it was introduced into linguistic semantics in Klein and Sag (1985).

We will add a few other composition rules that take care of situations in which neither $M_1(M_2)$ nor $M_2(M_1)$ in the sense above are defined later on, but FA alone will bring us a long way. For concreteness, we will assume that a constituent to which no semantic composition rule applies is uninterpretable and hence ungrammatical.

Interpreting flat structures

In chapter 1 we encountered examples which appear to involve flat structures, i.e. nodes with more than two daughters, e.g. double object VPs, NPs with two post-nominal PPs, and generally clausal structures in non-configurational languages:

(2.37)   (a)   I introduced the students to each other.
          (b)   (Ja čital) stat'ju   Tolstoja o   **sebe**.   (Russian)
                I   read article-ACC *T.*-GEN *about himself*-LOC
                '(I read) an article of Tolstoj about himself.'

---

[7] Confusion is lurking here: note that the *denotation domain* of an *expression E* is not identical to the *domain* of the *denotation* of E, even if E denotes a function. For example, the denotation domain of an intransitive verb is D_{et}, the set of functions from individuals to truth values, but the domain of the denotation of an intransitive verb is D_e, the set of individuals.

We suggested there that binding asymmetries among the daughters in such a multiply branching structure are encoded in a non-phrase structural aspect of syntactic representation, say the a(rgument)-list on which a command relation such as O(bliqueness)-Command can be defined. But, independent of the proper formulation of the Binding Conditions, we also need to say something about the interpretation of these structures, as our Function Application rule (2.36) (or its earlier incarnation [2.21]) obviously doesn't apply to such a structure. This can be done by adding a rule like the following:

(2.38) N-ary Function Application:

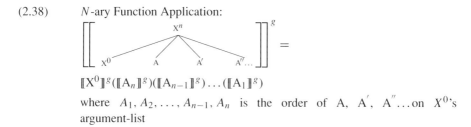

$$[\![X^0]\!]^g([\![A_n]\!]^g)([\![A_{n-1}]\!]^g)\ldots([\![A_1]\!]^g)$$

where $A_1, A_2, \ldots, A_{n-1}, A_n$ is the order of A, A$'$, A$''$...on X^0's argument-list

For example, *introduce Helena to Gwynn* will be interpreted as $[\![\text{introduce}]\!]^g$ $([\![(\text{to}) \text{Gwynn}]\!]^g)$ $([\![\text{Helena}]\!]^g)$, provided that the a-list of *introduce* looks like $\langle \text{NP}, \text{NP}_{\text{acc}}, \text{PP} \rangle$.[8] Note that this rule is strictly compositional, since it assigns a meaning to every node, based on the meanings of its daughters.

2.4   Extensions and alternatives©

2.4.1   A note on non-C-command anaphora

Above, we somewhat boldly called g (part of the representation of) the 'context'. However, nothing in our theory tells us how g relates to an actual context. Consider, for example, the following:

(2.39)   (a) A dog is sitting at the bar. (b) Suddenly, it sees a man come in. (c) The man has a dog too. (d) It is wearing a tie.

Here's a selection of what our treatment so far tells us: (i) *the bar* cannot be bound by *a dog* in (a); (ii) *it* in (b) can refer to the dog from (a), or some other neuter individual; (iii) *the man* in (c) refers to the unique man, which can be the man from (b); etc. etc. Here's what our treatment doesn't tell us, though native speakers could:

---

[8] Notice that the FA notation is left-associative, i.e. X(A)(A$'$)(A$''$) is equivalent to ((X(A))(A$'$))(A$''$). In other words, semantic composition still proceeds 'binary,' combining with one argument 'at a time.' We will justify this approach (rather than, say, one which combines the verb meaning with a tuple consisting of all its argument meanings at once) in chapter 4 below.
   Note, too, that (2.38) is built on the assumption that all but the least oblique argument A_0 on the a-list are sisters to X^0, though this could easily be refined.

(2.40)   (a)   *it* in (b) is very likely to be taken to refer to the dog mentioned in (a), rather than to any other individual

          (b)   *it* in (b) cannot possibly refer to the other dog (the one with the tie)

          (c)   *the man* in (c) is very likely to be interpreted as the man mentioned in (b)

          (d)   *a dog* in (c) cannot be the dog mentioned in (a) and (b)

          (e)   *it* in (d) is very likely to be taken to refer to the second dog

In short, what is missing is a theory about how a given sentence *changes* the context, including the referential options for sentences to follow. How do referents become available? How do speakers choose among different grammatically possible antecedents for a given pronoun?

Informally, such a theory would start from the assumption that at the beginning of a discourse there are no anaphoric possibilities; technically, a discourse starts with an assignment function with an empty domain. NP occurrences can then be classified into those that *introduce discourse referents*, hence add their index to the domain of the assignment function, and those that don't, hence rely on their index being in the domain of the assignment function already; the latter are the anaphoric NPs.

Whether or not an NP belongs to the introducing or the anaphoric type is not merely a matter of its morphological shape. Proper names, for example, can be used anaphorically, or to introduce a new discourse referent; so can definite NPs (*the moon* versus *the guy*), demonstratives, and first and second person pronouns (though the latter could be argued to be 'anaphoric' by definition). Even third person pronouns, though most commonly used anaphorically, can be used without an antecedent, for example when using, say, *she* to refer to a person who just walked in, or whom I point to, or whom we both watch on a TV monitor (though one could argue that their very appearance, or my pointing at them, actually introduces the discourse referent, which is then anaphorically picked up by the use of the pronoun). Indefinite NPs, including cardinals and certain quantifiers such as *few, most*, etc. are perhaps the only morphological class that is consistent, in that they always introduce new referents, and cannot, it seems, be used anaphorically.

Discourse Representation Theory provides a framework in which notions such as 'having a discourse antecedent,' 'introducing a discourse referent,' or 'being incapable of having a discourse antecedent' can be formalized; representative examples are Heim's (1982, 1983) *File Change Semantics*; Kamp's (1981) *Discourse Representation Theory*; and Groenendijk and Stokhof's (1991) *Dynamic Predicate Logic*. Useful introductory texts include Kamp and Reyle (1993) and Chierchia (1995).

In addition, a theory of discourse anaphora should address the question which type of NP will most likely be used anaphorically to pick up a particular referent (it seems that the choice between, say, a pronoun and a definite NP depends on roughly how long ago the pertinent discourse referent was introduced), and conversely, which one of a number of already introduced referents a given anaphoric NP is likely to pick out. Theories that address these questions include *Centering*

Theory (Grosz *et al.*, 1995; Walker *et al.*, 1998), *Accessibility Theory* (Ariel, 1999, 2001), and *Relevance Theory* (Sperber and Wilson, 1995) among many others; see also Kehler (2002) for a hybrid proposal.

I will not introduce a theory of context change, centering, or relevance in this book, which focuses mainly on binding within a sentence; that is, as far as our official theory goes, (b) in (2.39) for example, has as its possible meaning 'Fido sees a man come in,' where Fido is the dog mentioned in (a), but also 'Hasso sees a man come in,' where Hasso is the other dog mentioned in (c), and that it is up to a discourse theory to filter further among these.

It is worth noting that the question when an NP can pick up the referent introduced by another NP′ can sometimes influence our acceptability judgments on a simple sentence as well. For example, most speakers will find it very hard to interpret *his* and *Edson* as coreferential in (2.41a), while that interpretation is easy to get in (2.41b):

(2.41)   (a)   How did other mothers cope with this? For example, what did his mother think, when she learned Edson got arrested?

          (b)   How did other mothers cope with this? For example, what did *Edson*'s mother think, when she learned *he* got arrested?

The same sentence as in (2.41a), however, improves considerably on a coreferential reading if the preceding context is changed:

(2.42)   What did his family think of *Edson*? For example, what did *his* mother think, when she learned *Edson* got arrested?

This pattern suggests that the problem with (2.41a) is that *his* cannot pick up the referent introduced by *Edson*, presumably because it precedes it (whence the improvement if the NPs are swapped as in [2.41b]). If the previous sentence already talks about Edson as in (2.42), no such 'backwards link' is necessary, and *his* is naturally understood to refer to Edson. It seems appropriate to say that while *his* and *Edson* corefer in the second clause in (2.42), *his* is actually anaphoric to the occurrence of *Edson* in the first sentence in (2.42) (as is the second occurance of *Edson*, presumably).

To be sure, these remarks are not meant to provide a serious account of so-called *backwards anaphora*; it is quite possible that in some configurations, pronouns can be genuinely anaphoric to a full NP that *follows* them. If our remarks about the above examples are on the right track though, they do suggest that we were justified in separating out the purely structural Binding Conditions A–C, which have nothing to say about any of these cases, from a more general theory of introducing and anaphorically picking up discourse referents, which applies to intra- and inter-sentential anaphoric relations alike.[9]

---

[9] This doesn't mean that there can't be controversy about which kind of effect belongs to which theory. Evans (1980) claims that Binding Condition C effects are not structural but result from

2.4.2   Reflexives as reflexivizers

Above we assumed that reflexive and non-reflexive pronouns are semantically identical; they are interpreted like individual variables. Whatever differences we find between them are accounted for in the syntax, i.e. by indexing. An alternative approach is to view reflexives as *semantically* distinct from non-reflexive pronouns. As a starting-point, assume that the reflexive in a sentence like *Natasha painted herself* serves to map the relation denoted by *painted* onto the property of self-painting. Formally, this means that the meaning of *herself*, represented as SELF, maps a relation R onto the property of being an individual that stands in the R relation to itself, $\lambda x.R(x)(x)$:

(2.43)   (a)   SELF is that function from relations to properties such that $SELF(R) = \lambda x.R(x)(x)$ for all $R \in D_{e,et}$

           (b)   [[himself/herself/itself]]$^g = \lambda R\lambda x.(x$ is a male/female/neuter individual and) $SELF(R)(x)$

Interestingly, a reflexive on this view does not need to be indexed, since it is not a referring expression. The fact that it is 'locally bound' simply follows from its lexical meaning: it maps the predicate it combines with onto what we might call a 'reflexive property.' Thus something close to Binding Condition A actually follows from this analysis of reflexives.

Obviously, nothing about non-reflexives follows. One could formulate principles to re-establish complementary distribution again, however, e.g. (2.44):

(2.44)   (a)   No pronominal can be used where a reflexive would yield the same meaning.

           (b)   Unless a transitive verb V has a reflexive pronoun as its argument, interpret it as $\lambda x.\lambda y.[[V]]^g(x)(y) \& x \neq y$.

As just discussed, this approach is attractive in that it builds Binding Condition A into the lexical meaning of the reflexive: the reflexive will automatically be 'bound,' and it will be bound by a higher coargument. It is, however, well known that reflexives do not always combine with a relation denoting expression, cf. (2.45a) and (2.45b), and that in such cases the binder of a reflexive is not always the next higher coargument (in [2.45a] the 'highest' argument, the subject, binds the 'lowest,' the direct object, skipping, as it were, the indirect

---

the fact that a pronoun is trying to pick up its referent from a full NP it c-commands (he claims, in line with the other authors quoted at the end of section 1.2.3 in chapter 1, that a full NP c-commanding a coreferent full NP isn't ungrammatical at all). He adduces the acceptability of (i) below (his [59]) as evidence for that position. I believe though that (i) instantiates a special case of what Heim (1993) calls 'when structured meanings matter', which we will discuss briefly at the end of section 6.3 in chapter 6. Generally, a pronoun c-commanding a coreferent NP, even in the presence of an independent antecedent as in (ii), appears to be rather bad (compare [ii] to [2.42]), and should be ruled out on structural grounds:

(i)   What do you mean *John* loves no one? *He* loves *John*.
(ii)   *I wonder how *Edson* felt. What did *he* think when *Edson* got arrested?

object in the middle); indeed, the antecedent needn't be a coargument at all, cf. (2.45c) and (2.45d):

(2.45)   (a)   Gabi introduced herself to John.
          (b)   Gilbert$_1$ told Spencer$_2$ about himself$_{1/2}$.
          (c)   The president saw [himself give a speech].
          (d)   The CEO despised [those recent articles about herself].

In none of these cases can the reflexive be interpreted as in (2.43b); furthermore, to capture the two coreference options in (2.45b), we would have to assume two different meanings for the reflexive (or two different structures for the sentence). While appropriate meanings can be devised, the challenge is to show that the resulting class of meanings is constrained in some natural way. Otherwise, the distribution of reflexives reduces to an idiosyncratic case of lexical ambiguities, hardly a satisfactory state of affairs.[10]

On the other hand, even if this treatment turns out to be inadequate for English *himself*, there might be other elements in other languages that are amenable to it. In particular, many languages have a verbal reflexive marker which essentially de-transitivizes a transitive verb to give you an intransitive verb. This marker might aptly be characterized as denoting SELF. Consider the following examples from Finnish and Chichewa (from Sells *et al.* [1987]:177,187):

(2.46)   (a)   Jussi pese   -yty -i.   (Finnish)
                 J.   *washed self* PAST
                 'Jussi washed himself/self-washed.'
          (b)   Jussi puolusta -utu -i.
                 J.   *defended self* PAST
                 'Jussi defended himself/self-defended.'
(2.47)   Alenje a- na- dzi- lum -a.   (Chichewa)
          hunters SA PAST *self bite* INDICATIVE
          'The hunters bit themselves/self-bit.'

The affixes *-yty/-utu* and *dzi-* are not syntactic arguments or clitics (they cannot, for example, be separated from the verb or be coordinated with other NPs; see Mcahombo [1993a] for more evidence), and the derived form is syntactically intransitive (e.g. the *-yty/-utu* forms form causatives following the intransitive instead of the transitive pattern). It seems plausible that these affixes semantically function like SELF described above. Likewise, certain other reflexives with a more limited distribution than English *himself* are perhaps best treated this way (cf. Sells *et al.* [1987]).

Exercise 2.12

The relation that is reflexivized in (2.45a) can be written as $\lambda x.\lambda y.Gabi\ introduced\ y\ to\ x$. (2.48) gives the appropriate lexical entry for

---

[10] Another problem with this approach is what happens if the reflexive is coordinated, as in *Polsen painted himself and Mary*, especially on a *non-distributive* reading of the coordination, a matter we cannot go into here.

herself to derive this meaning (where R^3 is a variable over three-place relations, i.e. a variable in $D_{e,\langle e,et\rangle}$):

(2.48) $[\![\text{herself}_{dt1}]\!]^g = \lambda R^3.\lambda x_1.\lambda x_2.R^3(x_1)(x_1)(x_2)$
            $(= \lambda R^3.\lambda x_1.\lambda x_2.SELF(\lambda x_3.\lambda x_3.R^3(x_3)(x_4)(x_2))(x_1))$

Note that this rule assumes that the order of Function Application for *V NP₁ [to NP₂]* is actually $[\![V]\!]^g([\![NP_2]\!]^g)([\![NP_1]\!]^g$.

Characterize the relation that is reflexivized in (2.45b) in the same way. Then give a lexical meaning for *herself* that derives the correct meaning.

Exercise 2.13

Consider the following Kannada data (from Lidz [1995]):

(2.49)   (a)   shyaamu₁ raamu₂ tann-annu₁/* ₂ hoDe -d   -a
                 S.   R.   PRON-ACC   *hit*   -PAST-3SM
                 anta heeL -id   -a
                 that say PAST 3SM
                 'Shyamu said that Raamu hit him.'
            (b)   shyaamu₁ raamu₂ tann-annu₂/* ₁ hoDe -du   -koND
                 S.   R.   PRON-ACC   *hit*   -PAST *REFL.*
                 -a   anta heeL -id   -a
                 -3SM *that say* PAST 3SM
                 'Shyamu said that Raamu hit himself.'

What unexpected property do these sentences show? Discuss! Does this suggest alternative treatments for the Finnish and Chicheŵa cases above?

3 Domains and orientation

In chapter 1, section 1.2.5 we arrived at a general format for Binding Conditions, which I repeat here:

(3.1)   An NP of **class** must (**not**) be coindexed with a **commanding** NP within its **domain**.

We saw that the grammar of English contains three conditions of this form, pertaining to three disjoint **classes** of NPs. In the discussion up until now we have assumed that the relevant binding **domain** in which reflexives need to be bound, and non-reflexive pronouns need to be free, is the local clause.

In this chapter we are first going to refine this notion of binding domain. The discussion will start with English, again, showing that the correct description of the relevant domain should be something like 'smallest category containing a subject,' rather than just 'smallest clause.'

Second, we will introduce an additional parameter into the Binding Conditions, *orientation*. Whereas orientation doesn't seem to be central for the description of English pronouns (but see chapter 11), it is very important in many other languages. We will introduce three kinds of orientation: subject-orientation, anti-subject orientation, and logophoricity.

Third, we will then examine a range of data from other languages that requires Binding Conditions to make reference to different domains (both different from English, and different among the classes of NPs within a given language).

Fourth, we will briefly discuss so-called long-distance reflexives, that is, cases in which reflexive pronouns lead a 'double-life' as either locally bound (like in English) or bound in the sentence domain, like subject oriented pronouns and logophors.

With all these refinements in stock, then, we will fifth and finally look at a few complete pronominal systems in languages other than English.

3.1   Binding domains in English: governing category

3.1.1   Exceptional case marking (ECM)

Consider first so-called *exceptional case marking* (ECM) constructions. The hallmark of these is that a certain class of *ECM-verbs* case-mark an NP which is thematically the argument to an embedded verb. Examples are the verbs *believe* and *want* in English. The thematic subject of the lower verbs, *Georgina*, behaves like a grammatical object to the higher ECM-verbs: it is marked with accusative case, (3.2b), and gets promoted under passivization of the matrix verb, (3.2c). We will henceforth refer to these phrases, italicized in the following examples, as the *ECM-subjects*:

(3.2)   (a)   O'Leary wants/believes *Georgina* to lie.
         (b)   O'Leary wants/believes *her* to lie.
         (c)   *Georgina* is believed to lie.

Turning to binding, now, we observe that the ECM-subjects behave like they are clausemates to the matrix subject: coreference requires a reflexive and prohibits a pronominal:

(3.3)   O'Leary$_6$ believes himself$_6$/him$_{*6}$ to deserve the crown of England.

At the same time the ECM-subjects behave like clausemates with respect to NPs in the embedded clause: they trigger reflexivization in the lower clause and do not tolerate coreference with a non-reflexive object pronoun:

(3.4)   O'Leary wants Georgina$_8$ to protect herself$_8$/her$_{4/*8}$.

These two findings are yet unproblematic. They seem to suggest that all NPs in an ECM-construction, whether they thematically belong to the embedded verb or the matrix verb, populate the same binding domain in the sense relevant to Binding Conditions A and B. This, however, predicts that the matrix-subject should count as a clause-mate to the embedded non-subjects, too, which it patently does not:

(3.5)   O'Leary$_{12}$ wants Georgina to protect him$_{12}$/*himself$_{12}$.

At this point we are in a bind: whatever constituent is the binding domain for the embedded object must include the ECM-subject (because of [3.4]), but exclude the matrix subject (because of [3.5]). But then that constituent, even though containing the ECM-subject, cannot be the binding domain for the ECM-subject (because of [3.3]). In other words, the pertinent binding domains must *overlap* as in (3.6):[1]

(3.6)
$$[_{S^m} \text{SUBJ}^m \ldots V \ [_{S^e} \text{SUBJ}^e \ [\ V \ \text{OBJ} \ ]]]$$

binding domain for SUBJ^e (over SUBJ^e [V OBJ)

binding domain for OBJ (over SUBJ^e [V OBJ]])

These domains are correctly computed by the definition of *governing category* (GC) in (3.7):

---

[1] The schema in (3.6) assumes that the ECM-subject resides within the embedded clause. Essentially the same conclusion would hold, however, if we assumed that it raises to the matrix clause (i.e. if these sentences are to be analyzed as *raising to object*).

(3.7) γ is the *governing category* (GC) for NP if and only if (iff) γ is the smallest clausal category (S, $\bar{\text{S}}$, IP, CP, TP...) which dominates
    (a)   NP
    (b)   NP's case assigner

(3.8)   Binding Conditions (preliminary):
    (A)   A reflexive pronoun must be bound in its governing category.
    (B)   A non-reflexive pronoun must be free in its governing category.

The hypothesis expressed by (3.8), then, is that the binding domain for both reflexive and non-reflexive pronouns in English is their governing category. (3.7) can perhaps be understood best by looking at (3.6): the embedded object, OBJ, receives its case from the embedded V, hence its GC is the embedded clause. Accordingly, the embedded object must be reflexive if coreferent with the ECM-subject, but not if coreferent with the matrix subject. The ECM-subject, on the other hand, receives its case from the *matrix*-verb (exceptionally, as it were), which means that the embedded clause is *not* its GC: even though it contains the ECM-subject itself, it doesn't contain its case assigner. Indeed the smallest clausal category containing both the ECM-subject and its case assigner is the matrix clause. Accordingly, coreference of the ECM-subject with the matrix subject requires the former to be reflexive.

3.1.2   Infinitival clauses

Next, let us briefly look at infinitival complements other than ECM. At first, pairs of examples like those in (3.9) seem to provide contradictory evidence. (3.9a) suggests that the binding domain for the embedded object is the matrix clause, but (3.9b) suggests that it is something smaller than that, e.g. the infinitival clause/VP:

(3.9)   (a)   John$_3$ tried to educate himself$_3$/*him$_3$.
      (b)   Ana$_1$ told John to educate her$_1$/*herself$_1$.

The mystery is resolved, however, once we recognize that *try* is a *subject-control verb* (the understood subject of the embedded verb is the matrix subject), whereas *tell* is an *object-control verb* (the understood subject of the embedded verb is the matrix object). We can then establish the following generalization:

(3.10)   An infinitival clause functions as a G(overning) C(ategory), with the understood subject acting as a binder.

This generalization receives confirmation from sentences like (3.11) (compare to [3.9b]), and the structurally parallel Marathi example (3.12):[2]

---

[2] From Dalrymple (1993):17.

(3.11)   Ana told John$_3$ to educate himself$_3$/*him$_3$.

(3.12)   John$_1$ ne   Jane$_2$ laa swataahlaa$_{2/* 1}$ maraaylaa saangitle   (Marathi)
          John ERG *Jane* DAT *self*-ACC   *hit*   *told*
          'John told Jane to hit self (=Jane).'

In both examples the embedded reflexive corefers with the controller, which happens to be the matrix object. What makes the Marathi case interesting is that
the reflexive *swataah* is subject oriented; it cannot ever be bound by a non-
subject argument (see section 3.2 below). If the matrix object *Jane laa* were
the actual binder in (3.12), this sentence would constitute a mysterious exception to the subject-orientation of the reflexive. But assuming, as we did, that
the logical subject counts as a binder in these cases provides an immediate
explanation.

   How can we implement (3.10)? If we assume that phrase structural c-
command is the relevant notion, we will have to assume an actual empty NP
as the subject of the embedded infinitival clause, commonly called *PRO*. The
index on *PRO* depends on the matrix verb (subject, object, or arbitrary control),
but *PRO* is the inevitable binder for a reflexive or reciprocal in the embedded
clause. Representative structures are given in (3.13):

(3.13)   (a)   John$_4$ tried [*PRO*$_4$ to educate himself$_4$].   (subject control)
          (b)   Ana$_2$ told John$_4$ [*PRO*$_{4/*2}$ to educate himself$_4$/*herself$_2$].
                                                                  (object control)

It bears emphasizing that none of the binding principles discussed so far is responsible for the indexing of *PRO* in (3.13), e.g. that it must be indexed 4 rather
than 2 in (3.13b). BT as discussed here only governs the indexing of the embedded pronouns.[3]

   Alternatively, if we pursue an argument-structure based account of binding,
things are even more straightforward. All that needs to be assumed is that verbs
like *try*, *tell*, and adjective-based predicates like *be dangerous* select for a VP,
and encode that the index of the (unsaturated) subject-argument of that VP be
unified with the pertinent element on the a(rgument)-list of that verb:

(3.14)   (a)   a-list for *try*: $\langle NP_1, VP_{to}[SUBJ[\langle 1 \rangle]]\rangle$
          (b)   a-list for *tell*: $\langle NP, NP_{acc,1}, VP_{to}[SUBJ[\langle 1 \rangle]]\rangle$
          (c)   a-list for *promise*: $\langle NP_1, NP_{acc}, VP_{to}[SUBJ[\langle 1 \rangle]]\rangle$

The indices indicate that NP$_1$ is on the a-list of both the matrix verb and the
embedded verb (by virtue of being the SUBJ of the embedded VP). Accordingly,
more oblique elements on the a-list of the embedded verb can be bound by NP$_1$,
regardless of the position of NP$_1$ on the matrix a-list; for more details see Sag
and Pollard (1991); Sag and Wasow (1999).

---

[3] The interested reader is referred to Harbert (1995) and the references therein for attempts at sub-
suming the choice of (co)reference for *PRO* under BT as well; for a recent discussion of control
see Landau (2001a,b).

Exercise 3.1

The Marathi sentence in (3.12) made an argument that the reflexive is not bound by an NP in the matrix clause, but by the (invisible) subject of the infinitival clause. Make an argument to the same effect using the English sentences in (3.15):

(3.15)　　(a)　It is embarrassing to see yourself in the newspaper headlines like that.
　　　　　(b)　It is dangerous to trust each other like that.
　　　　　(c)　John agreed with Mary to bring each other's pictures to the meeting.

3.1.3　　NPs as binding domains

In this section we will briefly consider another modification of the definition of G(overning)C(ategory).

NPs with and without subjects

So far we have almost exclusively looked at NPs in verbal argument position (subject, object), when examining Binding Conditions. If we expand our data base, we find that NP positions in adnominal argument positions seem to behave as predicted:

(3.16)　　$John_5$ saw $[_{NP}$ a picture of $\left\{ \begin{array}{l} himself_5 \\ *him_5 \end{array} \right\}$]

The pronoun, functioning as an argument to the noun *picture*, receives its case from the preposition *of* within the NP. But the only clausal node dominating the pronoun is the matrix S, which also dominates the subject. Therefore the subject is in the GC of the nominal argument, which therefore must be reflexive if coreferent with the subject.

Things change, however, if we consider NPs with a prenominal argument (a *possessor*); now the non-reflexive is permitted, and, according to many authors, only the non-reflexive:

(3.17)　　$John_5$ saw $[_{NP}$ Mary's picture of $\left\{ \begin{array}{l} ^{??}himself_5 \\ him_5 \end{array} \right\}$]

Assuming these judgments, it seems that an NP functions like a (finite) clause with regard to BT if and only if it has a possessor. Accordingly, the following revision of the definition of GC in (3.7) suggests itself:

(3.18)　　γ is the *governing category* for NP, iff γ is the smallest category **that has a Subject** and dominates
　　　　　(a)　NP
　　　　　(b)　NP's case assigner
　　　　　(where a Subject is either a clausal subject or a possessive)

Applied to all cases in sections 3.1.1 and 3.1.2, this definition will yield the same results as before, given that clauses contain subjects (and clausal subjects are Subjects in the technical sense). If a pronoun is contained in an NP, however, that

NP, rather than the clause minimally containing it, can be the GC, if it contains a possessor. This is the case in (3.17): the GC for *him(self)* is the NP *Mary's picture of him(self)*, which implies that a reflexive has to be bound within that NP (which it evidently can't, given the gender mismatch). The NP in (3.16), on the other hand, is not the GC for *him(self)* because it contains no Subject, so the entire clause is. Accordingly, a pronoun must be free within the entire clause, and coreference with the clausal subject requires reflexivization.

This is probably the right time to note that at least one part of the generalization that motivates the formulation in (3.18) is not borne out by the facts, namely that post-nominal reflexives in NPs *with* a possessor only allow binding to the possessor. In a magnitude estimation experiment with 52 English speakers, Keller and Asudeh (2001) found that reflexives and non-reflexives are judged equally acceptable in a sentence like (3.19a) (in contradistinction, a reflexive in a sentence like *Joan's father respects herself* was clearly rejected). Similarly, Runner *et al.* (2002) found in an eye-tracking experiment that almost 25 percent of their subjects interpreted the reflexive to denote Ken in a sentence like (3.19b); similarly, examples of reflexives bound from outside a possessive NP are widely attested, e.g. (3.19c):[4]

(3.19)   (a)   *Hanna* found Peter's picture of *her(self)*.
          (b)   Have *Ken* touch Harry's picture of *himself*.
          (c)   "C.B.'s father had fared better in this respect than most of his fore-
                bears, but still resented his wife for *her low opinion of himself*, of
                the Whiting mansion, of Empire Falls, of the entire backward state of
                Maine . . . "

Asudeh and Keller's experiment also revealed that post-nominal non-reflexives bound to a possessor or a local sentential subject in possessor-less examples (essentially the *him$_5$* variant of [3.16]) – both of which are predicted to be ungrammatical by the account given here – while not fully acceptable, are significantly better than non-reflexive object pronouns bound to verbal coarguments.

It is a well-acknowledged fact that the data in this area of BT are complex and hard to judge (see e.g. Kuno [1987]:section 4.3; Reinhart and Reuland [1993]:683, 690). Experiments like Runner *et al.* (2002) and Keller and Asudeh (2001) are of utmost importance in that they provide a way of establishing a reliable data base even where individual speakers' introspective judgments are insecure or inconsistent. For a theoretical interpretation of some of these findings, see Asudeh and Keller (2002).

Non-complementary environments

Let me finally discuss an additional complication regarding pronouns within NPs, and briefly sketch a way of addressing them that roughly follows the proposals in Huang (1983) and Chomsky (1986):164ff. Although these proposals

---

[4] From Richard Russo, *Empire Falls (Kampf)*, p. 4, found by C. Potts (italics added).

have received a lot of attention in the literature, I believe they are superseded by the simpler and more accurate treatments afforded within the proposals discussed in chapter 11, so I will skip details wherever possible.

The complementarity between reflexive and non-reflexive pronouns has been at the heart of the definitions we have provided so far. It turns out, however, that while complementarity is observed in the vast majority of cases, it isn't always. (3.20) is a case in question:

(3.20)   John$_7$ believes [that [$_{S^e}$ pictures of $\left\{ \begin{array}{l} \text{him}_7 \\ \text{himself}_7 \end{array} \right\}$ are on sale]]

According to our definition (3.18) the GC for *him(self)* in (3.20) should be the embedded clause S^e: it contains the pronoun, its case assigner *of*, and a subject *pictures of him(self)*. This result yields the correct prediction for the non-reflexive *him*, which is free in S^e and can thus corefer with the matrix subject. By the same token, however, it blocks the reflexive, which is not bound in S^e.

It seems that reflexives and non-reflexives part company here: the GC for *himself* appears to be the matrix clause; that for *him* the embedded clause. Suppose this generalization is correct, then the question emerges if there is any way to define GC so as to get these two different domains for *him* and *himself* in (3.20). One ingenious attempt at that is found in Chomsky (1986).

Perhaps the best way to illustrate the gist of Chomsky's proposal is this: the GC for the reflexive in (3.20) doesn't contain any c-commanding NP (note that the embedded subject itself doesn't c-command an NP it contains). It is thus *in principle* impossible for the reflexive to meet the Binding Condition pertinent to it, Binding Condition A, within that GC. This is different for the non-reflexive, because a GC without any c-commanding NP is just a special case of a GC without a binder, so a non-reflexive can, and in fact always will, meet its Binding Condition, Binding Condition B, within such a GC. The idea then is that the GC for a given NP must be chosen 'mercifully,' in such a way that NP can at least in principle meet its Binding Condition in that GC. Consider the following revision of (3.18) (cf. Chomsky 1986:171f.):

(3.21) γ is the *governing category* for NP iff γ is the smallest category that has a Subject and dominates
             (a)   NP
             (b)   NP's case assigner
             (c)   an NP$'$ c-commanding NP, if NP needs to be bound

Take sentence (3.20) again, with a reflexive (*John believes that pictures of himself are on sale*). The GC for *himself* according to (3.21a–3.21b) would be the embedded clause S^e, but that clause doesn't contain any c-commanding NP, which could function as the binder of *himself*, as required by Binding Condition A. Accordingly, (3.21c) mercifully 'broadens' the GC to the next clause up, which indeed contains a binder for the reflexive.

In the case of a non-reflexive (*John believes that pictures of him are on sale*), (3.21a–3.21b) again determine S^e as the GC, but this time (3.21c) doesn't change anything about that because Binding Condition B, the Binding Condition pertinent for non-reflexive pronouns, doesn't require any binder at all. So S^e is the ultimate GC for *him*, in which it is free, as required.

It remains to verify that even the relaxed definition of GC in (3.21) doesn't rule in cases like (3.22):

(3.22)   (a) *Mary$_3$ said that [$_{S^{e1}}$ John believes that [$_{S^{e2}}$ [pictures of herself$_3$] are on sale]].

            (b) *John$_1$ believes that [[Mary's pictures of himself$_1$] are on sale].

The GC for *herself* in (3.22a) is S^{e1}, not the matrix clause, because S^{e1} already contains an NP which could bind the reflexive, meeting Binding Condition A; the fact that *John* cannot be the actual antecedent to *herself* is irrelevant to (3.21c). Likewise, *himself* in (3.22b) has the subject NP *Mary's picture of himself* as its GC, given that that NP contains a c-commanding NP, *Mary's*, that could serve as the binder (were it not for the gender mismatch).

The definition of GC in (3.21) predicts non-complementarity for two more positions: possessives and clausal subjects, as both of these, being the Subject in the sense of (3.21), do not have a c-commanding NP in their 'original' GC. This prediction turns out to be correct for the former case, but incorrect for the latter (we use a reciprocal here, since English doesn't have reflexive possessives):

(3.23)   (a)   They$_6$ love [$\left\{ \begin{array}{l} \text{their}_6 \\ \text{each other}_6\text{'s} \end{array} \right\}$ pictures].

            (b) *They$_3$ think [that each other$_3$ will win].[5]

An independent reason why (3.23b) is unacceptable has been proposed in Rizzi (1989), namely that reflexives universally cannot occur in agreeing positions.[6] But even if Rizzi's generalization is correct, reasonable doubts about the validity of the 'mercy-condition' on the definition of GC have been voiced, and alternative and more comprehensive accounts have been proposed (see chapter 11).[7]

---

[5] Lebeaux (1983) and many following him have claimed that sentences like (3.23b) are slightly better than full-blown Binding Condition A violations, and become virtually acceptable in the context of *wh*-extraction such as *??They don't know what each other are doing.* I am not aware of any coherent account of this contrast.

[6] A very different attempt at explaining the ungrammaticality of (3.23b), involving movement of the reflexives, is found in Chomsky (1986).

[7] It is also instructive to note that binding of reflexives and reciprocals in embedded finite subjects is by far not universally allowed. Languages as closely related as Dutch and German strictly prohibit this:

(i)   Martell hofft, dass eine Reportage über   ihn$_1$/*sich$_1$ im   Radio gespielt
          M.   hopes that a   report   about him/himself in-the radio played
          wird.   (German)
          becomes
          'Martell is hoping that a report about himself is going to be aired.'

Likewise, Kannada, Italian (Yang, 1983); Polish (Reinders-Machowska, 1992); Russian (Rappaport, 1986) do not allow this kind of binding for reciprocals and/or reflexives.

Exercise 3.2

Assume we replace (3.21c) by a clause that says 'enough material for NP to meet its Binding Condition (ignoring mismatches in person, gender and number),' while maintaining the rest of definition (3.21) and the Binding Conditions in (3.8). This would seem to express the idea of 'be merciful where appropriate' even better. Yet it is haunted by a fatal formal problem. Which?

3.1.4   PPs as binding domains

According to the definition of GC in (3.18), a GC needs to contain a Subject. Whatever the details of the technical Subject notion, it seems clear that PPs don't contain a subject and should therefore not constitute a GC for their complement NP. In other words, the prediction is that in $[_{PP}\ P\ NP]$, NP can be a reflexive bound from outside of the PP; by the same token, if NP is non-reflexive, it should have to be free within the next higher domain containing a subject (e.g. the clause of which PP is an immediate constituent). What are the data? Consider (3.24):

(3.24)   (a)   John$_1$ sent a letter to him$_{*1}$/himself$_1$.
            (b)   John$_1$ always relies on him$_{*1}$/himself$_1$.

These sentences are as expected. But they contrast with the superficially parallel (3.25):

(3.25)   (a)   John$_1$ looked around him$_1$/himself$_1$.
            (b)   John$_1$ pulled the blanket over him$_1$/himself$_1$.
            (c)   Muhammad$_1$ hid the book behind him$_1$/himself$_1$.

Here it seems as if the binding domain for *him* must be smaller than that for *himself*. For example Hestvik (1991), following unpublished work by Joan Bresnan, proposes that the binding domain for *him* is the PP, while it is the clause for *himself*; accordingly, complementarity between *him* and *himself* breaks down, as the former is free within PP, while the latter is bound within S.

If we adopt this kind of analysis, it means we give up on the assumption that there is *one* binding domain, the governing category, that is relevant for both Binding Condition A and Binding Condition B (we effectively gave up that assumption in section 3.1.3 above, but now it seems less likely that there could even be a uniform *formulation* of GC). While the binding domain for reflexives can remain what it was (the smallest category containing it, its case assigner, and a Subject), the binding domain for a non-reflexive pronoun should include the subject only if the pronoun is a complement of a verb (to block *He_4 likes him$_4$*), but not if it is a complement of a preposition (as in [3.25]).

Let us define NP's *coargument domain* as the smallest XP that contains NP, NPs case assigner C, and all other arguments of C (cf. section 3.3 below). Since subject and all objects are arguments of a verb, the coargument domain for any verb argument is its minimal clause. Given that a preposition has only a complement, but no subject, the coargument domain of an NP selected by a P is the PP. This is the distinction we're after:

(3.26)   Binding Conditions (final)
          (A) A reflexive must be bound within the smallest category containing it, its case assigner, and a Subject (=its GC).
          (B) A non-reflexive must be free in its coargument domain.

Given these definitions, we account for the non-complementarity in (3.25), but we lose our account of the complementary distribution in (3.24), because there, too, the non-reflexives would now be free within the PP. Now, there is arguably a difference between the PPs in (3.24) and those in (3.25). While they are all selected by the verb (or so we will assume), the prepositions in (3.25) make a clear semantic contribution to the sentences, while those in (3.24) seem semantically empty.

To be sure, it is not easy to motivate this distinction in every specific case (surely *on* and perhaps even *to* can have semantic content in other sentences). It is, however, suggestive that the Ps in the complements to *look, pull,* and *hide* can be exchanged for others as in *look behind NP, pull it around NP,* or *hide it next to NP,* and the whole PPs for proforms as in *look there, pull it up,* and *hide it away.* No such variation is possible in the case of *sent* or *rely* (*sent it on him, *rely there, etc.). Let us assume for concreteness, then, that *look, pull,* and *hide* truly select a PP that denotes a path (or location), while *sent to* and *rely on* are really complex verbs that semantically combine with the NP denotation, so that the P has no semantic function on its own.

Assuming this difference, how can it help us to explain the difference in the acceptability of non-reflexive pronouns? The intuition we are after is that the PPs in *rely [PP on NP], sent X [PP to NP]* and their likes are not the coargument domain for NP, because NP is 'really' an argument to V, whose arguments include the subject. Now, this would follow from our tentative definition of coargument domain above, if we could plausibly argue that V, not P, is the case assigner for NP in these cases. That, however, isn't obvious, and we will not pursue this option further here. Failing that, the non-domain status of these PPs would also follow if we replaced the notion of case assigner in the definition of coargument domain by the notion of thematic role (Θ-role) assigner, or semantic predicate. Consider the schemata in (3.27):

(3.27)   (a)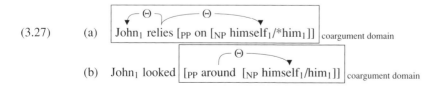

          (b)   John₁ looked [PP around [NP himself₁/him₁]] coargument domain

Since *him* receives a Θ-role from *relies* in (3.27a), all arguments to *relies* are within its coargument domain, in which it needs to be free. In (3.27b), on the other hand, *him* receives its Θ-role from *around* (while the entire PP in turn gets a Θ-role from *looked*), which doesn't have any further arguments and therefore makes PP the coargument domain, in which *him* must be, and is, free. This will be our account of the different behavior in these cases.

The alert reader will recall that a non-reflexive pronoun cannot be bound to a local subject, even if the subject and the pronoun aren't thematic coarguments. The crucial example involving exceptional case marking is repeated here:

(3.28)   O'Leary$_6$ believes himself$_6$/him$_{*6}$ to deserve the crown of England.

Note that by a purely semantic definition of coargument domain in terms of Θ-role assignment, *him*'s coargument domain in (3.28) should be the embedded clause, in which it is free, which wrongly predicts possible binding of *him* by *O'Leary* in (3.28). If, however, we defined the coargument domain to include the *case* assigner (rather than the Θ assigner) and its other arguments, we're back at predicting *him* to be possible in (3.24) (assuming that the case assigner is the semantically vacuous P). It seems we have to bite the bullet and adopt a disjunctive formulation of coargument domain as in (3.29):

(3.29)   NP's *coargument domain* is the smallest constituent X which contains (i) NP, (ii) NP's case assigner C, (iii) NP's Θ-role assigner T, and (iv) every XP whose case or Θ-role is assigned by C or T.

This, I grant, is an ugly definition, but it copes with both kinds of PP cases, as well as the ECM cases (and raising cases, to be discussed in chapters 11 and 12). We will return to some of the issues involved here in chapter 11, especially section (11.4.3), but the basic disjunction will stay with us.

In the discussion of binding domains in section 3.3 below, we will abstract away from these complications and use a simpler definition of coargument domain, ignoring the fact that similar data to the ones discussed in the present section are found in other languages as well (see e.g. Hestvik [1991] and the references there).

Before leaving the issue of PPs as binding domains, let me briefly mention cases of true and uncontroversial adverbial PPs, as opposed to selected PPs, as in (3.30):

(3.30)   (a)   Max$_1$ saw a ghost next to him$_1$/himself$_1$.
          (b)   John$_1$ found a dollar bill in front of him$_1$/$^{??}$himself$_1$.
          (c)   John heard a strange noise behind him/*himself.

The grammaticality marks in (3.30a), (3.30b), and (3.30c) are as given by Reinhart and Reuland (1993):686; Hestvik (1991); and Kuno (1987):65, respectively;[8] this variability of judgments is surprising, since the examples are parallel in all relevant respects, and no single author offers reasons to distinguish them.

How does our current approach fare here? The acceptability of the non-reflexive is expected and predicted, since clearly the P heading the adverbial PP is semantically potent and thus defines its own coargument domain. However, the impossibility or degraded acceptability of a reflexive – as reported in (3.30) – is unexpected, since the smallest category containing a Subject is obviously the clause. We could introduce yet another quirk in the definition of binding domain for reflexives, if we wanted to rule out reflexives in adjunct PPs systematically; examples of such a strategy can be found in Hestvik (1991) and Kuno (1987):ch. 2. Generally, though, reflexive pronouns in adjunct PPs are found rather frequently in actual text:[9]

(3.31)   (a)   Mrs B. who hears the steps behind herself feels rottenly and goes faster.
          (b)   He supplied the end of the cord near himself with a conductor in the shape of an iron key.
          (c)   Mr. Meynell, finding him in better health but suffering from the loneliness of his life, brought him to London and established him near himself.
          (d)   The seductress must be careful not to cast this spell near herself.

Given this, we will assume that reflexives in adjunct PPs can generally be bound from outside, leaving open the question of what accounts for the degraded status of (some of) these examples; see chapter 11, especially section 11.3.2, for further discussion.

This concludes our discussion of the distributional data from English. In the face of considerable unclarity in the data, we tentatively adopt the Binding Conditions A and B in (3.26), which fix the binding domains for reflexives and non-reflexives as the subject domain and coargument domain in the sense to be introduced in (3.3) below, respectively.

In the following sections we will extend our perspective to a wider variety of languages. We will see that neither the tripartition into reflexives (and reciprocals), non-reflexive pronouns, and full NPs, nor the notion of GC developed in this section seem directly applicable cross-linguistically. Nonetheless I will attempt to make visible the outlines of a general format of Binding Conditions.

---

[8] Reinhart and Reuland (1993):687 remark, though, that the reflexive in (3.30a) is 'much more marked' than in sentences like (3.24), which they attribute to the competing possibility of using a non-reflexive (though they don't say why that should be preferred); Kuno on the other hand uses stars but describes the contrast by merely stating that '...for many speakers the following sentences are better with a [non-reflexive; DB] pronoun than with a reflexive' (p. 65).

[9] From http://www.plew.de/english/Note.htm, a description of Benjamin Franklin's famous experiment at http://www.home.zonnet.nl/kitedude/VEK2.htm, the *Catholic Source Book* on Francis Thompson (http://www.newadvent.org/cathen/14703b.htm), and the *Realm of the Dragons* AD&D community and info. site, respectively.

A word on the terminology to be used. I will use the term *pronoun* in the usual sense, including forms that are not inherently anaphoric, such as first and second person pronouns. The term *reflexive* will be used in the text and the glosses for pronouns that need to be bound, including forms that can be bound across clause boundaries, where this is done by the authors whose presentation I allude to (a more apt term for these pronouns might be *command anaphor*, which would leave the term *reflexive* for a morphologically defined class).

I will use the general term *binding domain* instead of *governing category*. For one thing, it is unclear whether binding domains relevant in other languages are usefully described in those terms used in the definition of GC. For another, it is a particular property of English that the two relevant pronoun-classes, reflexives and non-reflexives, make reference to the same domain (if indeed they do) for their respective Binding Conditions. As we will see, different pronouns within the same language, and even different conditions pertaining to the same pronoun, can make reference to different domains. These domains will be designated by more informative names. The GC as defined in (3.18)/(3.26), for example, which is the binding domain for reflexives in English, will be called the *subject domain*.

3.2   Orientation

In this section we will extend our blueprint for binding conditions by one parameter, *orientation*. Orientation is not relevant in English, but has an important role to play in many other languages. To a first approximation, orientation means that a certain anaphoric element must be bound to or free from NPs with a particular grammatical function, in most cases a subject.

3.2.1   Subject orientation and anti-subject orientation

An illustrative example of subject orientation is the Chinese reflexive *ziji*. As widely discussed in the literature, *ziji* must be bound within its root clause, but not necessarily within any local domain. However, the antecedent has to be a subject:[10]

---

[10] Dalrymple (1993) (2.41); Tang (1989) (45); according to Huang (1982), *ziji* can only find a non-local antecedent if it is itself in subject position. But as Tang (1989) argues using (i), this doesn't seem correct:

(i)   Zhangsan$_3$ juede Lisi$_8$ dui **ziji**$_{3/8/*1}$ mei xinxin.
       Zhangsan think Lisi to   self   no confidence
       'Zhangsan thought that Lisi had no confidence in himself.'

Also, *ziji*'s antecedent can sometimes be an experiencer or a phrase contained in a subject (cf. Huang and Tang's [1992] notion of *subcommand*).

(3.32)   (a)   Zhangsan₁ shuo **ziji**₁ hui lai.   (Chinese)
Zhangsan say self will come
'Zhangsan says he will come.'

(b)   Zhangsan₁ renwei Lisi₂ zhidao **ziji**₁/₂/*₃ de taitai shi yige
Zhangsan think Lisi know self   DE wife is one-CL
da hao ren.
big good person
'Zhangsan thought that Lisi knew that his wife was a very good person.'

Subject orientation and domain restriction are not mutually exclusive. The Finnish reflexive *itse*, 'self,' must be bound by a subject within its minimal finite clause:[11]

(3.33)   (a)   Pekka₁ näki että Matti₂ katsoi   **itseään**₂/*₁   (Finnish)
Pekka saw that Matti watched self-POSS
'Pekka saw that Matti watched himself.'

(b)   * Puhuin   Pekalle₁ **itseään**₁/₂
spoke-1SG *Pekka   self*-POSS
'I spoke to Pekka about himself.'

Subject orientation of pronouns is cross-linguistically very pervasive; apart from the cases mentioned here, it is reported to hold for Chinese *taziji*,[12] Czech *si*, Danish *(sig) selv*, Dutch *zich*, French *soi*, Icelandic *(sjálfur) sig*, Italian *sè*, Japanese *zibun*, Kannada *hon* and *ta-nu*, Latin *se*, Malayalam *swa*,[13] Marathi *swataah*, Norwegian *seg self*, Russian *sebja* and *svoj(u)*,[14] and Spanish *se*.

Anti-subject orientation is exemplified by the weak pronoun form *ó* in Yoruba (Kwa, Niger-Congo). This pronoun can be unbound, or bound to a non-subject; it must not, however, be anaphorically related to any commanding subject:[15]

---

[11] Unless noted otherwise, the data and generalizations in this section and the next are taken from Tang (1989) (Chinese); Toman (1992) (Czech); Vikner (1985) (Danish); Enç (1991) (Dogrib, Turkish); Koster (1984) (Dutch); van Steenbergen (1992) (Finnish); Pica (1983) (French); Everaert (1992) (Frisian); Dalrymple (1993):157 (Fula); Iatridou (1986) (Greek); Mohanan (1990) and Yang (1983) (Hindi); É. Kiss (1992) (Hungarian); Koster and Reuland (1992b) (Icelandic, Italian); Katada (1991) (Japanese); Bhat (1978) (Kannada); Benedicto (1992) (Latin); Yang (1983) and Mohanan (1982) (Malayalam); Dalrymple (1993) (Marathi, Norwegian); Reinders-Machowska (1992) (Polish); Avrutin (1994) (Russian); Fontana and Moore (1992) (Spanish); and Pulleyblank (1986) (Yoruba).

[12] See also Koster and Reuland (1992b).

[13] Latin and Malayalam according to Yang (1983).

[14] Rappaport (1986).

[15] Cf. Pulleyblank (1986) and Pulleyblank (1990); data from Dalrymple (1993), (1.107) and (1.108). Pulleyblank (1990):987 actually provides an example in which *ó*, contained in an adverbial clause, is bound to the matrix subject. The purported generalization is that the anti-subject orientation only holds for pronouns embedded within complement clauses. Further investigation of this is beyond the scope of this book.

(3.34)   (a) Ṣẹ́gun₁ sọ pé Túndé₂ rò   pé ó₃/*₁/*₂ sanra.   (Yoruba)
              Segun say that Tunde think that he   fat
              'Segun₁ said that Tunde₂ thought that he₃/*₁/*₂ was fat.'
         (b) Tolú₁ sọ fún Ṣẹ́gun₂ pé Dúpẹ́₃ rò   pé ó₂/*₁/*₃/₄ sanra
              Tolu say to Segun that Dupe think that he   fat
              'Tolu₁ told Segun₂ that Dupe₃ thought that he₂/*₁/*₃/₄ was fat.'

Anti-subject orientation – sometimes within a delimited domain – is also found
in Danish *ham (selv)*, Dogrib *ye*, Kannada *ava*, Norwegian *ham (self)*, and
Russian *ego*.

   In the remainder, we will assume that the notion of 'subject' is available to
us in formulating Binding Conditions. In theories in which this notion is not a
primitive, it will have to be considered as a shorthand for some complex derived
notion. Binding Conditions will then take the following form, with an extra parameter added:

(3.35)   An NP of **class** must (**not**) be coindexed with a **commanding**
          $\begin{Bmatrix} \textbf{NP} \\ \textbf{Subject} \end{Bmatrix}$ within its **domain**.

3.2.2   Logophoricity

       In the previous subsection, we have seen pronouns which restrict the
class of their possible antecedents by reference to grammatical function (subject
vs. non-subject). In this subsection we turn to pronouns, so-called *logophors*,
which are oriented towards a semantically or pragmatically determined class of
antecedents.

   Various languages have a special set of pronouns used to refer to the 'source'
of an embedded statement. Consider the following examples from Ewe (Kwa,
Niger-Kordofanian):[16]

(3.36)   (a) kofi₁ be **yè**₁/*₂/*ₛ -dzo   (Ewe)
              Kofi say LOG   *left*
         (b) kofi₁ be **e***₁/₂/*ₛ -dzo
              Kofi say he   left
         (c) kofi₁ be **me***₁/*₂/ₛ -dzo
              Kofi say I   left
              'Kofi said that he/I left.'

The distribution of *e*, 'he,' and *me*, 'I,' is more or less as expected: *e* refers
to a non-speaker, non-addressee person (hence the subscript *ₛ, for 'not the
speaker'), while *me* must be the speaker; moreover, *e*, for reasons of no concern
here, cannot anaphorically relate to the matrix subject. What is of interest here
is the additional pronoun *yè*, which can only refer to the subject of *be*, 'say,' not

---

[16] From Clements (1975) by way of Sells (1987):448 and Kuno (1987):146.

to any other person, speaker or not. Pronouns like that are called *logophoric*, glossed LOG, following the terminology proposed in Hagège (1974).

Logophoric pronouns are not restricted to verbs of saying. As the following Ewe examples show, the subject of *be happy, know,* or *see* in Ewe can antecede logophoric pronouns; similarly, in Tuburi, the experiencer of a psychological verb can bind a logophor:[17]

(3.37) (a) ana$_1$ kpɔ dyidzo   be   **yè**$_{1/*2}$ -dyi vi   (Ewe)
             Ana see happiness COMP LOG   *-bear child*
             'Ana$_1$ was happy that she$_{1/*2}$ bore a child.'

        (b) kofi$_7$ (me-) nya   be   me -kpɔ **yè**$_{7/*2}$ (o)
             Kofi (not) know COMP *I   see* LOG
             'Kofi$_7$ knew/didn't know that I had seen him$_{7/*2}$.'

        (c) kofi$_7$ kpɔ be   **yè**wo$_{7+2/*2}$ -do   go
             Kofi see COMP LOG-PL   *-come out*
             'Kofi saw that they (including Kofi) had come out.'

(3.38) hí:ní dʒō nē$_1$ gā   **sɛ̄**$_{1/*2}$ lĩʔ tʃìgì   (Tuburi)
        fear make him COMP LOG   *fall illness*
        'He was afraid that he would fall ill.'

Before going on, let us briefly consider alternative characterizations of these pronouns. Couldn't they just be reflexives that need to be bound by a higher subject? After all, the 'source of an embedded proposition' often *is* (the referent of the) subject of the verb embedding (the sentence expressing) that proposition. Indeed, logophoricity and long-distance subject orientation aren't always easy to tell apart. There are two straightforward ways to distinguish them, though; consider the following examples involving the Japanese logophoric pronoun *zibun*:[18]

(3.39) (a) Takasi$_1$ wa Taroo$_2$ ni [Yosiko ga   **zibun**$_{1/*2}$ o   nikundeiru
             Takasi TOP *Taroo* DAT *Yosiko* NOM *self*   ACC *be-hating*
             koto] o   hanasita   (Japanese)
             COMP ACC *told*
             'Takasi told Taroo that Yosiko hated him (Takasi).'

        (b) Taroo$_2$ wa   Takasi$_1$ kara [Yosiko ga   **zibun**$_{1/*2}$ to   nikundeiru
             Taroo TOP *Takasi from Yosiko* NOM *self*   ACC *be-hating*
             to] kiita
             COMP *heard*
             'Taroo heard from Takasi that Yosiko hated him (Takasi).'

The only acceptable antecedent for *zibun* in both sentences in (3.39) is *Takasi*. *Takasi* is the subject and topic in (3.39a), but an oblique in (3.39b). If *zibun* were subject oriented, we would expect it to refer to *Taroo* in (3.39b), which has the same grammatical function and morphological marking as *Takasi* in (3.39a). It is clear from these examples that *zibun* is not subject oriented. Rather, it takes the

---

[17] Ewe data from Sells (1987):449; Tuburi from Hagège (1974).
[18] From Sells (1987):453f.

source of the embedded proposition as its antecedent, which in both sentences in (3.39) is *Takasi*.

A second hallmark of logophoric pronouns is that they can sometimes occur without a sentence internal antecedent at all. (3.40) illustrates this with an example from Icelandic, involving *sér*, the dative of the logophoric pronoun *síg*:[19]

(3.40)   Formaðurinn₁ varð   óskaplega reiður. Tillagan   væri   avívirðileg.
           *the chairman became furiously angry the proposal was-*SUBJ *outrageous*
           Væri   henni beint gegn   **sér**₁ persónulega?   (Icelandic)
           *was-*SUBJ *it   aimed against self personally*
           'The chairman became furiously angry. The proposal was outrageous. Was
           it aimed at him personally?'

Despite the sentence boundary, the second and third sentence are clearly reporting the chairman's thoughts (note also the subjunctive marking on the verbs in these sentences). As a consequence, the logophoric *sér* can be used here without any sentence internal binder. This again shows that we are not dealing with a reflexive that needs to be syntactically bound, however involved its syntactic binding domain.

Having demonstrated the difference between logophoric and (subject-oriented) reflexive binding, note secondly that logophoric pronouns are different from English non-reflexives, too. They do require an antecedent, and moreover one with a special pragmatic property. While one could argue that pronouns need (discourse) antecedents as well, the difference is clear. Contrast the Ewe example (3.36) above and a random English sentence like *Mary said that she left*. Out of the blue, the latter might tempt speakers strongly towards an interpretation in which *she* is bound by *Mary*, but a disjoint reading, in which *she* is discourse related, is clearly available. This is very different from the case of a logophor, which absolutely needs to take the source of information as its antecedent.

To get a better intuition about what counts as the 'source of information,' note the following paraphrases for the examples above:

(3.41)   (a)   Kofi said: "*I* left."
           (b)   Ana was happy thinking: "*I* am bearing a child."
           (c)   Kofi knew/didn't know: "X has seen *me*." (where X is the speaker of
                 the sentence)
           (d)   Kofi saw (something that triggered the mental representation): "*We*
                 have come out."
           (e)   He was afraid (of being in a state reflected by the mental representation): "*I* am falling ill."
           (f)   Takasi told Taroo: "Yosiko hates *me*!"
           (g)   Taroo heard from Takasi: "Yosiko hates *me*!"
           (h)   The chairman, furiously angry, thinks: "The proposal is outrageous. Is
                 it aimed at *me* personally?!"

---

[19] From Sigurðsson (1986), via Sells (1987):453.

In all these cases, I have replaced the embedded clause by a direct quotation. Accordingly, the logophoric pronouns of the original sentences are replaced by first person pronouns (in italics). We formulate this as our rule of thumb for logophoric pronouns:

(3.42)   A logophoric pronoun can be used if it is embedded in a constituent c such that (i) c is embedded, (ii) c denotes a proposition p, which (iii) can be paraphrased as a mental state or reported utterance of the pronoun's antecedent such that the paraphrase contains a first person pronoun in place of the pronoun.

What exactly qualifies as a logophoric antecedent, however, varies from language to language. Usually some lexical element indicates the presence of a 'logophoric environment,' e.g. a verb of saying, thinking, etc., or a special embedding complementizer. Further conditions may obtain. For example, in Ewe, only sentence embedding verbs license logophors, while verbs like *remember*, which selects an NP complement, or *hear*, with an ECM-type complement, do not (cf. [3.42ii]):[20]

(3.43)   (a)   * ama₁ do ŋku nyɔnuvi hi   dze yèı gbɔ dyi.   (Ewe)
                        Ama set eye girl   REL stay LOG side on
                        'Ama remembered the girl who stayed with her.'
           (b)   ama₁ gblɔ be   yè -do ŋku nyɔnuvi hi   dze yèı gbɔ dyi.
                        Ama say COMP LOG -set eye girl   REL stay LOG side on
                        'Ama said that she remembered the girl who stayed with her.'

(3.44)   (a)   *Ama remembered: "The girl who stayed with me." (not propositional)
           (b)   Ama said: "I remember the girl who stayed with me."

Logophoricity is attested in many languages of the world. It is important to keep the option of logophoricity in mind when attempting to describe Binding Conditions in a given language, precisely because it can so easily be mistaken for something else, e.g. long-distance subject-oriented anaphors.

3.2.3   Towards a formal treatment of logophoricity

Sells (1987) provides a formal implementation of logophoricity within the framework of Discourse Representation Theory (Kamp and Reyle, 1993). We will follow the gist, though not the letter, of his proposal in what follows; many details, however, will be omitted.

We take as our role model the treatment of first and second person pronouns from chapter 2, section 2.2.2:

(3.45)   (a) $[\![\text{I/me/my/myself}_n]\!]^{g,s,u} = g(n)$ if $g(n) = s$, undefined otherwise
           (b) $[\![\text{you/your}_n]\!]^{g,s,u} = g(n)$, if $g(n)$ is the person s addresses in u

---

[20] Cf. Sells (1987):449f.

Extending this treatment, we introduce another contextual parameter, which we call o for 'origo' (Latin for 'source', given that s is already in use). A logophoric pronoun will always refer to the individual o:

(3.46) $[\![\text{pronoun}_n^{log}]\!]^{g,s,u,o} = o$, if $o = g(n)$

Note that we assume here that logophors, just like first and second person pronouns, are indexed and that their lexical content is just a presupposition.

The origo-parameter can be shifted by verbs of saying, thinking, etc. to the sayer, thinker, etc. (all other aspects of these verbs' meanings are simplified as far as possible):

(3.47)   (a) $[\![\text{say (that) S}]\!]^{g,s,u,o} = \lambda x.x$ says something which entails $[\![\text{S}]\!]^{g,s,u,x}$

           (b) $[\![\text{hear from NP (that) S}]\!]^{g,s,u,o} = \lambda x.x$ hears y, $y = [\![\text{NP}]\!]^{g,s,u,o}$, says something which entails $[\![\text{S}]\!]^{g,s,u,y}$

           (c) $[\![\text{believe (that) S}]\!]^{g,s,u,o} = \lambda x.$ what x believes entails $[\![\text{S}]\!]^{g,s,u,x}$

           (d) $[\![\text{S frightens NP}]\!]^{g,s,u,o} = 1$ iff $x, x = [\![\text{NP}]\!]^{g,s,u,o}$, prefers a state of affairs in which $[\![\text{S}]\!]^{g,s,u,x}$ is false to one in which it is true

Note, in contrast, that the speaker parameter (just like the utterance-situation parameter) cannot be shifted, except for direct quotation. This can be seen, for example, from the fact that, unlike in a direct quotation, English first person pronouns cannot be used to refer to the speaker of an embedded sentence:[21]

(3.48)   (a)   *Gil_6 said that I_6 was happy.
           (b) Gil_6 said: "I_6 am happy."
           (c) Gil_6 said that she_6 was happy.

Rather, we appear to see ordinary coreference in these cases: *she* corefers with *Gil*, who happens to be the source or speaker of the embedded sentence. This is no different from the cases in (3.49), which don't involve reported speech or attitudes in the embedded clauses:

(3.49)   (a) Gil_6 met a pilot who liked her_6.
           (b) Gil_6 arrived even though Roger had said that she_6 wouldn't.

According to the treatment in (3.47), re-setting the logophoric center is a lexical property of verbs like *say, believe*, etc. Other sentence-embedding verbs do not have this option, just as little as, say, sentence-embedding prepositions:

(3.50)   (a) $[\![\text{look as if S}]\!]^{g,s,u,o} = \lambda x.$ the visual appearance of x makes it likely that $[\![\text{S}]\!]^{g,s,u,o}$ is true (**not:** . . . that $[\![\text{S}]\!]^{g,s,u,x}$ is true!)

           (b) $[\![\text{S unless S'}]\!]^{g,s,u,o} = 1$ iff $[\![\text{S}]\!]^{g,s,u,o}$ is true and will be as long as $[\![\text{S'}]\!]^{g,s,u,o}$ is

It is rather clear why *unless* cannot, in principle, establish a new logophoric center: there is no individual argument to the function denoted by *unless*, therefore

---

[21] The classical philosophical reference here is Kaplan (1977); see Schlenker (1999) for recent discussion.

a fortiori none that could serve as the new origo. This is different for *look like*, which does have an individual argument. We could thus give it a meaning as indicated in the parentheses in (3.50a), which would wrongly shift the origo to the person whose looks are described.

The intuition here is, of course, that *say* and *think*, but not *look like*, involve the report of an utterance or thought, and thus only they have a source to come along with it. This, however, is expressed nowhere in our formal treatment, and it is not easy to see how it could be.[22]

Exploring this issue further would be beyond the scope of this book. We will leave our formalization at this. Sells (1987) argues that we need in fact not just one origo parameter but three different ones, which he calls 'source,' 'self,' and 'pivot' (plus, of course, the familiar 'external speaker'). As these present nothing fundamentally new, I refer to Sells' work for further details.

There are a number of essential points we leave unaddressed or unresolved: first, the formal counterpart of the 'origo' intuition (i.e. the point just mentioned above); second, cases such as (3.40) above, in which the re-set origo parameter extends beyond the scope of the embedding element (these should follow from a general treatment of *modal subordination*, cf. Roberts (1987, 1989, 1996)); and third, cases in which the origo is not introduced by a specific lexical element, but nonetheless seems to represent a 'source' in the intuitive sense (Sells' *third person point of view* cases; see Sells [1987] for details).

3.3   Binding domains cross-linguistically

In section 3.1 we defined the notion of *governing category* and *coargument domain*, which could serve to identify the binding domain for reflexive (must be bound within) and non-reflexive (mustn't be bound within) pronouns, respectively. Other languages make reference to different domains. It seems, however, that the number of binding domains cross-linguistically might still be rather limited. For the purpose of the presentation to follow, I will focus on four different domains, listed in table 3.1.[23]

It is important to realize that these domains are collapsed in a great number of structures. In a simple transitive clause like (3.51), all four domains for the object NP are the same, namely the root clause:

---

[22] It may be tempting to try to give the logophoric pronouns a presupposition similar to the first and second person pronouns, e.g. $[\![\text{pronoun}_n^{log}]\!]^{g,s,u,o} = o$, presupposition: o is the source of P. But the question here is: what is P? Unlike u in the definitions above, P is not a contextual parameter. We want it to refer to the reported utterance or thought, but where should this come from?

[23] These domains correspond, from bottom to top, to the domains Root S, Minimal Finite Domain, Minimal Complete Nucleus, and Coargument Domain in Dalrymple (1993); and to Domains 3, 2, and 1 in Koster and Reuland (1992b) (who deny the relevance of the C-Domain, a point we will return to later). Interestingly, it is noted in both works that these domains seem to be the only ones required for their quite comprehensive, though not typologically representative, sample of languages.

Table 3.1 *Cross-linguistic binding domains*

Domain	Definition
the ... for A is	the smallest constituent containing A, A's case assigner C and ...
Coargument domain, CD	all arguments of C
Subject domain, SD	a Subject (within NP or S)
Tense domain, TD	a finite clause
Root domain, RD	the entire sentence

(3.51)   The Schindlers provoked the Flaunders.

Below, on the other hand is a maximally complex example in which the four domains, relative to the NP *Kim*, are different:

To find out which domain is crucial for a given pronoun type thus requires constructing intricate and often somewhat involved sentences. A lot of studies, especially older ones, on Binding Theory in particular languages do not distinguish between the different categories, which is why our cross-linguistic knowledge about these distinctions is very incomplete and likely to be in need of revision.

The root domain

The root domain is significant in English only as a negative domain for full NPs. There are languages, however, in which certain pronouns must be bound in the root domain, though not necessarily locally. Examples of such pronouns mentioned in the literature are Chinese *ziji*, Fula *Dum*, Greek *o idhios* and *ton idhios*, Icelandic *sig*, Italian *sè* and *proprio*, Japanese *zibun*,[24] Kannada *ta-nu*, Latin *se*, Malayalam *swa* and *taṇne*, Marathi *aapaṇ*, and Yoruba *ó*. It should be noted that many of these are also subject oriented, and also that the data provided are often not sufficient to rule out the possibility that some of these are actually logophoric.[25] For the remaining core cases, however, the pertinent Binding Condition will take the general form in (3.52), with illustrative examples given in (3.53) and (3.54):[26]

---

[24] Also Sportiche (1986).

[25] In the same vein, it is not clear in all of these cases that the antecedent actually needs to c-command, or command at all for that matter, the pronoun (this is, for example, not the case in Chinese and Fula).

[26] From Iatridou (1986):769 and Yang (1983):183, respectively; *o idhios* must also be locally free, hence it cannot be bound by *Maria* in (3.53).

(3.52)   *o idhios/caki (ziji/zibun/swa . . .)* **must** be coindexed with a commanding NP within its **root domain**.

(3.53)   O Yanis₁ ipe ston Costa₂ [oti i   Maria₃ aghapa **ton idhio**₁/₂/*₃/*₄]
         the Y.   said to-the C.   that the M.   loves   himself

         (Greek)

         'Yanis told Costa that Maria loves him.'

(3.54)   John₁ -in [Bill₂ -i   [Mary₃ -ka [Tom₄ -iy   **caki**₁/₂/₃/₄/*₅**-e**
         J.   -TOP *B.*   -NOM *M.*   -NOM *T.*   -'s   *self*

         tæhan thæto] -lil silhəha -n   -ta   -ko] sængkakha -n
         toward attitude   -ACC *hate*   -ASP -DEC -COMP *think*   -ASP

         -ta -ko] mit   -nin -ta.   (Korean)
         -DEC -COMP *believe* -ASP -DEC

         'John₁ believes that Bill₂ thinks that Mary₃ hates Tom₄'s attitude toward self₁/₂/₃/₄/*₅.'

The Korean example aptly illustrates how a Binding Condition like (3.52) is to be read: *caki* can be bound within *any* domain up to the root domain, but not from outside of the root domain (not: in the root domain, but not in any smaller domain). So, generally, if a Binding Condition says that an element needs to be bound in domain D, this means that its antecedent has to be somewhere within D, not necessarily at the 'top' of D. Note, on the other hand, that certain elements may be subject to more than one Binding Condition. On top of (3.52), Greek *o idhios*, for example, also needs to be *free* in its tense domain (which is why it can't be coindexed with *Maria* in [3.53]), so that effectively its binding domain 'starts' at the next higher clause and 'ends' at the root node.

The tense domain

The tense domain functions as the binding domain, for example, for Czech *se/sebe* and *svůj*,[27] Danish *sig*, Finnish *hän, itse*, and *hän itse*, French *soi*, Marathi *swataah* (in the less restrictive version), Norwegian *seg* and *sin*, Polish *siebie* and *swój*, and Russian *sebja* and *svoj(u)*.[28] Tense-domain-bound reflexives might look like subject-domain-bound reflexives (i.e. like English) at first glance, cf. (3.56a) and (3.57a). What is distinctive, however, is that the pronoun can be bound across subjects in NPs and non-finite complements such as gerunds or infinitival clauses (i.e. the subject domain, marked by parentheses):[29]

(3.55)   *swataah/seg (sig/soi/siebie/uskii . . .)* **must** be coindexed with a commanding NP within its **tense domain**.

---

[27] According to Toman (1992):154f., the exact domain seems to be 'inflected clause' (including infinitival clauses), as Czech reflexives cannot be bound across infinite sentence boundaries; they can be bound across small clause and NP subjects though, which is why I group them here.

[28] Also Rappaport (1986).

[29] Examples are Dalrymple's (1993) (1.49), (1.42), (1.43), (1.87), and (1.86).

(3.56) (a) * Tom$_1$ mhanat hota [$_{TD=SD}$ ki   Sue ni   **swataahlaa$_1$** maarle]
            Tom   said   that Sue ERG self   hit
                                                                    (Marathi)
            'Tom said that Sue hit himself.'

        (b) [$_{TD}$ Jane$_2$ laa [$_{SD}$ Tom ne   **swataaci$_2$** pustake phekun dilyaace]
            Jane DAT   Tom ERG self   books   throw
            kalle]
            learned
            'Jane learned about Tom throwing away (her)self's books.'

        (c) [$_{TD}$ Jane$_2$ [$_{SD}$ John ne **swataahlaa$_2$** maarlyaavar] rusun]
            Jane   John ERG self   hitting   angry
            'Jane remained angry upon John hitting (her)self.'

(3.57) (a) * Jon$_1$ var ikke klar   over [$_{TD=SD}$ at   vi hadde snakket om
            Jon was not aware of   that we had   talked about
            seg$_{1/2}$]   (Norwegian)
            self
            'Jon was not aware that we had talked about him.'

        (b) Jon$_1$ likte [$_{SD}$ din artikkel om   **seg$_1$**]
            Jon liked   your article about self
            'Jon likes your article about him.'

The subject domain

Ignoring the non-complementary cases (i.e. those where a reflexive
or reciprocal is contained in a subject), the subject domain is the relevant one
for English reflexives. It furthermore appears to be the binding domain for reciprocals in all languages I could find information about on this issue, including
Danish *hinanden*,[30] Dutch *elkaar*, English *each other*,[31] Finnish *toiset*, Hungarian *egymas*, Icelandic *hvor annar*, Italian *l'uno, l'altro*, Norwegian *hverandre*,
the reciprocal use of Polish *siebie*, and, shown here, Russian *drug druga*:[32]

(3.58) (a) [$_{SD}$ Pisateli$_1$ čitali [vospominanija **drug** o   **drug**
            writers-NOM *read   reminiscences*-ACC *each about other*
            -e$_1$]]   (Russian)
            -LOC
            'The writers read reminiscences about each other.'

        (b) * Pisateli$_1$ čitali [$_{SD}$ vospominanija   Tolstoja   **drug**
            writers-NOM *read   reminiscences*-ACC *Tolstoi*-GEN *each*
            o   **drug** -e$_1$]
            about other -LOC
            'The writers read the reminiscences of Tolstoj about each other.'

[30] Pica (1983).
[31] But see Lebeaux (1983).
[32] Rappaport (1986) (18). Yang (1983) actually speculates the SD is the binding domain for reciprocals universally, but see Huang (2000):n. 46, pp. 101f. for possible exceptions.

Cases of (non-reciprocal) pronouns that need to be bound in the subject domain alongside English *herself/himself* are Chinese *taziji*,[33] all Danish *-self* pronouns, Dutch *-zelf* pronouns, French *se*, Frisian *'m(sels)*, Greek *ton*,[34] Hungarian *maga*, Icelandic *sjálfur* forms, Italian *si* and *se stesso*, Japanese *-zibun* forms, Marathi *swataah* (in the restricted dialect), Norwegian *-self* forms and possessive *sin*, and Turkish *kendi*:[35]

(3.59)   *zichzelf (hvor hanna/toiset/each other/ton/si/swataah . . .)* **must** be coindexed with a commanding NP within its **subject domain**.

(3.60)   (a)   Peter$_1$ zag [$_{SD}$ Mary$_2$'s foto   van **zichzelf**$_{2/*1/*3}$].   (Dutch)
                P.   saw   M.'s   pictures of self
                'Peter saw Mary's pictures of him/herself.'

        (b)   Mary$_1$ liet [$_{SD}$ Peter$_2$ op **zichzelf**$_{2/* 1/* 3}$ schieten]
                M.   let   P.   at self   shoot
                'Mary let Peter shoot at himself.'

The subject domain is also significant as a *negative* domain. Dogrib *ye*, Finnish *hän*, Greek *ton (idhios)*, Italian *lui*, and Turkish *o* need to be free in their subject domain.

Moreover, Danish *ham/hende* and *ham selv*, Finnish *hän (itse)*, Icelandic *hann sjálfur*, Malayalam *taan*, Norwegian *ham (self)*, Polish *nim* and possessive *jej*, Russian *ego* must be *subject*-free within the subject domain:

(3.61)   *nim (jej/ham (selv)/hän (itse)/ taan . . .)* **must not** be coindexed with a **commanding subject** within its **subject domain**.

(3.62)   Piotr$_1$ czytał [$_{SD}$ Janka$_2$ artykuł o   **nim**$_{?1/* 2}$]   (Polish)
            P.   read   J.'s   article about him
            'Piotr read Janek's article about him.'

The coargument domain

Turning finally to the coargument domain, it appears that this domain is only relevant as a negative domain. For example, Marathi *to* at first glance behaves like a non-reflexive pronoun in that it cannot be bound in its local clause, but across a finite sentence boundary, cf. (3.63a/3.63b); however, unlike a non-reflexive pronoun in English, it can occur with an antecedent within its subject domain, as long as the antecedent is not a coargument, cf. (3.63c/3.63d):[36]

(3.63)   (a)   Jane$_1$ ne   **tilaa**$_{2/*1}$ bockaarle.   (Marathi)
                Jane ERG her-ACC scratched
                'Jane scratched her.'

        (b)   Mary$_2$ dukhi hoti. **tilaa**$_2$ jaataa aale   naahi.
                Mary sad   was she-DAT go   could not
                'Mary was sad. She could not go.'

---

[33] Koster and Reuland (1992b); Tang (1989).
[34] Also Enç (1989).
[35] Examples are Koster's (1984) (45) and (23).
[36] Examples are Dalrymple's (1993) (1.63), (1.64), (1.60), and (1.61).

    (c)   Jane₁ ne **ticyaakartaa**₁ saaḍi gheṭ   li.
          Jane ERG *her for*   *sari* *bought*
          'Jane bought a sari for her (Jane).'

    (d)   Jane₁ ne   John laa **ticyaabaddal**₁ maathiti   dili.
          Jane ERG *John* DAT *her about*   *information gave*
          'Jane gave John information about her (Jane).'

Danish *ham* and *hende*, Dutch *zich*, Frisian *'m*, Kannada *ava-*, Marathi *to* and *aapan*, and Norwegian *seg* all need to be free in their coargument domain:

(3.64)   *to (hende/zich/ava-...)* **must not** be coindexed with a commanding NP within its **coargument domain**.

It is worth emphasizing that all these elements can be 'locally' bound (e.g. by a non-coargument subject within a finite clause), as in (3.63c/3.63d), and indeed some of them actually *must* be bound within the next higher tense domain (Norwegian), or subject domain (Frisian, Dutch, Danish).

   These pronouns have thus a very limited distribution, essentially as arguments to prepositions and inherent-reflexives (cf. chapter 1, section 1.4). In chapter 11 we will explore a possible rationale behind the peculiarities of this domain, namely that all elements that must be free in the coargument domain are simply incapable of marking a predicate as reflexive.

This concludes our cross-linguistic discussion of domains. It is worth stressing that the choice of binding domain is not made once per language (say, tense domain for Marathi and Norwegian, subject domain for English), or even twice (say subject domain as negative domain for non-reflexives, and first clause with an *accessible* subject as positive domain for reflexives, as is sometime suggested for English). Rather, the choice of domain appears to be morpheme-specific, where within the same language different forms can have different binding domains (for example, tense domain as positive domain for Norwegian *seg*, but subject domain for *ham selv* and the reciprocal *hveandre* in the same language). This challenges attractive ideas about setting a single 'domain parameter,' and leaves us with what appears to be a less restrictive approach to the acquisition of binding domains (cf. Manzini and Wexler [1987]; and Wexler and Manzini [1987]).[37]

Exercise 3.3

    Indicate all four domains relative to *Y* in the following schematized structures. Provide labeled bracketings for clarity:

---

[37] There is, of course, the possibility that something about the *form* of a given pronoun, coupled with a universal theory of binding domains, yields the different domains (Déchaine and Wilschko [2000]; Reuland [2001, a.o.]). There are, however, to the best of my knowledge no cross-linguistically valid generalizations about form–domain correspondences that could serve as the basis for such a theory, and, accordingly, such approaches often remain stipulative.

(3.65)   (a)   X loves Y
           (b)   Z says that X loves Y
           (c)   Z left upon X's hitting Y
           (d)   X has information about Y

Exercise 3.4

(i) Formulate, as far as the following data warrant, the positive and negative binding condition for Greek *ton eafton tou* and *o idhios* (cf. also [3.53]):[38]

(3.66)   (a)   O   Yanis$_1$ aghapa   ton eafton   tou$_{1/*2}$/   *ton   idhio$_{1/2}$.
                 the Y.   loves   PRON
                 (Greek)
                 'Yanis loves himself.'
           (b)   O   Yanis$_1$ theori   oti   o idhios$_{1/*2}$ ine   o   kaliteros
                 the Y.   thinks   COMP   PRON   *is   the   best*
                 ipopsifios.
                 candidate
                 'Yanis thinks that he is the best candidate.'
           (c)   O   Yanis$_1$ theli   o   Costas$_2$ na voithisi   ton   idhio$_{1/*2}$/ton
                 the Y.   wants   the C.   *helps   PRON*
                 eafton tou$_{2/*1}$.
                 'Yanis wants Costas to help him(self).'
           (d)   O   Yanis$_1$ theori   ton eafton tou$_{1/*2}$ ton   kaliero
                 the Y.   considers   PRON   *the   best*
                 ipopsifio.
                 candidate
                 'Yanis considers himself the best candidate.'

(ii) Would you expect that *ton eafton tou* in (3.66d) can be replaced by *o idhios*? Explain!

Exercise 3.5

Complete, as precisely as the data allow, the following Binding Condition for the Hindi pronoun *uskii*:[39]

(3.67)   *uskii*   must_____be   coindexed   with   a   commanding_____in
           its _____

---

[38] Data from Iatridou (1986).
[39] Data from Mohanan (1990), via Dalrymple (1993):37f.

(3.68) (a) ravii₁ **uskii**∗₁ saikiḷ -par baiᵗʰaa   (Hindi)
             Ravi his   bicycle -LOC *sit*-PERF
             'Ravi sat on his bike.'

        (b) vijay -ne₁ ravii -ko₂ **uskii**₂/∗₁ saikiḷ -par biᵗʰaayaa
             Vijay -ERG *Ravi* -ACC *his   bicycle* -LOC *sit*-CAUSE-PERF
             'Vijay seated Ravi on his (Ravi's) bike.'

        (c) raajaa -ne₁ kahaa   ki   mantrii₂ **uske**₁/∗₂ gʰar   gayaa
             king   -ERG say-PERF *that minister his   house*-LOC *go*-PERF
             'The king said that the minister went to his (the king's) house.'

        (d) raajaa -ne₁ mantrii -ko₂ **uske**∗₁/∗₂ gʰar   jaanee -kii
             king   -ERG minister -ACC his   hous-LOC *go   NONFIN*-GEN
             aagyaa dii
             order give
             'The king ordered the minister to go to his (someone else's)
             house.'

3.4   Long-distance reflexives (LDRs)

There are many languages in which reflexives lead a 'double life':
they can be locally bound, similar to English *herself*; or they can find an antecedent outside their minimal clause. In the latter case, that antecedent often
needs to be a subject and/or a logophoric center. Such languages include Latin,
Icelandic, and Japanese. We will follow the custom in the literature in this section and refer to such pronouns as *long-distance reflexives* (LDRs). For example,
the Latin reflexive *se* (acc.)/*sibi* (dat.) can be bound to a non-local antecedent
if that antecedent is a verb of saying, cf. (3.69a); we do not of course have ungrammatical examples, but note that in embedded clauses that are not embedded
under verbs of saying, only plain pronominal forms are found, cf. (3.69b):[40]

(3.69) (a) Iccius nūntium mittit, nisi   subsidium **sibi**₇ submittātur ...
             *Iccius message sends if-not relief   REFL *furnished*-PASSIVE
             (Latin)
             'Iccius sends a message that unless relief be given to himself, ... '

        (b) Ibi   in proximiīs villīs   ita bipartītō   fuērunt₍₁₎, ut
             there in nearest   farmhouse so in two parts made-they that
             Tiberis inter   **eōs**₁ et pōns   interesset.
             Tiber   between them and bridge lay between
             'They set (themselves) up in farmhouses very nearby, divided in two,
             so that the Tiber and the bridge were in between them.'

There are two general lines of analysis for LDRs: movement analyses, according
to which LDRs are locally bound after covert movement into the local clause of
their antecedent; and non-movement analyses. Among the latter some analyze

[40] Examples from Kuno (1987):137.

LDRs as command anaphors bound within a certain (rather large) syntactic domain (e.g. Progovac (1992); Manzini and Wexler (1987)), while most claim that LDRs fall outside the domain of sentence grammar and are purely a matter of logophoricity (e.g. Hellan (1992); Kameyama (1984); Kuno (1987); Maling (1984); Thráinsson (1992)).[41]

We do not intend to review the rather extensive literature on the issue here (see e.g. Huang (2000):ch. 2.3 for a critical overview). Generally, proponents of movement accounts claim to offer a unified analysis of the short-distance and long-distance binding cases of LDRs, and stress the parallelism to languages with clitic climbing (it is noteworthy that LDRs are overwhelmingly prosodically weak, monosyllabic forms; see below). Furthermore, these analyses often capture specific restrictions on LDRs connected to things like intervening subjects or mood.

Proponents of non-movement accounts, on the other hand, often point out counter-examples to the restrictions dealt with on the movement analyses. Also, they argue that the existence of logophoric pronouns needs to be acknowledged anyway, and that LDRs can sometimes be found without any sentence-internal antecedent, which is, of course, typical for logophoric pronouns, but finds no natural account under movement approaches. Furthermore they point out that the purported movement of LDRs often needs to violate established restrictions on movement.

It is probably fair to say that the problems for movement accounts are considerable and severe, but that logophoric approaches are only as restrictive as their underlying theory of logophoricity, an area where more work is required.

Maling (1984), Sells (1987), and Thráinsson (1992), among others, make a convincing case that Icelandic LDRs are logophoric in nature. Their data also provide some nice examples of what does and what doesn't count as a logophoric antecedent. To emphasize this latter point, I have provided the direct speech paraphrases below the examples:[42]

(3.70)   (a)   Hann$_2$ sagði [að **sig$_2$** vantaði hæfileika].   (Icelandic)
                he   said   that self lacked ability
                'He said that he lacked ability.' – 'He said: "I lack ability."'
          (b) * Honum$_2$ var sagt [að **sig$_2$** vantaði hæfileika].
                he   was said   that self lacked ability
                'He was told that he lacked ability.' – 'He was told: "You/# I lack ability."'

---

[41] Among the movement analyses, we can furthermore distinguish between analyses that assume LDRs to move as heads (essentially parallel to clitics in clitic-climbing languages; cf. Cole *et al.* [1990]; Cole and Sung (1994); Cole and Wang (1996); Cole *et al.* [2000]; Hestvik (1992); Pica (1983, 1987)), and those that assume them to move as phrases (Huang and Tang (1992)), as well as mixed ones (e.g. Katada [1991]).

[42] (3.70) is Maling (1984)'s (37a/b), (3.71), and (3.72) are from Sigurðsson (1986), both via Sells (1987):450ff.

(3.71)   (a)   Barnið₁   lét ekki í   ljós [að   það   hefði verið hugsað vel
                  child-the₁ let not in light that there had   been though well
                  um   **sig₁**]
                  about self
                  'The child didn't reveal that it had been taken good care of.'
                  'The child didn't say: "I've been taken good care of."'
          (b) * Barnið₁   bar þess ekki merki [að   það   hefði verið hugsað
                  child-the₁ bore it   not signs   that there had   been though
                  vel um   **sig₁**]
                  well about self
                  'The child didn't look as if it had been taken good care of.'
                # 'The child didn't look: "I've been taken good care of."'

As mentioned before, logophoric pronouns can, under the right circumstances, appear without a sentence-internal antecedent at all. This is the case, too, for Icelandic LDRs:

(3.72)   Formaðurinn₄ varð   óskaplega reiður. Tillagan   væri avívirðileg.
          The chairman became furiously angry. The proposal was outrageous.
          Væri henni beint   gegn **sér₄** persónulega.   (Icelandic)
          Was it   aimed at   self personally?

Because LDRs usually occur in subjunctive, rather than indicative, subordinated sentences (where such a distinction exists), it has been suggested that their binding domain could be syntactically described as 'first dominating clause with independent (=indicative) inflection' (plus, possibly, subject-orientation). While this might be the case for some languages, Thráinsson (1992) shows that subjunctive mood is neither a necessary nor a sufficient condition for LDRs in Icelandic. Rather, the connection appears to be an indirect one: subjunctive mood marks certain embedded contexts (e.g. non-factual ones), which, in turn, coincide to a large degree with those created by verbs of saying and thinking.

   A striking generalization about LDRs is that they are morphologically simple. Languages that have only complex reflexives (like English) systematically lack LDRs, and in those that have simple and complex forms (e.g. Icelandic) only the simple ones are found to be LDRs. In some movement approaches to LDRs, this remarkable property has been taken to correlate with the head/phrase distinction: complex forms like *himself* are syntactically branching and thus inherently phrasal, confined to phrasal movement, while simple forms like Icelandic *sig* can act as heads and undergo head-movement (Pica, 1983, 1984). The success of such a story partly relies on how plausible it is to assume that head-movement is less local than phrasal movement (the natural expectation might be that it is the other way around), an issue we won't go into here. Non-movement accounts, on the other hand, have little to offer in the way of explaining the general morphological simplicity of LDRs (either) (see Hellan [1992]:29 for a few speculative remarks).

Exercise 3.6

Explain the grammaticality contrast between the two Icelandic examples in (3.73) below (Maling [1984]'s [29a/b]) by paraphrasing them as direct speech:

(3.73)   (a)   Jón$_4$ trúir   [að   hann$_4$ verði   alltaf   froskur [nema
               John *believes* *[that* *he*   *will be* *forever* *a frog* *[unless*
               konungsdóttir   kysse sig$_4$]]
               a king's daughter kisses self]]
               'John believes that he will remain a frog forever unless a princess kisses him.'

    (b) * því er trúað   [að   hann$_4$ verði   alltaf   froskur [nema
                it   *is* *believed* *[that* *he*   *will be* *forever* *a frog* *[unless*
                konungsdóttir   kyssi sig$_4$]]
                a king's daughter kisses self]]
                'It is believed that he will remain a frog forever unless a princess kisses him.'

3.5 Some pronominal systems

Now that we've seen a broader array of possibilities for domains and orientation, we can have a glance at some complete pronominal systems different from English.

3.5.1 Danish and Norwegian

Many Germanic languages other than English show a four-way split in their pronominal system, cf. table 3.2 (the labels SE- and P-form are taken over from the literature, reminiscent of the French reflexive clitic *se* and the generative term 'pronominal').

Table 3.2 *Germanic pronoun systems*

		SE-form:	P-form:
bare	Danish	sig	ham
	Dutch	zich	hem
	German	sich	ihn
	Norwegian	seg	ham
+'self'	Danish	sig selv	ham selv
	Dutch	zich self	hem self
	German	sich selbst	ihn selbst
	Norwegian	seg selv	ham selv

Table 3.3 *Danish and Norwegian pronoun system*

	SE-form bound to subject in tense domain	P-form free from subject in coargument domain
bare free in c-dom.	D: *sig* N: *seg*	D: *ham, hende* N: *ham*
+'self' bound in s-dom.	D: *sig selv, hende selv* N: *seg selv*	D: *ham selv* N: *ham selv*

Typically, the plain SE-form is found in all non-referring constructions, e.g. inherent reflexives and detransitivized forms such as middles. When referring, SE-forms tend to be locally subject oriented, while P-forms are often locally anti-subject oriented. Bare forms (SE- or P-) are usually locally free, whereas 'self' forms must be locally bound.

I will illustrate this using Danish and Norwegian, which provide particularly neat illustrations of such a system. As suggested in table 3.2, their pronominal systems can be thought of as arranged by two binary choices: SE-form vs. non-reflexive pronoun; and bare form vs. 'self' form. Each value for these choices is associated with one binding requirement. As the choices cross-classify, so do the conditions, as shown in table 3.3.[43]

The examples given below illustrate these systems.[44] (3.74) illustrates the simple case in which tense, subject, and coargument domain coincide. No bare forms can be used, given that these need to be free in the coargument domain, which includes all NPs here. Among the *selv*-forms, *sig/seg selv* must be chosen if the antecedent is a subject, but *hende/ham selv*, if it is a non-subject:

(3.74)   (a)   Susan$_1$ fortalte Anne$_2$ om $\left\{ \begin{array}{l} *\text{hende}_1/ *\text{hende selv}_1/*\text{sig}_1/ \textbf{sig selv}_1 \\ *\text{hende}_2/ \textbf{hende selv}_2/*\text{sig}_2/*\text{sig selv}_2 \end{array} \right\}$
            Susan told   Anne   about
            (Danish)

   (b)   Harald$_1$ fortalde Jon$_2$ om $\left\{ \begin{array}{l} *\text{ham}_1/ *\text{ham selv}_1/*\text{seg}_1/ \textbf{seg selv}_1 \\ *\text{ham}_2/ \textbf{ham selv}_2/*\text{seg}_2/*\text{seg selv}_2 \end{array} \right\}$
            Harald told   John   about
            (Norwegian)

[43] Note that both 'self' and SE correspond to 'bound in domain D,' while both 'bare' and P correspond to 'free in domain D.' It is tempting to think that +/−SE corresponds to '+/− bound to subject in domain D$_1$,' and that +/−self corresponds to '+/− bound (at all) in domain D$_2$.' But note that neither D$_1$ nor D$_2$ are the same across positive and negative conditions. Therefore, the formal similarity between the conditions associated with the opposing values cannot be captured in any straightforward way.

[44] I did not differentiate between tense domain and coargument domain for the sake of simplicity; cf. Dalrymple (1993) for evidence for the choice of the latter. Danish examples from Vikner (1985).

Let us now turn to a case where coargument domain and tense domain are distinct. Since *bad*, 'asked,' is an object control verb, the understood subject of the embedded clause in (3.75) is Anne, not Susan. Therefore, coreference with *Susan* is a case of binding outside the coargument domain (and subject domain), but within the tense domain. In such a case, the *selv*-forms are excluded because they require an antecedent within the subject domain. The bare SE-form *sig/seg* is possible, because it is free in its coargument domain and at the same time bound to a subject within the tense domain; the bare P-form *hende/ham* is possible, too, because it is (subject-)free in the smaller coargument domain:

(3.75)   (a)   Susan₁ bad   Anne om at ringe til   **hende₁**/ *hende selv₁/
                 Susan   asked   Anne for to ring   to
                 sig₁/ *sig selv₁   (Danish)
                 'Susan asked Anne to call her.'
           (b)   Jon₁ bad   oss snakke om   **ham₁**/ *ham selv₁/ **seg₁**/ *seg
                 Jon   asked   us   to talk   about
                 selv₁   (Norwegian)

As expected, *sig/seg* will no longer be available if the binding is to a non-subject (note that the understood subject of *ringe* is *Susan*, i.e. the pronoun is indeed bound by the matrix object):

(3.76)   Susan₁ lovede   Anne₂ at ringe til   **hende₂**/ *hende selv₂/*sig₂/
           Susan   promised   Anne   to ring   to
           *sig selv₂   (Danish)

Note finally that the bare SE-forms (and only those) are used in non-thematic positions such as with inherently reflexive verbs:[45]

(3.77)   Peter sov over * ham/ *ham selv/ **sig**/ *sig selv   (Danish)
           Peter slept over
           'Peter overslept.'

This contrasts with the reflexive object in true transitive constructions, which, as seen in (3.74) above, cannot be bare SE. It looks as if the subject qualifies as a binder in the sense of the SE-vs.-P distinction (otherwise we would expect to see *ham*), but not in the sense of the bare-vs.-'self' distinction (otherwise we would expect *sig selv*). We will return to some of these issues in chapter 11.

---

[45] As Vikner (1985):8f. notes, certain verbs that allow either thematic or non-thematic objects give the misleading impression that *sig* and *sig selv* have a similar distribution, e.g. in (i):

(i)   Peter vaskede sig / sig selv.   (Danish)
           Peter washed

It turns out, however, that *vaskede* simply has two argument frames, one transitive and one inherently reflexive. Thus *Peter vaskede sig selv* corresponds to English *Peter washed himself*, while *Peter vaskede sig* corresponds to English *Peter washed*. As Vikner shows convincingly, the non-complementarity disappears as soon as one uses verbs that are either always transitive (*sig selv*), or always inherently reflexive (*sig*).

Table 3.4 *Marathi pronoun system*

	bound to	free in
swataah	subject in subject-domain	–
aapaṇ	(logical) subject in root-domain	coargument-domain
to	–	coargument-domain

3.5.2   Marathi

Marathi, as discussed in Dalrymple (1993), has three different pronoun forms, two of which require a binder; cf. table 3.4.[46]

As discussed in section 3.3 above, *to*, like English *her/him*, must be locally free, but unlike *her/him* (and like bare pronouns in Danish and Norwegian) only in its coargument domain (as opposed to subject domain). *Swataah* plays the role of a reflexive pronoun, except that its domain is slightly larger than that of English, Danish, or Norwegian 'self'-forms (tense domain in Marathi vs. subject domain in the Germanic languages), and it is subject oriented. In addition there is the long-distance reflexive *aapaṇ*, which must be locally free, but bound within the root S;[47] it can thus occur in embedded clauses, within NPs, and as the object of prepositions that assign their own θ-role:[48]

(3.78)   (a)   Tom$_1$ mhanat hota ki   Sue$_2$ ni   **aaplyaalaa**$_{1/*2/*3}$ maarle (Marathi)
                  Tom   said   that Sue   ERG self-ACC   hit
                  'Tom said that Sue hit him.'
          (b)   Jane$_1$ ni   **aaplye**$_1$ pustak phekun dile
                  Jane   ERG self-GEN book   threw   give
                  'Jane threw away self's book.'
          (c)   Jane$_1$ ne   **aaplyaakartaa**$_1$ saaḍi gheṭ li
                  Jane   ERG self-for   sari   bought
                  'Jane bought a sari for herself.'

Note once again that the distribution of *aapaṇ* significantly overlaps with that of *swataah* (for all positions whose tense domain is bigger than the coargument domain), and is even a proper subset of that of *to*. This kind of non-complementarity is common among languages: the Turkish pronoun *kendi* is a domain reflexive – it needs to be bound within the root-domain. But Turkish also has a second form *kendisi*, which obeys no Binding Conditions at all. The distribution of *kendi* is thus a proper subset of that of *kendisi*:[49]

---

[46] The line for *swataah* describes what Dalrymple calls the 'restrictive' dialect of Marathi. For speakers of the less-restricted dialect, the relevant domain is the tense domain.
[47] Dalrymple (1993):21–24 convincingly shows that *aapaṇ* is not a logophor.
[48] Dalrymple (1993)'s (1.49), (1.35), (1.31).
[49] Keenan (1988):134, following Enç (1989).

(3.79)   Herkes₁ ayna-da $\left\{ \begin{array}{l} \textbf{kendisi-(n)i}_{1/2} \\ \textbf{kendi-(n)i}_{1/*2} \\ \textit{(him)self-}\text{ACC} \end{array} \right\}$ gördu   (Turkish)
           everyone mirror-LOC   *saw*
           'Everyone saw themselves in the mirror.'

Even more extreme, Fijian (Oceanic, Austronesian) has no reflexives at all. The Fijian pronoun *koya* occurs in all kinds of configurations, from locally bound, to non-locally bound, to free:[50]

(3.80)   a   mokuti **koya**₁/₂ o ira kece₁   (Fijian)
           PAST *hit*   *him(self)*   PL *all*
           'They all hit themselves.'

These are but a few illustrative examples of pronominal systems found in the languages of the world. Our general schema for Binding Conditions at this point looks as in (3.81):

(3.81)   An NP of **class** must (**not**) be coindexed with a **commanding**

$\left\{ \begin{array}{l} \textbf{NP} \\ \textbf{subject} \end{array} \right\}$ within its $\left\{ \begin{array}{l} \textbf{coargument} \\ \textbf{subject} \\ \textbf{tense} \\ \textbf{root} \end{array} \right\}$ domain.

A **class** can be just one lexical item (with all its different case, person, and number forms, e.g. Marathi *aapan*, Turkish *kendisi*), or a set of (all forms of) stems that have a certain morphological shape in common ('self' vs. bare, SE-based vs. P-based in Germanic), or, of course, their complement (all non-pronominal NPs). Any one of the parameters in (3.81) can serve to define natural super-classes of forms (e.g. all that need to be bound vs. all that need to be free, only the subject-oriented, etc.).

Different languages distinguish different numbers of classes, and whether there is a minimal or a maximal number of classes, whether there are any implicational relations between the different classes cross-linguistically, and whether any super-classes (e.g. Chomsky [1981]'s anaphors versus pronominals) play a cross-linguistically privileged role, remains yet to be found out. What should have become clear, however, is that it is not useful to ask which elements in a given language are the counterparts of, say, reflexive and non-reflexive pronouns in English, or what *the* binding domain (or governing category) in a given language is.

Exercise 3.7
Define the following classes using the schema in (3.81):

1.   the class of *domain reflexives*, i.e. all pronouns that must be syntactically bound at all
2.   the class of logophors
3.   the class of bare SE anaphors in Danish and Norwegian

---

[50] Keenan (1988):132.

Exercise 3.8

Using table 3.4, predict which of the three pronouns *swataah, aapan,* and *to* can occur in the position of PRONOUN in the Marathi sentence frames in (3.82a) and (3.82b) (Dalrymple [1993] [1.60/61]):

(3.82) (a) Jane$_1$ ne PRONOUN$_1$-FOR saaḍi gheṭ li   (Marathi)

     Jane ERG *self-for*   *sari bought*

     'Jane bought a sari for herself.'

  (b) Jane$_1$ ne John laa PRONOUN$_1$-ABOUT maahiti

     Jane ERG *John* DAT *self-about*   *information*

     dili

     gave

     'Jane gave John information about herself.'

4   Binding versus coreference

In this chapter we will refine the interpretation procedure developed in chapter 2. An important distinction – that between coreference and binding – will be introduced, motivated, and technically implemented. An early and very lucid explication of the distinction is found in Bach and Partee (1980), so lucid, in fact, that I'll simply quote it:

> Let's summarize the places where something like coindexing is used in the literature:

(1)   The same pronoun appears in several places in a sentence:
He said *he* was OK.

(2)   A pronoun appears together with a referring NP:
John said that *he* was OK.

(3)   A pronoun appears together with a quantificational NP:
No woman doubts that *she* is OK.

(4)   A pronoun occurs in a relative clause:
... the *woman* who said that *she* had found the answer.

(5)   A reflexive or other obligatorily bound pronoun appears in a sentence:
John loves *himself*
Oscar is out of *his* head.

> It is really only in situation (1) (in some sentences), and (2) that it seems appropriate to talk about coreference. In every other case (...) coindexing a pronoun with some other expression is a shorthand way of saying that the pronoun in question is being interpreted as a bound-variable...

Other authors have emphasized this point, too, in particular Tanya Reinhart (Reinhart, 1982, 1983a, b). Up to now we have uniformly interpreted coindexing to mark *coreference*. If, as Bach and Partee, and Reinhart in the aforementioned works, point out, coreference is only one of two semantic concepts that fall under the pre-theoretic concept of 'binding,' the other being *variable binding*, we should explore how this second concept can be implemented in our little grammar.

To get a better understanding of what is behind this distinction it is perhaps best to look at prototypical examples:

(4.1)   Coreference: $\begin{Bmatrix} He_5 \\ John_5 \end{Bmatrix}$ said that *he$_5$* was okay.

(4.2)   Variable binding: *No woman$_5$* doubts that *she$_5$* is okay.

As the name coreference suggests, we can think of the embedded pronoun in (4.1) as a referring expression of its own, which just picks out the same individual as its antecedent. Accordingly, apart from the awkwardness resulting from a Binding Condition C violation, the sentence in (4.3) is a semantically accurate paraphrase of (4.1):

(4.3)   *John* said that *John* was okay.

This is as expected. If *John* and *he* in (4.1) are coreferential, that means that both expressions refer to the same individual, John. In other words, they have the same denotation (under the given indexing, that is). Therefore the two expressions should be exchangeable *salva veritate* (preserving the truth conditions), which they turn out to be. In striking contrast to that, no paraphrase similar to (4.3) can be given for the example that illustrates variable binding. Consider (4.4):

(4.4)   *No woman* doubts that *no woman* is okay.

(4.4) patently differs in meaning from (4.2): if (4.2) is true, women in general have a high opinion of themselves (and possibly other women, though nothing is said about that); if (4.4) is true, women in general think lowly of women.

Also, (4.4) doesn't feel like a Binding Condition C violation in the way that (4.3) does. It is, in fact, just unclear what it is *supposed* to mean to interpret the two occurrences of *no woman* as coreferent. This is very much unlike Binding Condition C violations with names as in (4.3), where we have a perfectly sensible and easily expressible meaning, albeit expressed in a way that is felt to be syntactically deviant.

The conclusion is that *she* in (4.2) does not denote the same as *no woman*, and can therefore not be analyzed as coreferent with its antecedent. What we are going to see next is that *no woman* does not *refer* in the first place, which is why no pronoun can *co*refer with it. It turns out that there is an entire class of NPs which are, by their very semantic nature, incapable of reference, and hence coreference. These are *quantified noun phrases* (QNPs) such as *no woman* or *each of the women*, and *wh*-phrases such as *which man* or *who*. It will be useful to start with an exploration of these (in particular, to abstract away from unnecessary complications: the QNPs) in order to find out more about what variable binding is. We will return to the question of whether ordinary, non-quantified NPs like *John, the soprano*, or even pronouns like *she* can function as variable binders in chapter 5, and to the question of whether (some) QNPs can refer in chapter 7.

A terminological remark: in chapter 1 we defined the notion of a binder in syntactic terms (a c-commanding, coindexed NP). In this chapter we focus on a semantic distinction between variable binding and coreference. To keep matters clear, we will therefore distinguish between *syntactic binding* or *syn-binding* for short, and variable binding, which we will mostly refer to as *semantic binding*, or simply *sem-binding*. As a cover term for both, and for coreference without syntactic binding, we will henceforth use the term *anaphoric relation*.

To exemplify, there is no doubt that both antecedent NPs in (4.1) *and* (4.2) – *John/he* and *no woman* – syntactically bind the pronouns, but what is at issue here is which anaphoric relation that syntactic binding expresses semantically: semantic binding (a.k.a. variable binding) or coreference.

4.1   Quantified NPs and variable binding

Above we saw that we cannot simply replace a bound pronoun by a copy of its antecedent, if the antecedent is a QNP. The result is not a Binding Condition C violation, as predicted, but, curiously, a well-formed sentence that means something completely different. To get an idea of what is going on in these sentences, let us start with a simple example like (4.5). We assume, as before, that VPs such as *is happy* denote functions from individuals to truth values, here the function that maps all and only the happy creatures to 1. Additionally, we assume that *common nouns* such as *manager* also denote such functions, here: that function which maps all and only the managers to 1. (4.5) is true, then, if every individual that is a manager is a happy creature, (4.5b):

(4.5)   Every manager is happy.
   (a) $[\![\text{is happy}]\!]^g = [\![\text{happy}]\!]^g = \lambda y.y$ is happy (the characteristic function of the set of happy creatures, $\{y \mid y \text{ is happy}\}$)
   (b) $[\![\text{Every manager is happy}]\!]^g = 1$ iff for every x, if x a manager,
      (i) $[\![\text{happy}]\!]^g(x) = 1$ or
      (ii) x is in $\{y \mid y \text{ is happy}\}$

The two alternative renderings in (4.5b-i) and (4.5b-ii) relate back to the set/function equivalence and the convention related to it we introduced in chapter 2, section 2.3.1. Each function of type $\langle et \rangle$ (such as the denotation of an intransitive verb, or of a common noun such as *manager*) characterizes a set of individuals (cf. [4.5a]). Instead of saying that the function maps an individual to 1, as done in (4.5b-i), we can, and often will in the discussion to follow, say that the individual is in the corresponding set (cf. [4.5b-ii]). Other cases of QNPs can be interpreted in an analogous manner:

(4.6) $[\![\text{One manager is happy}]\!]^g = 1$ iff
                  for (at least) one x such that $[\![\text{manager}]\!]^g(x) = 1$, $[\![\text{happy}]\!]^g(x) = 1$

(4.7) $[\![\text{No manager is happy}]\!]^g = 1$ iff
                  for no x such that $[\![\text{manager}]\!]^g(x) = 1$, $[\![\text{happy}]\!]^g(x) = 1$

The interested reader will find more about the meaning of QNPs in subsection 4.5.2 below. For the moment, all we need to know is that sentences of the form *QNP VP* are interpreted as in (4.8), where the VP meaning is a regular property/set of individuals, but the QNP meaning is a more complicated logical construct, not just an individual or plurality of individuals:

(4.8)

	QNP		VP	
for $\left\{\begin{array}{l} \text{every} \\ \text{some} \\ \text{(at least) } n \\ \text{no} \end{array}\right\}$	x such that x is an N, x is in	$\{y \mid y$	$\left\{\begin{array}{l} \text{is happy} \\ \text{sleeps} \\ \ldots \end{array}\right\}$	$\}$

There is something curious about this schema, as well as the examples in (4.5–4.7), to wit that it doesn't mention any indices on the QNP. There is a reason for this, namely that the meaning of the QNP isn't dependent on the assignment function at all, and doesn't even relate to it. That is, while pronouns rely on the assignment functions to be interpreted in the first place, and names and definite NPs can at least be related to the assignment function because they denote individuals after all (see chapter 2), QNPs are simply not sensitive to assignments, period. This makes sense semantically, given that an assignment assigns *referents* to NPs, and that QNPs don't refer. It raises the embarrassing question, however, of whether the index on a QNP does anything at all. It is this question we will turn to next.

Let us thus look at a case that involves coindexing. What do our interpretation rules predict as the denotation for an example like (4.9)? By the interpretations given in chapter 2, the denotation of the matrix VP will depend on the assignment g – (4.9a) – and so will the interpretation of the entire sentence – (4.9b) ($[\![(4.9)]\!]^g$ stands for the meaning of the entire sentence in (4.9); we'll ignore the gender and number presuppositions of pronouns throughout this chapter):

(4.9)   Every tenor$_2$ thinks that he$_2$ is competent.
  (a) $[\![$thinks that he$_2$ is competent $]\!]^g = \lambda x.x$ thinks that $g(2)$ is competent ($\approx$ the set of people who think that $g(2)$ is competent)
  (b) $[\![(4.9)]\!]^g = 1$ iff for every x such that x is a tenor, x is in the set of people who think that $g(2)$ is competent

Under the interpretation (4.9b), *he$_2$* is a free pronoun, which receives its value from the context. This reading is clearly available for the sentence *per se*, but it shouldn't be under the indexing given in (4.9).

What we rather want the example to denote is (4.10a). We will get this denotation if we can make the matrix VP have the denotation in (4.10b):

(4.10)   (a)   wanted: $[\![(4.9)]\!]^g = 1$ iff for every x, x a tenor, x is in the set of people who think that x is competent
  (b)   required: $[\![$thinks that he$_2$ is competent $]\!]^g = \lambda x.x$ thinks that x is competent ($\approx$ the set of people x who think that x is competent)

How can we get this denotation for the VP? Suppose we treat the presence of a quantified NP with index n as an indicator that, within the c-command domain of that NP, pronouns bearing the index n are no longer referring pronouns, but *bound* pronouns. That means that their value is no longer determined by the contextual assignment, but by the argument slot filled by the NP. Our official implementation of this will have two parts: one syntactic; one semantic:

(4.11)   Index Transfer (preliminary):
For any quantified noun phrase QNP with index n, adjoin β_n to QNP's sister constituent:

(4.12)   Binder Index Evaluation rule (BIER) (final):

For any natural number n, $\left[\!\!\left[\begin{array}{c} \\ \beta_n \quad Y \end{array} \right]\!\!\right]^g = \lambda x.[\![Y]\!]^{g[n \to x]}(x)$

Index Transfer in (4.11) implements the observation made above that an index on a QNP doesn't play a role for the interpretation of QNP, but rather expresses that any coindexed pronoun within QNP's sister (its c-command domain) is to be interpreted as a bound variable. The BIER (4.12) consecutively interprets such a configuration. It states that β_n's sister constituent Y is not to be interpreted relative to the original assignment g, but to a changed assignment $g[n \to x]$, which is just like g except that the index n is mapped to the individual x. Since x is also the individual argument to $[\![Y]\!]^{g[n \to x]}$, this means in effect that any pronoun bearing the index n in Y is bound by the open argument slot of Y (if you are unfamiliar with the $g[n \to x]$ notation for assignment modifications, you might want to skip to subsection 4.5.1 below before reading on). Let us see this in a sample derivation:

(4.13)   Every tenor$_4$ thinks that he$_4$ is competent.

after Index Transfer:

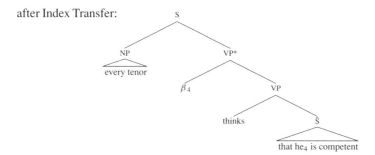

(a) $[\![_{V^0}\text{ thinks }]\!]^g = \lambda p_t \lambda z_e.z$ thinks (that) p
(b) $[\![_{\bar{S}}\text{that he}_4\text{ is competent}]\!]^g =$ the proposition that $g(4)$ is competent
(c) $[\![_{VP}\text{ thinks that he}_4\text{ is competent}]\!]^g =$
$\lambda z.z$ thinks that $g(4)$ is competent
$\approx$ the set of those who think that $g(4)$ is competent

(d) $[[_{VP*} \beta_4 [_{VP} \text{ thinks that he}_4 \text{ is competent}]]]^g$
  $= \lambda x.[[_{VP} \text{ thinks that he}_4 \text{ is competent }]]^{g[4 \to x]}(x)$ (by BIER)
  $= \lambda x.[\lambda z.z \text{ thinks that } g[4 \to x](4) \text{ is competent }](x)^1$
  $= \lambda x.x \text{ thinks that } g[4 \to x](4) \text{ is competent}^2$
  $= \lambda x[x \text{ thinks that } x \text{ is competent }]$
  $\approx$ the set of those x who think that x is competent
  $\approx$ the set of people who consider themselves competent

It is very important to understand the difference between (4.13c) and (4.13d): (4.13c) denotes the set of people who have a belief about a particular individual $g(4)$. (4.13d) denotes the set of people who have a belief about themselves. It is precisely the transition to the latter that accounts for binding.

What remains to be done is to combine (4.13d) with the meaning of the subject *every tenor* in the standard way (the standard way being [4.8], or some reasonable generalization thereof), which gives us the desired truth conditions:

(4.14) $[\![\text{every tenor}_4 [\beta_4 [\text{thinks that he}_4 \text{ is competent}]]]\!]^g =$
  for every y such that y is a tenor, $[\lambda x.[[_{VP} \text{ thinks that he}_4 \text{ is competent}]]^{g[4 \to x]}(x)](y) = 1$
  $\equiv \dots y$ is in $\{x \mid [[_{VP} \text{ thinks that he}_4 \text{ is competent}]]^{g[4 \to x]}(x)\}$
  $\equiv \dots y$ is in $\{x \mid x \text{ thinks that } x \text{ is competent}\}$
  $\equiv$ every tenor is in the set of those who consider themselves competent

Note in particular that the denotation of the entire sentence is not dependent on the assignment g at all, despite the fact that it contains indexed NPs. The reason is that the index on *every tenor* is interpreted by the BIER, rather than as a referential index on an NP, and that the pronoun is semantically bound within the clause (by the QNP).

In what follows, I will call the adjoined β_n a *binder prefix*, and the NP minimally c-commanding it the *(semantic) binder NP*. The index on a binder NP (before Index Transfer) or on a binder prefix (after Index Transfer) will be called a *(semantic) binder index*. I will use the term *semantic binder* both for binder prefixes and, derivatively, binder NPs. Semantic binding (sem-binding) is defined as follows:

(4.15)   Semantic binding (final):
  A binder prefix β *sem(antically)-binds* an NP if and only if
  (a) β and NP are coindexed
  (b) β c-commands NP
  (c)   there is no binder prefix β' which is c-commanded by β and meets (a) and (b)
  If an NP is not bound by any binder prefix β in a phrase marker P, we say that NP is *semantically free* in P.

---

[1] $[\lambda z.z \text{ thinks that } g[4 \to x](4) \text{ is competent}]$ is copied from (4.13c), with $g[4 \to x]$ replacing g.
[2] Note that 'x thinks that $g[4 \to x](4)$ is competent' is the result of applying the function $[\lambda z.z \text{ thinks that } g[4 \to x](4) \text{ is competent}]$ to the variable x.

In the example (4.13) above, the adjoined β_4 is a binder prefix with binder index 4; it sem-binds the pronoun he_4, which is therefore semantically bound. Derivatively, the NP *every tenor* sem-binds he_4, and is thus a semantic binder as well.

Applying Index Transfer (4.11) is a necessary condition for semantic binding, but not a sufficient one. If a pronoun is in the c-command domain of a QNP, but not coindexed with it, it will still be interpreted as a free pronoun whose denotation is determined by the global assignment.[3] This is demonstrated in (4.16) below:

(4.16) Every tenor$_3$ thinks that he$_2$ is competent.
  (a) after Index Transfer:
       Every tenor $[_{VP*} \beta_3 [_{VP}$ thinks that he$_2$ is competent.$]]$
  (b) $[\![_{VP}$ thinks that he$_2$ is competent$]\!]^g = \lambda z.z$ thinks that $g(2)$ is competent
       ($\approx$ the set of those who think that *g(2)* is competent)
  (c) $[\![_{VP*} \beta_3 [_{VP}$ thinks that he$_2$ is competent $]]\!]^g = \lambda x [\![_{VP}$ thinks that he$_2$ is competent $]\!]^{g[3 \to x]}(x)]$
       $= \lambda x.x$ thinks that $g[3 \to x](2)$ is competent
       $= \lambda x.x$ thinks that $g(2)$ is competent
       $\approx$ the set of those x who think that g(2) is competent
  (d) for every y such that y is a tenor, $[\lambda x [\![_{VP}$ thinks that he$_2$ is competent $]\!]^{g[3 \to x]}(x)]](y) = 1$
       $\approx$ every tenor is in the set of those who think that $g(2)$ is competent

Crucially, the BIER manipulates the assignment in (4.16c) to $g[3 \to x]$, but this change doesn't have any effect on the VP-denotation, which doesn't contain an NP indexed 3. In particular, the denotation of the pronoun he_2, $g[3 \to x](2)$, remains unaffected by the change, which is why we could simply write $g(2)$ instead (recall that $g[3 \to x]$ is just like g except perhaps which value it assigns to 3). That is, he_2 remains a free pronoun that receives its value from the context.

Note that even though there isn't any sem-bound NP in (4.16), the prefix β_3 and the NP *every tenor* qualify as semantic binders. In such a situation we speak of *vacuous binding*: the index 3 is null and void. There is no immediate reason to prohibit indexings that lead to vacuous binding; the indexing in (4.16) leads to an interpretation in which *he* and *every tenor* are independent of one another, which is intuitively satisfactory.

One last terminological remark: indices which are not binder indices (i.e. not on a QNP or a binder prefix β) will be referred to as *referential indices*. This makes sense, since these indices – unlike binder indices – determine the denotation of the NP they are on, which is an individual. Confusion might arise, though, given that not every NP that bears a referential index refers to one particular individual. For example, the index 2 on *he* in (4.16) is a referential index, as is

---

[3] The interpretation of a bound pronoun is, of course, dependent on the assignment, too, but only locally.

the index 4 on *he* in (4.13). However, the latter is semantically bound in the sentence, which means that it will not refer to a particular individual or referent, but rather covary with its semantic binder. So only semantically free pronouns are referential in the intuitive sense, while semantically bound pronouns are not. However, both types carry referential indices. Put in other words, the distinction between referential indices and binder indices is a local one (it only regards the NP and possibly its neighboring binder prefix), while the distinction between bound and referential NPs is a global one (an NP is bound or free only within a larger syntactic domain).

We observed earlier that since QNPs do not refer, we don't really have any use for an index on them. Given the workings of the Index Transfer rule in (4.11) we no longer need to worry about that, since it doesn't just adjoin an index to the QNP's sister constituent, but strips that index off the QNP at the same time, leaving a 'bare' QNP.

Having two notions of binding, semantic and syntactic, the question arises which of these is relevant for our Binding Conditions. We will return to this question in chapters 5 and 6. For the moment, we will assume that all Binding Conditions regard syntactic binding. This implies that Binding Conditions have to apply *before* Index Transfer, while all NPs still bear their indices. Let us henceforth refer to the result of applying Index Transfer as the *Logical Form* or *LF* of a sentence. We then require:

(4.17)   The Binding Conditions apply before LF. (to be revised)

Also, we must make sure that Index Transfer applies obligatorily to all QNPs (and *wh*-NPs, see below); otherwise we could have a pronoun be syntactically bound by a QNP, without being semantically bound by that QNP at LF. To ensure this, we demand:

(4.18)   No QNP (or *wh*-NP) bears an index at LF.

Not too much should be read into the LF terminology. As will be discussed in chapters 5 and 6, the LF/pre-LF distinction is entirely reducable in the present context and merely serves expository purposes. An equivalent non-derivational formalism can easily be formulated. By the same token, the introduction of the binder prefix as a separate *syntactic* constituent is merely for expository convenience; alternative systems that don't involve an actual extra node in the tree can be defined, but are considerably less transparent.

Exercise 4.1

Which of the following statements are true? Which are false and why? Add qualifications where necessary.

1.   If a pronoun ϕ is semantically free in S, its meaning in S will depend on the contextual assignment g.
2.   If a pronoun ϕ is semantically bound in S, its meaning in S will depend on the contextual assignment g.

3.   If a pronoun ϕ_n is semantically bound by an *NP* in a configuration like $[_S NP[_\alpha \beta_1 [_\gamma \ldots \phi_1 \ldots]]]$, ϕ is free in S.

4.   If a pronoun ϕ_n is semantically bound by an *NP* in a configuration $[_S NP\ [_\alpha \beta_1 [_\gamma \ldots \phi_1 \ldots]]]$, ϕ is free in γ.

5.   If a pronoun ϕ_n is coindexed with an *NP* in a configuration $[_S NP_3\ [_\alpha [_\gamma \ldots \phi_3 \ldots]]]$, ϕ is semantically bound in S.

6.   If a pronoun ϕ_n is coindexed with an NP in a configuration $[_S NP_3\ [_\alpha [_\gamma \ldots \phi_3 \ldots]]]$, ϕ is free in S.

7.   If a pronoun is not c-commanded by any coindexed NP in S, that pronoun is semantically free in S.

8.   If a pronoun is syntactically bound by an NP in S, it cannot be semantically free in S.

9.   If a pronoun is syntactically bound by a QNP in S, it cannot be semantically free in S.

10.   If a pronoun is syntactically bound by a QNP in S, it cannot be semantically free in any subtree of S.

11.   If an LF contains an adjoined binder prefix β_n, it also contains a semantically bound pronoun indexed n.

12.   If a structure S contains an NP indexed n at s-structure, and NP is not semantically bound, the denotation of S will depend on the contextual assignment g.

13.   If all indices within a structure S are on QNPs or NPs that are semantically bound in S, the denotation of S will not depend on the contextual assignment g.

Exercise 4.2

Suppose that structures of the form *NP[β_n Y]* are base-generated (rather than derived by Index Transfer).

1.   Formulate a definition of *syntactic binding* that will derive the familiar Binding Condition A–C effects both for quantificational and non-quantificational antecedents under this assumption.

2.   Provide an indexing and prefixing procedure which generates all and only the interpretable structures under this assumption.

4.2   The syntax of semantic binding

Let us now turn to the syntactic conditions that need to hold for semantic binding to occur. I will demonstrate that two central aspects of the binding behavior of QNPs follow directly from the semantic assumptions we made in the previous two sections.

4.2.1   The C-command requirement on semantic binding

Consider the examples in (4.19):

(4.19)   (a) *He$_2$ exploits the secretary that Felix$_2$ hired.
           (b) He$_2$ exploits the secretary that he$_2$ hired.
           (c) *He$_2$ exploits the secretary that each of the tenors$_2$ hired.

The fact that *he* and *Felix* in (4.19a) cannot corefer is due to a Binding Condition C violation: the name is syntactically bound (whence the contrast with [4.19b]). The fact that *he* cannot be coindexed with *each of the tenors* in (4.19c) can likewise be attributed to Binding Condition C. Quantified noun phrases such as *each of the tenors* are full NPs and are therefore subject to Binding Condition C. Consider next the examples in (4.20):

(4.20)   (a) The secretary he$_2$ hired thinks that Siegfried$_2$ is despotic.
           (b) *The secretary he$_2$ hired thinks that each of the tenors$_2$ is despotic.

Intuitively, (4.20b) does not allow for a bound variable reading for *he*, i.e. it cannot mean 'each of the tenors is considered despotic by the secretary he hired'; this is why the sentence is starred under the given indexing. The unavailability of this reading cannot be attributed to Binding Condition C, given that *he* does not c-command *each of the tenors*. This is also confirmed by the fact that the otherwise parallel (4.20a) is perfectly well-formed on a reading where *he* and *Siegfried* are coreferent. It seems that – unlike names – QNPs don't allow for coindexing without c-command.[4] One way to block cases like (4.20b) is by a stipulation like (4.21) (I'll return to the *wh*-trace part below):

(4.21)   Bound Anaphora Condition (BAC, Reinhart, 1983a:122/137)
           Quantified NPs and *wh*-traces can have anaphoric relations only with pronouns in their c-command syntactic domain.

Since *each of the tenors* is a quantified noun phrase, (4.21) requires it to c-command the pronoun *him* in order to be coindexed ('have an anaphoric relation') with it. This is not the case in (4.20b), which is therefore correctly ruled out.

It is interesting to note that (4.21) also renders ungrammatical our earlier example (4.19c), repeated here as (4.22):

(4.22)   *He$_2$ exploits the secretary that each of the tenors$_2$ hired.

On top of violating Binding Condition C (because the pronoun syn-binds the QNP), this sentence is now ruled out because it violates the BAC (since the QNP doesn't c-command the pronoun it is coindexed with).

As Reinhart argues, however, it is dubious that something like the BAC in (4.21) is needed as an independent principle of grammar. We have already established that QNPs (and *wh*-expressions) do not refer and therefore don't allow for coreference. The only option to interpret the coindexing is thus via semantic binding, as discussed in section 4.1. Given this much, the BAC can be reduced to the restriction in (4.23) (cf. also Heim and Kratzer [1998]:264):

---

[4] See e.g. Reinhart (1983a):112f. for more examples.

(4.23)   Semantic binding requires syntactic binding (i.e. that the binder be coin-
           dexed with and c-command the pronoun).

In neither one of the examples (4.20a) and (4.20b) does the full NP *Siegfried*
and *each of the tenors*, respectively, c-command – and hence syn-bind – the
pronoun. In the case of (4.20a) this doesn't matter since the coindexing is simply
interpreted as coreference, which doesn't require c-command. The QNP *each
of the tenors* in (4.20b), however, can neither corefer with the pronoun (since it
doesn't refer), nor can it semantically bind it (since it doesn't c-command, hence
syntactically bind it, as required by [4.23]). Therefore the indexing can neither be
interpreted as coreference nor as semantic binding. The same dilemma is found
for the QNP in (4.22).

    We can go further than reducing (4.21) to (4.23); the effect of the restric-
tion in (4.23) actually follows from the way we defined semantic binding, in
particular two aspects of it: first, the binder prefix is adjoined immediately
c-commanded by the QNPs; its c-command domain is the same as that of the
QNP (prior to Index Transfer); second, the BIER manipulates the assignment
function and thereby binds all free coindexed pronouns *within β's sister constituent*; a pronoun outside of that constituent will remain unaffected by it, regardless of its index. In other words, if a coindexed pronoun is outside of the
c-command domain of a QNP, coindexing between the two will be semantically
vacuous.

    Exactly this case is found in our sentence (4.20b), repeated here. Its pertinent
representation is (4.24a). Applying the BIER, the pronoun *he_6* will be contextually interpreted as *g(6)*, while *each of the tenors$_6$* will bind vacuously, as there
are no free occurrences of the index 6 within its sister constituent, the VP *is
despotic*, cf. (4.24b):

(4.24)   The secretary he$_6$ hired thinks that each of the tenors$_6$ is despotic.
      (a)   LF (i.e. after Index Transfer): The secretary he$_6$ hired thinks that each
             of the tenors $[\beta_6[\text{is despotic}]]$
      (b) $[\![(4.24a)]\!]^g =$ the secretary $g(6)$ hired thinks that for each x, x a tenor,
             x is in $\{z \mid [\![\text{despotic}]\!]^{g[6 \to z]}(z)\}$
             $=$ the secretary $g(6)$ hired thinks that for each x, x a tenor, $x \in \{z \mid$
             z is despotic$\}$

The important fact in (4.24) is that the pronoun *he_6* will end up as a free pronoun
with the interpretation *g(6)*, while the binder index 6 doesn't get to bind anything.

    This result is more general and thus bears restating: semantic binding involves
adjunction of a binder prefix β. Coindexed pronouns are interpreted as bound
variables only within the c-command domain of that prefix. And the c-command
domain of β after Index Transfer equals that of the QNP before. Taken together
this means that:

(4.25)   Theorem:
           Coindexing between a QNP and a pronoun results in semantic binding only
           if the QNP c-commands the pronoun.

It should be easy to see that this captures the *effect* of Reinhart's BAC and Heim and Kratzer's (4.23) above. It is derived that the indexing in (4.24) does not result in a bound variable reading for the pronoun *him*. We have not, however, excluded the coindexing itself. To do that, we would still have to evoke a principle like the Bound Anaphora Condition in (4.21).

The question we should ask ourselves at this point is whether we should do this or not. If our task is to generate intuitively correct indexing patterns, we obviously still need the Bound Anaphora Condition. But, as pointed out at the end of section 2.3 in chapter 2, indices are not part of the linguistic data, but merely ancillary devices to predict the data, in particular the range of possible interpretations. If that is the task, then there is no need to ban the indexings in (4.22) and (4.24), as long as our interpretation procedure correctly predicts that no semantic binding (let alone coreference) results from it.

Consequentially we will not adopt the BAC or (4.23). The indexing in (4.24) (*The secretary he₆ hired thinks that each of the managers₆ is despotic.*) is thus grammatical (though misleading), but won't result in any anaphoric relation.

4.2.2   Why QNPs cannot be bound

Let us now return to a case in which a QNP is illicitly c-commanded by another coindexed NP, e.g. (4.19c), repeated here:

(4.26)   ∗He₂ exploits the secretary that each of the tenors₂ hired.
          LF: he₂ exploits the secretary that [each of the tenors][β_2 [hired]].

As discussed above, the indexing in (4.26) is ruled out by Binding Condition C, since *each of the tenors* is a full NP. But interestingly, the coindexing will also be semantically vacuous: the pronoun is not semantically bound by the QNP, due to lack of c-command (cf. last subsection). The index on the QNP has been stripped off it and acts as a binder index, which binds vacuously (since there are no coindexed pronouns in the binder prefix's c-command domain); since binder prefixes don't refer, there is no coreference here either. The interpretation we assign to (4.26) is thus the same we would assign to it if *he* and *each of the managers* were contra-indexed.

The situation in which a NP c-commands a coindexed QNP is thus technically no different from that in which neither c-commands the other: the coindexing is simply vacuous. So while Binding Condition C blocks the *indexing* in (4.26) (as would the BAC), even without Binding Condition C this sentence would receive only its intuitively available interpretation, in which *he₂* is free.

Exercise 4.3
Consider the following sentence with the indexing given:

(4.27)   Every girl₄ told her₄ mother that every boy₄ forgot his₄ books.

1.   Does this structure violate any Binding Principles before Index Transfer? If so, which and how?
2.   List all pairs of syntactic binders and bindees in this structure.
3.   Give the LF representation(s) for this sentence.
4.   List all syntactic binder/bindee pairs for this LF.
5.   List all semantic binder/bindee pairs for this LF.
6.   Does this LF representation violate any Binding Principles? If crucial, specify which elements in your LF fall under which Binding Principle(s).
7.   Calculate the interpretation for this LF. Be sure to give the meanings of all VPs and VP-segments as intermediary steps.
8.   Does your interpretation match with your intuitions about the meaning of this sentence? Comment!

Exercise 4.4
Contrast (4.27) with the following:

(4.28)   Every girl$_4$ told her$_4$ mother that every boy$_4$ stole her$_4$ books.

1.   What interpretation will this sentence get, and why?
2.   Give at least one indexing which represents an intuitively available reading for this sentence.

Exercise 4.5
Give an LF and calculate the denotation for the following sentence:

(4.29)   Every girl$_4$ told her$_4$ mother that every boy$_2$ showed her$_4$ his$_2$ books.

4.3   *Wh*-expressions

Before closing this chapter, a few words should be said about *wh*-expressions, in particular those that are NPs such as *which crocodile* or *what*. Our intuition, presumably even stronger than with QNPs, is that *wh*-expressions do not refer: after all, it is the point of asking a *wh*-question to learn about the referent of the pertinent NP.[5] So thinking of another NP, say a pronoun, as coreferent with a *wh*-expression makes no sense.

Things are different with regard to semantic binding. Consider the sentence in (4.30):

(4.30)   *Which girl* told Suzie that *she* had detention?

This sentence has two plausible interpretations. One where we ask which girl said to Suzie: 'You have detention'; and one where we ask which girl said to

---

[5] The term 'referential *wh*-expression' is sometimes applied in the syntactic literature to phrases like *which of the boys* (or even just *which boy*) and is presumably meant in the sense of 'wh-phrase with lexical content,' or 'wh-phrase containing a referential expression' (as opposed to e.g. *how* or *who the hell*). It should be clear that the *wh*-phrases themselves are in no sense referring.

Suzie: 'I have detention.' In addition there is a less salient, but nonetheless plausible, reading where the girl said: 'She has detention.' We can represent these different readings by different coindexings:

(4.31)   *Which girl₁* told Suzie₂ that *she*₁/₂/₃ had detention?

The different indices represent different anaphoric relations: *she*₁ is the teller (the 'I have dentention' reading), *she*₂ is Suzie ('you have detention'), and *she*₃ is some third party ('she has detention'). It is straightforward to get the second and third interpretations: *she* gets its referent from the contextual assignment g, which is the same as that of *Suzie* (index 2) or some other antecedent NP (index 3). The 1-indexing, however, encodes a bound variable reading. The denotation for the question should be something along the lines of (4.32):

(4.32)   for which girl x is the following the case: x told Suzie that x has detention

This contrasts with the two other readings, which we might represent as in (4.33):

(4.33)   for which girl x is the following the case: x told Suzie that $\left\{ \begin{matrix} g(2) \\ g(3) \end{matrix} \right\}$ has detention
(where $g(2) =$ Suzie, and $g(3) =$ some contextually given female person)

To derive an interpretation along these lines, we fortunately don't have to go into the semantics of questions at all. All we need to concern ourselves with is the part after the colon in (4.32) and (4.33). Assume the following LF for (4.31) under the 1-indexing:

(4.34)   which girl $[_{VP*}\beta_1 [_{VP}$ told Suzie₂ that she₁ had detention $]]$

Here, Index Transfer has adjoined a binder index β_1 to the sister of *which girl*, VP (this is assuming that *which girl* has not been displaced, which we will for the sake of the exposition; I will return to the issue of *wh*-movement in chapter 8). By the BIER, the interpretation of VP* will be (4.35):

(4.35) $[\![[_{VP*}\beta_1 [_{VP}$ told Suzie₂ that she₁ had detention $]]\!]^g$
$= \lambda x.[\![[_{VP}$ told Suzie₂ that she₁ had detention $]]\!]^{g[1 \to x]}(x)$
$= \lambda x.x$ told Suzie that $g[1 \to x](1)$ had detention
$= \lambda x.x$ told Suzie that x had detention

This is precisely the meaning we assumed in (4.32). We see thus that while *wh*-expressions must have a denotation very different from QNPs (roughly something to get us from [4.35] to [4.32]), their behavior with regard to the Binding Theory is parallel: they do not corefer, but can act as semantic binders. The derivation of readings where they do behaves parallel to that of examples with QNPs in all relevant respects.

We can close by noting that this parallelism extends to the structural prerequisites for semantic binding. For example, neither sentence in (4.36) can get a reading in which *which girl* can have anaphoric relations with the pronoun:

(4.36) (a) *She*₁ wondered *which girl*₁ had detention.

(b) *Her*₁ mother wondered *which girl*₁ had detention.

These examples display violations of the BAC and, in the case of (4.36a), Binding Condition C. Independent of that, and in full parallelism to the case of QNP-binding discussed in 4.2, they also fail to get an interpretation on which the *wh*-phrase and the pronoun are anaphorically related (in fact, it is unclear what such a reading would be). This again falls out from our semantics, given that the *wh*-expressions fail to c-command the pronouns, which would be a prerequisite to interpret the coindexing as semantic binding.

4.4   Summary

This concludes our main discussion of coreference vs. variable binding. Let me summarize the main points:

- Coindexing between two NPs can be interpreted in two essentially different ways: as coreference (both NPs denote the same individual); or as semantic binding (the bound NP covaries with its binder).
- Quantified NPs and *wh*-expressions do not refer, hence *a fortiori* do not corefer. The only available interpretation of coindexation with such an expression is thus semantic binding.
- Semantic binding is restricted to configurations in which the binder (the QNP) c-commands the bound pronoun. In a slogan, semantic binding requires syntactic binding. Coindexing without c-command can only be interpreted as coreference (if no QNPs are involved) or not at all (if QNPs are involved).
- This restriction can very plausibly be attributed to the way the interpretation of binding dependencies works. In other words, the c-command restriction on coindexing with a QNP doesn't have to be stipulated, since it follows from the interpretive semantics that any other coindexing simply doesn't result in a bound variable interpretation of the pronoun at all.

We distinguished different syntactic and semantic relations between NPs: coindexing and coreference are symmetric relations; if NP₁ is coindexed and/or coreferent with NP₂, then NP₂ is coindexed/coreferent with NP₁. Syntactic and semantic binding are asymmetric notions: among two NPs in a binding relation, one is the binder, the other one the bindee. As things stand, the two pairs are not in a one-to-one correspondence: coindexing encompasses all types of anaphoric dependencies (not just coreference), and syntactic binding may or may not coincide with semantic binding (though semantic binding always presupposes syntactic binding, as discussed). This situation is schematically summarized in table 4.1.

Table 4.1 *Syntactic and semantic relations between NPs*

SYNTAX		
coindexing		non-coindexing
syntactic binding (one NP c-commands the other)	no syntactic binding (no c-command)	
semantic binding (binder is a QNP)	coreference (no QNP involved) SEMANTICS	non-coreference

4.5   Semantic details$^{\text{©}}$

4.5.1   Assignment modification

The BIER in (4.12) above makes crucial use of assignment modification, using the notation $g[n \rightarrow x]$, which is defined as follows:

(4.37)   Assignment modification:
For any assignment g, $g[n \rightarrow a]$ is that assignment which is like g, except that $g(n) = a$.

Modifying an assignment is thus to exchange one individual in the sequence for another. To illustrate, let's take our assignment g_1 from chapter 2.

(4.38) $g_1 =$

1	2	3	4	5	6	7	...
↓	↓	↓	↓	↓	↓	↓	
Bo	Kim	Sven	Ana	Kurt	Eszter	Tanya	

We can now modify g_1 to, say, $g_1[4 \rightarrow Marge]$:[6]

(4.39) $g_1[4 \rightarrow Marge] =$

1	2	3	4	5	6	7	...
↓	↓	↓	↓	↓	↓	↓	
Bo	Kim	Sven	**Marge**	Kurt	Eszter	Tanya	

Modification can be done iteratively ...

(4.40)   (a) $g_1[4 \rightarrow Marge][1 \rightarrow Ana] =$

1	2	3	4	5	6	7	...
↓	↓	↓	↓	↓	↓	↓	
Ana	Kim	Sven	**Marge**	Kurt	Eszter	Tanya	

---

[6] We could also 'modify' g_1 to $g_1[4 \rightarrow Ana]$, i.e. assignment modification can be vacuous.

(b) $g_1[4 \to Marge][1 \to Ana][5 \to Carl] =$

1	2	3	4	5	6	7	...
↓	↓	↓	↓	↓	↓	↓	
Ana	Kim	Sven	**Marge**	**Carl**	Eszter	Tanya	

... and even to the same argument slot:

(4.41)   (a) $g_1[4 \to Marge][5 \to Carl][4 \to Sylvie] =$

1	2	3	4	5	6	7	...
↓	↓	↓	↓	↓	↓	↓	
Bo	Kim	Sven	**Sylvie**	**Carl**	Eszter	Tanya	

(b) $g_1[4 \to Marge][5 \to Carl][4 \to Ana] =$

1	2	3	4	5	6	7	...
↓	↓	↓	↓	↓	↓	↓	
Bo	Kim	Sven	**Ana**	**Carl**	Eszter	Tanya	

Note that in (4.41a), the change brought about by $[4 \to Marge]$ is 'overwritten' by the later modification $[4 \to Sylvie]$. In (4.41b) the later modification $[4 \to Ana]$ even changes the value of $g(4)$ back to the original value, 'cancelling' the first modification $[4 \to Marge]$. Modifications are thus carried out left-to-right.

Obviously, if an XP contains a free pronoun, changing the assignment can change the denotation of the XP as a whole:

(4.42)   (a) $[\![\text{like him}_4]\!]^g =$ the set of all those who like g(4), for any g

(b) $[\![\text{like him}_4]\!]^{g[4 \to Abraham]} =$ the set of all those who like $g[4 \to Abraham](4)$, for any g

= the set of all those who like Abraham, for any g

= the set of all those who like Abraham, regardless of g

Accordingly, if an XP denotes a proposition, changing the assignment can change the proposition denoted by XP:

(4.43)   (a) $[\![\text{she}_2 \text{ is asleep}]\!]^g = 1$ iff $g(2)$ is asleep.

(b) $[\![\text{she}_2 \text{ is asleep}]\!]^{g[2 \to Clara]} = 1$ iff Clara is asleep.

(c) $[\![\text{she}_2 \text{ is asleep}]\!]^{g[2 \to Betsy]} = 1$ iff Betsy is asleep.

(d) $[\![\text{she}_2 \text{ is asleep}]\!]^{g[2 \to x]} = 1$ iff x is asleep.

In (4.43d), the second slot in the assignment is replaced by a variable x. Since our meta-language – English – doesn't contain free variables, this expression doesn't describe any denotation. We can, however, use this technique to form a predicate out of an expression by 're-opening' an argument slot. Thus (4.44a) denotes the set of all individuals who, if replaced for slot 2 in the assignment g, would make the sentence *she$_2$ is asleep* true. That, of course, is the set of all (female) sleepers (or rather: the characteristic function thereof):

(4.44)   (a) $\lambda x.[\![\text{she}_2 \text{ is asleep}]\!]^{g[2 \to x]} \approx$ the set of those who are asleep

(b) $[\lambda x.[\![\text{she}_2 \text{ is asleep}]\!]^{g[2 \to x]}](\text{Betsy})$

Accordingly, (4.44b) expresses the same proposition as (4.43c).

Exercise 4.6

Which sets of people do the following functions characterize?

(4.45)   (a) $[\text{like her}_9]^g$

        (b) $[\text{like her}_9]^{g[9\to Arabella]}$

        (c) $[\text{like her}_9]^{g[4\to Arabella]}$

        (d) $[\text{like her}_4]^{g[4\to Arabella]}$

        (e) $[\text{introduce her}_4 \text{ to him}_9]^g$

        (f) $[\text{introduce her}_4 \text{ to him}_9]^{g[9\to Kim]}$

        (g) $[\text{introduce her}_4 \text{ to him}_9]^{g[4\to Kim]}$

        (h) $[\text{introduce her}_4 \text{ to him}_9]^{g[4\to Kim][9\to Sandy]}$

        (i) $[\text{introduce her}_4 \text{ to him}_9]^{g[4\to Sandy][9\to Kim]}$

        (j) $[\text{introduce her}_4 \text{ to him}_9]^{g[9\to Kim][4\to Sandy]}$

        (k) $\lambda x[[\text{introduce her}_4 \text{ to him}_9]^{g[9\to Kim][4\to Sandy]}](x)$

        (l) $\lambda x[[\text{introduce her}_4 \text{ to him}_9]^{g[9\to x][4\to Sandy]}](x)$

        (m) $\lambda x[[\text{introduce her}_4 \text{ to him}_9]^{g[9\to Kim][4\to x]}](x)$

        (n) $\lambda x[[\text{introduce her}_4 \text{ to him}_9]^{g[9\to Kim][4\to x]}](Sandy)$

        (o) $\lambda x[[\text{introduce her}_4 \text{ to him}_9]^{g[9\to x][4\to x]}](Sandy)$

4.5.2   The semantics of quantified NPs

Above we never concerned ourselves with what QNPs actually denote. Rather, we concentrated on logical paraphrases of entire sentences containing QNPs such as in (4.46a):

(4.46)   Every manager is happy.

        (a) $[\text{Every manager is happy}]^g = 1$ iff for every x, if $[\text{manager}]^g(x) = 1$, then $[\text{happy}]^g(x) = 1$

        (b) $\{x \mid x \text{ is a manager}\}$ is a subset of $\{x \mid x \text{ is happy}\}$

(4.46a) is equivalent to (4.46b) (recall that $\{x \mid x \text{ a manager}\}$ and $\{x \mid x \text{ is happy}\}$ are the sets characterized by $[\text{manager}]^g$ and $[\text{happy}]^g$, respectively). Similar renderings can be given for the other examples discussed in 4.1:

(4.47)   One manager is happy.

        there is some x such that $[\text{manager}]^g(x)=1$ and $[\text{happy}]^g(x) = 1$

        $\{x \mid x \text{ is a manager}\}$ and $\{x \mid x \text{ is happy}\}$ have a common element

(4.48)   No manager is happy.

        there is no x such that $[\text{manager}]^g(x)=1$ and $[\text{happy}]^g(x) = 1$

        $\{x \mid x \text{ is a manager}\}$ and $\{x \mid x \text{ is happy}\}$ do not have a common element

We will not go into the meaning of quantificational determiners like *every* or *no* in isolation here (see e.g. Heim and Kratzer [1998]:ch. 6:4); we will, however, give meanings for selected QNPs such as *every manager* in (4.49):

(4.49) $[\text{every manager}]^g = \lambda P \in D_{et}$.for all x, if $[\text{manager}]^g(x) = 1$, then $P(x) = 1$

        (the set of all properties P which maps every manager to 1; i.e. the set of all properties that characterize a superset of the manager-set)

(4.50)   Every manager is happy.

    (a) $[\![$every manager is happy$]\!]^g$ $=$ 1 iff $[\lambda P \in D_{et}.$for all $x,$ if $[\![$manager$]\!]^g(x) = 1,$ then $P(x) = 1]([\![$is happy$]\!]^g)$

    (b) $= 1$ iff for all $x,$ if $[\![$manager$]\!]^g(x) = 1,$ then $[\![$is happy$]\!]^g(x) = 1$

    (c) $= 1$ iff for all $x,$ if $[\![$manager$]\!]^g(x) = 1,$ then $[\lambda x.x$ is happy$](x) = 1$

    (d) $= 1$ iff the set of managers is a subset of the set of happy creatures

The sample calculation in (4.50) shows how such a meaning combines with a VP meaning. Three things are particularly important to note: first, the semantic argument of the QNP meaning, corresponding to the variable P in (4.49), is not an individual, but a property; it is of type $\langle e,t \rangle$. This is explicitly written in (4.49), but henceforth we will just stick to the convention introduced in table 2.1 of chapter 2 and use variables $P, P_1, P_2 \ldots$

Second, the denotation of an NP headed by a quantificational determiner like *every* in (4.49) is not an individual, but something more complicated: a function from properties (which themselves are functions from individuals to truth values) to truth values (which corresponds, in set talk, to a set of sets of individuals); this kind of semantic object is called a *generalized quantifier*, following Barwise and Cooper (1981). It denotes a property of properties (e.g. that the property of being a happy creature has the property of mapping every element of the manager-set to 1), and crucially not an individual, even broadly construed as including pluralities of individuals. This is why it was said earlier that QNPs do not refer, given that reference is the subcase of denotation in which the denotation is an individual.

Third, the Function Application rule applies the NP denotation to the VP denotation in (4.50a), not the other way around, i.e. $[\![$NP VP$]\!]^g = [\![$NP$]\!]^g([\![$VP$]\!]^g)$ instead of $[\![$VP$]\!]^g([\![$NP$]\!]^g)$, as we used to do. This is a direct consequence of the fact that NP denotes a generalized quantifier, as just discussed. The reader may verify that the choice of functor and argument for Function Application follows from the types of the NP and VP denotations, according to the type-driven interpretation rule given in chapter 2, section 2.3.3.

Readers with further interest in the compositional interpretation of QNPs are invited to consult a textbook on formal semantics such as Heim and Kratzer (1998):ch. 6, at this point.

Exercise 4.7

Define analogous meanings for *one of the managers* and *none of the managers*.

4.5.3   Object QNPs

The discussion in the main text concerned only QNPs in subject position. The reason for that is not specific to Binding Theory, but pertains to the general question of how to interpret QNPs in object positions. Consider, for example, (4.51):

(4.51)

$\llbracket$met$\rrbracket^g$ is a function in $D_{e,et}$, it corresponds to a relation. *Jenny* denotes an individual, so she is in the domain of $\llbracket$met$\rrbracket^g$, so that $\llbracket$met$\rrbracket^g(\llbracket$Jenny$\rrbracket^g)$ yields a well-formed interpretation by our rule of Function Application (FA) from chapter 2. *Every gymnast* denotes a generalized quantifier (type $\langle$et,t$\rangle$). The problem is that neither $\llbracket$met$\rrbracket^g(\llbracket$every gymnast$\rrbracket^g)$ nor $\llbracket$every gymnast$\rrbracket^g(\llbracket$met$\rrbracket^g)$ are defined; since neither function is in the domain of the other, Function Application is simply not defined for types $\langle$e,et$\rangle$ and $\langle$et,t$\rangle$.

One way of remedying this is by a syntactic transformation, *quantifier raising*, which we will briefly discuss in chapter 8 (see e.g. Heim and Kratzer [1998]:ch. 7.3). In our official grammar, we will use a semantic combinator instead. The idea is this: a standard generalized quantifier q can combine by FA with a property P to yield $q(P)$. Now, if we want to combine q with a relation R, we want the result to be $\lambda x.Q([\lambda y.R(y)(x)])$. In other words, q 'targets' the innermost argument slot of R, y, while the higher one, x, is 'transferred to the outside.' If q combines with a three-place relation R^3, the *two* outermost arguments are 'transferred,' as in $\lambda x \lambda y.Q([\lambda z.R^3(z)(x)(y)])$, and so forth.

To implement this idea, we first define a two-place composition function C (for *combine*), which can interpret QNPs and verbal meanings (among others) of any arity:

(4.52) $C(\phi, q)$ is defined if q is of type $\langle$et,$\tau\rangle$ (with τ being any type) and ϕ is a predicate denotation (see below). If defined, $C(\phi, q) =$
    (a) $q(\phi)$ if $\phi \in D_{et}$,
    (b) $\lambda\psi[C(\lambda y[\phi(y)(\psi)], q)]$ otherwise

(4.53)   (a)   Predicate denotation:
        If τ is a conjoinable type, $\langle$e,$\tau\rangle$ is a predicate type. For any predicate type τ_p, all elements in D_{τ_p} are *predicate denotations*.
    (b)   Conjoinable type:
        (i) $\langle$t$\rangle$ is a conjoinable type
        (ii)   if τ_1 is a conjoinable type, then for any type τ_2, $\langle\tau_2, \tau_1\rangle$ is a conjoinable type

A predicate denotation, sloppily speaking, is a denotation of any type that starts with e and ends in t, i.e. the type of an expression that 'wants' an individual argument. C as defined in (4.52) above can combine a generalized quantifier (where $\tau = \langle$t$\rangle$) with any predicate denotation, i.e. with any denotation that wants an individual argument. In other words, C can combine a generalized quantifier with whatever an individual could be combined with by plain Function Application.

As a last step, we define a syntactic operator κ (again reminiscent of 'combinator'):

(4.54) $\left[\!\!\left[\begin{smallmatrix} & \text{NP*} \\ \kappa & \text{NP} \end{smallmatrix} \right]\!\!\right]^g$ is that function which maps any ϕ onto $\mathcal{C}(\phi, [\![\text{NP}]\!]^g)$

Since $\mathcal{C}$ can only combine generalized quantifiers with predicate meanings, it follows that NP must be a quantified NP (or in any case, denote a generalized quantifier), and that $[\kappa\ NP]$ can only combine with expressions that denote predicate denotations.

The workings of κ and $\mathcal{C}$ are demonstrated below, where EC abbreviates $[\![\text{every cake}]\!]^g$ (in $D_{et,t}$) and ATE abbreviates $[\![\text{ate}]\!]^g$ (in $D_{e,et}$):

(4.55) Muni ate every cake.

(a) 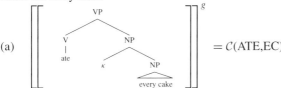 $= \mathcal{C}(\text{ATE,EC})$

(b) $\mathcal{C}(\text{ATE,EC}) = \lambda x[\mathcal{C}(\lambda y[\ \text{ATE}(y)(x)]],\ \text{EC})]$ (by [4.52b])

   (i) $\mathcal{C}(\lambda y[\ \text{ATE}(y)(x)],\ \text{EC}) = \text{EC}(\lambda y[\text{ATE}(y)(x)])$ (by [4.52a])

(c) $\mathcal{C}(\text{EC,ATE}) = \lambda x[\text{EC}(\lambda y[\text{ATE}(y)(x)])]$ (from [4.55b], [4.55b-i])

(d) $[\![\text{Muni ate every cake}]\!]^g = \lambda x[\ \text{EC}(\lambda y[\text{ATE}(y)(x)])])(\text{Muni})$

   $= 1$ iff $\text{EC}(\lambda y\ [\text{ATE}(y)(Muni)])$

As the reader is invited to verify for her/himself, these rules work fully generally, i.e. generalized quantifiers can combine with ditransitive verbs, verbs that take an additional sentential object, and so forth.

Exercise 4.8

Calculate the meaning for *no student solved every problem* in the way shown in (4.55).

Exercise 4.9

Assume that $[\![\text{her}_n\ \text{desk}]\!]^g =$ the desk of $g(n)$ (type $\langle e \rangle$). Give a complete LF based on the following unindexed tree for a reading on which *every girl* binds *her*. Make sure to include all necessary indices, prefixes, etc. Then interpret that LF (I chose a verb-final structure here to abstract away from complications with the English double object construction; think of this structure as German with English words):

(4.56)

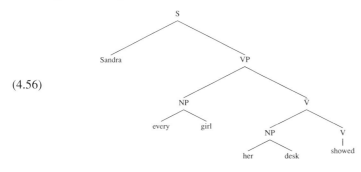

4.5.4   Semantic binding in flat structures

In section 2.3 of chapter 2 we introduced a rule to interpret n-ary branching structures as found, by assumption, in English VPs, Russian $\bar{\text{N}}$'s, and any sort of 'flat' structure. This rule is repeated in (4.57):

(4.57) N-ary Function Application:

$$\left[\!\!\left[\begin{array}{c} X^n \\ X^0 \quad \text{A} \quad \text{A}' \quad \text{A}''... \end{array} \right]\!\!\right]^g =$$

$[\![X^0]\!]^g([\![A_n]\!]^g)([\![A_{n-1}]\!]^g)\ldots([\![A_1]\!]^g)$

where $A_1, A_2, \ldots, A_{n-1}, A_n$ is the order of A, A$'$, A$''$...on X^0's argument-list

This rule only works if all arguments A, A$'$...denote individuals. As a first step, then, we change this rule so as to apply $[\![NP]\!]^g$ to $[\![X^0]\!]^g$ instead, in case $[\![NP]\!]^g$ is a generalized quantifier; to facilitate readability, we define an operation '+':

(4.58)   P+A $=_{\text{def}}$ P(A) if defined, $\mathcal{C}(P, A)$ otherwise (cf. [4.52])

Like Function Application, we understand + to be left-associative, i.e. $P + A + A' = (P + A) + A'$. The + operation has the combinator $\mathcal{C}$ built into it. It will deliver a well-formed denotation for a generalized quantifier or an individual combined with any predicate denotation. Thus κ prefixing is superfluous when using our new n-ary FA rule:

(4.59) N-ary Function Application with generalized quantifiers:

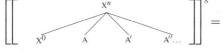

$[\![X^0]\!]^g + [\![A_n]\!]^g + [\![A_{n-1}]\!]^g + \ldots + [\![A_1]\!]^g$

where $A_1, A_2, \ldots, A_{n-1}, A_n$ is the order of A, A$'$, A$''$...on X^0's argument-list

(4.59) still does not allow for binding. In fact, the Index Transfer rule (4.11) is undefined for NPs in an n-ary branching structure, given that it wants to adjoin β to *the* sister of the QNP bearing a binder index.

The correct generalization about semantic binding in flat structures is, not surprisingly, that it is possible wherever syntactic binding is. That is, an NP can bind (into) another XP if and only if NP commands XP. Descriptively speaking, NP can semantically bind (into) XP iff NP can, under the right circumstances, bind a reflexive (in) XP or block a non-reflexive (in) XP:

(4.60)   (a)   I showed every boy$_3$ $\left\{ \begin{array}{l} \text{himself}_3 \text{ (in the mirror)} \\ \text{his}_3 \text{ desk} \end{array} \right\}$.

(b)   *I showed $\left\{ \begin{array}{l} \text{himself}_3 \\ \text{his}_3 \text{ friend} \end{array} \right\}$ every boy$_3$ (in the mirror).

(4.61)   (a) I showed every girl$_8$ to $\left\{ \begin{array}{l} \text{herself}_8 \\ \text{her}_8 \text{ sister} \end{array} \right\}$.

(b) *I showed $\left\{ \begin{array}{l} \text{herself}_8 \\ \text{her}_8 \text{ sister} \end{array} \right\}$ to every girl$_8$.

To get this to follow from the semantic interpretation requires a little work. The reason is that (4.59) above gets the meanings of the argument NPs A, A', ... *relative to the assignment g* as its input. But if NP$_1$ were to bind NP$_2$, it would have to change the assignment for NP$_2$. In order for that to work composition-ally, we must input the composition rule not with $[\![NP_2]\!]^g$, but with $\lambda g.[\![NP_2]\!]^g$, a function from assignments to ordinary NP-denotations. We then define a *se-mantic* binding operator $\mathcal{B}$, the counterpart to the syntactic binder prefix β:

(4.62)   let ϕ be a function from assignments to elements in $D_{e,\tau}$ (where τ can be any type), then $\mathcal{B}_n(\phi) = \lambda g \lambda x . \phi(g[n \rightarrow x])(x)$

There is nothing essentially new in this definition. Our BIER from above, for example, is equivalent to the following:

(4.63)   Binder Index Evaluation rule, notational variant:
$[\![\beta_n \text{ Y}]\!]^g = \mathcal{B}_n(\lambda g.[\![\text{Y}]\!]^g)$

We now assume that the binder prefix β is inserted on the a(rgument)-list of the head of an *n*-ary branching structure. The a-list of *introduce* in *introduce every soprano$_2$ to her$_2$ partner*, for example, looks like (4.64); no β is adjoined in the syntactic tree:

(4.64) $\langle NP_{nom}, NP_{acc}, \beta_2, [_{PP} \text{ to NP}] \rangle$

We then replace (4.57) with the following rule:

(4.65)   *n*-ary Function Application with Binding:
Let X^0's argument-list be $\langle A_0, \ldots, A_i, \beta_n, A_j, \ldots, A_m \rangle$,[7] then

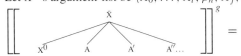

$(\mathcal{B}_n([\![X^0]\!] + [\![A_m]\!] + \ldots + [\![A_J]\!]) + [\![A_I]\!] + \ldots + [\![A_1]\!])(g),$

where $P + A =_{\text{def}} \lambda g . P(g)(A(g))$ if defined, $\lambda g.\mathcal{C}(P(g), A(g))$ otherwise (to replace [4.58] above)

Exercise 4.10
Convince yourself of the equivalence between (4.63) and the origi-nal (4.12) by calculating through a simple example such as *every girl painted her desk*.

Exercise 4.11
Give a complete calculation for (4.60a) and (4.61a).

---

[7] Where $0 < m, 0 < i < m - 1$ and $j = i + 1$.

5   Other cases of semantic binding

In the last chapter we distinguished between NPs that act as semantic binders (quantified NPs, *wh*-words), and those that don't (names, pronouns, definite NPs). Depending on whether or not a syntactic binder is a semantic binder as well, different rules apply:

(5.1)   She$_7$ knows her$_7$ rights.   (no LF rules apply)
    (a) $[\![(5.1)]\!]^g = 1$ iff $[\![$knows her$_7$ rights$]\!]^g(g(7)) = 1$
    (b) $= 1$ iff $g(7)$ is in $\{y \mid y$ knows $g(7)$'s rights$\}$

(5.2)   Every woman$_3$ knows her$_3$ rights.   (invokes Index Transfer)
    (a)   LF: every woman [β_3 [knows her$_3$ rights]]
    (b) $[\![(5.2a)]\!]^g = 1$ iff for every z, z a woman, $[\lambda x.[\![$knows her$_3$ rights $]\!]^{g[3 \to x]}(x)](z) = 1$
    (c) $= 1$ iff for every z, z a woman, z is in $\{x \mid x$ knows x's rights$\}$

(5.1) is a case of mere *coreference*: two NPs happen to be assigned the same referent; (5.2) features true *semantic binding*. However, note that we would get an equivalent meaning for (5.1) if we treated *she* as a semantic binder, i.e. if we allow Index Transfer to apply to the NP *she$_7$*, while retaining the index on it:

(5.3)   (a)   LF: she$_7$ [β_7[knows her$_7$ rights]]
    (b) $[\![(5.3a)]\!]^g = 1$ iff $g(7)$ is in $\{x \mid x$ knows x's rights$\}$

(5.1b) and (5.3b) are truth conditionally equivalent. Their LFs, however, are crucially different. Below I have connected those NPs that get their meaning from the contextual assignment g by arrows to their referent:

(5.4)   LF(5.1):   she$_7$ knows   her$_7$ rights (coreference)
              ↓   ↓
              Ana   Ana

(5.5)   LF(5.3):   she$_7$ $\lambda x.x$ knows x's rights (binding)
              ↓
              Ana

The case of coreference is like two positions that are contingently (or accidentally, if you like) occupied by the same person: in 1559–60 Scotland and France had the same queen as the consequence of a series of marriages and heritages.

But there is no intrinsic relation between the two regencies. This resembles coreference. On the other hand, England and Canada have the same queen, generally. Whoever is the queen of England is automatically the Canadian queen. This is like binding.

Exercise 5.1

What was the name of the aforementioned Scottish/French queen?

The reason we can't tell from the truth conditions whether the relation between *she* and *her* in (5.1) is a case of binding or a case of coreference is that the reference of *she* doesn't vary, so we cannot see whether the reference of *her* would covary with it (as expected if true binding is involved), or not (as with coreference). In contrast, *her* in (5.2) is obviously bound by *every woman*, for its reference covaries with the quantifier. If it didn't, *her* would be a free pronoun, i.e. refer to a particular woman determined by the contextual assignment.

We might thus ask ourselves whether the option to treat pronoun–pronoun relationships, and referential NP–pronoun relationships in general, as semantic binding *or* coreference is: (i) a harmless, consequence-less ambiguity (which we might or might not want to eliminate to avoid spurious ambiguities); or (ii) a real option with yet-to-be-found linguistic consequences (which, if correctly predicted, would force us to have both in the theory). As we will see, (ii) is the correct choice.

But how can we tell? The answer is: we need to make non-quantificational NPs which are suspected binders 'switch' their reference, similar to the way that quantifiers do. What we'll find then is aptly summarized in the following quote from Reinhart (1983a):150:

> In fact, all [syntactically bound; DB] pronouns can be interpreted as bound variables, regardless of whether the antecedent is a quantified NP or not . . .

How do we get referential NPs to betray semantic binder status? In the next section we will look at a first case, focus constructions. Then, after refining our theory in various respects in section 5.4, we will present a second case, strict and sloppy identity in VP ellipsis, in section 5.5.

5.2   Focus constructions

Example (5.6) has two prominent readings which are paraphrased in (5.6a) and (5.6b) below (additionally there is a less-prominent reading [5.6c]); capitals indicate a prominent pitch accent, which we assume indicates *focus*:

(5.6)   I only said that TATJANA should stay in her room.
          (a)   I didn't say anyone other than Tatjana should stay in Tatjana's
                room.   (*her* coreferent with *Tatjana*)

(b) I didn't prohibit anyone other than Tatjana to leave his/her
room.   (*her* bound by *Tatjana*)

(c) I didn't say anyone other than Tatjana should stay in Marijana's
room.   (*her* refers to someone totally different)

As indicated below the examples, the two prominent readings will be traced back
to different interpretation strategies, namely coreference versus semantic binding. For this analysis to go through, we have to assume that referential NPs like
Tatjana can be semantic binders, which is what we set out to do.

To understand these cases, we need to introduce some new assumptions regarding focus and the adverbial *only*. The following are simplified adaptations
of the proposal in Rooth (1985):

(5.7)   (a) $[\![\text{only VP}]\!]^g = \lambda x.[\![\text{VP}]\!]^g(x) = 1$ and x has no other property $P \in$ P-
SET(VP)

(b) P-SET(VP) = the set of all properties $P = [\![\text{VP}']\!]^g$, where VP' is the
result of replacing the focused constituent in VP by some alternative

The notion of a *P-set* is crucial to this analysis. The P-set of a constituent α is
a second 'layer' of meaning, if you will, which is associated with α in addition
to α's ordinary meaning. The meanings in a P-set will always be of the same
general type as the ordinary meaning, i.e. the P-set of a VP will be a set of
properties, the P-set of a transitive verb will be a set of relations, and the P-set of
a name will be a set of individuals. As indicated in (5.7b), the elements in the P-
set are restricted to certain *alternatives* to the ordinary meaning: P-set elements
may differ from the ordinary meaning only in those parts that are focused in the
constituent in question. Rooth (1985) provides a compositional way of deriving
these P-sets, which we do not need to concern ourselves with here. Instead, let's
acquaint ourselves with the idea by way of a dry run (i.e. an example that doesn't
involve bound pronouns):

(5.8)   (a) Pjotr only likes TATJANA.

(b) $[\![\text{likes TATJANA}]\!]^g = \lambda x.x$ likes Tatjana ($\approx$ the set of Tatjana-likers)

(c) P-SET(*likes TATJANA*) = {$[\![\text{like Marijana}]\!]^g$, $[\![\text{like Claudia}]\!]^g$, $[\![\text{like}$
Steven$]\!]^g$, $[\![\text{like Tatjana}]\!]^g \dots$}

The P-set of *likes TATJANA* contains all properties that can be described as an
instantiation of the schema *likes x*, or, more formally, are in the following set:
$\{[\lambda x.x \text{ likes } y] \mid y$ is an individual$\}$. According to (5.7b), *only* (and other adverbs
of its kin, such as *even* and *also*) take both the ordinary meaning and the P-set of
their VP complements as semantic arguments, and deliver another VP meaning:

(5.9) $[\![\text{only likes TATJANA}]\!]^g = \lambda y.y$ likes Tatjana, and y has no other properties
$P \in$ P-SET(*like TATJANA*)
$\approx$ the set of all people who like Tatjana and don't like anyone else

That Pjotr is in the set of Tatjana-likers, and in no other set of X-likers, is a
roundabout way of saying that his feelings are exclusively for Tatjana, which is
an intuitively satisfying paraphrase.

Given this much we can return to the original example (5.6). Consider first an LF in which the indices on *Tatjana* and *her* are both interpreted as referential indices:

(5.10) LF_1: I only said that $TATJANA_8$ should stay in her_8 room.

      (a) $[\![TATJANA_8 \text{ should stay in } her_8 \text{ room}]\!]^g = 1$ iff ($g(8)$ is Tatjana and) Tatjana is in $\{y \mid y \text{ should stay in } g(8)\text{'s room}\}$

      (b)   P-SET(*TATJANA_8 should stay in her_8 room*): {Claudia is in $\{y \mid y$ should stay in $g(8)$'s room$\}$, Marijana is in $\{y \mid y$ should stay in $g(8)$'s room$\}$, Steven is in $\{y \mid y$ should stay in $g(8)$'s room$\}$, Tatjana is in $\{y \mid y$ should stay in $g(8)$'s room$\}$, ...$\}$[1]

Note that in all the alternatives in the P-Set in (5.10b) the room is the room of $g(8)$, which is Tatjana. No meaning like 'Claudia should stay in Julia's room' could be in that set, given that *her* is not focused. When we combine the embedded clause with *said* and then *only*, we get the property of saying that Tatjana should be confined to her room and not saying that anyone else should stay in Tatjana's room. It is true if I also said 'Marijana, stay in your room,' but false if I also said 'Mirko, stay in Tatjana's room.'

Consider now the alternative LF in (5.11), in which we let the name *Tatjana* semantically bind the pronoun *her*. The ordinary meaning of the embedded clause is (5.11a):

(5.11) LF_2: I only said that $TATJANA_8[\beta_8 [\text{ should stay in } her_8 \text{ room}]]$

      (a) $[\![TATJANA_8 \; \beta_8[\text{ should stay in } her_8 \text{ room}]]\!]^g = 1$ iff ($g(8)$ is Tatjana and) Tatjana is in $\{x \mid [\![\text{should stay in } her_8 \text{ room}]\!]^{g[8 \to x]}(x)\}$

            $= \ldots$ is in $\{x \mid x \text{ should stay in } g[8 \to x](8)\text{'s room}\}$

            $= \ldots$ is in $\{x \mid x \text{ should stay in } x\text{'s room}\}$

Crucially, since this ordinary meaning in (5.11a) has the pronoun bound by the local subject, the meaning of the embedded VP is $[\lambda x.x \text{ should stay in } x\text{'s room}]$, the characteristic function of $\{x \mid x \text{ should stay in } x\text{'s room}\}$. Given that the VP doesn't contain anything focused, the alternatives in the P-Set of VP and any constituent containing VP will be built around that property, i.e. the P-Set will look something like (5.12):

(5.12)   P-SET(*TATJANA_8 β_8 should stay in her_8 room*): { Claudia is in $\{x \mid x$ should stay in x's room$\}$, Marijana is in $\{x \mid x$ should stay in x's room$\}$, Steven is in $\{x \mid x$ should stay in x's room$\}$, Tatjana is in $\{x \mid x$ should stay in x's room$\}$, ...$\}$

The meaning of the matrix VP will now be the property of saying that Tatjana should stay in her room and not saying that anyone else should stay in *their* room. It is false if I also said 'Marijana, stay in your room,' but true even if I also said

---

[1] Note that the alternatives to $[\![TATJANA_8]\!]^g$ are individuals, not names (i.e. they are meanings, not words). Accordingly they don't bear indices and cannot enter into any systematic coreference patterns.

'Mirko, stay in Tatjana's room' – the exact mirror image of the situation with LF$_1$ in (5.10).

We see, thus, that the two readings of this sentence correspond to two different LFs, one of which has *Tatjana* semantically bind the pronoun *her*. For that to be possible, we have to allow the non-quantificational NP *Tatjana* to undergo Index Transfer, which is what we set out to show.

Exercise 5.2

Calculate ordinary meanings and P-SETs for VP, S1, and S2 in (5.13), once under the assumption that *Bill* and *his* are coreferent, once under the assumption that the former binds the latter. Then give the truth conditions for the whole sentence in each reading (you don't need to give an LF):

(5.13)   We only [$_{VP}$ know that [$_{S1}$ she told BILL where [$_{S2}$ his bicycle is parked]]].

Exercise 5.3

Above we assumed that Index Transfer needs to retain the index on the binder NP itself. This was argued for regarding example (5.1)/(5.3a), where Index Transfer applied to a pronoun. Show that a pronoun can indeed semantically bind another pronoun by constructing and discussing an example parallel to (5.6).

Exercise 5.4

Use (5.14) to make an argument that Index Transfer needs to retain the index *even on a full NP*:

(5.14)   She only said that TATJANA would stay in her room.

Exercise 5.5

Which of the following variants of (5.13) are ambiguous in the same way as (5.13); discuss why (not):

(5.15)   (a)   We only know that SHE told Bill where his bicycle is parked.
          (b)   We only know that SHE told BILL where his bicycle is parked.
          (c)   We only know that she told Bill where HIS bicycle is parked.
          (d)   We only know that SHE told Bill where her bicycle is parked.
          (e)   We only know that she told BILL where HER bicycle is parked.

Exercise 5.6

Consider the sentence *I only knew that GANDALF had lost his mind*. Give all possible LFs for this sentence and explain why these and only these are possible.

Exercise 5.7

Consider a case of *bare contrastive focus* such as (5.16):

(5.16)   I told KATHRIN to write down her name (not SABINA).
   (a)   Give paraphrases that indicate the three different readings of (5.16)
         analogous to the different readings of (5.6) above.
   (b)   Give the LFs for the non-parenthesized part on the different readings
         and classify them as coreferent/semantically bound, where applicable.
   (c)   Sketch a treatment to interpret the parenthesized part that interacts in
         the desired way with your LFs above.

5.3   Double indexing

We have established in section 5.2 that the Index Transfer rule, orig-
inally designed for use with QNPs, can apply to referring NPs, too. As noted
in passing, the latter case requires us to amend the rule so that it *copies* the index on NP onto the binder prefix (rather than literally transferring it); otherwise
the binder NP would wind up with no index whatsoever, which, in the case of a
referential NP (unlike a QNP), leaves us with no way to interpret it (this is true
in particular if the NP is a pronoun). In this section, we will formulate the final
version of this rule, which will function yet differently from that: it will freely
introduce an index on the binder prefix, retaining the index on the NP, if there is
one:

(5.17)   Binder rule (final version):

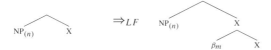

The major difference to a rule that *copies* the index onto the β-prefix and then
optionally deletes it on the NP is that (5.17) allows the index m on the binder
prefix to be different from the index n on the binder NP. Why would this be
useful? Consider example (5.18) below:

(5.18)   We only know that MARY parked her car in her garage.

Consider this example in the context of a question like 'Did Mary and Sue both
park their cars in Mary's garage?' In such a context, (5.18) as an answer would
entail that

(5.19)   (a)   we know that Mary parked Mary's car in Mary's garage, but
           (b)   we don't know that anyone else parked their car in Mary's garage (in
                 particular, we don't know if Sue parked Sue's car in Mary's garage)

And, intuitively, (5.18) can serve to express just that. Let us now ask ourselves
what an LF for (5.18) that expresses this reading would have to look like. A
straightforward guess would be (5.20):

(5.20)   we only know that MARY$_1$ [β_1 parked her$_1$ car in her$_1$ garage]

In (5.20), *Mary* semantically binds the pronouns, which appears to be correct, given that we are not interested in a purely referential reading, in which we don't know if anyone else parked Mary's car in Mary's garage (this reading, to be sure, is generally available, but it is pragmatically odd in this particular example). But despite that, (5.20) is not what we are after, because it says (5.21) instead of (5.19):

(5.21)　　(a)　we know that Mary parked Mary's car in Mary's garage, but
　　　　　(b)　we don't know that anyone else parked their car in their garage (in particular, we don't know if Sue parked Sue's car in Sue's garage)

Again, this reading is available for (5.18), but it is not the one we are after. It turns out that in order to get the interpretation in (5.19), we need to have one pronoun be referential, but the other one be semantically bound. (5.22) is an LF that expresses that reading:

(5.22)　　we only know that MARY$_1$ [β_2 parked her$_2$ car in her$_1$ garage]

Here the car, but not the garage, covaries with the focus alternatives to Mary, as desired. But this LF crucially assumes that the binder prefix next to *Mary* has an index different from the referential index on *Mary*. That is, (5.22) cannot be derived by copying the index in *Mary* onto the binder prefix; rather, we have to allow the binder prefix to introduce its own index.

In this particular example, *Mary* sem-binds the first *her*, but corefers with the second. But the same effect can be seen in the more complex variant of this example in (5.23) below:

(5.23)　　Almost every woman only admitted that SHE parked her car in her garage.

Suppose that we are trying to get confessions of the form: 'Sue parked her car in my garage, too.' (5.23) can be used to report the futility of that endeavor. In order for that reading to arise, the LF must be as in (5.24):

(5.24)　　almost every woman [β_1 only admitted that SHE$_1$ [β_2 parked her$_2$ car in her$_1$ garage]]

Here, both occurrences of *her* are bound; extending our terminology we will say that *she$_1$* and *her$_1$* are *co-bound* (by *almost every woman*), while *she$_1$*, mediated through the binder prefix β_2, *binds* the pronoun *her$_2$*, as in (5.22). Formal definitions of these notions and the reformulated Binding Conditions will be provided in section 5.4.

5.4   A new system

In this chapter we have established so far that any NP, quantificational or not, can serve as a semantic binder, as witnessed by the interpretive options in focusing constructions (a second construction that leads to the same conclusion will be discussed in section 5.5 below). This situation in some sense represents the zero-hypothesis. Index Transfer, or its successor, the Binder rule, is a syntactic operation available to any NP by the rules of our grammar. The opposite situation – that only QNPs can act as semantic binders – would have required us to make its applicability sensitive to the semantic type of the NP in question (referring vs. quantificational).[2] The way things are stated now, all NPs are treated as equal, although the effect of semantic binding with referential NPs can be detected only in special contexts like the ones involving focus explored in this chapter.

We formulated a new Binder rule, to replace our earlier Index Transfer rule, repeated here:

(5.25)   Binder rule (final version):

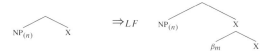

The BIER from chapter 4 remains the same. In chapter 4 we saw that the index on a QNP cannot be interpreted as a referential index, and we used the Index Transfer rule to strip it off such an NP. Since its successor, the Binder rule, doesn't remove indices any more, we need to amend our indexing conventions:

(5.26)   Indexing convention (preliminary):
          All and only non-quantificational NPs bear an index.[3]

Where a QNP acts as a semantic binder, the Binder rule will introduce the prerequisite index; in all other cases, QNPs are indexless. As for the Binding Conditions, we will need a couple of reformulations. Note first that LFs derived using (5.25) do not correspond to any 'normal' surface indexings, the obvious reason being that the (indices on) binder prefixes no longer correspond to indices on NPs. Heim (1993) approaches this problem by assuming that NPs can bear two indices at s-structure: an *inner index*, corresponding to our referential indices, i.e. those found on NPs at LF; and *outer indices*, corresponding to our binder indices, i.e. those found on binder prefixes at LF. She then goes on to formulate the pertinent Binding Conditions on s-structures thus enriched. We will follow the opposite strategy here and formulate our binding conditions so as to apply at LF ([5.28] repeated from chapter 4):

---

[2] A similar issue is discussed in the transformationalist literature regarding the question whether only quantificational NPs can undergo Quantifier Raising. Since there, Quantifier Raising is considered a prerequisite for semantic binding, our conclusion about semantic binding carries over to this question, *contra* e.g. May (1985).

[3] Since no rules delete or add indices on NPs, nothing needs to be said about where in the derivation (5.26) applies.

(5.27)   Syntactic binding (final):
          NP syn(tactically)-binds NP′ if and only if (iff)
          (a)   NP and NP′ are coindexed
          (b)   NP c/o/...-commands NP′
          If an NP′ is not syntactically bound by any NP in a phrase marker P, we say
          that NP′ is *syntactically free* in P.

(5.28)   Semantic binding (final):
          A binder prefix β *sem(antically)-binds* an NP iff
          (a) β and NP are coindexed
          (b) β c-commands NP x
          (c)   there is no binder prefix β' which is c-commanded by β and meets (a)
                 and (b)
          If an NP is not bound by any binder prefix β in a phrase marker P, we say
          that NP is *semantically free* in P.

Binding Conditions A and C for English then say:

(5.29)   Binding Conditions
          (A)   A reflexive pronoun must be semantically or syntactically bound in its
                 domain.
          (C)   A full NP must be semantically and syntactically free in the root
                 domain.

The (implicit) disjunctions[4] in (5.29) are the price we pay for our new Binder
rule, given that semantic binding no longer presupposes syntactic binding (in
those cases where the binder is a QNP). We will address the issue of unifying
these definitions in chapter 6. For the moment, we will leave it at this, and turn
to Binding Condition B.

   By our new Binder rule, we get LFs in which a pronoun is (locally) semantically bound without being syntactically bound, (5.30a), and vice versa, (5.30b);
furthermore it can end up being anaphorically related to a local NP without being
locally sem- *or* syn-bound, as in (5.30c); all of these express intuitively unavailable readings and need to be blocked:

(5.30)   (a)   *Jeanne$_1$ β_2 saw her$_2$.
          (b)   *Jeanne$_1$ saw her$_1$.
          (c)   *Jeanne$_1$ β_2 thought that she$_2$ saw her$_1$.

To predict all these stars by Binding Condition B, we need a notion that encompasses all these possibilities, a notion we will call *codetermination*:[5]

---

[4] Note that 'semantically and syntactically free' is the same as 'not semantically *or* syntactically
bound.'
[5] A term from Heim (1993):233f.; the original insights behind double indexing and codetermination
seem to go back to Higginbotham (1983):404 and 406.

(5.31)   Codetermination:
NP and NP′ *codetermined* if any of the following holds:
(a)   they are coindexed
(b)   one semantically binds the other
(c)   there is an NP″ such that NP and NP″ are codetermined and NP″ and
NP′ are codetermined

We will revisit (and ultimately render obsolete) this rather motley set of sub-conditions in chapter 6. For the moment it allows us to formulate Binding Condition B as follows:

(5.32)   Binding Condition B: A non-reflexive pronoun must not be codetermined
with a c-commanding NP in its domain.

To see how this works, reconsider the unacceptable bindings in (5.30): *Jeanne* and *her* are illicitly codetermined in (5.30a) by (5.31b) because the former sem-binds the latter, and in (5.30b) by (5.31a) because they are coindexed (in this particular case, coindexing corresponds to coreference, but the same would apply to an example like *Jeanne$_1$ β$_1$ thinks that she$_1$ saw her$_1$* in which it corresponds to being co-bound). Finally, in (5.30c), *Jeanne* and *she* are codetermined because the former binds the latter, *Jeanne* and *her* are codetermined because they are coindexed, and therefore *she* and *her* are codetermined by (5.31c), with NP″ = *Jeanne*, triggering a Binding Condition B violation, as desired.

This concludes the introduction of our new system. The novel elements, in a nutshell, are that referential NPs can act as semantic binders, and that we have double indexing, i.e. an NP with referential index n binding a different index m. Since, by the latter innovation, an NP can semantically bind a pronoun without actually syntactically binding it, we had to reformulate our Binding Conditions so as to apply at LF, after the Binder rule, and take into consideration both syntactic and semantic binding, as well as any combination thereof (codetermination). It may seem that these reformulations are a high price to pay for double indexing, and that we should have made more of an effort to avoid it. Readers who feel that way might be consoled to know that the system as set up in this section is only a transitional one, and will be replaced by a more parsimonious one in chapter 6.

In the discussion to follow, it will often be useful to present an example and mark two NPs as anaphorically related without committing to the exact nature of that relation (coreference, semantic binding, or co-binding). Where this is intended, I will henceforth simply italicize the NPs in question, without adding any indices or binder prefixes.

Exercise 5.8

Reformulate Binding Conditions A and C using the notion of co-determination. Are there empirical differences? Argue!

5.5   Verb phrase ellipsis℮

5.5.1   Strict and sloppy identity

A famous argument for non-quantificational NPs as semantic binders comes from Verb Phrase Ellipsis (VPE). Observe that (5.33) can have two kinds of interpretations:

(5.33)   Every woman in Culver City hates her neighbor, but no woman in Los Feliz does.

On the first, *her* refers to some contextually given female person, call her Ms. Jones, whose neighbor is universally hated by Culver City women, but not Los Feliz women. Call this a *strict* reading. On the second reading, every woman in Culver City hates *her own* neighbor, whereas no Los Feliz woman hates the people she herself lives next door to; call this reading *sloppy*. Obviously, on the first, strict, reading the pronouns in the overt VP and in the elided VP are both referential (since no NP referring to Ms. Jones syntactically binds them), whereas on the second, sloppy, one, they are each sem-bound (since their binder is a QNP).

It is, however, impossible to 'mix and match' these two options. (5.33) cannot mean that all Culver City woman hate Ms. Jones' neighbor, while no Los Feliz woman hates her own neighbor, nor vice versa. Likewise, if neither pronoun is bound, they actually need to *co*refer. There is no reading for (5.33) on which Ms. Jones' neighbor is hated in Culver City, while, say, Ms. Smith's neighbor is well liked in Los Feliz. We can capture this in the following generalization:

(5.34)   VP-Ellipsis generalization:
           If a pronoun p in the antecedent VP is semantically bound, the corresponding pronoun p' in the elided VP must be semantically bound in parallel. If p is referential, p' must corefer with it.

Crucially, (5.34) applies to non-quantificational NPs as well. Consider (5.35):

(5.35)   Felix hates his neighbor, and Max does, too.

Here again, we find a strict reading, in which Felix and Max both hate some third guy's, say John's, neighbor, and a sloppy reading, in which Felix hates Felix's neighbor, and Max hates Max's. But, again, no mixed readings are possible (e.g. Felix hates John's neighbor, and Max Bill's; or Felix hates Max's neighbors, and Max Felix's; or Felix Felix's and Max Bill's ...).

There is one special reading, though, on which Felix's neighbor is hated by Felix *and* Max. This, however, turns out to be just another instance of the strict reading on closer inspection, one where *Felix* and *his* happen to corefer. The three readings can be represented as follows (where strikeout marks the elided VP):

(5.36)   (a) $Felix_1$ hates his_3 neighbors and
                     Max_2 does ~~hate his_3 neighbors~~, too   (strict, 3rd party)
          (b) $Felix_1$ hates his_1 neighbors and
                     Max_2 does ~~hate his_1 neighbors~~, too   (strict, coreference)
          (c) $Felix_1$ β_1 hates his_1 neighbors and
                     Max_2 β_2 does ~~hate his_2 neighbors~~, too   (sloppy, sem-binding)

This pattern exactly follows the generalization in (5.34): either both pronouns are bound, or both are referential. The generalization only captures (5.35) though – and this is the heart of the argument – if it is assumed that *Felix* and *Max* can function as semantic binders, as in (5.36c).

Suppose we assumed instead that non-quantificational NPs can*not* act as semantic binders; then sloppy identity in (5.35), unlike in (5.33), would have to be captured by allowing the elided pronoun to have a different *referent* from the one in the overt VP if and only if they are both *coreferent* with an antecedent in their respective conjunct. While such a condition is not unimaginable, it seems preferable to avoid it, if the alternative hypothesis – that sloppy identity always involves semantic binding – is viable.

Exercise 5.9

Why doesn't example (5.33) have a strict reading analogous to the 'Felix hates Felix's neighbors, and Max hates Felix's neighbors too' reading for (5.35)?

Exercise 5.10

One plausible idea to capture the generalization in (5.34) is to say that the elided VP has to be *syntactically identical* to the overt one. This identity is warranted in the strict reading (5.36b) for VP $=$ *hate(s) his$_1$ neighbors*, and in the sloppy reading if we assume the LF in (5.37) instead of (5.36c) above, so that the VP in both conjuncts is β_1 *hates his$_1$ neighbors*:

(5.37) $Felix_1$ β_1 hates his_1 neighbors and Max_2 β_1 ~~hates his_1 neighbors~~, too

In other words, the strict/sloppy alternation is a function of whether the elided VP contains a β or not (this is, in fact, more or less the solution put forth in Sag [1976]).

1.   Discuss the details of the LF in (5.37). In particular, address issues regarding (i) auxiliary verbs, and (ii) the choice between Index Transfer and the Binder rule.

2.   Discuss the implication that examples like (5.38) (from Jacobson [1992]:206f.) have for this idea.

(5.38)   Tom wanted Sue to water his plants, while
                     John wanted Mary to ~~water his plants~~.

5.5.2   Deriving the generalization

In the discussion so far we implicitly assumed that pronouns in VP ellipsis can be freely indexed and bound, with the resulting structures subject to the following filter, repeated from above:

(5.39)   VP-Ellipsis generalization:
          If a pronoun p in the antecedent VP is semantically bound, the correspond-
          ing pronoun p' in the elided VP must be semantically bound in parallel. If p
          is referential, p' must corefer with it.

Let us ask now whether (5.39) can be derived in a systematic way. Let us start with the second half of the generalization. Can we derive the requirement that referential pronouns in the two VPs must be coreferent? An obvious idea is to have a syntactic condition on VP ellipsis that requires that the two VPs must be syntactically identical, *including indices*. From this it will follow that the pronouns are coindexed. This, however, only guarantees that they corefer if neither of them is bound. As pointed out above, we need to exclude the possibility that one of them is semantically bound, while the other is referential. That is, we have to exclude LFs as in (5.40) below:

(5.40)   (a) *every woman in Culver City β_2 *hates her$_2$ neighbors*, but
                            no woman in Los Feliz does hate her$_2$ neighbors
          (b) *Felix$_1$ β_2 *hates his$_2$ neighbors*, and
                            Max$_3$ does hate his$_2$ neighbors, too

In both of these LFs, the pronouns are coindexed, but the elided pronoun is referential, referring to some contextually given $g(2)$, while the overt one is bound. This is excluded by the original generalization (5.39), but would wrongly be allowed if syntactic identity was the only condition on VP ellipsis. Let us call such LFs *pseudo-strict*.

We can get rid of pseudo-strict readings, and thus derive the second half of (5.39) from the strict syntactic identity, if we add the following condition:[6]

(5.41)   No Spurious Coindexing:
          No LF representation may contain both semantically bound and free occur-
          rences of the same pronoun.

(5.41) effectively requires that indices used to express semantic binding are a disjoint set from those used to express (co)reference. It straightforwardly rules out the pseudo-strict readings in (5.40) since the index 2 is bound in the first conjuncts, but free in the second. For the general case it requires that the overt pronoun and the elided pronoun – since they bear the same index – be either both free, i.e. (co)referential, or both bound, yielding sloppy readings.

---

[6] From Heim and Kratzer (1998):254; a constraint along these lines is also proposed in Heim (1997):202, for more or less the same reasons; see the discussion in Heim and Kratzer (1998):9.3.2.

Let us turn to the first half of the generalization in (5.39), bound readings, then. Note that even if we require strict syntactic identity, we can still derive sloppy readings, given that we are allowed by the new Binder rule to use the same index on different binders. So we can derive sloppy readings of our standard examples, including the one discussed in section 5.5.1 above, by LFs such as (5.37), repeated here, and (5.42b):

(5.42)   (a)   Felix$_1$ β_3 hates his$_3$ neighbors, and

                              Max$_2$ β_3 does hate his$_3$ neighbors, too

            (b)   Tom$_1$ β_2 wanted Sue to water his$_2$ plants, while

                              John$_3$ β_2 wanted Mary to water his$_2$ plants.

So strict syntactic identity is compatible with sloppy readings, and, together with (5.41), No Spurious Coindexing, it will derive (5.34). We will return to these issues in section 6.5.1 of chapter 6, where we will weaken the strict syntactic identity condition on VP ellipsis.

Exercise 5.11

In section 5.3 above, the possibility of double indexing was motivated using examples (5.18) and (5.23).

1.   Make a parallel argument from the realm of ellipsis using (5.43) instead of (5.18):

          (5.43)   Mary parked her car in her garage, and Lee did, too.

2.   Find a variant of (5.43) which is parallel to (5.23) and discuss those aspects of it in which that variant differs from (5.43).

6 The Coreference rule

6.1 The proposal

In chapters 4 and 5 we introduced the central distinction between coreference and binding. We have formally implemented the notion of a semantic binder by introducing binder prefixes, i.e. indexed elements adjoined not to the actual NP but to the sister of the binding NP. We saw that, in a number of constructions, the question of whether coindexing among two NPs (with one c-commanding the other) is to be interpreted as coreference or as semantic binding can be answered on semantic grounds:

- If the higher NP is quantified (or a *wh*-expression), it semantically binds the lower NP.
- Embedded under focus-sensitive particles like *only*, the coreference/semantic binding distinction leads to different truth conditions.
- In the context of VP ellipsis, the coreference/semantic binding distinction leads to different resolutions for the elided constituent (strict versus sloppy).

Nothing in our system, however, allows us to decide in a run-of-the-mill case, like (6.1), whether the anaphoric relation between the italicized NPs is to be interpreted as coreference, as in LF (6.1a), or as semantic binding, as in LF (6.1b):

(6.1)   *John* thinks *he* is sick.
      (a)   John$_1$ thinks he$_1$ is sick
      (b)   John β_1 thinks he$_1$ is sick

In Reinhart (1983a):ch. 7 it is proposed that in such a configuration, coindexing *has* to be interpreted as semantic binding. Following Grodzinsky and Reinhart (1993):79 and Heim (1993):209 we can render the pertinent condition as follows:[1]

---

[1] Grodzinsky and Reinhart (1993) call this rule *Rule I*. The original condition in Reinhart (1983a):167 is: "Where a syntactic structure you are using allows bound-anaphora interpretation, then use it if you intend your expression to corefer, unless you have some reason to avoid bound anaphora." We will return to the particulars of this formulation below.

(6.2)   Coreference rule (CR)
             α cannot corefer with β if an indistinguishable interpretation can be gener-
             ated by replacing α with a variable bound by β.

Applied to (6.1), α is *he* and β is *John*. In (6.1a), α and β corefer, in (6.1b), α
is semantically bound by β. Since both sentences have the same interpretation,
only (6.1b), the LF with semantic binding, accords with the CR (6.2); (6.1a) violates it, and since the CR is a principle of grammar, (6.1a) is ungrammatical. We
say that the bound variable construal (6.1b) *blocks* the coreferent construal (6.1a)
by virtue of the CR.

    At first glance, the CR in (6.2) rules out coreference in all those cases in which
we couldn't tell the difference from a bound variable construal anyway. In other
words, it removes certain spurious ambiguities, but never seems to make any
novel predictions. Is this really all there is to it? In the following sections we will
discuss cases in which the CR yields significant simplifications in our theory,
and moreover yields different empirical predictions.

6.2   Theoretical consequences

6.2.1   Eliminating codetermination

    In chapter 5 we saw that our new device of double indexing forces
certain complications in the formulation of the binding principles. In particular, we saw that an additional notion, *codetermination*, needed to be defined to
block anaphoric relations between the subject and the object in a simple clause
like (6.3), given that any of the LFs in (6.3a)–(6.3c) could yield such a reading
and hence needs to be excluded by Binding Condition B:

(6.3)   *she* saw *her*
             (a) $*$she$_1$ β_2 saw her$_2$
             (b) $*$she$_1$ saw her$_1$
             (c) $*$Jeanne$_1$ β_2 thought that she$_2$ saw her$_1$

Using the CR, we can actually alleviate the need for this notion. To see how, note
first that (6.3b) is ruled out by the CR: *she* ($=\beta$) and *her* ($=\alpha$) corefer, where an
indistinguishable reading could be achieved by semantic binding as in (6.3a);
therefore, (6.3a) blocks (6.3b) by virtue of the CR. The star on (6.3b) is thus
explained independent of Binding Condition B.

    Next consider (6.3c): here, *Jeanne* ($=\beta$) and *her* ($=\alpha$) corefer, instead of the
former binding the latter. A structure in which α is replaced by a variable bound
by β is (6.4):

(6.4)   Jeanne$_1$ β_2 thought that she$_2$ saw her$_2$

(6.3c) above and (6.4) have the same interpretation, so the latter blocks the former, which means that (6.3c), too, is rendered ungrammatical by the CR, independent of Binding Condition B.

So far so good, but note that *she* ($=\beta$) and *her* ($=\alpha$) in (6.4) are coindexed, and neither sem-binds the other. Let's assume for the moment that this configuration counts as 'coreference' in the sense of the CR, too, and must therefore be avoided, preserving meaning, in favor of the LF in (6.5):

(6.5)   Jeanne$_1$ β_2 thought that she$_2$ β_3 saw her$_3$

Here, *Jeanne* sem-binds *she*, which in turn sem-binds *her* (the choice of actual indices is irrelevant, of course). None of the NPs corefers, but the interpretation is still the same. Therefore (6.5) blocks (6.4) and (6.3c) by the CR.

The only LFs allowed by the CR are thus (6.3a) and (6.5); all others are blocked. But these two involve *bona fide* local violations of Binding Condition B: a pronoun is bound within its local domain. Moreover, it is *semantically* bound in both cases. We can thus do away with the notion of codetermination and simply state Binding Condition B as in (6.6):

(6.6)   Binding Condition B (final version)
             A non-reflexive pronoun must be semantically free in its domain.

We thus see that the CR, apart from blocking spurious binding/coreference ambiguities, yields a significant simplification of our Binding Condition B.

Before going on, we have to amend the Coreference rule in (6.2) slightly. The intended effect of the CR in an example like *Jeanne thought that she saw her* (=[6.3c] above) was to force local semantic binding wherever possible. There is an LF for this sentence, however, that has no coreference in it but still involves non-local binding:

(6.7)   Jeanne$_1$ β_2 β_3 thought that she$_2$ saw her$_3$

She and *her* are co-bound, but aren't coindexed. But, with neither coreference nor coindexing, the CR, even on its most favorable interpretation, cannot block this LF. Still, (6.7) has an interpretation in which *she* and *her* have the same referent, i.e. one that is intuitively unavailable. This was blocked under our previous formulation of Binding Condition B, since *she*$_2$ and *her*$_3$ are codetermined in (6.7), but it is no longer under the simplified (6.6), since *her*$_3$ is not semantically bound in (6.7).

How can we block this LF, then? One possibility is to replace '. . . cannot corefer . . .' in the formulation of the CR by '. . . cannot corefer or be co-bound by the same NP . . .'. Then (6.7) is blocked by (6.5) in a way analogous to the way that (6.4) was.

Another possibility is to disallow by stipulation one NP from binding two indices at once (i.e. two βs next to one another), as *Jeanne* does in (6.7). Then the only way to get *her* to be sem-bound by *Jeanne* is again (6.4), which we already saw is blocked by (6.5).

Both these amendments, however, would fail to block the more complex example in (6.8), which involves neither coreference nor co-binding nor double βs, but poses the exact same problem in the lowest clause as (6.5):

(6.8)   Jeanne$_1$ β_2 said that she$_2$ β_3 thought that she$_2$ saw her$_3$

Let us, then, invoke an additional constraint that prohibits non-minimal binding of a pronoun. The idea is that *Jeanne/she$_2$* mustn't sem-bind *her$_3$* in (6.7)/(6.8) (or [6.4] for that matter) because *she* could *minimally* bind *her* as in (6.5) with the same interpretation. Such a principle is proposed as *Rule H* in Fox (2000):ch. 4:[2]

(6.9)   Rule H
             A pronoun, α, can be bound by an antecedent, δ, only if there is no closer an-
             tecedent, γ, such that it is possible to bind α to γ and *get the same semantic*
             interpretation.

The CR and Rule H in tandem enforce something like a 'closest antecedent re-quirement'; the former forces semantic binding among c-commanding NPs that are supposed to receive the same interpretation, and the latter forces semantic binding among more than two c-commanding NPs to be strictly transitive, local, and non-overlapping. Since the closest binder structure is automatically the one most likely to violate Binding Condition B, we can thus stick with the much simpler version of it given in (6.6).

Despite this successful elimination of the notion of codetermination (and, effectively, co-binding), we are left with the somewhat unsatisfactory division of labor between the Coreference Rule and Rule H, which moreover formally resemble each other. A rule which subsumes them both under one roof is (6.10):

(6.10)   Have Local Binding!
             For any two NPs α and β, if α could bind β (i.e. if it c-commands β and β
             is not bound in α's c-command domain already), α must bind β, unless that
             changes the interpretation

In a sentence like *Jeanne thought that she saw her*, the only way in which (6.10) can be met for all pairs of (relevant) NPs is indeed the binding pattern in (6.5), i.e. the one that violates Binding Condition B, as desired. In (6.7), for example, *her* is free within the c-command domain of *she* and could thus be bound by it. Since this will yield an indistinguishable interpretation, it *must* be bound by it. The resulting LF has *her* locally bound by *she*, and *Jeanne* vacuously binding the index 3, which is equivalent to (6.5). Similarly in (6.4) and (6.3c), where *she* fails to bind *her*; the necessary insertion of β_2 (β_1 in [6.3c]) right next to *she* will yield another LF equivalent to (6.5).

---

[2] Fox (2000):111ff. attributes his Rule H (though not by this name) to Heim (1993), but it is unclear to me that Heim's (1993) proposal, which, unlike Fox's, distinguished between semantic and syntactic binding, actually entails something like Rule H (unfortunately, Fox doesn't provide any page references).

Officially, we will adopt (6.10), which subsumes the CR and Rule H. I will, however, continue to refer to the CR in the arguments that follow, where the minimality of pronoun binding isn't at issue.

Exercise 6.1

Give a step-by-step treatment of examples (6.3), (6.4), and (6.8) using the rule in (6.10).

6.2.2   Eliminating Binding Condition C

In Reinhart (1983a), the CR (or its counterpart there) is used to eliminate yet another part of BT, namely Binding Condition C. To see how, note first that the CR blocks the following LFs for sentences like *He/John likes John* or *He/John likes John's mother*:

(6.11)   (a) *he_1/$John_1$ likes $John_1$
          (b) *he_1/$John_1$ likes $John_1$'s mother

The reason is that we could replace *John* by a variable sem-bound by *he*, in accordance with the CR:

(6.12)   (a) he_1/$John_1$ β_2 likes $himself_2$
          (b) he_1/$John_1$ β_2 likes his_2 mother

Obviously, these LFs receive the same interpretations as those in (6.11), but avoid coreference in favor of sem-binding (note that the choice between *him* and *himself* is determined by Binding Conditions A and B, as before). We have thus successfully ruled out the Binding Condition C violations in (6.11) without invoking Binding Condition C, but just the CR.

One question left open by this is whether we couldn't also sem-bind *John*, as in (6.13):

(6.13)   (a) he_1/$John_1$ β_2 likes $John_2$
          (b) he_1/$John_1$ β_2 likes $John_2$'s mother

Obviously, if we want to do away with Binding Condition C, we have to block this possibility. There is now a rather radical way to do so, by adopting the following:

(6.14)   Full NPs don't carry referential indices.

We have already adopted something like this for quantified NPs in chapter 4. How will the generalization proposed here work? First, note that we never used referential indices on full NPs to determine their reference. That, by assumption, was done by the lexical content of the NP. Indeed, we had to go somewhat out of our way actually to make the indices on full NPs do something at all. Adopting (6.14), then, does away with all of that: since there are no indices on full NPs, there is no need to have anything but the lexical content enter into their interpretation.

Second, indices on full NPs were never used to signal that they were bindees, since full NPs couldn't be bound due to Binding Condition C. In other words, although full NPs were technically bindable in the same way that pronouns are, this option was effectively blocked in the syntax. Doing away with referential indices on full NPs altogether resolves this situation: full NPs cannot be bound because they don't have a bindable index in the first place.

Third, indices on full NPs *were* required to induce Binding Condition B violations in a sentence like *Peter shaved him*. But this is taken care of by a conspiracy now: the LF in (6.15a) is ruled out by the CR, because the same interpretation could be gotten by *Peter* binding *him*, as in (6.15b). But that LF is ruled out because it constitutes a Binding Condition B violation: *him* is bound in its local domain, not syntactically by a referential index, but semantically by β_1:

(6.15)   (a) ∗Peter shaved him_1 (violates CR)
           (b) ∗Peter β_1 shaved him_1 (violates Binding Condition B)

In sum, we see that the CR allows us to do away with referential indices on full NPs, and, accordingly, with Binding Condition C.

In closing this section, let me point out that it wasn't claimed that it *makes no sense* to bind a full NP. On the old account, $Karen_2$ was interpreted as $g(2)$, with the presupposition that $g(2)$ was Karen. Thus a sentence like *every girl β_2 voted for $Karen_2$* would have received an interpretation like 'for every x, if x is a girl, then x is Karen and voted for herself.' Granted, this sentence can only be uttered in a situation where there is only one girl, Karen; but it certainly is an *imaginable* proposition that would be expressed here.[3]

The case seems even clearer for descriptive NPs or *epithets* like *the idiot*: there is no reason whatsoever why *I told every boy β_5 that the $idiot_5$ should stay home* wouldn't denote the perfectly reasonable proposition that I told every boy that he is an idiot and should stay home. That none of these readings exists is thus a fact about the way full NPs happen to function in natural language. Unlike with QNPs, there is no logical reason why definites and names couldn't be bound, but it seems that they just can't. If we assume that they do not bear referential indices, we have a natural way of capturing this fact (more natural, arguably, than imposing an extra condition such as Binding Condition C), but I wouldn't claim that we have explained it in any deeper sense.

It has been reported in passing in the literature that some languages like Thai or Vietnamese, and possibly even English (see Lasnik [1986], and the references at the end of chapter 1, section 1.2.3), don't display Binding Condition C effects:[4]

---

[3] Note that an NP like *her_2 bicycle* is usually interpreted as 'the bicycle of $g(2)$' with the presupposition that $g(2)$ has a bicycle. *Every girl β_2 rode her_2 bicycle* is a perfectly well-formed sentence, and it is usually understood to quantify only over girls who own bicycles. So it wouldn't be unreasonable even to expect that *every girl β_2 voted for $Karen_2$* would generally denote something like 'every girl who is Karen voted for herself,' which is an even more sensible proposition than the one mentioned in the main text.

[4] Data from Lasnik (1986):153.

(6.16)   (a)   cɔɔn khít   waâ cɔɔn chàlaàt   (Thai)
               John thinks that John is smart

          (b)   John tin   John s̄ e thăńg   (Vietnamese)
               John thinks John will win

Does the reduction of Binding Condition C to the CR allow for such languages? It does, and in several ways. One simple possibility is that the CR is language particular (I deliberately refrained from claiming above that the CR follows from any general maxims of cooperative communication, as is sometimes done); if a languages doesn't have it, it shouldn't show Binding Condition C effects (but it also, crucially, should lack the other empirical effects of the CR discussed in the present chapter). Another possibility is that the CR in such languages lacks, as it were, the 'replaced by a pronoun' part of our formulation in (6.2), that the CR in such languages prohibits α from coreferring with β only if α could itself be a bound variable instead (rather than be replaced by one), i.e. it blocks pronouns coreferential with a c-commanding NP, but never full NPs. A third possibility is that some languages do have indices on full NPs, so that full NPs can, in fact, be *semantically* bound. In all these cases, there might additionally be independent restrictions on full NPs (it seems, for example, that speakers of Thai and Vietnamese, as well as those of English who allow sentences of the 'full NP . . . full NP' variety, still reject 'pronoun . . . full NP' under c-command). There hasn't been enough research on languages that appear to lack Binding Condition C effects to determine which (if any) of these options may indeed occur.

Exercise 6.2

Explain step by step how anaphoric relations are blocked between pronoun and full NP in *The dog howls at it* and *It howls at the dog*.

6.2.3   Upshot: BT regards semantic binding only

Let me point out once more the arguably most interesting consequence of adopting the CR, with or without indices on full NPs: all Binding Conditions now regard semantic binding only. This might not be obvious at first, but the reasoning is quite simple: first, the Binding Conditions refer to pairs of c-commanding NPs only (where by 'c-commanding NPs' I mean NPs one of which c-commands the other[s]); second, Binding Conditions aside, c-command is a sufficient condition for semantic binding; third, by the CR, coreference is blocked by semantic binding, wherever the latter is possible, which means: among c-commanding NPs, which means, among all pairs of NPs for which Binding Conditions are relevant.

Another way of saying this is that only binding relations of the form $\beta_n \ldots NP_n$ are relevant to BT. Or, put yet the other way around:

(6.17)   Consequence of the CR: (semantically) unbound indices are irrelevant to BT.

To illustrate, consider (6.18):

(6.18) (a) Nina's mother visited her$_2$.
     (b) Her$_{1/2}$ mother visited her$_2$.

Both sentences allow coreference between the possessive *Nina's*/*her* and the object pronoun (note that binding is not an option, since the possessive doesn't c-command the object). However, in the pronoun case (6.18b) this is indicated by coindexing, while in the name case (6.18a) it isn't, and can't be, given that names no longer bear indices. But, even in the case of (6.18b), the indices on the two occurrences of *her* are irrelevant to the BT, as claimed in (6.17): since neither pronoun c-commands the other, Binding Conditions won't apply to them.

 Reinhart (1983a) proposes therefore that the pronouns in (6.18) shouldn't bear indices either. Rather, being referring pronouns, their reference should be determined by principles outside of core grammar, i.e. pragmatic principles. The only anaphoric relation that *is* encoded in the grammar proper, by indexing, is that of semantic binding. Reinhart thus advances the following radical hypothesis, which subsumes our earlier (6.14):

(6.19) Reinhart's (1983a) hypothesis:
     Only semantic binding is represented in the syntax. Coreference is not.

Implementing this hypothesis into our current system amounts to adopting the following conditions:

(6.20) (a) NPs may, but need not, bear an index.
     (b) All indices on NPs must be sem-bound at LF.

Unsurprisingly, adopting (6.20) doesn't change the predictions made about the sentence in (6.18). With or without indexing, the two NPs may, but need not, corefer. Indeed, it doesn't change the predictions about the core BT cases either, again thanks to the CR. Consider a simple case like (6.21):

(6.21) (a) she likes her   (no coreference possible by CR)
     (b) *she β_2 likes her$_2$ (out by Binding Condition B)

While it is now possible to have a structure devoid of any indexing, as in (6.21a), the two pronouns, unlike those in (6.18b), are not allowed to corefer, due to the CR: since semantic binding is possible in this configuration, any coreference is blocked. True semantic binding, on the other hand, introduces indices as in (6.21b), which in turn betray the Binding Condition B violation. So, even if we adopt (6.19)/(6.20), we still block pronouns with local antecedents by a conspiracy of the CT and Binding Condition B.

 Reinhart's conjecture that, once we adopt the CR, indices on referential NPs are irrelevant for deriving BT-violations and thus superfluous syntactic objects is certainly correct. It leaves us with the task of *interpreting* referential NPs without the help of indices, however. This, as noted above, seems simple enough for full NPs, but far less obviously so for referential pronouns. We will add some comments about this in section 6.5.2 below. For the moment, let us register that all Binding Conditions will refer to semantic binding only, and that the choice to maintain referential indices on some (or perhaps all) referential NPs would merely be motivated by semantic considerations.

6.3   Binding Theory obviations

So far we have reviewed a number of theory-internal changes that result from the CR. But there are empirical differences as well. Note that all our formulations of the CR invoke the notion of 'indistinguishable interpretation.' Why haven't we simply said that an NP cannot corefer with another NP if it can be bound by it? The reason is that, in a few cases, coreference and binding do *not* yield indistinguishable interpretations. An example are the focus constructions discussed in chapter 5:

(6.22)   I only said that TATJANA should stay in her room.

    (a)   coreference: I only said that TATJANA should stay in her$_1$ room
          entailment: I didn't say anything else of the form 'x should stay in $g(1)$'s room' $\equiv$ I didn't say anything else of the form 'x should stay in Tatjana's room'[5]

    (b)   binding: I only said that TATJANA β_1 should stay in her$_1$ room
          entailment: I didn't say anything else of the form 'x should stay in x's room'

Here, *her* is α and *Tatjana* is β in the sense of the CR; β corefers with α in (6.22a), and binds α in (6.22b). But, as we discussed at length in chapter 5, the two LFs yield distinct interpretations: (6.22a) is true if I also said 'Marijana, stay in your room', but (6.22b) is false then. (6.22b) is true even if I said 'Mirko, stay in Tatjana's room,' but (6.22a) is false then. Since the two LFs don't yield the same interpretation, CR doesn't apply here and neither LF blocks the other, i.e. both are grammatical, correctly predicting the ambiguity.

This ambiguity, however, would have been predicted, too, if we had never adopted the CR in the first place, so this case doesn't provide an argument *in favor of* the CR. But, as Reinhart (1983a) points out, in exactly those cases where the CR allows for exceptional coreference among c-commanding NPs, Binding Conditions seem to be suspended. Consider for example, the following cases of what might be thought Binding Condition C violations:

(6.23)   (a)   Only JOHN thinks John is smart.
         (b)   Even LARA voted against Lara.

The argument here is straightforward: a grammatical LF for e.g. (6.23a) is (6.24):

(6.24)   only John$_F$ thinks John is smart
         interpretation: no one other than John thinks that John is smart

(6.24) does not violate any Binding Conditions, since it doesn't contain any semantic binding (this holds even if we index names, since this will be mere

---

[5] Assuming that $g(1) =$ Tatjana.

coreference). But shouldn't it be ruled out by the CR? The CR wants us to compare this representation to (6.25):

(6.25)   only John$_F$ β_2 thinks he$_2$ is smart
           interpretation: no one other than John considers himself/herself smart

Here the lower NP has been replaced by a bound pronoun. But crucially, as indicated below the representations, the interpretations aren't identical, so the CR doesn't apply; (6.25) does not block (6.24), and both (6.25) and (6.24) are predicted to be grammatical. Generally, an NP *can* occur c-commanded by a coreferring NP if coreference yields a different interpretation from sem-binding. If this is the case, Binding Conditions do not apply, and we find *obviations* (though not literally violations) of Binding Conditions B and C.

As Heim (1993) points out, the same argument can be made for cases of exceptional co-binding. According to her, examples like (6.26) are slightly more complex than, but generally as acceptable as, (6.24):

(6.26)   Everyone feared that only he voted for him.

Why doesn't it have to be ... *that only he voted for himself*? The LF for (6.26) is (6.27):

(6.27)   everyone β_1 feared that only he$_1$ voted for him$_1$

This LF doesn't violate Binding Condition B because *him*, although coindexed with *he$_1$*, is not semantically bound by it. If we bind it locally, we get (6.28) instead:

(6.28)   everyone β_1 feared that only he$_1$ β_2 voted for himself$_2$

(Note that β_2 *voted for him$_2$* would be a sem-bound reading, too, but blocked by Binding Condition B.) This LF, however, expresses a different meaning from that of (6.27). The former says that everyone feared 'No one but me voted for me!'; the latter expresses the fear that 'No one but me voted for themselves.' Given the non-synonymy of these sentences, the CR remains silent here and both structures are allowed, each with its respective interpretation.

These cases present strong empirical evidence for the CR or something like it.[6] A similar class of examples is constituted by what Heim calls 'when structured meanings matter':[7]

(6.29)   (a) I know what John and Bill have in common. John thinks that Bill is
                terrific and Bill thinks that Bill is terrific.
           (b) Look, fathead. If everyone loves Oscar's mother, then certainly Oscar
                must love Oscar's mother.

---

[6] Heim's (1993) proposal doesn't, in fact, use the CR but rather allows for violation of the Binding Conditions in exactly those cases in which a non-distinguishable reading results.

[7] Both examples from Evans (1980):356.

The reasoning here is, informally, that the rhetorical effect of these examples rests on ascribing the *same property* to John and Bill, and to Oscar and the rest. While, say, *Oscar loves Oscar's mother* and *Oscar loves his (own) mother* denote the same proposition, *loves Oscar's mother* and β_1 *loves his$_1$ mother* do not denote the same property. If we understand these two as 'distinguishable interpretations' in the sense of the CR, we correctly predict cases like (6.29) to be acceptable (for closer examination of these cases cf. Heim [1993], especially pp. 216ff.).

Reinhart's and Heim's works contain more examples of exceptional anaphora, which we will not go into here. One case that is often subsumed here, too, is that of unknown or mistaken identity, which we will discuss separately in 7.2.

What we saw in this section is that the CR doesn't generally block coreference among c-commanding NPs, but only if the same reading can be expressed via binding. While this justifies the particular way the rule is formulated, and provides a strong empirical argument in its favor, it also highlights one of its noteworthy, and to some worrisome, properties: The CR, Rule H, and Have Local Binding are all genuinely *transderivational constraints*. They don't just (dis)allow a particular structure by checking certain properties of that structure, but by comparing different structures within a certain set of 'similar' structures. None of the other rules and conditions employed in this book is transderivational, and some researchers regard the inclusion of transderivational constraints as a problematic step (see e.g. Potts [2001] for recent discussion).

Exercise 6.3
Construct and discuss an example of exceptional coreference involving a focus construction with an element other than *only*.

Exercise 6.4
What is remarkable about the example *Only MILLI brought her own lunch*. What is the reason? Speculate!

Exercise 6.5
Do we find exceptional coreference in *Only MILLI talked to her teacher*?

Exercise 6.6
The following statement is false: 'Binding Condition obviations only occur if there is no way to have a coreferent reading without violating a Binding Condition.' Show why! (Hint: look at exceptionally coreferring full NPs.)

6.4   Summary: the final system

In this chapter we have discussed the consequences of adding Reinhart's CR, or its generalization in (6.10), repeated in (6.32) below, to our theory.

This constraint, which encodes a general preference for local binding over coreference and codetermination, immediately yields two consequences: one theory-internal, one empirical:[8]

- Binding Conditions can be formulated using the notion of semantic binding only. There is no need to make reference to the more complex notion of codetermination, or to syntactic binding, in addition.
- We get an account of exceptional coreference and exceptional co-binding, including the Binding Condition obviations that can go along with them.

In addition, adopting (6.10) allows for further simplifications in the theory:

- We can eliminate indices on full NPs, and, consequentially, Binding Condition C.
- We can eliminate unbound indices altogether, simplifying the syntactic representations and – as we will see momentarily in section 6.5.1 – alleviating the need for the ban against spurious coindexing ([5.41] in chapter 5, section 5.5) in the treatment of VP ellipsis.

These last two steps are logically independent of the first two, and one might choose to refrain from them on independent grounds (see e.g. the arguments in Lasnik [1986] against dropping Binding Condition C, and the discussion in 6.5.2 regarding referential indices on pronouns).

For the remainder of this book, we will adopt (6.32) and the assumption that full NPs are indexless. We will stop short of implementing Reinhart's full proposal, though, and continue to index referential pronouns, for reasons of perspicuity (see the remarks in 6.5.2 below). A summary of our conventions and definitions is given below:

(6.30)   Indexing Convention (final)
           All and only pronouns (and binder prefixes) bear an index.

(6.31)   Binding Conditions (final)
           (A) A reflexive pronoun must be semantically bound in its domain.
           (B) A non-reflexive pronoun must be semantically free in its domain.

(6.32)   Have Local Binding!
           For any two NPs α and β, if α could bind β (i.e. if it c-commands β and β is not bound in α's c-command domain already), α must bind β, unless that changes the interpretation

Semantic binding is defined as per chapter 4, section 4.2 (and syntactic binding, if required, as per chapter 5, section 5.4). In addition to these definitions, we continue to use the Binder rule from chapter 5, section 5.3, the Binder Index Evaluation Rule (BIER) from chapter 4, section 4.1, and the Prohibition against Accidental Coreference (PACO) from chapter 2, section 2.2.2:

---

[8] In addition, (6.32) has welcome consequences for the analysis of various 'many pronoun puzzles' in VP ellipsis, as discussed in Fox (2000):ch. 4.

(6.33)   Semantic binding (final):

A binder prefix β *sem(antically)-binds* an NP if and only if

(a) β and NP are coindexed

(b) β c-commands NP

(c)   there is no binder prefix β' which is c-commanded by β and meets (a) and (b)

If an NP is not bound by any binder prefix β in a phrase marker P, we say that NP is *semantically free* in P.

(6.34)   Binder rule (final version):

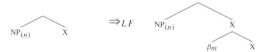

(6.35)   Binder Index Evaluation rule (BIER) (final):

For any natural number n, $\left[\!\!\left[\begin{array}{c} \overset{\frown}{\beta_n \quad Y}\end{array}\right]\!\!\right]^{g} = \lambda x.[\![Y]\!]^{g[n \to x]}(x)$

(6.36)   Prohibition against Accidental Coreference (PACO):

$[\![S]\!]^g$ is a possible interpretation of sentence S only if $g(n) \neq g(m)$ if $m \neq n$, for any natural numbers n, m.

In the remainder of this book I will often use the term 'binding' without specification. Assuming that our conjecture about the irrelevance of syntactic binding is correct, this is a shorthand for 'semantic binding'; for the most part, however, little in the exposition hinges on this distinction.

6.5   Extensions

6.5.1   VP ellipsis revisited ©

Before concluding our discussion of the CR, we need to revisit VP ellipsis (VPE), as discussed in chapter 5. There we saw that a sentence like (6.37) is ambiguous between a strict reading, on which the two pronouns corefer, as in LF (6.37a), and a sloppy reading, on which they are each bound in their own conjunct, as in LF (6.37b); to make coreference assumptions more perspicuous I will index names throughout this discussion, contrary to our official treatment, but nothing in the argument hinges on this:

(6.37)   John saw his sister, and Bill did, too.

(a)   John$_1$ saw his$_1$ sister, and Bill$_3$ did ~~see his$_1$ sister~~, too.

(b)   John$_1$ β_2 saw his$_2$ sister, and Bill$_3$ β_2 did ~~see his$_2$ sister~~, too.

In section 5.5 of chapter 5 we discussed how to derive these two readings and, in subsection 5.5.2, how to allow for the prerequisite LFs while blocking any LF that leads to 'mixed' readings. It was proposed that two conditions are needed to capture the correct generalization, namely a strict syntactic identity condition on VP ellipsis, requiring that the indexing in the elided VP be identical to that in the overt one, and a condition No Spurious Coindexing, which prohibits the same index to be used referentially in one conjunct, and semantically bound in the other.

As the alert reader might have noticed, however, (6.37a) violates the CR in the first conjunct, since *John* corefers with, yet c-commands, *his*. What if *John* binds *his* instead? Two possible LFs for this option would be:

(6.38)   (a)   John$_1$ β_1 saw his$_1$ sister, and Bill$_3$ did ~~see his$_1$~~ sister, too
          (b)   John$_1$ β_2 saw his$_2$ sister, and Bill$_3$ did ~~see his$_1$~~ sister, too

Both LFs express a strict reading, as intended. But (6.38a) violates the prohibition against spurious coindexing: the index 1 is used both as a referential index (on *John* and the elided *his*) and as a bound index (on β and the first *his*), which is precisely what that condition prohibits. (6.38b), on the other hand, doesn't violate this prohibition (index 1 is only used referentially), but fails the VP identity condition instead: since the indices on the two pronouns aren't identical, the VPs aren't either.

Given that none of these sem-binding LFs seems to work, then, one might try to grab the other end of the dilemma. Maybe (6.37a) is the correct LF after all, and coreference in the first conjunct is exceptionally possible precisely because the only well-formed sem-bound structure, (6.37b), leads to a different interpretation, namely the sloppy one. This requires us to think of the CR as applying at the higher level: while bound and coreferent construal yield the same reading for the first conjunct alone, they yield distinguishable interpretations for the coordinate structure as a whole.[9]

While this is certainly a plausible idea, it is undermined by the facts. To see how, simply recall that exceptional coreference structures are generally immune to Binding Condition violations (since Binding Conditions by assumption only 'see' semantic binding). The consequence of this for the VP-ellipsis case would be (6.39) below:

(6.39)   Consequence of assuming that strict identity in VP ellipsis always involves binding theory obviations in the first conjuncts:
          All first conjuncts in strict identity VP ellipsis should be exempt from Binding Conditions B and C.

This prediction, however, is clearly wrong, as can be seen in (6.40) below. To interpret *John* and *him/John* as anaphorically related in the examples in (6.40) is as hard or impossible as it is if you consider their first conjuncts in isolation, regardless of whether construed as strict or sloppy; but in contrast to that, both examples should, according to (6.39), have a grammatical strict construal as given in (6.41):

(6.40)   (a)   *$*$John* saw *him* and Bill did, too.
          (b)   *$*$John* saw *John*'s sister, and Bill did, too.

---

[9] Note that this 'higher level' isn't always the sentence level, since the same ambiguity shows up in cross-sentence VP ellipsis such as *John saw his sister. Bill did, too.* See Fox (2000) for much more discussion of these issues.

(6.41)   (a)   John₁ saw him₁ and Bill₂ did see him₁, too.
          (b)   John₁ saw his₁ sister, and Bill₂ did see his₁ sister, too.

We conclude that strict identity in VP ellipsis cannot involve exceptional coreference in the first conjunct. To the contrary, to render the sentences in (6.40) ungrammatical, the CR *must* apply to these, forcing semantic binding and thus provoking a Binding Condition violation. The correct LF for the strict reading of (6.37) must thus be either (6.38a) or (6.38b) above.

Let us assume that (6.38b), repeated here, is the correct LF. We are then forced to give up the strict identity condition on VP ellipsis, replacing it by something like (6.43):

(6.42)   John₁ β₂ saw his₂ sister, and Bill₃ did see his₁ sister, too

(6.43)   VP Identity Condition (final):
          An elided VP must find a syntactic antecedent that is identical *except perhaps for indices*.

This condition obviously allows for (6.42), but along with it for a whole new set of unwanted LFs in which the elided pronoun has a completely new, referential index, e.g.:

(6.44)   *John₁ β₂ saw his₂ sister and Bill₃ did see his₄ sister, too.

The correct generalization about pronouns in VP ellipsis seems to be the following (cf. e.g. Fox [2000]:116f.):

(6.45)   NP Parallelism:
          NPs in the antecedent and elided VPs must either
          (a)   have the same referential value, or
          (b)   be bound (in parallel) in their respective conjuncts

(6.46)   Ancillary definition: individual *a* is the *referential value* of NP in sentence
          S if
          (a)   NP refers to *a*,   or
          (b)   NP is semantically bound in S to an NP′ with referential value *a*

The innovation with respect to the generalization (5.34) discussed earlier in section 5.5 of chapter 5 (roughly: pronouns must either corefer or be bound in their respective conjuncts) lies in clause (6.45a): The pronouns now don't need actually to corefer, as long as they end up denoting the same individual. The prerequisite notion of (same) *referential value* is defined in (6.46).

Unfortunately, (6.45), unlike our earlier stricter condition, doesn't follow at all from the theory of binding and ellipsis. That is, an intuitively clearly unavailable reading such as that expressed by LF (6.44) isn't ruled out by conditions on VP ellipsis or the prohibition No Spurious Coindexing, but only by explicitly stipulating (6.45) in addition.

A way to improve on this unsatisfactory situation might be provided by the VP-ellipsis condition proposed in Rooth (1992a). Simplifying considerably, Rooth argues that the relation between the first conjunct and the second in VP ellipsis is one of *focus-matching*, along the following lines:

(6.47)   VP$_E$ can be elided if there is an antecedent constituent C$_A$ that is *focus-matched* by some C$_E$ dominating VP$_E$.

(6.48)   C$_E$ *f(ocus)-matches* C$_A$ if $[\![C_A]\!]^g$ is an element of P-SET(C$_E$).

As indicated, the formal rendering of focus-matching uses the P-SETs introduced in chapter 5, section 5.2. For all intents and purposes, we can think of C$_E$ focus-matching C$_A$ if some substitution for the focused elements in C$_E$ yields a C$'_E$ that is synonymous to C$_A$ under any assignment g. Consider third-party readings first:

(6.49)   (Everybody liked Amanda$_1$.) Tim$_2$ asked her$_1$ out for dinner.
          ROBERTA$_3$ did ask her$_1$ out for dinner, too.

What is crucial for VP ellipsis according to (6.47) is not the relation between the VPs themselves, but between constituents dominating them. Let's look at the Ī-level: we find *asked her$_1$ out for dinner* (=C$_A$) and *did ask her$_1$ out for dinner* (=C$_E$), which are synonymous under any assignment g; this is a trivial case of focus-matching (no foci, hence no replacements), meeting (6.47). Thus VP ellipsis is predicted to be possible.

Suppose now, for illustration, that we looked at the IP level instead: although we find *Tim$_2$ asked her$_1$ out for dinner* and *ROBERTA$_3$ asked her$_1$ out for dinner*, which are not synonymous, we still meet (6.47), given that *ROBERTA* is focused, and therefore its P-SET contains the proposition 'Tim asked her out for dinner.' Informally, we replace the focused *ROBERTA$_3$* by *Tim$_2$*, notated as in (6.50):

(6.50)   Tim$_2$ asked her$_1$ out for dinner ⇔ $\boxed{\begin{matrix}\textbf{Tim}_2\\ \text{ROBERTA}_3\end{matrix}}$ asked her$_1$ out for dinner

IP$'_E$ – *Tim$_2$ asked her$_1$ out for dinner* – is synonymous with IP$_A$, thus IP$_E$ – *ROBERTA$_3$ asked her$_1$ out for dinner* – focus-matches IP$_A$, and ellipsis is, again, predicted possible. The gist of this proposal is thus that ellipsis is possible if you can replace focused material around the elided VP so as to match the antecedent site.

Turning now to strict identity, note that if the pronoun in the antecedent VP is semantically bound (as required by the CR if it is c-commanded by its antecedent), the pronoun in the ellipsis site cannot be coindexed with it, unless it is bound, too. This is a consequence of No Spurious Coindexing. The LF for (6.51) must thus be (6.51a) (= [6.42]), which meets Rooth's condition (6.47) by virtue of focus marking on *Bill*, cf. (6.51b):

(6.51)   John saw his sister and BILL did, too.
          (a)   John$_1$ β_2 saw his$_2$ sister, and Bill$_3$ did see his$_1$ sister, too
          (b)   John$_1$ β_2 saw his$_2$ sister ⇔ $\boxed{\begin{matrix}\textbf{John}_1\\ \text{BILL}_3\end{matrix}}$ did see his$_1$ sister

Note that, in this example, the fact that the matching takes place at a higher constituent is crucial; *did see his$_1$ sister* doesn't focus-match either *saw his$_2$ sister* or β_2 *saw his$_2$ sister* (it isn't synonymous – thanks to the different indices – and it doesn't contain any focused items). But *BILL$_3$ did see his$_1$ sister* f-matches *John$_1$ β_2 saw his$_2$ sister*, as shown in (6.51b).

Note, too, that focusing *Bill* in (6.51) is a necessary condition for this to go through. Presumably a theory of focus will derive this fact independently,[10] but for the moment we can be content with the observation that in all the cases of VP ellipsis we looked at, such focusing is indeed found.

In this case of strict identity, then, the two pronouns aren't coreferring, although they have the same referential value in the sense of (6.46) above. This comes out to be a case of semantic focus-matching in the sense of (6.47), since 'viewed from the IP level,' both pronouns denote John for every assignment g.

Turning now to sloppy identity, (6.47) licenses parallel binding in the familiar way, but regardless of the actual choice of indexing:[11]

(6.52)   John saw his sister, and BILL did, too.

    (a) $John_1$ β_2 saw his_2 sister, and $BILL_3$ β_4 did see his_4 sister

    (b) $John_1$ β_2 saw his_2 sister $\Leftrightarrow$ $\boxed{\begin{array}{c}John_1\\ Bill_3\end{array}}$ β_4 did see his_4 sister

(6.53)   Tom wanted Sue to water his plants,

                                      while JOHN wanted MARY to.

    (a) Tom_1 β_2 wanted Sue_5 to water his_2 plants,

            while $JOHN_3$ β_4 wanted $MARY_6$ to water his_4 plants

    (b) Tom_1 β_2 wanted Sue_5 to water his_2 plants

       $\Leftrightarrow$ $\boxed{\begin{array}{c}Tom_1\\ JOHN_3\end{array}}$ β_4 wanted $\boxed{\begin{array}{c}Sue_5\\ MARY_6\end{array}}$ to water his_4 plants

Finally, what of the possibility of arbitrarily changing the indexing in the elided VP, as allowed by (6.43)? Note that this option is now severely constrained by (6.47): if both pronouns are referential, they have to be coreferential, and hence – by PACO – coindexed, in order to ever meet (6.47). If one of them is bound and the other one isn't, (6.47) can only be met if the bound one is eventually bound by (an NP bound by) an NP that is coreferent with the referential one, as in (6.51) (i.e. same referential value). If both are bound, their binding has to be parallel to meet (6.47), as in (6.52) and (6.53). Thus, while (6.44), repeated below, is possible as far as the identity condition (6.43) is concerned, it violates (6.47) because his_4 is not coreferent with $John_1$, nor ever bound by something that is, so focus-matching will fail at every node in the structure, which is therefore correctly ruled out.

(6.54)   *$John_1$ β_2 saw his_2 sister and $Bill_3$ did see his_4 sister, too.

In sum, adopting (6.48) together with the more lenient VP identity condition (6.47) gives us a way of deriving sloppy readings and strict readings with c-commanding antecedents without actually having to stipulate NP Parallelism as in (6.45) and without using the notion of referential value. Coupled with No

---

[10] Cf. Rooth (1992a,b); Schwarzschild (1999); Tomioka (1999) among many others.

[11] If one chooses to use the same index on both binder prefixes (e.g. replace 4 by 2 in these examples), (6.47) is actually met at the $\bar{I}$ level here as well. While this doesn't do any immediate harm in this example, it effectively provides a loophole to circumvent the parallelism requirement otherwise enforced by (6.47). To evaluate whether this is problematic is beyond the scope of this book, though.

Spurious Coindexing, it derives the complex range of strict/sloppy facts in VP ellipsis in full compatibility with the CR and our earlier treatment of exceptional coreference.

An interesting consequence of this setup is that the actual *name* of an index never plays a role in the theory. That is, while in the treatment of VP ellipsis of chapter 5, identity of indices on the overt and elided pronoun was a crucial ingredient to derive strict readings, this is no longer the case in the present, revised, system, nor could it be, given that we allowed mere sameness of referential values as in (6.51) in strict identity cases.

Note furthermore that, by the same token, this treatment of VP ellipsis is compatible with Reinhart's suggestion, mentioned in subsection 6.2.3, to omit indices on referring NPs, including referential pronouns, altogether. Focus-matching, as defined in (6.47), checks sameness of denotation in the semantics, not by looking at indices. It therefore doesn't matter how the theory actually assigns a denotation to referential pronouns. Adopting Reinhart's proposal can actually lead to a simplification of our theory, namely the elimination of No Spurious Coindexing. Consider again a potentially problematic case like (6.55) below:

(6.55)   every boy β_1 loves his$_1$ mother and
                        almost every man β_2 does love his$_1$ mother, too

Under full indexing, (6.55) above meets (6.47) at the $\bar{\text{I}}$-level (*loves his$_1$ mother* is synonymous with *does love his$_1$ mother* for any assignment g), predicting an unattested reading. This had to be blocked by No Spurious Coindexing, which bans the index 1 from being bound in the first conjunct, but referential in the second. If we dispense with referential indices altogether, the second conjunct is ungrammatical independently, because it shows an unbound index, in violation of (6.20b) above. Dropping the index on the elided *his* altogether yields a grammatical LF, but one which doesn't yield synonymous expressions at the $\bar{\text{I}}$ (or any other) level.

6.5.2   Indices on referential pronouns©

In this section I will briefly explore what it would take to adopt Reinhart's idea of eliminating unbound indices completely, even on referential pronouns. As remarked earlier, given our reformulations of the Binding Conditions, there is clearly no *syntactic* reason to maintain referential indices, once we have followed Reinhart to the point of eliminating both indices on full NPs, and Binding Condition C. Our concern in this section, then, will be with the *semantic* consequences of this move.

For the purpose of the discussion, we will refer to a theory as outlined in the summary above (i.e. one that uses the CR/(6.32), doesn't index full NPs, but does index referential pronouns) as the *official theory*. Its Reinhartian extension, in which *all* unbound indices are eliminated, will be called the *R-theory*.

How is a non-indexed element interpreted on the R-theory? Full NPs, including in particular names, don't pose a problem (remember that we only made them assignment dependent in order to derive Binding Condition C effects in the first place). But what about referential pronouns? Technically, we could be content assuming that the pronoun gets assigned a random individual (of the right sex and number, that is). But this would run counter to our intuitions that pronouns are context-dependent.[12] So far we have assumed that the assignment g is all the context we need. But if pronoun meanings are context-dependent, but not assigned by the assignment function g, it is obviously time to revise that assumption. Let us assume therefore that expressions are evaluated with respect to an assignment g and a *context*, c. It is the context that provides referents for indexless expressions, in the way illustrated in (6.56):

(6.56) $[\![she]\!]^{c,g}$ = the most salient female person in c if there is one, undefined otherwise

We don't really need to decide just what kind of object c is, as long as it allows us to define 'maximally salient individual.' Let us consider an example: (6.57) gives the interpretation of a sentence relative to an assignment g and a context c in the official theory and the R-theory (parentheses mark presuppositions):

(6.57)   She$_{(6)}$ is writing a book.
      (a)   official: ($g(6)$ is a female individual and) $g(6)$ is writing a book
      (b)   R-theory: (there is a maximally salient female person in c and) the most salient female person in c is writing a book

Both denotations capture the context-dependency of the pronoun meaning as well as its lexical content. Moreover, the R-theory definition captures an aspect of the pronoun meaning that isn't mentioned in the official one, namely salience. It opens the door for an explanation of why *she* in (6.58) is understood to be Sally, rather than any other female individual: using a name creates a context in which the referent of that name is maximally salient; therefore, a following pronoun will pick up that referent:

(6.58)   I saw Sally this morning. She was riding a bicycle.

No such explanation is available in the official theory (though see the remarks in chapter 2, section 2.4.1). On the other hand, the official theory could easily represent the two most salient interpretations of a text like (6.59) as an ambiguity; *she* can be coindexed with either *Norma* or *Sally*:

(6.59)   Norma saw Sally this morning. She was riding a bicycle.

Within the R-theory, these different interpretations are not discriminated in the grammar proper. Furthermore, it is necessary to assume that there exist at least two different contexts which can result from an utterance of *Norma met Sally*

---

[12] It is also not trivial to implement. After all, $[\![pronoun]\!]^g$ should be a semantic object of type $\langle e \rangle$. But what object would this be?

this morning, which differ in who is the more salient woman in them. More precisely, while for any given context, the coreference pattern in (6.59) is uniquely determined, because the utterance of *Norma met Sally this morning* will make one woman maximally salient, to which *she* in the next sentence will then refer; in two different *initial* contexts, the utterance of *Norma met Sally this morning* might yield a different maximally salient woman, resulting in a different coreference pattern. Since a number of facts outside of the scope of this book become relevant here (for example intonation of the pronoun and its antecedent), we will leave the issue at these remarks.

Note finally that contexts in the R-theory must be able to change sentence internally. Otherwise, two agreeing pronouns within the same sentence would inevitably end up with the same referent. Consider e.g. (6.60):

(6.60)   Norma saw Sally and her son this morning. Her son invited her for tea.

The first and the second *her* in the second sentence of this example can (and, in fact, are most likely to) be interpreted as referring to two different women: Sally and Norma, respectively. To derive this possibility, we need to assume that the context for the two is not the same. In other words, we need to acknowledge that uttering *her son invited* changes the saliency in the context (note that coreference between the two *her*s is grammatically possible since neither c-commands the other; this is also evident from the possibility of a coreferent reading in the structurally parallel example *Her son was helping her with the groceries*). Once again, implementing this properly is beyond the scope of this book, but the idea should be clear by now. Likewise, we cannot explore here what facilitates a change in contextual saliency and what does not (e.g. *invite for dinner* vs. *help with groceries*). Note in passing, though, that for a sentence like *She greeted her* to get an interpretation at all, the saliency change *must* be available.

In sum, making the R-theory semantically adequate requires us to develop a complete theory of context, and reference assignment to pronouns by contexts. While perhaps such a theory would be beneficial in other respects, in particular if it could say more about the preferred interpretation of referential pronouns in particular contexts, it is beyond the scope of this book. Mostly for this reason, we will continue to index all pronouns, bound or free, in our official theory. It should be borne in mind, though, that, apart from technical questions, the choice between the two theories seems to reflect in part our opinion about the more substantial question whether referential pronouns are more akin to bound pronouns (official theory), or to other deictic and, in particular, demonstrative expressions (the R-theory, as sketched here).

Exercise 6.7

English, like many other languages, uses the same elements as bound and free pronouns. Suppose this was universally so; would that provide evidence for/against the R-theory? Suppose some languages did use different forms for the two. Which position would *that* argue in favor of?

6.5.3   More on reflexives©

The arguments presented in this chapter all argued in favor of a version of Binding Theory which regards semantic binding only, and is blind to syntactic binding. We were thus able to simplify the Binding Conditions and avoid disjunctive formulations such as given in chapter 5. For Binding Condition A, which we haven't discussed in this chapter so far, this yields a formulation as in (6.61) (argued for in particular in Grodzinsky and Reinhart [1993]):

(6.61)   Binding Condition A
          A reflexive pronoun needs to be semantically bound in its domain.

The reasoning here is transparent: we know that reflexives are always anaphorically related to a c-commanding NP; but, according to the CR, two NPs cannot, *ceteris paribus*, corefer if one c-commands the other. Therefore, reflexives will have to be sem-bound. The question we may ask now is if there are any empirical effects of (6.61), similar to the obviation effects observed above. For example, (6.61) is often argued for on the grounds that it allows one to derive the following (purported) generalization about VPE:

(6.62)   Reflexives do not allow strict identity readings in VPE.

Let us ask, first, whether (6.62) is empirically correct; and, second, whether it actually follows from (6.61). For English, it has been argued e.g. in Hestvik (1992):1 that a ' . . . strict reading is only weakly acceptable or impossible' in a sentence like (6.63) (a strict reading, recall, would have the second conjunct interpreted as 'Bill defended John'):

(6.63)   John defended himself well, and Bill did, too.   (?*strict)

On the other hand, Sag (1976) claims that (6.64a) is acceptable on a strict reading (i.e. Sandy could imagine Betsy dating Bernie), and speakers report similar judgments on sentences like (6.64b) and (6.64c):

(6.64)   (a)   Betsy couldn't imagine herself dating Bernie, but Sandy could.
          (b)   Bill was scared to introduce himself to Monica. Thankfully, the officer
                 had already agreed to.
          (c)   I could see myself having a romantic dinner with Winona Ryder, but
                 my girlfriend couldn't.

Cross-linguistically, strict readings with reflexives are attested, e.g. in Icelandic, Norwegian, Finnish, and Swedish:[13]

---

[13] See Thráinsson (1992):60; and Huang (2000):99f.

(6.65)   Jón₁ sagði að þú hefðir svikið   sig₁ og Pétur gerði það líka.

J.   said   that you had   betrayed self and Peter did   so   too
(Icelandic)
'Jon said that you had betrayed yourself and Peter said so (that you had be-trayed Jon/Peter), too.' (strict or sloppy)

Supposing that sentences like these are the rule, rather than the exceptions (contrary to e.g. Hestvik [1992]), would (6.61) rule them out? No! As we have seen in section 6.5.1 above, strict identity readings can, and usually do, involve sem-binding in the overt VP (cf. e.g. [6.42] and the discussion around it). Therefore, the problematic generalization (6.62) doesn't follow, even if (6.61) is assumed. A licit LF for e.g. (6.64a) is given in (6.66) (as in section 6.5.1, I continue to index full NPs for ease of discussion):

(6.66)   Betsy₂ β₁ couldn't imagine herself₁ dating Bernie, but SANDY₃ β₁ could_F imagine her₂ dating Bernie.

SANDY_F 3 β₁ could imagine her₂ dating Bernie f-matches *Betsy₂ β₁ couldn't imagine herself₁ dating Bernie* ('replace' *SANDY* by *Betsy* and *COULD* by *couldn't*), making (6.66) a well-formed ellipsis structure given the assumptions made in section 6.5.1 above. In other words, (6.61) can be adopted *despite* the fact that (6.62) is too strong, because it doesn't entail it anyway.

It should be mentioned, though, that this state of affairs is not without problems either. For one thing, it *is* true that strict readings involving reflexives seem much harder to get than with non-reflexives, a fact that remains to be captured given the present proposal.

For another, as Hestvik (1992) shows convincingly, strict readings with reflexives are much more readily acceptable in *subordinate ellipsis* such as (6.67):

(6.67)   John defends himself better than Peter.   (sloppy or strict)

Speakers immediately accept a reading of (6.67) on which John defended himself better than Peter defended John, i.e. a strict one. This contrast is reported to be even stronger with the Dutch reflexive *zichzelf*, which doesn't allow strict readings in coordinations like (6.68a) at all, but is fine, just like its English counterpart, in subordinated ellipsis like (6.68b):[14]

(6.68)   (a)   Jan wast   zichzelf en Piet ook.   (Dutch)
               J. washes himself and P.   also
               'Jan washes himself, and Piet does, too.'   (sloppy/*strict)

---

[14] Everaert (1986):254; these examples, as well as those in n. 15, are all found in the discussion of VP ellipsis. It should be noted, though, that they actually resemble the English *stripping* or *bare argument ellipsis* construction (*John defends himself better than Peter.*) more than English VP ellipsis. To the extent that these constructions behave differently (see e.g. Kennedy and Lidz [2001]), conclusions based on these examples have to be taken with a grain of salt.

(b) Zij verdedigde zichzelf beter dan Peter.
     she defended   herself better than P.
     'She defended herself better than Peter.'   (sloppy/strict)

As Hestvik points out, the crucial element in subordinate ellipsis that is lacking from coordinate ellipsis is that the antecedent of the overt reflexive actually
c-commands the ellipsis site, and can thus bind the pronoun in the elided VP. In
present terms, the elided pronoun can be semantically bound by the antecedent
of the overt pronoun, as is the case in the LF in (6.69):

(6.69)   John$_1$ β_1 [defends himself$_1$ better than Peter$_2$ defends him(self)$_1$]

It seems that there is at least a *preference* for an elided pronoun to be semantically bound, if its overt counterpart is a reflexive, be it in its own conjunct, as in
sloppy identity coordinate ellipsis, or across the board, as in (6.69). Again, this
preference is not captured by the rules we have so far.[15]

Finally, it should be noted that (6.61) *does* make very clear predictions for the
case of focus constructions, namely that focus constructions involving reflexives – unlike those involving non-reflexive pronouns – are unambiguous:

(6.70)   (a)   Only IDI voted for his proposal.
           (i)   strict: only IDI$_{1,F}$ voted for his$_1$ proposal
           (ii)   sloppy: only IDI$_{(1),F}$ β_1 voted for his$_1$ proposal

---

[15] To make things worse, a whole number of reflexive markers cross-linguistically don't allow for
strict identity with reflexives at all, not even in subordinate ellipsis, among them the verbal reflexive suffixes *-utu* and *koḷ* in Finnish and Kannada (Sells *et al.* [1987]:178; Lidz [2001]:129),
the pronouns *zich* and *se/sebe* in Dutch and Serbo-Croatian (Sells *et al.* [1987] [123]), and even
the long-distance reflexive *zibun* in Japanese (Sells *et al.* [1987]:186):

(i)   Jussi puolusta -utu -i   paremmin kuin Pekka.
           J.   defended self PAST better   than P.-NOM
(ii)   Rashmi Siita-ginta cheenage tann-annu rakshisi -koḷ -utt   -aaḷe.
           R.   S.-COMP   better   self-ACC defend -self NONPAST 3SGFEM
(iii)   Zij verdedigde zich beter dan Peter.
           she defended   self better than P.
(iv)   Petar se branio   bolje nego Ana.
           P.   self defended better than A.
(v)   Petar je branio   sebe bolje nego Ana.
           P.   AUX defended self better than A.
(vi)   Taroo wa   Jiroo yori zibun   -o   umaku bengosi -ta.
           T.   TOPIC Jiroo than himself -ACC better defend -PAST
           'Jussi/ Rashmi/ she/ Petar/ Taroo defends/defended self better than Pekka/ Sita/
           Peter/ Ana/ Jiroo does/did (defend self/*her/*him).'

(According to Huang [2000]:99f.,141, Hindi/Urdu, Marathi, and Telugu don't allow strict identity either, but all his examples involve coordinate ellipsis.) It is interesting to note that verbal
reflexive suffixes do not generally block strict identity, as they do in Kannada and Finnish: at least
in subordinate ellipsis, the reflexive affix *-dzi* in Chicheŵa (Sells *et al.* [1987]:187; Mchombo
[1993a]:195) allows for strict identity.

(b)   Only IDI voted for himself.
    (i)   ∗strict: only $IDI_{1,F}$ voted for $himself_1$
    (ii)   sloppy: only $IDI_{(1),F}$ β_1 voted for $himself_1$

As discussed in chapter 5, section 5.2, semantic binding as in the (ii) examples results in a 'sloppy' reading, according to which no one else voted for themselves/their own proposal. Without semantic binding the reflexive and its antecedent simply corefer, resulting in a 'sloppy' reading: no one else voted for Idi/Idi's proposal. If reflexives needed to be sem-bound, this latter construal should be out for the reflexive case, given that the reflexive in (6.70bi) is syntactically, but not semantically, bound. In other words, (6.70b), unlike (6.70a), is predicted to be unambiguous. This, however, does not accord with speakers' intuitions. While the sloppy reading for (6.70b) is generally preferred, the strict one is clearly judged possible. As far as I know, this wrong prediction has not been addressed in the pertinent literature. The only immediate way to capture this behavior would seem to be to reformulate Binding Condition A so as to require that reflexives be *either* semantically *or* syntactically bound within their local domain, accepting the fact that Binding Conditions A and B are simply not on a par.

In sum, then, whether (6.61) is the correct way to state Binding Condition A seems unclear. At least under the generalizations about VPE put forward in section 6.5.1, it predicts that strict and sloppy readings should generally be possible in VPE, which is a good approximation to the facts, though not obviously correct. Its predictions for focus constructions, on the other hand, are arguably wrong.

It is, of course, conceivable that the assumptions in section 6.5.1 are in need of changing, and that strict identity *does* require coreference in the antecedent clause as well as the ellipsis site. In that case, strict readings are predicted to be generally *im*possible in coordinated ellipsis, but possible in subordinated ellipsis (the position advocated in Hestvik [1992]). But that assumption doesn't help with the focus constructions either, and is faced with the problem of acceptable strict readings in coordinate ellipsis such as (6.64a) and (6.65). It seems that, in either case, something is missing from the picture as of yet.

Exercise 6.8

Throughout the discussion in this section we have assumed that the pronoun in the ellipsis site doesn't itself impose any syntactic Binding Conditions. A conceivable alternative, explored e.g. in Kitagawa (1991), is that the elided pronoun itself must be a reflexive if its overt counterpart is, and that Binding Condition A directly applies to the elided pronoun in its local clause.

(1)   Discuss the predictions of such a proposal for the cases discussed here (coordinate ellipsis, subordinate ellipsis, focus constructions), and show where it is advantageous and where it is problematic.

(2)   Try to construct examples that could help you to determine whether
             similar assumptions would be reasonable for Binding Conditions B
             and C. (For much more on this see the discussion of 'vehicle change'
             in Fiengo and May [1994].)

Exercise 6.9

What are the possible interpretations for the elided pronoun in the examples in (6.71)? Discuss these data in the light of the various proposals floated
around in this section. What conclusions, if any, can you draw?

(6.71)   (a)   John wanted to introduce himself to Mary, but Carl hoped that Bill
                    would.
             (b)   John wanted to introduce his plans to Mary, but Carl hoped that Bill
                    would.

7 Descriptive pronouns and individual concepts

7.1 Anaphoric pronouns that don't corefer

7.1.1 Introduction

So far, we have assumed that a pronoun can be either semantically bound or free. In the latter case, it might or might not have the same referent as some other pronoun, name, or definite NP. Consider now (7.1) on a reading where *he* is anaphorically related to the direct object of the preceding sentence:

(7.1)   Janet brought $\left\{ \begin{array}{l} \text{him} \\ \text{Fido} \\ \text{her dog} \\ \text{a dog} \\ \text{exactly one dog} \end{array} \right\}$ to the party. But *he* had to wait outside.

Evidently, *he* in (7.1) cannot be semantically bound by its antecedent, given that they occur in different sentences (remember that c-command is a precondition for binding). If the antecedent is *him* (which, in turn, is likely to have a full NP antecedent in the context), the two pronouns corefer, and are coindexed. If it is *Fido* or *her dog*, which we take to be referring expressions, too, the anaphoric dependency involved is again coreference (which *could* be marked in the grammar by coindexing, though we saw in chapter 6 that indexing full NPs, even referential ones, can be omitted). However, neither *a dog* nor *exactly one dog* refer – they are quantified noun phrases (QNPs) – and thus cannot, *a fortiori*, corefer with *he*, given that they are genuinely quantificational NPs.

What we see, then, is that, as things stand, all these anaphoric dependencies, with the exception of the pronoun–pronoun case, are not represented in the grammar at all.[1] The pronoun in the second sentence is a referential pronoun, which, depending on its index, can refer to any individual, including Fido the dog.[2]

---

[1] As discussed in chapter 6, sections 6.2.3 and 6.5.2, even pronoun–pronoun cases need not be, as far as Binding Conditions are concerned.

[2] It is worth while to stress that the question of the grammatical representation of anaphoric relations is independent of the question of preferred reference. That is, even if we did express the anaphoric dependencies above by means of coindexing, we would still need a theory of indexing that explains why coindexing is so strongly preferred, i.e. why *he* almost inevitably has to refer to Fido rather than anyone else.

While there is nothing wrong with this formally, there is at least a persistent intuition that the pronoun *he* in some sense *stands for* a repetition of the description *her dog*, or goes proxy for a description like *the (one) dog Janet brought to the party*. But, honorable though such intuitions are, is there any way to *show* that there is more to the anaphoric dependency in (7.1) than so far assumed? Put the other way around: assume, for the sake of the argument, that *he* does in fact 'expand' to a full-fledged definite NP at LF. What empirical difference would that make? None for the case of (7.1) – not at least until we have a restrictive theory of *which* description a pronoun expands into in a given context. But we can construe cases in which a definite should allow for more readings than a plain referential pronoun; we will turn to these cases now.

Exercise 7.1

Suppose, contrary to what was assumed above, that *a dog* and *exactly one dog* can somehow bind the pronoun in the second sentence. That is, assume an LF for these cases which essentially looks like (1) (more realistically, the first *him$_1$* should be a trace of sorts, but since we haven't discussed the binding of traces yet, and nothing hinges on this here, we will go with this representation):

(7.2) $\left\{ \begin{array}{l} \text{a dog} \\ \text{exactly one dog} \end{array} \right\}$ β_1 [[Janet brought him$_1$ to the party] but [he$_1$ had to wait outside]]

Derive the truth conditions for these sentences, assuming the following NP meanings. Then argue whether the derived truth conditions are intuitively adequate. They shouldn't be for at least one case; show this using concrete scenarios about dogs brought to the party.

(7.3)   (a) $[\![\text{a dog}]\!]^g = \lambda P$. there is at least one dog x s.t. $P(x) = 1$
          (b) $[\![\text{exactly one dog}]\!]^g = \lambda P$. there is one and only one dog x s.t. $P(x) = 1$

7.1.2   Pronouns as descriptions

Evans (1980):342 points out that the conditional in (7.4) has a natural reading on which *a man* or *a man in the garden* antecedes *him*:

(7.4)   If there is *a man* in the garden, John will tell *him* to leave.

Note, however, that the antecedent clause of the conditional does not talk about a particular man in the garden. And, accordingly, there is no particular referent for *him* that would yield the intuitively correct truth conditions for this sentence. If we interpret *him* as a full-fledged NP, on the other hand, we get the intuited reading:

(7.5)   If there is a man in the garden, John will tell **the man who is in the garden** to leave.

The same point can be illustrated using the following variant of our original example:

(7.6)   Every woman brought *her dog/exactly one dog* to the party, but left *him* outside.

Here we have embedded sentences of the type in (7.1) under another QNP. Accurate paraphrases for these sentences seem to be those in (7.7):

(7.7)   (a)   *every woman* brought *her* dog to the party but left ***her* dog** outside.
         (b)   *every woman* brought exactly one dog to the party but left **the dog *she* brought to the party** outside.

Starting with Geach (1962), pronouns like in (7.7a), which can be replaced by a literal repetition of their antecedent NPs, have been called *pronouns of laziness*; pronouns like those in (7.7b), whose paraphrase involves a description that has to be 'distilled' from the preceding context, were christened *e-type pronouns* in Evans (1977). In the discussion to follow we will give the same analysis to pronouns of laziness and e-type pronouns, and use the term e-type pronoun indiscriminately to refer to pronouns of laziness and 'proper' e-type pronouns alike.

Can we get meanings as in (7.7) by assuming that *him* is a referential pronoun? Clearly not, because no particular dog can serve as the referent of that pronoun. Rather, dogs need to covary with women, which is what makes the paraphrases in (7.7) work so well, in which the pronouns are replaced by definite descriptions containing a variable bound by *every woman*.

Can we assume instead that *him* is a bound pronoun? No again, since for one thing, *her dog/exactly one dog* doesn't c-command *him* and, hence, cannot bind it. For another, even if it somehow could, the resulting truth conditions would be wrong at least in the case of (7.7b), namely something like (7.8):

(7.8)   for every woman x, there is one and only one dog y such that x brought y to the party and left y outside

In (7.8), *exactly one dog* takes scope over both conjuncts, which it has to to bind the pronoun in the second one. But, as a result of that, the sentence is true as long as the number of dogs brought to the party and left outside was exactly one. In other words, a woman could have brought any number of dogs to the party, as long as she left exactly one of them outside. But these are not the truth conditions this sentence intuitively has (rather, they would correspond to a sentence like *Every woman has exactly one dog she brought to the party and left outside*). Rather, there must be exactly one dog per woman that she brought to the party, and that dog must have had to wait outside. In other words, *exactly one dog* must crucially not scope over the second conjunct and, hence, *him* cannot be a bound pronoun (cf. section 7.1.1 above).

Examples like these prompted Evans (1977, 1980) to conclude that it must be possible actually to interpret pronouns as definite descriptions. That is, the paraphrases in (7.7) and (7.5) – or something very similar to them – are the correct *representations* for (7.6) and (7.4).

There are two extreme ways of formalizing this idea in our grammar: either
we assume that these pronouns transform into full-fledged definite NPs at LF,
i.e. (7.7a) and (7.7b) essentially *are* the LFs for the sentences in (7.6); or we
do this in the semantics, assuming that a pronoun such as him_n is, or at least
can be interpreted not as $g(n)$, but as $f(g(n))$, where f is some contextually
given function from individuals to individuals, e.g. one that maps individuals to
the dogs they brought. The specific proposal we will adopt here is somewhere
in the middle between these two. Following Cooper (1979), we assume that the
pronouns are represented as full NPs at LF, but that their terminal nodes are
filled by special, phonologically inert, elements. Concretely, the LF representation for an e-type pronoun will look as in (7.9) (cf. also Heim and Kratzer
[1998]:ch. 11):

(7.9)   Pronoun expansion: pron $\Rightarrow_{LF}$

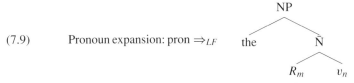

(a) $[\![R_m]\!]^g = g(R_m)$, where $g(R_j) \in D_{e,et}$ for all j
(b) $[\![v_n]\!]^g = g(n)$

According to these definitions, R will always be a contextually determined relation (i.e. an element in $D_{e,et}$). The symbol v is an empty pronoun, i.e. it denotes
the same as $he/she/it_n$ for all g and n (ignoring gender, of course). In a context in
which $g(R_8)$ is the dog-of–relation, *the R_8 v_3* will denote the unique element in
the set of $g(3)$'s dogs, that is: $g(3)$'s dog. Its denotation is thus the same as that
of the full NPs *the dog of hers$_3$* or, less awkwardly, *her$_3$ dog*.

In the examples of proper e-type pronouns, the relation R is more complicated.
For (7.7a) it must be the 'be-a-dog-brought-to-the-party-by' relation, formally:
$[\lambda x \lambda y . y$ is a dog and x brought y to the party$]$. The meaning of the pronoun as a
whole will be 'the (unique) dog $g(1)$ brought to the party':

(7.10)   every woman β_1 $[_{VP}[_{VP}$ brought exactly one dog$]$ but $[_{VP}$ left **[the R_3/dog
             brought by** v_1**]** outside$]]$

The variable v_1 in (7.10) is bound by β_1, that is, by *every woman*, which properly
c-commands it. The variable R_3 on the other hand is free, hence contextually
determined. In (7.10) and the examples to follow, I have indicated the relevant
assignment to the variable R – here: *dog brought by* – next to the variable in
the LF; note crucially, though, that this is just a convenient notation. Nothing
in the 'official' representation – *the R_3 v_1* – indicates that R_3 is anaphorically
related in any way to the previous clause. That is, we did not, for example, write
[exactly one dog]$_3$ to indicate what the value of R_3 is. This is so because for one
thing, *exactly one dog* is a QNP and, hence, does not denote an individual nor a
relation; for another, the actual relation assigned to R_3 – $[\lambda x . \lambda y . y$ is a dog and x
brought y to the party$]$ – is not the denotation of any constituent, not the NP, nor
the N̄ within it (that is what makes it a true e-type pronoun). For this reason, and

because there are no known instances of semantically bound relational variables, we treat the assignment of values to relational variables as a purely pragmatic phenomenon.[3]

The first conjunct *brought exactly one dog to the party* must establish the relation in the discourse, i.e. make it salient (or somehow induce that some R_n denotes that relation). We will assume this much and ignore the question of how exactly this saliency of the relation comes about, a question known in the literature as the question of the *formal link*.[4]

Exercise 7.2

Other common labels for pronouns of the kind discussed here are *paycheck pronouns* and *donkey pronouns*, each owing their names to the classical example used to present them:[5]

(7.11)   (a)   The woman who deposited *her paycheck* in the bank was wiser than the woman who deposited *it* in the Brown University Employees' Credit Union.

           (b)   Every farmer who owns *a donkey* beats *it*.

Give paraphrases for the examples in (7.11a) and (7.11b). Decide for each whether it is, descriptively, a pronoun of laziness or an e-type pronoun (cf. the discussion in section 7.1.2 above).

Exercise 7.3

Give an LF for the examples in (7.12), and specify the denotation of the relation variables R. What accounts for the ungrammaticality with *no*, *every*, and *two*?

(7.12) $\left\{\begin{array}{l}\text{One/only one/some journalist}\\ *\text{No/*every journalist}\\ *\text{Two journalists}\end{array}\right\}$ admire(s) Kennedy. *He* is very junior.

---

[3] An alternative, in the spirit of Reinhart's proposal (1983a) regarding free pronouns discussed in sections 6.2.3 and 6.5.2 of chapter 6, would leave R altogether unindexed and let its denotation be determined through a *context parameter c*, roughly as 'the most salient relation in c.' At present, nothing hinges on this choice. Since the variable R is not of type $\langle e \rangle$, and since its index is not an index on an NP (or a binder prefix), it is by definition not subject to Binding Theory. There cannot be any interactions between indices on relation variables and pronouns, full NPs or traces. Whether other conditions apply for these variables, and if they can be bound at all, is a topic beyond the scope of this book.

[4] Recent formal approaches to this issue include the proposal in Elbourne (2000, 2001) to treat all e-type pronouns as pronouns of laziness and derive them as instances of N̄-deletion, as well as van Rooy (1997, 2001)'s extension of dynamic semantics to include relational discourse referents.

[5] (7.11a) is the example used in Jacobson (2000):87; Geach's original example is the, with hindsight rather gender stereotypical, (i):

(i)   John gave *his paycheck* to his wife, but Bill gave *it* to his mistress.

Exercise 7.4

Explain the following contrast:

(7.13)   (a) *No one brought *a blanket*, so we can't sit on *it*.

(b) I can't believe this house has *no bathroom*. *It*'s got to be somewhere!

Exercise 7.5

Consider the distribution of singular and plural pronouns anteceded by a QNP (7.14). What is the generalization? Can you predict when a singular and when a plural pronoun is used?

(7.14)   (a) $\left\{\begin{array}{l}\text{At least one}\\\text{Less than five}\\\text{More than zero}\\\text{One or more}\\\text{Between one and six}\end{array}\right\}$ journalist(s) left.

(b) $\left\{\begin{array}{l}\textit{He}\text{ was}\\\textit{They}\text{ were}\end{array}\right\}$ very drunk.

Does your generalization predict the correct form for NPs headed by *an even number of*?

Exercise 7.6

Describe the pattern found in the examples in (7.15):

(7.15) $\left\{\begin{array}{l}\text{very few}\\\text{(almost) no}\\\text{*half of the}\end{array}\right\}$ journalists came to Kennedy's party. *They* stayed at home to watch the world series.

Exercise 7.7

Sentences involving e-type pronouns, particularly pronouns of laziness, bear a certain resemblance to cases of VP ellipsis. A constituent containing a pronoun is present at LF, but not at s-structure, and that constituent is (more or less) 'copied from' a linguistic antecedent. With this in mind, discuss the following non-existing readings for the sentences (7.16a) (from Sternefeld [1993]:948) through (7.16c). Provide LFs that would yield the reading in question, and indicate what would be necessary to block them:

(7.16)   (a) I don't know his wife but everyone loves her. (not: '... but *everyone* loves *his (own) wife*')

(b) Every woman testified that some girl took her purse and then threw *it* away. (not: '...took the girl's purse and threw the woman's purse away' nor vice versa)

(c) (i) Bastian buried his share of the money, while Claude hid *it* in a hollow tree trunk (OK: *it* = Claude's share of the money)

(ii) Bastian buried his share of the money, while the policeman who interrogated Claude thinks *it* is hidden in a hollow tree trunk (not: *it* = Claude's share of the money)

7.1.3   **E-type pronouns of varying arity**

Consider the example in (7.17):

(7.17)   Almost every boy wants his present girlfriend to keep the letters he wrote
          her, but no boy wants any ex-girlfriend to publish them.

The pronoun *them* is naturally understood to denote 'the letters he wrote her',
i.e. it contains two dependent variables. Its formal representation could be *[the
R_n^3 v_m v_j]*, where $g(R_m^3)$ is a (contextually salient) three-place relation – here:
[$\lambda x.\lambda y.\lambda z.z$ are letters x wrote to y] – and v_m and v_j are bound by *no boy* and
any ex-girlfriend, respectively.

More in general there appears to be a whole family of e-type pronoun meanings, differing in the arity of the relational variable, as well as the number of
individual variables provided to saturate it. Formally, the representation of the
variable has to be augmented so as to show its arity (the superscript on R_m^3 above,
indicating it ranges over three-place relations), and clause (7.9a) above has to be
modified so that the assignment function assigns a relation of the appropriate
arity to any relational variable (i.e. $g(R_j^2) \in D_{e,et}$, $g(R_j^3) \in D_{e,\langle e,et\rangle}$, etc.).

There is probably no upper limit to the arity of the relation, though examples
of more than two- or three-place relations will be rare and hard to process. Is
there a lower limit? Consider our original example (7.1) repeated here, again:

(7.18)   Janet brought *a/exactly one dog* to the party. But *he* had to wait outside.

We concluded at the very beginning of this chapter that *he* could simply be a
referring pronoun in this sentence. On the other hand, nothing prevents us from
assuming that *he* is expanded to *[the R_n^1]*, where R_n^1 is a contextually salient property, here: [$\lambda x.x$ is a dog brought to the party by Janet]. On this analysis, (7.18)
involves an e-type pronoun, but one with a 'one-place relation' variable, i.e. a
property; we'll call such e-type pronouns *constant e-type pronouns*.

Can we distinguish between those two analyses – referential vs. constant e-
type pronoun – on empirical grounds? Evans (1980) argues that we can in plural
cases: a sentence like (7.19) implies that Harry vaccinates *all* John's sheep:

(7.19)   John owns some sheep, and Harry vaccinates them in the spring.

Suppose that *them* is a constant e-type pronoun, represented at LF as *[the R^1]*; if
the context assigns to R^1 the property 'be a sheep owned by John,' the whole NP
is interpreted as 'the sheep John owns' (we ignore the exact semantics of plural
definite NPs; suffice it that the e-type pronoun means the same as its overt plural
counterpart). This accounts for the above-mentioned intuition that Harry needs
to vaccinate *all* (i.e. *the*) sheep owned by John.

The same does not hold if we assume that *them* is a plain variable pronoun.
Suppose that John owns three sheep, Albert, Bruno, and Clarissa, of which Harry
vaccinates the former two, but not the latter. Assume furthermore that *them* is
indexed 3 (it is an ordinary referring pronoun), and $g(3)$ is the plurality consisting
of Albert and Bruno. Since it is the case that there is an x, x a plurality of sheep

John owns, and that Harry vaccinates $g(3)$, the sentence is predicted to be true, even though our intuition is that the sentence is false in that scenario.[6]

To allow a (constant) e-type analysis for this case, however, doesn't completely remove this problem. The somewhat mysterious fact about these constructions is that even if we have convinced ourselves that an e-type analysis, and only an e-type analysis, can derive the correct truth conditions for (7.19), this does not yet explain why the other, weaker, reading using a referential pronoun is absent. Nothing in our system blocks the alternative LF under which *them* is a non-e-type pronoun which simply refers to a subplurality of John's sheep. To exclude this, we'd have to make additional assumptions about what makes a plurality accessible or salient as a referent for a free pronoun, which we are not in a position to do here. The most radical amendment of this sort would obviously be to say that referential pronouns can *never* occur with just a quantificational antecedent. That is, every sequence of the form *a/one/only one/some/few N ... he/she/it/they ...* must be analyzed as involving constant e-type pronouns, rather than referential pronouns.[7]

Exercise 7.8

The following so-called *crossing coreference* sentence allows for a reading on which *it* is anaphorically related to the object NP, and *him* to the subject NP:

(7.20)   Every/No boy who found it could keep the prize made for him.

(1)   Explain why this sentence was used as an argument against the idea that *every* pronoun is replaced by the NP it is anaphorically related to at LF (cf. Bach [1970]).

(2)   Find an LF representation for (7.20) which captures the pertinent reading. Be explicit about the values assigned to any variables within e-type pronouns (cf. Jacobson [1977, 2000], also Higginbotham and May [1981]; Keenan [1972]).

Exercise 7.9

As things stand, we effectively assume an ambiguity in pronoun meanings between e-type (with or without a variable inside), and variable

---

[6] Note incidentally that there is no guarantee that the x instantiating the truth of the first clause in (7.19) is actually the *maximal* plurality of sheep John owns; instantiating x as the plurality consisting of Albert and Bruno alone would make the first clause true just the same. This alone, however, doesn't pose any problems.

[7] In chapter 2, section 2.4.1 and chapter 6, section 6.5.2 we have speculated a little on the correct treatment of free pronouns, sketching a variable-like treatment (chapter 2) as well as a salience-based one (chapter 6). E-type pronouns, as implemented here, are a hybrid form, in that we treated their descriptive content as variable-like, but their actual choice of referent is partly salience-based (to the same extent, that is, that definite NPs are). Extending the theory of e-type pronouns to cover *all* occurrences of free pronouns via the use of constant e-type pronouns, as considered above, thus provides something of a 'third way' between the analyses sketched previously.

(bound or free). As discussed above, free variable pronouns can always be replaced by constant e-type pronouns. Devise a meaning for bound pronouns that has the form of an e-type pronoun (i.e. *the $R^n v_1 \ldots v_m$*) that can function like a simple bound variable pronoun. Demonstrate the workings of this using the sentence *every woman thinks she will win.*

7.2   Unknown and mistaken identity

Let us now turn to a second class of NPs that seem neither referential nor bound. Consider sentences like the following, which have long been pointed out as a challenge for BT:

(7.21)   (a)   (I think they gave my paper to Zelda Jones for review.) The reviewer praises Zelda to high heavens (and totally ignores my stuff).
           (b)   Scandalous! The guy in the hallway is putting on John's coat!

Take (7.21a): if the reviewer is, in fact, Zelda Jones, as the speaker insinuates, *the reviewer* and *Zelda* corefer. The sentence should thus violate the Binding Theory: under our earlier set of assumptions, because coreference requires coindexing, and if *the reviewer* and *Zelda* are coindexed, the former illicitly binds the latter, violating Binding Condition C; under the theory in chapter 6, because *Zelda* corefers with the c-commanding *the reviewer*, it should thus be replaced by a bound pronoun, on pain of violating the Coreference rule.

Similarly, if the speaker observes a man putting on his coat, without realizing that that man is actually John, she can felicitously utter (7.21b). But since, in actuality, *the guy in the hallway* and *John* refer to the same person, shouldn't this be a violation of the CR?

There is an immediate response to this challenge, which, for the case of (7.21a), we can phrase as follows (the account for [7.21b] is parallel):

(7.22)   Common sense account of (7.21a):
           Regardless of whether *the reviewer* and *Zelda* refer to the same person *in reality*, the speaker of (7.21a) conceptualized them as different entities, so there is no issue of BT involved. That is, Binding Theory regards *intended or presupposed coreference*, not *accidental coreference*.

There is definitely a ring of truth to this common sense account, but things aren't as simple as that. If NPs refer, then any two NPs either corefer or they don't. There is no place for a concept such as 'conceptualizing the same individual as two different entities.' If we want to incorporate this notion into our formal theory, we have to give up the simple idea that the denotation of an NP is its referent, and that will inevitably lead to a very different theory of coreference and binding.

According to Reinhart (1983a,b), sentences like (7.21a) provide additional evidence in favor of the Coreference rule (as opposed to Binding Condition C). She points out that there is a very clear intuition that *The reviewer praises Zelda to high heavens* has a different interpretation from its bound variable counterpart in (7.23):

(7.23)   The reviewer praises herself to high heavens.

According to the Coreference rule, (7.23) would block (7.21a) only if they had indistinguishable interpretations; since they don't, both sentences are predicted to be grammatical. But, once again, if *the reviewer* and *Zelda* both simply denote Zelda Jones, we have no explanation for *why* (7.21a) and (7.23) are felt to have different interpretations; both should denote the proposition that Zelda Jones praised Zelda Jones. To get a better understanding of what is going on, it will be useful to step back and scrutinize our notions of *meaning* and *reference* in cases that don't involve binding issues.

7.2.1   Meaning and reference

Constant and non-constant reference

Consider inspector Callas talking to detective Brunswinkle at the crime scene, saying:

(7.24)   The murderer left a shoe behind.

Who is the referent of *the murderer*? If Callas is correct in assuming that there is a murderer (rather than a murderer collective, or an accident that happens to look like a murder), *the murderer* clearly has a referent. However, Callas doesn't know who this referent is, and therefore we cannot claim that Callas uttered, say, the proposition 'Bobby left a shoe behind,' even if Bobby, in fact, was the murderer.

Let us say that an *information state* is an assemblage of ways things could be. It is a set of *possibilities*. Each possibility has one and only one murderer (for the pertinent case) in it. We can associate with each person a particular information state, which reflects that person's knowledge (sometimes called their *doxastic alternatives*). The possibilities in Callas' (as well as Brunswinkle's) information state differ in who the murderer is, but there is one and only one in each. With respect to a single possibility, *the murderer* refers to a particular individual. With respect to Callas' (or Brunswinkle's) information state as a whole, it doesn't.

We can derivatively say that an NP refers with respect to an information state as a whole, but just in case it refers to the same individual in every possibility of that information state. Assume that our detectives have identified the victim as Sir Gandalf, then the NP *the victim* refers to Sir Gandalf in each possibility in their information states, and derivatively, with respect to the information states as a whole. We can say that *the victim* has a *constant reference* in these information states.

What determines the information state with respect to which a sentence must be evaluated? We can assume for the moment that that information state, which we call the *contextual information state* (IS^C), consists of all and only those possibilities which at least one participant in the conversation thinks could be reality. We can now rephrase the common sense account of (7.21a) more precisely as follows:

(7.25)   NP and NP′ corefer in the sense of the CR iff NP denotes the same individual as NP′ in all possibilities of the contextual information state IS^C.

The speaker who utters (7.21a) (*The reviewer praises Zelda to high heavens*), instead of using a reflexive (as in [7.23]) can do so despite the CR because the identity of Zelda Jones and the reviewer is not yet an established fact, i.e the contextual information state between her and her addressee(s) contains possibilities in which someone else is the reviewer. Before going on, it is worth while to note that our judgments about these examples remain the same if we replace *the reviewer* by *she*:

(7.26)   (I think they gave my paper to Zelda Jones for review.) She praises Zelda to high heavens (and totally ignores my stuff).

Again, the intuition is that *she* somehow *means* 'the reviewer,' and since the identity of the reviewer and Zelda is not established in IS^C, the two NPs *she* and *Zelda* don't corefer in the sense of the CR, as put down in (7.25). But note that, for this to go through, we have to assume that pronouns, just like definite NPs, must be able to refer to different individuals in different possibilities. That is, for a given assignment g, $[\![she_n]\!]^g$ cannot simply be the individual $g(n)$, but has to be something else. We will return to this in the formalization below.

Formalization I: definite NPs

In order to implement the intuitions above, we have to introduce the notions of possibilities and information states into our formal theory. First, we have to relativize the denotation of expressions to possibilities. Although we are only interested in noun phrase meanings, we'll assume that *any* meaning is relativized to possibilities. Since possibilities are commonly referred to as *possible worlds*, we'll write $[\![\alpha]\!]^{w,g}$ to mean 'the denotation of α relative to assignment g in possibility (world) w,' e.g.:

(7.27)   (a) $[\![reviewer]\!]^{w,g} = \lambda x.x$ is a reviewer in w
           (b) $[\![murderer]\!]^{w,g} = \lambda x.x$ is a murderer in w
           (c) $[\![know]\!]^{w,g} = \lambda y \lambda x.x$ knows y in w
           (d) $[\![the\ reviewer]\!]^{w,g} =$ the unique individual x such that $[\![reviewer]\!]^{w,g}(x) = 1$, if there is one, undefined otherwise (i.e. the unique reviewer in w)
           (e) $[\![the\ reviewer\ knows\ the\ murderer]\!]^{w,g} = 1$ iff the unique reviewer in w knows in w the unique murderer in w

For entire sentences, we can now define their *intension* relative to an information state (and an assignment) as:

(7.28) $Int_{IS}^g(S) =_{def} \{w \in IS \mid [\![S]\!]^{w,g} = 1\}$

Let W be the set of all possibilities/worlds, however unlikely, then $Int_W^g(S)$ is the *proposition* expressed by S (relative to g), i.e. the set of all possibilities in which S is true.

We can now define the notion of '(in)distinguishable interpretation,' as used in the Coreference rule and its generalization (repeated here):

(7.29)   Sentences S_1 and S_2 have indistinguishable interpretations in context C = $\langle g,IS \rangle$ iff $Int_{IS}^g(S_1) = Int_{IS}^g(S_2)$, else they have distinguishable interpretations.

(7.30)   Coreference rule (CR), revised:
α cannot corefer with β in S in context C if an indistinguishable interpretation in C can be generated by replacing α with a variable bound by β.

(7.31)   Have Local Binding!, revised:
For any two NPs α and β in S in context C, if α could bind β (i.e. if it c-commands β and β is not bound in α's c-command domain already), α must bind β, unless that results in a distinguishable interpretation in C.

We thus simply need to understand '(in)distinguishable interpretation' to mean '(in)distinguishable interpretation in C.'

For NPs that have constant reference with respect to (w.r.t.) an information state, it will be useful to speak of the *referent of an NP in an IS*, which is simply the x such that $[\![NP]\!]^{w,g} = x$ for any $w \in IS$, if such an x exists. It is furthermore useful to be able to speak of NP_1 and NP_2 as being *coreferent relative to IS (and g)*, namely iff $[\![NP_1]\!]^{w,g} = [\![NP_2]\!]^{w,g}$ for all $w \in IS$. The notion of presupposed coreference (in a context C) mentioned above can then be understood to mean that the NPs in question are coreferent w.r.t. IS^C.

In short, then, our new treatment incorporates the generalization that two c-commanding NPs may refer to the same individual in the real world (whichever that may be), as long as they don't corefer in the context.

Formalization II: pronouns

As we saw in (7.26) above, unknown identity phenomena are not restricted to full NPs; we find parallel cases with pronouns. These could be accounted for by assuming that the pronouns *are* full NPs at LF. Thus, an example like (7.32a) would be represented at LF as (7.32b):

(7.32)   (a)   (Billy's teacher resembles the famous actress). She also dresses like her.
         (b)   LF: Billy's teacher also dresses like the famous actress

Since the pronouns *are* full NPs at LF, they are governed not by Binding Condition B, but by the CR/HLB. Thus they will be allowed to corefer (in the real world), as long as they don't in the context (i.e. as long as there are possibilities in IS^C in which they don't).

Upon closer examination, we seem to have already allowed for such pronouns when we introduced constant e-type pronouns, i.e. e-type pronouns built around 'one-place relations' (i.e. properties) in section 7.1.3. On this view, the LF representation of *she* and *her* in (7.32a) are not actually *Billy's teacher* and *the famous actress*, respectively, but rather *the R_2^1* and *the R_8^1*, where R_2^1 and R_8^1 are variables over properties, which will be contextually instantiated by the properties 'be Billy's teacher' and 'be a famous actress,' respectively. The only thing we have to change to make e-type pronouns truly equivalent to definite NPs is to assume that the relational variables are actually *intensional*, i.e. functions from possibilities to n-place relations:

(7.33)   For any integers n, m, and assignment g, $g(R_m^n)$ is a function from worlds to n-place relations; $[\![R_m^n]\!]^{w,g} = g(R_m^n)(w)$ for all $w \in W$

Let $g(R_2^1)$ be the function that maps a possibility w to the set of Billy's teachers in w, and $g(R_8^1)$ the function which maps a w to the set of famous actresses in w, then the actual LF for (7.32a) is (7.34):

(7.34)   **the** R_2^1 also dresses like **the** R_8^1

Int_{IS}^g (7.34) is thus the same proposition as Int_{IS}^g (*Billy's teacher also dresses like the famous actress*) in any information state *IS*; like the latter, it will be allowed by the CR/HLB in any IS in which *the R_2^1* ('Billy's teacher') and *the R_8^1* ('the famous actress') are not coreferent, in the technical sense defined above.

As in the discussion in section 7.1.2, we do not concern ourselves with what determines the actual assignment of values to these variables. That is, the fact that *she is her* in this context is not understood to mean 'the queen of the Netherlands is Ptolemy XII's daughter' is not accounted for under this treatment – just as little as the fact that it doesn't mean 'Beatrix is Cleopatra' is under the assumption that pronouns denote individuals; but the fact that whatever descriptions they go proxy for must not denote the same individual in all possibilities in the context follows from the CR/HLB.

7.2.2   Identity statements

With the formal apparatus in place, let us finally look at a borderline case of unknown coreference, identity statements:

(7.35)   (A) I wonder if the guy in the hallway is John. He put on John's coat ...
           (B) He *is* John!

The first two utterances in this dialogue are familiar in nature: *the guy in the hallway* might actually refer to John, but in the current information state IS^C, this identity is not established (hence the question), so there are possibilities $w \in IS^C$ in which $[\![$the guy in the hallway$]\!]^{w,g} \neq [\![$John$]\!]^{w,g}$, so the sentence expresses a different proposition in IS^C than *I wonder if the guy in the hallway is himself*.

A's second utterance behaves exactly the same, assuming that *he* expands at LF to *the R_6^1*, where $[\![R_6^1]\!]^{w,g} = g(R_6^1)(w)$ is the property of being a guy in the hallway in w.

But, assuming the same about *he* in B's reply, is it still possible that *he* (alias 'the guy in the hallway') has no constant reference in IS^C and is, hence, different from *John*? Clearly, if B is honest in what she claims, *the guy in the hallway* and *John* must refer to the same individual, John, in every possibility corresponding to B's knowledge. But recall that we took IS^C, the contextual IS, not to be the speaker's IS, but the information shared by speaker and hearer. Obviously, A does not know that the guy in the hallway is John, so there are possibilities in B's IS in which $[\![\text{the guy in the hallway}/R_6^1]\!]^{w,g} \neq [\![\text{John}]\!]^{w,g}$, and these possibilities will necessarily also be part of IS^C. So we see that our earlier decision to define the CR/HLB relative to the shared assumption of all participants is crucial in allowing for identity statements.

We have limited our discussion of unknown or mistaken identity, as well as identity statements, to cases of descriptive NPs, to which we've assimilated pronouns. Some of these phenomena have counterparts with proper names; one can, for example, say *Cicero is Tully* and be at the same time truthful and grammatical. We are not prepared to embark on a discussion of these cases, since many of the fundamental issues regarding the semantics of proper names are not well understood or at least highly controversial.[8]

7.3   Descriptive NPs and indexing©

Throughout the preceding discussion we have assumed that full NPs, including e-type pronouns, do not bear indices, and that their coreference restrictions follow from the CR/HLB (rather than Binding Conditions B or C). Indeed, at least the unknown identity cases might, at first glance, be taken as additional evidence against a theory that assigns indices to referential expressions. Thus suppose that both NPs in (7.21a) *were* indexed, as in (7.36a); then a Binding Condition B/C violation obtains iff $n = m$. How could context influence this?

(7.36)   (a) $\left\{ \begin{array}{l} \text{She}_n \\ \text{The reviewer}_n \end{array} \right\}$ praises Zelda$_m$ to high heavens.

(b)   She$_n$ is her$_m$.

Upon closer inspection, however, it turns out that the existence of unknown identity cases doesn't bear on the question of indexing. Rather, it merely bears on our interpretation of counter-indexing. To see this, let us start with (7.36b), on a reading where each pronoun corresponds to a constant e-type pronoun, i.e. one whose paraphrase doesn't contain a bound variable (Heim [1993]'s *guises*). These are effectively interpreted as functions from possibilities/worlds to individuals, also called *individual concepts*.

---

[8] See the seminal Kripke (1972) as well as any survey on the philosophy of language.

For example, *she* in (7.36b) becomes *the* R_i^1 at LF, which is interpreted the same as *the reviewer*, i.e. as the unique reviewer (if there is one) in w for arbitrary g, w. The same effect could be achieved without expanding the pronoun at LF, assuming it to be she_n instead; for that, we have to assume that the assignment g directly assigns to pronouns an individual concept, in this case a function that maps a possibility onto a (female) individual:

(7.37)　　(a)　for all indices n on pronouns, $g(n) \in E^W$
　　　　　　　　(read: $g(n)$ is a function from possibilities/worlds to individuals)
　　　　　(b)　$[\![\text{pron}_n]\!]^{w,g} = g(n)(w)$

Given any assignment g, we can now say that two pronouns $pron_1$ and $pron_2$ corefer *relative to a possibility* w iff $g(pron_1)(w) = g(pron_2)(w)$. Derivatively we say that $pron_1$ and $pron_2$ corefer w.r.t. an information state IS iff they corefer with reference to every possibility $w \in IS$. The generalization discussed above is that coindexing corresponds to coreference with reference to an IS.

This can be implemented straightforwardly: if the assignment assigns individual concepts, rather than individuals, to pronouns, we can make PACO sensitive to these, rather than their value in a particular possibility. The following reformulation will achieve this:

(7.38)　　PACO (revised): An information state *IS* and an assignment g qualify as a *context* iff for any indices n, m, if $g(n)(w) = g(m)(w)$ for all $w \in IS$, then $n = m$

By the revised PACO, two pronouns may be coindexed even if they, in fact, corefer, as long as they aren't coreferential with reference to the contextual information state.[9]

Turning to full NPs now, we first have to become clear about what the index on a full NP means; we therefore repeat the relevant part of (2.10) from chapter 2, with possibilities/worlds added:

(7.39)　　For all names and definite NPs, $[\![\text{NP}_n]\!]^{w,g} = g(n)(w)$ if $g(n)(w) = [\![\text{NP}]\!]^{w,g}$, undefined otherwise

Relative to an information state IS, then, NP_n is defined if it is defined for all possibilities $w \in IS$. In other words, an indexed NP denotes exactly what a pronoun with the same index denotes, namely an individual concept, except that it additionally presupposes that its lexical content denotes the same individual concept.

---

[9] An alternative is to assume that assignments differ with each possibility, i.e. that an information state is a set of pairs consisting of a possibility and an assignment function. On this view, $[\![\text{pron}_n]\!]^p = g(n)$ for any $p = \langle w,g \rangle$. PACO would then say that IS is a context for S if for any indices n, m, if $g(n) = g(m)$ for all g in IS (to be exact: all $g \in \{g' \mid \exists w[\langle w,g' \rangle \in IS]\}$), then $n = m$. This is the route taken in much of *dynamic semantics*, e.g. Groenendijk and Stokhof (1991); Heim (1982). Nothing in the present context hinges on this distinction.

Given this much, referential full NPs behave just like pronouns with reference to PACO: they can be counter-indexed in C if and only if they denote different individuals with reference to at least one possibility $w \in IS^C$. Thus in (7.36a), we can index the NPs e.g. as follows:

(7.40) $\left\{ \begin{array}{l} \text{She}_3 \\ \text{The reviewer}_3 \end{array} \right\}$ praises Zelda$_6$ to high heavens.

(7.40) will be possible in a given context $\langle IS, g \rangle$ only if for any $w \in IS$, first, $g(3)(w)$ is the unique reviewer in w and $g(6)(w)$ is Zelda, and second, there is at least one possibility $w' \in IS$ such that $g(3)(w') \neq g(6)(w')$.

We see, thus, that mistaken identity cases can be accommodated in essentially the same way with or without indexing of full NPs and constant e-type pronouns.

The system as revised in this subsection seems to acknowledge two kinds of pronouns: free pronouns, interpreted as individual concepts; and bound pronouns, interpreted as individuals. There is no need to accept this bifurcation, though. After all, an individual denoting pronoun can simply be viewed as an individual concept denoting pronoun, but one that assigns the *same* individual to each possibility/world. This can be encoded in the definition of the binder prefix as follows:

(7.41) $[\![\beta_n \, X]\!]^{w,g} = [\![X]\!]^{w,g[n \to f]}(x)$, where f is that function from W to E such that $f(w) = x$ for any w

According to (7.41), bound pronouns always denote constant individual concepts, which are equivalent to individuals.

Appendix: Indexing problems

It should be pointed out that this section only showed that mistaken identity is in principle compatible with a full indexing theory that maintains Binding Condition C. This is not to say, however, that all cases adduced in favor of the CR can be handled using the intensionalized indexing just introduced. Recall from chapters 5 and 6 the cases of BT obviations involving focus particles and the like:

(7.42)   (a)   Only Oscar voted for Oscar.

(b)   (If everybody likes Oscar, then necessarily) Oscar/he likes Oscar/him.

The individual concept denoted by *Oscar* is clearly the same for all instances of that name. And, even with the pronouns, it is not the case that (7.42b) is only felicitous if the conversationalists have two different descriptions of Oscar (e.g. 'the guy called Oscar' and 'the most popular guy in our school') to assign to them. In other words, there is no sense in which the identity of *he* and *him* (let alone *Oscar* and *Oscar*) must be unclear or under debate for these sentences to be felicitous. Accordingly, all NPs must be coindexed, and a Binding Condition B/C violation obtains, contrary to intuitions. It thus seems that these cases do still pose a problem for the full indexing theory.

Exercise 7.10

Consider (7.43a). (i) Show why this indexing, or any other, on the NP *his country* cannot be interpreted given the rules we have. (ii) Can such a *functional NP* remain unindexed instead? Argue using (7.43b) (I omitted any grammaticality judgment here, so make it clear how you judge which reading first)! (iii) How does the CR or Have Local Binding! fare w.r.t. these examples? (iv) What does this tell us about the possibility of indexing e-type pronouns?

(7.43)　　(a)　Every head of state β_2 represented [his$_2$ country]$_8$.
　　　　　(b)　*Every head of state* secretly knows that *his* country won't be able to maintain *his* country's standard of living in the long run.

7.4   Summary

What we saw in this chapter is that certain pronouns must be interpreted as something akin to a full definite NP. The reasons are that pronouns can be anaphorically related to quantificational NPs; that they can be dependent on commanding QNPs without being bound by them; and that they can show intensional behavior in contexts of mistaken or unknown identity. We also saw that coreference should more accurately (but forbiddingly) be called 'descriptive contextual equivalence.' Two referential NPs may denote the same individual for certain possibilities/worlds. Only, however, if they do for all worlds in the contextual information state IS^C – roughly corresponding to the shared assumptions of all participants – do they count as 'coreferent' in the sense of the Coreference rule (or its successor, Have Local Binding!).

Exercise 7.11

Consider the following text:

(7.44)　　Hey, John is the guest of honor!

　　　　　#He's putting on $\left\{ \begin{array}{l} \text{his} \\ *\text{John's} \end{array} \right\}$ coat. He can't be leaving already!

Suppose that *he* in the second sentence expands as *the R_9*, where $g(R_9)(w)$ is the property of being a guest of honor in w (for any w), while $[\![\text{his}]\!]^{w,g} = [\![\text{John}]\!]^{w,g}$ = John for all w. Obviously, there are worlds w' then such that $[\![\text{the } R_9]\!]^{w',g} \neq [\![\text{John}]\!]^{w',g}$. Why is the second sentence bad nonetheless?

7.5   An extension: unexpected sloppy identity

With e-type pronouns at our disposal, we can now turn to a class of puzzling cases of anaphoric dependency. In chapter 5, sections 5.2 and 5.5, we showed how pronoun binding is crucial in deriving a certain type of reading for focus constructions, as well as so-called sloppy identity readings for VP ellipsis. Given that, and given that pronoun binding in our system requires c-command, a clear prediction is (P):

(P)   Bound readings in focus constructions and sloppy identity in VP ellipsis are possible only if the antecedent c-commands the pronoun.

At first glance, this prediction is borne out. For example, Reinhart (1983a):151f. points out the contrast in (7.45):

(7.45)   (a)   *Los Angeles* is adored by *its* residents, and *New York* is, too.

(OK: ... adored by NY's residents → strict/sloppy)

(b)   The people who were born in *Los Angeles* adore *its* beaches, but the people who were born in *New York* do not.

(only: ... adore LA's beaches → strict/?*sloppy)

Reinhart's judgment on these cases, however, is not uncontroversial, and there are, in any event, other cases, discussed in Dalrymple *et al.* (1991); Fiengo and May (1994); Hardt (1993); Tomioka (1997, 1999), among others, which constitute clear counter-examples to (P):[10]

(7.46)   (a)   The police officer who arrested John insulted him, and the one who arrested Bill did, too.

(OK: ... insulted Bill → strict/sloppy)

(b)   *The policeman who arrested *every murderer* insulted *him*.

Bill in the second conjunct of (7.46a) does not c-command *him*, nor can an NP in that position in general take scope over (or bind into) the matrix clause, as the impossibility of a bound variable reading for *him* in (7.46b) shows; this is as expected. What is unexpected, though, is that there is, nonetheless, a sloppy identity reading in (7.46a), contrary to (P).

We can see an equally unexpected case of semantic binding in focus constructions such as (7.47). On its most prominent reading, the sentence is false if we know that Bill, too, was insulted by the police officer arresting him:

(7.47)   So far, we only know that the policeman who arrested *JOHN* insulted *him*.

Logical paraphrases of these sentences are given in (7.48):

---

[10] Example from Tomioka (1999):219. Generally, the availability of these kinds of readings seems subject to variation – perhaps depending on speakers, perhaps on context (see e.g. n. 4 in Tomioka [1999]). Hirschberg and Ward (1991) show convincingly, though, that a majority of speakers accepts at least some of these cases on the pertinent readings.

(7.48)   (a)   John has the following property: λx. the police officer who arrested x insulted x; Bill has the same property

         (b)   so far, John is the only person who we know to have the property: λx. the police officer who arrested x insulted x

Details aside, it should be evident that, in both cases, we need to refer to the property $[\lambda x$. the police officer who arrested x insulted $x]$; but there is no constituent that denotes that property. One might assume that some covert syntactic movement could create such a constituent (e.g. Rooth [1992a]; see chapter 8 for details). But note that that movement would have to move *John* out of a relative clause and a subject NP, which are usually said to be islands for movement. Furthermore, if such movement was mysteriously possible in these sentences, we would expect (7.46b) above to have the same option and hence a bound variable reading, which it doesn't.

Tomioka (1997, 1999) proposes to use e-type pronouns to derive the surprising readings. Assume, for example, that (7.47) has the following LF:

(7.49)   so far, we only know that [the police officer who arrested *JOHN*] [β_1 insulted **the R_8/person arrested by** x_1]

Here we have expanded *him* as an e-type pronoun *the R_8 x_1* at LF, where x_1 is bound by *the police officer who arrested John*, which, *nota bene*, c-commands it. The relational variable R_8 is assigned the function 'be arrested by,' as indicated, which yields the meaning: 'the police officer who arrested John insulted the person he arrested.' This meaning is synonymous with one where *him* is an ordinary pronoun referring to John. It behaves differently, and advantageously, though, when embedded under *only*, yielding the following:

(7.50)   (a) $[\![$we only VP$]\!]^g = 1$ iff $[\![$VP$]\!]^g($we$) = 1$, and if for no other $p \in$ P-SET(VP), $p($we$) = 1$ (cf. chapter 5, [5.7])

         (b) $[\![$VP$]\!]^g =$ knowing that the police officer who arrested John is in $\lambda x.x$ insulted the person x arrested

         (c)   P-SET(VP) $=$ {knowing that the police officer who arrested y is in $\lambda x.x$ insulted the person x arrested $\mid y \in D_e$}

         (d)   we know that the police officer who arrested John insulted the person he arrested, and we don't know that the police officer who arrested y insulted the person he arrested, for any $y \neq$ John

As can be seen, the property of insulting the person he arrested covaries with focus alternatives to *John*, but only indirectly; in particular, *John* doesn't bind any variables it doesn't c-command. The analysis of VP ellipsis works in parallel:

(7.51)   the police officer who arrested John [β_1 insulted **the R_8/person arrested by** x_1], and the one who arrested Bill did [β_1 insult **the R_8/person arrested by** x_1], too.

Obviously, the two VPs are identical, and the variable x_1 within the VPs is bound by a c-commanding NP in each conjunct (I leave it to the reader to verify that these cases of VP ellipsis also meet the refined identity condition discussed in chapter 6, section 6.5.1).

We see, then, that e-type pronouns provide a general analytical tool for (re-)analyzing anaphoric dependencies that don't involve c-command as instances of binding that do involve c-command. Despite that appealing quality, and despite the fact that for some constructions – to wit: simple paycheck sentences like (7.11a) and anaphora to non-referential NPs as in (7.6) – no alternative analysis exists, e-type analyses need to make good on two promises: the *problem of the formal link*, i.e. the question how the value of the relational variable is construed (or can't be construed, in some cases); and the *uniqueness problem*, i.e. the problem that arises from analyzing e-type pronouns as definite descriptions, which therefore should presuppose uniqueness of its denotation.

The literature on these issues is huge, and valid alternatives to the e-type treatment have been proposed, in particular for donkey sentences and some of the cases discussed in section 7.5 (Chierchia [1992, 1995]; Groenendijk and Stokhof [1991]; Heim [1982]; von Heusinger [1997]; Higginbotham and May [1981]; Kamp [1981]; Kamp and Reyle [1993]; Tomioka [1997], a.m.o), which cannot be discussed here. We will come to yet another application for e-type pronouns in chapter 8, section 8.3.3.

8   Semantic binding and c-command

In chapter 4 we discussed the binding behavior of QNPs and *wh*-elements and observed that they can semantically bind only under c-command, and that they cannot be bound at all. While additional mechanisms are required to rule out the co*indexings* that might suggest that (the BAC/[4.23] and Binding Condition C, respectively), it was argued that the correct interpretations can be made to follow from the way semantic interpretation works alone, without invoking such principles.

In this chapter I will present cases in which that generalization seems too weak in that semantic binding, even under c-command, doesn't seem possible. These involve the so-called *weak crossover effect* (WCO effect). I then introduce some cases where it appears too strong, namely so-called *indirect binding*.

8.1   The weak crossover phenomenon

8.1.1   Weak crossover in *wh*-constructions

The first set of cases we are going to look at involves the weak crossover effect in *wh*-constructions. Consider (8.1):

(8.1)   Who phoned his uncle?
    (a)   for which person x is it the case that: x phoned $g(3)$'s uncle (assuming that *his* is indexed 3)
    (b)   for which person x is it the case that: x phoned x's uncle

As discussed in chapter 4, section 4.3, a sentence like (8.1) can have two interpretations, as indicated, differing in whether or not the pronoun is bound by the *wh*-phrase. Strikingly, the bound pronoun option is absent in the following example:

(8.2)   Whom did his uncle phone?
    (a)   for which person x is it the case that: $g(3)$'s uncle called x
    (b)   *for which person x is it the case that: x's uncle called x

What (8.2) is trying to mean is most naturally expressed by the bound variable reading of 'Who was called by his uncle?' The fact that this reading is absent is surprising, given that *whom* in (8.2) clearly c-commands *his* and should therefore be able to bind it.

To see what exactly is going on semantically, we have to make some assumptions about movement constructions. Fortunately for us we don't have to be concerned with the semantics of the *wh*-phrase itself, or that of the entire sentence, so we won't. We assume that *wh*-questions like (8.1) and (8.2) are derived by a movement rule that leaves behind a coindexed trace. Both the movement rule itself and the interpretation of the resulting configuration will be formalized following Heim and Kratzer [1998]:ch. 5:

(8.3)   *Wh*-movement:
         Move a *wh*-NP or QNP α to the clause initial position, leave a trace indexed
         n, and adjoin a trace binder prefix μ_n to the sister of α's landing site:

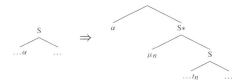

(8.4)   Trace rule (preliminary):
         for all numbers n, $[\![t_n]\!]^g = g(n)$

(8.5)   Movement Interpretation rule (MIR), preliminary:
         for all numbers n, $[\![\mu_n X]\!]^g = \lambda x.[\![X]\!]^{g[n \to x]}$

This Movement Interpretation rule (MIR) is very similar to the BIER introduced in chapter 4. The only difference is that it doesn't saturate an argument position of X, but only binds variables in X. This corresponds to the fact that an NP in a derived position is not sister to a constituent that has an open argument slot. To keep trace binders distinct from pronoun binders I use the prefix μ (for 'movement') rather than β. Let us now look again at those LFs from above that involve pronoun binding:

(8.6)   *Who* phoned *his* uncle?
         (a)   LF: who $[\mu_2 \; [t_2 \text{ phoned his}_2 \text{ uncle}]]$
         (b) $[\![\mu_2 \; [t_2 \text{ phoned his}_2 \text{ uncle}]]\!]^g = \lambda x.[\![t_2 \text{ phoned his}_2 \text{ uncle}]\!]^{g[2 \to x]}$
                $= \lambda x.x$ phoned x's uncle

(8.7)   **Whom* did *his* uncle phone?
         (a)   LF: whom $[\mu_2 \; [\text{did his}_2 \text{ uncle phone } t_2]]$
         (b) $[\![[\mu_2 \; [\text{did his}_2 \text{ uncle phone } t_2]]\!]^g = \lambda x[\![\text{did his}_2 \text{ uncle phone}$
                $t_2]\!]^{g[2 \to x]} = \lambda x.x$'s uncle phoned x

In both these LFs the trace-binder prefix c-commands the coindexed trace and the coindexed pronoun at LF and should thus bind them. However, only (8.6) allows for this reading.

This curious restriction on binding is known as the *weak crossover restriction* or *weak crossover effect* (WCO). The name owes itself to the idea that in the bad example (8.7), but not in the good example (8.6), the *wh*-phrase has 'crossed over' the pronoun on its way to the left-peripheral position in the sentence. There are numerous ways in which the WCO effect has been stated; a relatively theory-neutral one is given in (8.8):

(8.8)   The weak crossover restriction
         An NP in a derived position can semantically bind only those pronouns
         which it c-commands already from its base position.

(8.6) doesn't violate this restriction, since the base position of the *wh*-phrase is the subject position, which c-commands the object position containing the bound pronoun. (8.7), on the other hand, violates it, since the base position of the *wh*-phrase is the object position, which does *not* c-command the subject position.

What makes the WCO restriction relevant in our context is the fact that it constitutes a counter-example to the generalization that the domain in which an NP can semantically bind pronouns is its s-structural c-command domain.

Could Binding Conditions A–C help us rule out the indexing in (8.7)? In particular, could it be that the *wh*-phrase, in binding the pronoun *his*, violates Binding Condition B? Unfortunately no such explanation seems possible. Recall from the discussion in chapter 3 that the binding domain or governing category for *his* in (8.7) is the NP *his uncle*. Since *his* is free in this domain, no Binding Condition B violation emerges. That the NP, rather than anything bigger like the clause, is the relevant binding domain for the pronoun is also confirmed by the fact that none of the cases of WCO can be rescued by using a reflexive instead of a non-reflexive pronoun; for example both versions of the sentence in (8.9) are equally out:

(8.9) $*Who$ did a friend of $\left\{ \begin{array}{c} his \\ himself \end{array} \right\}$ call?

Note in addition that it would become mysterious why (8.6) should be grammatical if the pronoun needed to be free in the entire clause. Finally, even a pronoun embedded within a constituent as big as a finite clause falls victim to WCO:

(8.10) $*Who$ did a woman who wanted to sell *him* stock options call?

We conclude that the WCO effect will not follow from Binding Condition B. Additional machinery is needed.

In section 8.2 we will discuss ways to incorporate the WCO restriction into the grammar. In the next subsection we will first discuss a second case where the WCO restriction arguably applies. This subsection can be skipped by readers who are in a hurry.

8.1.2   Inverse scope and weak crossover

The second case to look at is that of sentences in which QNPs don't seem to be interpreted in their surface position. In transformational generative theories these cases are generally analyzed as involving an application of the *quantifier raising* (QR) transformation which raises QNPs to a scope position

[May, 1977, 1985]. This operation is, for example, assumed to derive the most natural reading for a sentence like (8.11a) via an LF representation like (8.11b). As is usual with movement operations (cf. e.g. [8.3] above), QR leaves behind a coindexed trace in the base position of the raised QNP:

(8.11)   (a)   A picture was standing on every desk.

            (b)   every desk$_2$[a picture was standing on t_2]

In fact, we can interpret this structure straightforwardly if we assume that quantifier raising is the same operation involved in the *wh*-constructions above:

(8.12)   (a)   LF: every desk[μ_2[a picture was standing on t_2]]

            (b) $[\![\mu_2$[a picture was standing on t_2]$]\!]^g$
                  $= \lambda x.[\![$a picture was standing on $t_2]\!]^{g[2 \to x]}$
                  $= \lambda x.[$a picture was standing on $g[2 \to x](2)]$
                  $= \lambda x.[$a picture was standing on $x]$

            (c)   for every desk y, y is in $\{x \mid$ a picture was standing on $x\}$

Now, interestingly, while QR can enlarge the scope of a QNP, it cannot extend the domain in which a QNP can bind pronouns. In other words, even though the QNP *every desk* in (8.11b) c-commands the subject NP, it cannot bind a pronoun within that subject NP; this is shown in (8.13):

(8.13)   ∗A picture of *its* owner was standing on *every desk*.

(8.13) cannot mean 'every desk had a picture of its owner on it.' This is surprising, now, given that the QNP *every desk* can be quantifier-raised to an LF position where it c-commands the pronoun *its* (it does follow from our current account that the QNP in its surface position can't semantically bind *its*):

(8.14)   LF$_{(8.13)}$: every desk[μ_2[a picture of its$_2$ owner was standing on t_2]]

This LF receives exactly the intuitively unavailable interpretation:

(8.15)   (a) $[\![\mu_2$[a picture of its$_2$ owner was standing on t_2]$]\!]^g$
                  $= \lambda x.[\![$a picture of its$_2$ owner was standing on $t_2]\!]^{g[2 \to x]}$
                  $= \lambda x.[$a picture of $g[2 \to x](2)$'s owner was standing on $g[2 \to x](2)]$
                  $= \lambda x.[$a picture of x's owner was standing on $x]$

            (b)   for every desk y, y is in $\{x \mid$ a picture of x's owner was standing on $x\}$

The impossibility of this reading is thus another instance of the WCO effect: *every desk$_2$* in (8.14) tries to bind the pronoun *its$_2$* within the subject NP, which it doesn't c-command at s-structure.

8.2   Blocking weak crossover

How can the WCO effect be captured? There is a rich literature on this topic which we cannot review in detail here. Two general strategies are conceivable: to filter out representations which would lead to the incriminated readings, and to block the generation of those readings in the first place.

8.2.1   Filtering accounts

Consider the following filter from Koopman and Sportiche [1983]:[1]

(8.16)   Bijection principle:
An operator can bind at most one variable.

Operator here is used as a cover term for quantifier raised NPs and *wh*-phrases, and *variable* subsumes traces of these, and pronouns. Since operators by definition bind a trace, the principle essentially prohibits binding of pronouns by an operator (it also prohibits binding of more than one trace, which doesn't interest us here). Evidently, *whom* in (8.7a) and *every desk* in (8.15) – both of which are repeated here – violate the Bijection Principle in that they – or rather the trace binder prefix μ_2 introduced by them – bind a trace *and* a pronoun:

(8.17)   (a)   whom $[\mu_2 \ [\text{did his}_2 \ \text{uncle phone } t_2]]$
          (b)   every desk$[\mu_2[\text{a picture of its}_2 \ \text{owner was standing on } t_2]]$

This leaves us with the question how there could ever be a pronoun bound by a QNP or *wh*-phrase. Consider a good *wh*-case:

(8.18)   *Who* do you think phoned *his* uncle?
          (a)   *who $[\mu_2 \ [\text{do you think } [t_2 \ [\text{phoned his}_2 \ \text{uncle}]]]]$
          (b)   who $[\mu_2 \ [\text{do you think } [t_2 \ [\beta_2[\text{phoned his}_2 \ \text{uncle}]]]]]$

The LF for (8.18) cannot be (8.18a), given that it violates the Bijection Principle. LF (8.18b), however, obeys the Bijection Principle and yields the reading we want. The trick here is that the moved phrase binds its trace, and only its trace, as required, but the trace in turn binds the pronoun.

The critical difference between the LFs in (8.17), on the one hand, and those in (8.18), on the other, then, is that not only the moved NPs but also its trace c-commands the pronoun in the latter, but not in the former. This was, of course, our earlier generalization (8.8).

Exercise 8.1
Does the *wh*-expression in (8.18b) semantically bind the pronoun?

Exercise 8.2
Give an LF for *Some person wanted every boy to bring his guitar* on a reading where *every boy* takes scope over *some person* and binds the pronoun *his*.

---

[1] Other filtering accounts along these lines include the Leftness Condition of Chomsky [1976], the Parallelism Constraint on Operator Binding of Safir ([1984]: 607), and the various accessibility relations on linking developed in Higginbotham [1983, 1987].

8.2.2   A non-filtering account

One way of rationalizing weak crossover is that it emerges when a movement index simultaneously acts as a binding index, which it shouldn't. A possible conclusion is that, although both pronouns and traces are aptly interpreted as individual variables, grammar keeps them distinct; an operator that binds a trace can therefore never, as a 'side-effect' as it were, bind pronouns (nor can a pronoun-binding operator accidentally bind a trace).

Such an account of WCO has been developed within the framework of variable-free semantics [Jacobson, 1999, 2000]. Within our current setting, we can implement this idea through a minimal change to our system. Given that we already discriminate trace-binder prefixes from ordinary binder prefixes (μ versus β), all we need to do is to make the interpretation procedure sensitive to whether a semantic variable is amenable to binding by μ or by β. So far we have assumed that a trace indexed n is simply interpreted as $g(n)$, and thus has the same meaning as a coindexed pronoun (relative to that assignment g, that is, and ignoring number and gender presuppositions of the pronoun).

We will now give up this assumption and assume that while $[\![it_2]\!]^g$ is still $g(2)$, $[\![t_2]\!]^g$ is $g(t_n)$, that is, in the case of a trace, the argument to the assignment function is no longer just the index but the indexed trace; as a crucial consequence, it doesn't necessarily hold that $[\![pronoun_n]\!]^g = [\![t_n]\!]^g$, since $g(n)$ may be different from $g(t_n)$ even for the same n (technically, this involves changing our definition of what an assignment function is; see the appendix to this section). As a consequence of this change, the pronoun in a configuration like (8.19a) will not semantically depend on the trace-binder prefix μ (though the coindexed trace will), despite the fact that it is c-commanded by, and coindexed with, it; the same holds for the pronoun in (8.19b):

(8.19)   (a) μ_2 [t_2 phoned his$_2$ uncle]
           (b) μ_2 [did his$_2$ uncle phone t_2]

In order to bind traces, we have to slighly amend the MIR, as in (8.20). The interpretations for the structures in (8.19) will then be (8.21a) and (8.21b), respectively:

(8.20)   Movement Interpretation rule (MIR), final:
           for all numbers n, $[\![\mu_n X]\!]^g = \lambda x.[\![X]\!]^{g[t_n \to x]}$

(8.21)   (a) $\lambda x.g[t_2 \to x](t_2)$ phoned $g[t_2 \to x](2)$'s uncle
                 $= \lambda x.x$ phoned $g[t_2 \to x](2)$'s uncle
           (b) $\lambda x.g[t_2 \to x](2)$'s uncle phoned $g[t_2 \to x](t_2)$
                 $= \lambda x.g[t_2 \to x](2)$'s uncle phoned x

The resulting question meaning will still contain free pronouns:

(8.22)   (a)   who μ_2 phoned his$_2$ uncle
                 for which person x is it the case that: x phoned $g[t_2 \to x](2)$'s uncle
           (b)   whom μ_2 did his$_2$ uncle phone
                 for which person x is it the case that: $g[t_2 \to x](2)$'s uncle phoned x

Note that once again we have blocked the incriminated reading, but not the co-indexing. That is, both (8.22a) and (8.22b) have licit indexings but neither of them expresses variable binding. Rather they express the exact same meaning that they would if the pronoun were indexed, say, $3.^2$

Now, in (8.22a) we can, alternatively, bind the pronoun to the trace of *who*, as before, to give us the bound variable reading:

(8.23)   LF: who $\mu_2[t_2[\beta_2[\text{phoned his}_2 \text{ uncle}]]]$
        for which person x is it the case that:
        $[\![\mu_2[t_2[\beta_2[\text{phoned his}_2 \text{ uncle}]]]]\!]^g(x) = 1$
        $= \ldots$ that x is in $\{y \mid [\![t_2[\beta_2[\text{phoned his}_2 \text{ uncle}]]]]\!]^{g[t_2 \to y]} = 1\}$
        $= \ldots x$ is in $\{y \mid [\![\beta_2[\text{phoned his}_2 \text{ uncle}]]\!]^{g[t_2 \to y]}(g[t_2 \to y](t_2)) = 1\}$
        $= \ldots x$ is in $\{y \mid [\![\beta_2[\text{phoned his}_2 \text{ uncle}]]\!]^{g[t_2 \to y]}(y) = 1]$
        $= \ldots x$ is in $\{y \mid [\lambda z. [\![\text{phoned his}_2 \text{ uncle}]\!]^{g[t_2 \to y][2 \to z]}(z)](y) = 1\}$
        $= \ldots x$ is in $\{y \mid [\![\text{phoned his}_2 \text{ uncle}]\!]^{g[t_2 \to y][2 \to y]}(y) = 1\}$
        $= \ldots x$ is in $\{y \mid y \text{ phoned } g[t_2 \to y][2 \to y](2)\text{'s uncle }\}$
        $= \ldots x$ is in $\{y \mid y \text{ phoned } y\text{'s uncle}\}$

Can we do the same for (8.22b), the WCO case? To do so, we would have to adjoin β on top of μ, as in the LF in (8.24):

(8.24)   whom$_2[\beta_2[\mu_2[\text{did his}_2 \text{ uncle phone } t_2]]]$

To express our earlier generalization that binding cannot proceed from a position derived by *wh*-movement, and hence derive the WCO effect, we have to block LFs like (8.24). We will do this by adding a stipulation to our Binder rule: we allow for β-prefixing only next to a non-derived position:

(8.25)   Binder rule with WCO, final version:

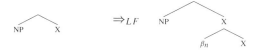

    (where NP has not undergone *wh*-movement)

---

[2] The pronouns *his*$_2$ in (8.22) can remain free, or subsequently get bound by a binder prefix, e.g. in (i):

  (i)   Every man$_2$ knew whom$_2$ his$_2$ uncle phoned.
        (a)   LF: every man $\beta_2[\text{knew whom } \mu_2[\text{his}_2 \text{ uncle phoned } t_2]]$
        (b)   for every man x, $[\![\beta_2[\text{ knew whom } \mu_2[\text{his}_2 \text{ uncle phoned } t_2]]]\!]^g(x) = 1$
            $=$ every man is in $\{x \mid [\![\text{knew whom } \mu_2[\text{his}_2 \text{ uncle phoned } t_2]]\!]^{g[2 \to x]}(x) = 1\}$
            $= \ldots$ is in $\{x \mid x$ knew for which person y, $[\![\mu_2[\text{his}_2 \text{ uncle phoned } t_2]]\!]^{g[2 \to x]}(y) = 1\}$
            $= \ldots$ is in $\{x \mid x$ knew for which person y the following is the case: y is in $\{z \mid [\![\text{his}_2 \text{ uncle phoned } t_2]\!]^{g[2 \to x][t_2 \to z]}\}\}$
               $\ldots y$ is in $\{z \mid g[2 \to x][t_2 \to z](2)\text{'s uncle phoned } g[2 \to x][t_2 \to z](t_2)\}$
               $\ldots y$ is in $\{z \mid x\text{'s uncle phoned } z\}$
            $=$ every man is in $\{x \mid x$ knew for which person y the following is the case: $x\text{'s}$ uncle phoned $y\}$

By (8.25), β must not be adjoined to a derived position, blocking LF (8.24). It is easy to check that this treatment derives results equivalent to those of the filtering accounts discussed in section 8.2.1. In the remainder of this book, we will adopt (8.25) as our Binding rule with a 'built-in' WCO restriction.

This concludes our discussion of weak crossover. We have seen that the WCO effect can be accounted for directly in the syntax–semantics mapping. As with the c-command condition on semantic binding and Binding Condition C effects involving syntactically bound QNPs discussed in chapter 4, we have blocked the generation of the intuitively unavailable readings rather than the coindexing, which we take to be sufficient. Unlike with these earlier cases, however, the derivation of WCO required us to make a stipulative addition to the Index Transfer rule.[3]

Nonetheless this account arguably has an advantage over filtering approaches as discussed in section 8.2.1 above, namely that it is extremely local: there is no reference to the bound element in the pertinent rule (8.25) at all, i.e. the rule doesn't have to "look into" the structure of the constituent β is attached to (X in the rule above) to see what the relation between the trace and coindexed pronouns, if present, is. That is, the account proposed in this subsection – unlike the filtering solutions – is naturally compatible with syntactic frameworks in which phrase markers (or some impoverished version thereof such as strings of words) are generated incrementally and, once built, become opaque to further grammatical rules, such as Categorial Grammar[4] or certain approaches in the spirit of the "Minimalist Program" [Chomsky, 1995].

Exercise 8.3
Calculate the denotation for (8.24) above.

Appendix: Assignments (final)
At this point, the assignment maps pronouns, variables (as found in e-type pronouns) and traces to individuals, as well as relational variables (again as in e-type pronouns) to relations *in intenso*. While pronouns and variables are interpreted the same (and thus are coreferring or co-bound if coindexed), traces are not:

---

[3] This account is not unlike the proposal in Ruys [2000], according to which traces left by *wh*-movement, including QR, are of a non-individual type. The assignment function will assign a meaning to each pronoun or trace, depending on its index *and logical type*, so that $[\![t_n]\!]^g$ can never be equal to $[\![pron_n]\!]^g$, since they are of different logical types in the first place. Unlike the present solution, which simply stipulates the different treatment for traces and pronouns, Ruys' explanation goes deeper in that it offers a reason why they *have* to be different. Since the net effect of both treatments is the same, and the details of the semantics assumed in Ruys [2000] are rather complicated, the reader is referred to that work and the references therein.

[4] Unsurprisingly, given that this proposal, as mentioned, is inspired by Jacobson [1999]'s Categorial Grammar treatment, in which the counterpart to our β, the *z-rule*, can only apply to predicates.

(8.26)   let G, the set of *assignments*, be the set of all partial functions from
$N \cup \{R_m^n \mid n, m \in N\} \cup \{t_n \mid n \in N\}$ (where N = the set of natural numbers)
such that

    (a)   for all $x \in N \cup \{t_n \mid n \in N\}$, $g(x)$ is an individual

    (b)   for all $x \in \{R_m^n \mid n, m \in N\}$, $g(x)$ is a function from worlds to n-place
    relations,

then for all $g \in G, n \in N$,

    (a) $[\![t_n]\!]^{w,g} = g(t_n)$

    (b) $[\![pron_n]\!]^{w,g} = [\![v_n]\!]^g = g(n)$ (if $[\![pron]\!]^g = g(n)$ in the pronoun case,
    undefined otherwise)

    (c) $[\![R_m^n]\!]^{w,g} = g(R_m^n)(w)$

8.2.3   Weakest crossover

Our discussion above has shown how to block NPs in derived positions from semantically binding pronouns, and argued that that is the correct
treatment of weak crossover. An immediate prediction of this is that nothing
should stop an NP from *coreferring* with a pronoun it has 'crossed over.' Obviously, this is not an option for the cases of *wh*-phrases and QNPs as discussed in
sections 8.1.1 and 8.1.2, respectively, as these kinds of NPs are unable to refer in
the first place (cf. chapter 4). But cases of the pertinent kind can be found with
topicalization, as in the following examples of so-called *weakest crossover*:[5]

(8.27)   (a)   *John*$_1$, I believe *his* mother loves t_1.

    (b)   *This book*$_1$, I would never ask *its* author to read t_1.

A well-formed LF for e.g. (8.27a) would look as in (8.28):

(8.28)   John $[\mu_1$ [I believe [his$_2$ mother] loves $t_1]]$

The pronoun *his* can now corefer with John (which could be indexed 2, were we
to index full NPs), and thereby end up having the same *referent* as it, without
semantic binding.

It is worth while to note that it is not topicalization *per se* that alleviates WCO
effects; we merely chose this construction because it allows us, in principle, to
move a referring NP. Topicalizing a quantificational NP immediately incurs a
WCO violation again, as pointed out in Postal [1993]:

(8.29)   (a)   *Jack*, I told *his* wife that I had called t_{Jack}.

    (b)   **Everybody else*, I told *his* wife that I had called t_{QNP}.

While (8.29a) is as fine as (8.27a), the otherwise parallel (8.29b) shows a typical
WCO effect. To be sure, (8.29b) is a perfectly good sentence if *his* is understood
as a referring pronoun, but it can't be bound by *everybody else*, nor can it corefer

---

[5] From Lasnik and Stowell [1991]:697; ideas similar to those developed in this subsection are also
found in Ruys (2004), which appeared when this book was at the page-proof stage.

with it. So both sentences support LFs like (8.30), but only if the topicalized element is a name can $g(2)$ be the referent of that name:[6]

(8.30) $\begin{Bmatrix} \text{Jack} \\ \text{everybody else} \end{Bmatrix}$ μ_1 [I told his$_2$ wife that I called t_1]

Topicalization is not the only construction of this kind, others being appositive relative clauses, clefts, and parasitic gap constructions (see the references above). Observe for example the contrast in (8.31):[7]

(8.31)   (a) *The/every book which its author wrote within a week was a hit.
                   (b) This book, which its author wrote within a week, is a hit.

Without going into the details, we assume that relative pronouns in general function as trace binders from derived positions; so the relative clauses in (8.31) have a structure as in (8.32) (cf. Heim and Kratzer [1998]:ch. 5):

(8.32)   which μ_4 its author wrote t_4 in a week

It is clear that *its* in (8.32) cannot be bound by *which* on pain of creating a WCO effect. Hence it must be a free pronoun, which, in the case of the appositive relative construction in (8.31b), can corefer with *this book*. With the restrictive relative in (8.31a), neither *the/every book* nor *the/every book that* . . . refers in the first place, so the only option for *his* to anaphorically depend on it would be to be bound by *which*, which is blocked by WCO.

    Cases of weakest crossover thus provide evidence in favor of our treatment of WCO as a fact about semantic binding, not anaphoric dependencies or indexing in general.[8]

8.2.4   Strong crossover

        Our treatment of weak crossover also blocks so-called *strong crossover* (SCO) cases:

(8.33)   *Who does *he* love?

(8.33) is trying to mean 'who is loved by himself'; but to derive that meaning, *who* would have to bind *he* from a derived position, which is impossible by

---

[6] One might wonder whether the Coreference rule should have anything to object to in the good cases above. Shouldn't the topicalized NP, say *Jack* in (8.29a), have to bind *his*, instead of coreferring with it? The answer must be that the CR doesn't regard that option, arguably precisely because it is in principle impossible, given the way binding works.

[7] Cf. Lasnik and Stowell [1991]:698.

[8] It should be pointed out that Postal (1993) notices a number of curious exceptions to the picture drawn above, among them that WCO seems to return if the intermediary pronoun is within what he calls a scope island, cf. the contrast in (i). This might suggest that weakest crossover somehow involves c-command between the pronoun and the trace after all (cf. n. 6 above), an issue we cannot further explore here.

(i)   (a) *Sidney*, I'm sure *his* job/mother/beard is important to.
                 (b) **Sidney*, I'm sure your carving/description/opinion of *him* is important to.

the Binder rule. In addition, and unlike in the WCO cases, the pronoun in SCO c-commands the trace of its would-be binder. We can stipulate an additional condition to rule out that configuration, e.g. (8.34):

(8.34)   A *wh*-moved NP must not bind any pronoun c-commanding its (NP's) trace.

Why should we have some extra principle to the effect of (8.34) in our grammar; why doesn't it suffice that our treatment of WCO rules out SCO? Let me briefly mention three reasons: first, strong crossover violations – as the name suggests – are perceived as more severely degraded than weak crossover ones, suggesting that some additional, stronger principle is at work. Second, strong crossover is found in non-quantificational ('weakest crossover') cases, where weak crossover is not found at all (cf. section 8.2.3 above):

(8.35)   this suspect, whom his mother/ *he claims never left the house,...

Third, languages may display strong crossover effects, while lacking weak crossover effects, as is the case in German:

(8.36)   (a)   *Wen* hat *seine* Mutter lieb?
                who has his   mother dear
          (b) ∗ *Wen* hat *er* lieb?
                who has he dear
                'Who is his mother/he fond of ?'

Though we cannot go into why the weak crossover effect is absent in (8.36a) (see Fanselow [1993]; Grewendorf [1988]; Müller [1993] as well as Vanden Wyngaerd [1989]; Mahajan [1990] for cross-linguistic data), it seems clear that strong and weak crossover (at least in such languages) cannot be due to the same cause.

We conclude that an extra condition must rule out SCO; (8.34) does this, though, in an entirely stipulative way. A suggestion often found in the literature is that the correct rendering of (8.34) is that traces of *wh*-movement are subject to Binding Condition C. Since *he* binds the trace of *who* in (8.33), we derive a violation of that condition, explaining the ungrammaticality of the example. This suggestion actually rules out many more cases than the generalization in (8.34); the latter only requires that a trace be 'free' within the c-command domain of the moved element, but says nothing about any element binding both the trace *and* its binder. As long as we look at cases where the moved element is a *wh*-phrase, it is hard to tease these predictions apart, since *wh*-elements cannot themselves be bound. But, if we look at other instances of *wh*-movement such as topicalization, we find that there is nothing wrong with a topicalized pronoun being bound from a higher clause, whereas embedding a full NP in the position of the trace of the pronoun yields a typical Binding Condition C effect; this holds true for the somewhat stilted case of English topicalization in the translations below, and even more clearly so for embedded topicalization in verb second languages such as Danish:[9]

(8.37)   (a)   *Henrik/ han* tror   at   *ham* kunne ingen   lyve over for t_{ham}.
                 H./   he   thinks that him   could no-one lie   over for
                 'Henrik/he thinks that him, nobody could lie to.'

         (b)   * *Henrik/ han* tror   at   her   kunne ingen   lyve over for
                 H./   he   thinks that here could no-one lie   over for
                 H.
                 H.
                 'Henrik/he thinks that here, no one could lie to Henrik.'

These facts cast doubts on the idea that traces of *wh*-movement should be subjected to Binding Condition C in order to derive the strong crossover effect. We will leave open the question of what, instead, is the correct analysis of SCO.

I should mention in closing that strong crossover, whatever its correct rendering, is sometimes used to derive negative Binding Conditions. To illustrate, suppose that for some reason non-reflexive pronouns in English always had to move to a clause initial position in English. It would then follow by (8.34) that they couldn't be anaphorically related to any NP that c-commanded them before movement.[10] So the LF for *John likes him* would be *him John likes*, and since *John* c-commands the trace of *him* at LF, it cannot be anaphorically related to *him* on pain of violating (8.34). Generally, any condition of the form 'An NP of class X must be free in domain Y' can thus be re-rendered as 'An NP of class X must move to the top (specifier . . .) of Y at LF.'[11]

Quite arguably, little is won by "explaining" Binding Conditions in this way, given that we replace one stipulation – the initial Binding Condition – by another – the LF-movement requirement; therefore, we will not pursue SCO as an analysis of negative binding requirements any further.[12]

8.3   A challenge: indirect binding

Let us now look at a phenomenon that raises serious problems for the treatment of variable binding provided so far, *indirect binding*.[13] By indirect

---

[9] Example courtesy of Line Mikkelsen (p.c.).

[10] Note, in passing, that this line of analysis crucially relies on an explanation of SCO that doesn't require traces of *wh*-movement to be free in the entire sentence, as a Binding Condition C treatment along the lines discussed in the last paragraph would, since otherwise an LF-moved pronoun would always have to be free in *any* domain.

[11] Suggestions along these lines are found e.g. in Déchaine and Wilschko (2002); Demirdache (1997).

[12] In general, independent evidence for such an approach could be found. For example, an SCO account for pronouns would seem to predict that if a pronoun needs to be free in domain X (since it moves to the top of X at LF) it also cannot be anaphorically related to any NP *within* a c-commanding constituent in X (since that would trigger a weak crossover violation). I am not aware of such arguments, however.

[13] We discuss indirect binding here because it is the exception to the WCO generalization presented in the previous section that is best studied and – though perhaps not fully explained – understood.

binding, we refer to a class of examples in which a pronominal NP covaries with a QNP or *wh*-phrase that does not c-command it. Examples are *genitive binding* in (8.38) and *inverse linking* in (8.39):[14]

(8.38)   (a)   *Whose* mother loves *him/his* sister?
          (b)   *Every senator*'s portrait was on *his* desk.
          (c)   *Some boy*'s father's best friend's daughter wants *him* to marry her.

(8.39)   (a)   Somebody from *every city* despises *it/its* architecture.
          (b)   *Every daughter* of every professor in *some small college town* wishes *she* could leave *it*.

For the purpose of the following discussion, we will refer to the larger NPs that c-command the pronoun (*whose mother, every senator's portrait*, etc.) as the *container* NP, and to the QNP that antecedes the pronoun (*whose, every senator*) as the *embedded QNP*.

8.3.1   Extraction analyses

Starting with the inverse linking construction, let us first look at the interpretation of a non-quantificational case such as *some person from Berlin*, which is straightforward. We assume that *from* denotes a relation between individuals and cities (which are individuals as well), and that the meaning of *from Berlin* is combined with that of *person* by *predicate modification*:

(8.40)   (a) $[\![\text{person}]\!]^g = \lambda x.x$ is a person
          (b) $[\![\text{from}]\!]^g = \lambda y \lambda z.z$ is from y
          (c) $[\![\text{Berlin}]\!]^g = $ Berlin (the city)
          (d) $[\![\text{from Berlin}]\!]^g = \lambda z.z$ is from Berlin (from [8.40b] and [8.40c] by function application)
          (e) $[\![\text{person from Berlin}]\!]^g = \lambda z.z$ is a person and z is from Berlin (from [8.40d] and [8.40a] by predicate modification)
          (f)   Predicate modification:
                 $[\![Y\ Z]\!]^g = [\lambda x_e.[\![Y]\!]^g(x) = 1$ and $[\![Z]\!]^g(x) = 1]$ if Y and Z are of type $\langle et \rangle$ (cf. Heim and Kratzer [1998]:ch. 4.3).

The meaning of *some*, recall, maps sets of individuals to sets of properties:

(8.41)   (a) $[\![\text{some}]\!]^g = \lambda P_1 \lambda P_2.$ there is some x such that $P_1(x) = 1$ and $P_2(x) = 1$
          (b) $[\![\text{some person from Berlin}]\!]^g = \lambda P_2.$ there is some x such that x is a person and x is from Berlin and $P_2(x) = 1$

Other rather mysterious exceptions to the generalization cannot be discussed here, e.g. that WCO effects – at least with overt *wh*-movement – disappear with certain focusing particles (Postal, 1993:549), or if the pronoun is within an adjunct (Lasnik and Stowell, 1991:690):

(i)   (a)   *Which lawyer* did even *his* clients/only *his* older clients/*his* own clients hate?
       (b)   *Who* did Jan say she admired in order to please *him*?

[14] From May (1988):89f.; Hornstein (1995):108; and Higginbotham (1980b):690f.

In *some person from every city*, the embedded QNP *every city* occupies the place of *Berlin*, which poses a problem. For one thing, QNPs don't denote individuals, so *every city* can't combine with *from* by function application. For another thing, note that *every (city)* takes logical scope over *some*: *some person from every city sleeps* doesn't say that some person, who is from every city sleeps (perhaps there is such a reading, too, but it is rather nonsensical, and doesn't concern us here), but rather that for every city, there is some person from it who sleeps.

Assume, then, that at LF, *every city* is quantifier raised from the container NP *some person from every city* and adjoined to the clause. The LF we get is thus:

(8.42)

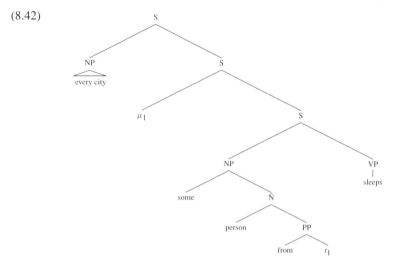

This LF contains our familiar trace binding operator μ. Its interpretation is, as desired:

(8.43)   for every city z, there is some person x who is from z, and x sleeps

So far so good. What if we replace *sleeps* with *likes its beaches*, where we co-index *its* with *every city*? Intuitively, we want to derive a logical form like (8.44):

(8.44)   for every city z, there is some person x who is from z, and x likes z's beaches

Alas, we won't derive this reading. To see this, remember that traces and pronouns are not interpreted on a par. In particular, $[\![\text{likes its}_1\text{ beaches}]\!]^g$ is $[\lambda x.x$ likes $g(1)$'s beaches]; $[\![\text{some person from t}_1]\!]^g$ is $[\lambda P.$ there is a person y who is from $g(t_1)$ and $P(y) = 1]$. If we combine these two, we get:

(8.45) $[\![\text{some person from } t_1 \text{ likes its}_1 \text{ beaches}]\!]^g =$ there is a person y who is from $g(t_1)$ and likes $g(1)$'s beaches

Now we interpret the μ-operator, which yields:

(8.46) $\lambda z.$ there is a person y who is from $g[t_1 \to z](t_1)$ and likes $g[t_1 \to z](1)$'s beaches
           $= \lambda z.$ there is a person y who is from z and likes $g(1)$'s beaches

At this point it should be clear what went wrong: the μ-prefix has bound the trace but not the pronoun. Accordingly, the pronoun will remain free, and the sentence will mean 'for every city, there is some person who is from that city and likes $g(1)$'s beaches' – certainly an available reading, but not the one we're after.

To get the pronoun to be bound, then, we have to insert a binder prefix, β, as in (8.47):

(8.47)

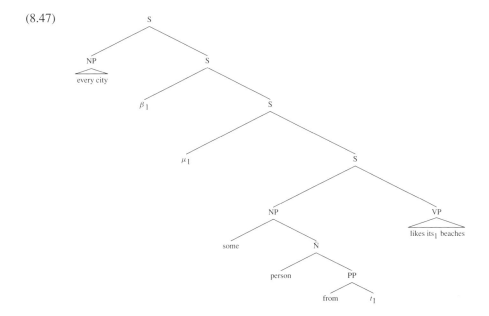

This LF gets us the correct reading, but it is not derived by our rules. In particular, the insertion of the β prefix is not licensed by the Binder rule (8.25), given that *every city* is in a derived position.

This is not just an oversight. The Binder rule was formulated precisely so as to exclude binding from derived positions, and (8.47) is as clear an instance of that as can be.

Without going into the details, note that an analogous problem haunts cases of genitive binding such as (8.38b). Let *portrait* denote a relation (the one that holds between a portrait and the person portrayed on it), then we can derive a case like *Mary's portrait* as follows:

(8.48)   (a) $[\![portrait]\!]^g = \lambda x \lambda y. y$ is a portrait of x
         (b) $[\![\text{'s}]\!]^g = \lambda R \lambda x.$ the unique z such that $R(x)(z) = 1$ (undefined if there is no such z)
         (c) $[\![\text{'s portrait}]\!]^g = \lambda x.$ the unique z such that z is a portrait of x (undefined if there is no such z)
         (d) $[\![\text{Mary's portrait}]\!]^g =$ the unique z such that z is a portrait of Mary (undefined if there is no such z)

Once again, to derive the correct reading for an example with a quantified genitive NP, we have to apply QR:

(8.49)

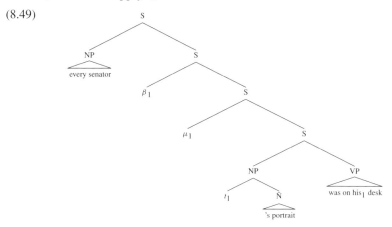

This LF gets both the pronoun (by β) and the trace (by μ) bound, but again,
is not licensed by the Binder rule, since β is adjoined next to an NP in derived
position.

Before going on, it is worth while to note that these indirect binding cases
are also incompatible with the filtering accounts of crossover discussed in section 8.2.1. For example, the QR-ed NPs *every city* and *every senator* bind a trace
and a pronoun at the same time, in violation of Koopman and Sportiche (1983)'s
Bijection Principle.

8.3.2   Accessibility

We saw above that the correct interpretation for indirect binding
structures can be derived if we give up the extra clause in our Binder rule in (8.25)
which restricts β adjunction to non-derived positions. Let us assume we do (I
will suggest in section 8.3.3 that we don't have to); the new task, then, is to find
a different way of blocking standard WCO cases such as (8.24), while allowing
for LFs like (8.47) and (8.49). I will not here go through all the proposals found
in the literature, but zoom right in on one that provides the empirically correct
results; this system is largely built on work by James Higginbotham.[15] To start,
we define a new notion of *accessibility*; based on that, we then define a filter to
rule out WCO:

(8.50)   NP$_1$ is *accessible* to NP$_2$ iff

    (a)   NP$_1$ c-commands NP$_2$ from a non-derived position (it is *directly ac-
    cessible*), or

    (b)   NP$_1$ binds a trace accessible to, or within an NP accessible to, NP$_2$

(8.51)   Crossover filter: NP$_1$ can bind NP$_2$ only if it is accessible to NP$_2$.

---

[15] Higginbotham (1980a,b, 1983, 1985, 1987) cf. also Haïk (1984); Reinhart (1987); Safir (1984);
    alternative proposals include May (1988); and Hornstein (1995):ch. 6.

Consider how these definitions apply to simple cases of direct binding: by clause (8.50a), *Mona* in *Mona likes her mother* is directly accessible to *her* and may thus bind it (it is in a c-commanding, non-derived position). This holds even if *Mona* for some reason undergoes QR, because then it binds a trace accessible to *her*, which, by (8.50b), is sufficient.

A crossover violation like (8.2) will still be derived by the definitions in (8.50)/(8.51):

(8.52)   ∗*Whom* did *his* uncle call t_{who}?

Here *whom* doesn't c-command *his* from a non-derived position, so it doesn't qualify as directly accessible by (8.50a); nor does it bind a trace that is accessible to *his*, or contained in an NP that is. Thus *whom* isn't accessible to *his*, and by (8.51) can't bind it.

Turning to indirect binding, then, note that *every city* in (8.47) binds a trace within the subject NP *some person from t*; the subject NP in turn is directly accessible to *its* in *its beaches*, which, by (8.50b), makes *every city* accessible to it as well. Therefore the structure is predicted to be fine by (8.51); similarly for (8.49).

The crossover filter (8.51) also correctly predicts cases of so-called *secondary weak crossover* (2WCO). 2WCO is found e.g. in (8.53):[16]

(8.53)   (a) ∗*Whose* mother does *his* sister love?
          (b) ∗*Its* climate is hated by everybody from *some city*.

Take (8.53b): to get the reading we are after, *some city* has to be QR-ed above *its climate*. One possible LF for this looks as in (8.54):

(8.54)   [[some city] β_8 μ_8 [its$_8$ climate is hated by [everybody from t_8]]]

Obviously, *some city* is not directly accessible to *its*, because it is in a derived position. But since the NP containing its trace, *everybody from t_8*, isn't accessible to *its* either (it doesn't c-command it), *some city* is not accessible to *its* and thus violates the crossover filter (8.51). What about the following LF?

(8.55)   [[some city] β_8 μ_8 [[everybody from t_8] μ_4 [its$_8$ climate is hated by t_4]]]

Now, *everybody from t_8*, after QR-ing itself, does c-command *its (climate)*, but from a derived position. Hence, it is still not accessible to *its*, and neither is *some city*. The crossover effect thus remains.

We can summarize the crossover generalization embodied by (8.51) by the following slogan:

(8.56)   Surface generalization about WCO and 2WCO:
          A(n embedded) QNP can bind a pronoun only if it(s container NP) c-commands the pronoun from a non-derived position.

---

[16] From Safir (1984):627; and Higginbotham (1980b):693.

Before closing, it is important to point out that (8.51) and its rendering in (8.56) provide necessary, but not sufficient, conditions on pronoun binding. Not every QNP that meets them can therefore bind a pronoun it doesn't c-command. For example, *every city* in (8.57) clearly cannot, in contrast to (8.39a):

(8.57)   *Somebody who lives in *every city* likes *its* beaches.

Every city's container NP c-commands *its* from a non-derived position; put differently, if *every city* raises by QR, even just within the relative clause, its trace will be contained in an NP accessible to *its*. So *every city* is accessible to *its* and should be able to bind it, contrary to fact.

The crucial observation here is that, regardless of pronoun binding, *somebody who lives in every city VP* cannot mean 'for every city, there is somebody who lives in that city and who VP'; that is, *every city* cannot scope over *some*. We assume that this restriction will be derivable from a general theory of scoping – e.g. that quantifiers cannot be raised out of relative clauses. As far as Binding Theory is concerned, the relevant conclusion is simply that accessibility to a pronoun is not the only precondition for (indirect) binding, scope over the pronoun being another one.

Exercise 8.4
Give an LF for (8.38c) above. Show that each binder is accessible to its bindee.

8.3.3   Indirect binding and e-type pronouns

Is there a way to reconcile indirect binding with our earlier restriction embodied in (8.25) that pronoun binding can only proceed from non-derived positions, thereby avoiding a filter like (8.51)? In passing, Bach and Partee (1980) suggest an alternative treatment of possessor binding cases, which is compatible with our original treatment of WCO. They propose that the bound pronoun in these constructions should be analyzed as an e-type pronoun, as discussed in chapter 7. Adapting that proposal to our present system, (8.38b) for example would get an LF as in (8.58), where the apparently bound pronoun is expanded as an e-type pronoun *the R_5 v_2*:

(8.58)   every senator μ_1 [[t_1's portrait] [β_2 was on [[**the** R_5 v_2]'s desk]]]

Now we instantiate the variable R_5 with the relation 'be (the senator) portrayed on' (in boldface), and we get:

(8.59)   for every senator x, the portrait, y, of x is on the desk of **the senator/person portrayed on** y

This paraphrase is cumbersome to read, but it is intuitively correct: the person portrayed is the senator, so *the R_5 v_2 with v_2 bound to every senator's portrait* is the same as *his* bound to *every senator*. A completely parallel analysis can be given for inverse linking cases (Büring, 2001b, 2004):

(8.60)   (a)   every city μ_1 [[some person from t_1] [β_2 likes [[**the** R_7 v_2]'s beaches]]]

          (b)   for every city x, there is some person y from x who likes the beaches of **the city** y **is from**

Here, R_7 must be assigned the relation 'be the city of' to yield the intuitively correct paraphrase.

What makes this proposal interesting in the present context is that it allows us to maintain our original account of WCO in terms of restricting β to non-derived positions. Note that it isn't the embedded QNP that functions as the binder in (8.58) and (8.60a), but the container NP, which c-commands the pronoun (and, hence, the variable within the pronoun under the e-type account) from a non-derived position. Thus binding takes places under c-command from a non-derived position.

This analysis directly captures the 2WCO facts as well. Consider the contrast between (8.38b)/(8.58) and (8.61):

(8.61)   *His* file contained a portrait of *every senator*.

According to the e-type analysis of indirect binding, (8.61) has the LF in (8.62):

(8.62)   every senator μ_1 [[a portrait of t_1] [$\boxed{\beta_2}$ μ_3 [[**the** R_4 v_2]'s file] contained t_3]]

Let the relation R_4 be instantiated as 'being (a senator) portrayed on'; as in (8.58) before, this LF could only get the pertinent reading – 'for every senator, his portrait was contained in the file of the person on that portrait' – if *a portrait of* ... could bind the variable v_2 within the e-type pronoun from a derived position, via the boxed β in (8.62). But this, again, is not possible by our Binder rule (8.25).

Generally, the e-type pronoun analysis directly derives the generalization in (8.56): the embedded QNP can antecede a pronoun only if the container NP c-commands it from a non-derived position. Given that the container NP *is* the binder, this is simply our original generalization about WCO – indeed 2WCO turns out to be nothing but WCO after pronoun expansion.

Summing up this section so far, we have seen how to derive the correct scoping and binding for indirect binding constructions by QR at LF. After QR, we have two analytical choices: either we let the extracted embedded QNP directly bind the pronoun (since this binding takes place from a derived position, we have to give up our previous implementation of the crossover generalization in favor of the conditions in [8.51]); or we analyze the apparently bound pronoun as an e-type pronoun, the variable within which is actually bound by the container NP from a non-derived position, in keeping with our earlier WCO account.

8.3.4   Sub-extraction analyses [ⓔ]

The syntactic analysis of indirect binding presented in the previous subsections has been criticized for invoking extraction of the binder QNP from its container NP. For one thing, extraction from NPs, in particular from preverbal genitives, is generally impossible:

(8.63)   (a) *Who did [every person from t] get sick?
           (b) *Who/whose did [t ('s) sister] win the award?

While one might counter that observation by simply claiming that (covert) QR is simply not restricted in the same way as (overt) *wh*-movement (although such a move arguably weakens the plausibility of a movement account), no such maneuver seems forthcoming for the second objection: no other quantifier can ever take scope in between the sub-extracted QNP and its former container. For example, (8.64), from Larson (1987), has only two, instead of the predicted three, readings:

(8.64)   Two agents spy on some politician from every city.
           (a)   every – some – two
           (b)   two – every – some
           (c) *every – two – some

The pragmatically plausible reading that is missing here is one where there are two agents assigned to each city, each spying on some, possibly different, politician from that city. The question is what blocks the LF that leads to that reading, (8.65):

(8.65)

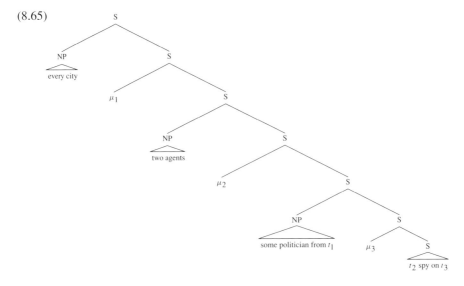

While not every conceivable option to block (8.65) can be discussed here, it should at least be noted that *some politician from every city* as a *whole can* scope over the subject, yielding a reading where some politician in each city has two agents spying on him ([8.64a] – this reading is different from the one we're after, since, on the missing reading, no politician needs to have two spies assigned to them). What seems impossible is for *every city* and its container to scope independently (see May [1985]:69ff.; Larson [1987]; and subsequently, Barker [2001a,b]; and Heim and Kratzer [1998]:232ff. for more discussion).

Both objections discussed point to the same conclusion: it seems unlikely that the QNP really leaves its container at LF. Rather, they remain one syntactic and semantic unit. Therefore May (1985):69f. proposes to assign an LF essentially like (8.66):

(8.66)

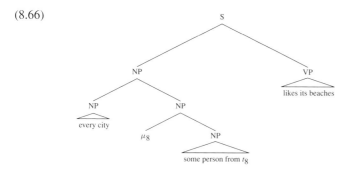

Here, *every city* has merely been *sub*extracted from its container, and adjoined to it. This LF neither involves actual extraction from NP, nor does it allow any clause-mate QNPs to scope in between *every city* and *some*, alleviating both problems discussed above. And, according to May, adjunction to NP is sufficient to give *every city* wide scope.

We will show that this is indeed the case in the appendix to this section. For the moment, let us take for granted that the container NP receives the following meaning:

(8.67) $[\![$every city $[\mu_8$ some person from $t_8]]\!]^g = \lambda P$.for every city x, there is some person y from x such that $P(y) = 1$

Note that *every city* in *some person from every city VP* counts as *accessible* (in the sense of section 8.3.2) to everything within VP, since it binds a trace within an NP which is accessible to VP (i.e. c-commands VP from a non-derived position). Still, *every city* does *not* bind anything inside VP, including *its* in (8.39a). More generally, while we derive the correct scoping, indirect binding is generally ruled out under the subextraction analysis. This is because we assume that binding, although not scope, requires c-command. More precisely, a β prefix that could bind *its* in *[VP likes its beaches]* has to c-command *its*. This could be achieved by adjoining β to the VP; but on the resulting reading *its* would wind up bound by *some person from every city*, which is, of course, not what we're after.

On the other hand, for *every city* to be the binder of *its*, it has to (minimally) c-command the β binding *its*. So we could adjoin β right above μ in (8.66). But then β wouldn't bind *its* because it doesn't c-command it, and β only affects variables within its c-command domain.

This problem is not easily fixed, and we will not be able to go into the details of conceivable solutions. Suffice it to say, at this point, that *some person from every city* cannot denote a plain generalized quantifier; that is, it cannot denote a set of properties, like 'ordinary' QNPs. Rather, it has to denote a set of relations, and VP has to denote a relation (instead of a property), as sketched in (8.68):

(8.68)   (a) $[\![\text{some person from every city}]\!]^g = \lambda R \in D_{e,et}$.for every city c, there is a person x who is from c such that $R(c)(x)$

          (b) $[\![\text{likes its beaches}]\!]^g = \lambda x \lambda y.y$ likes x's beaches

Clearly, neither our binder prefixes nor our composition rules for NPs allow for the derivation of such meanings. Furthermore, it should be noted that the procedure is not limited to two-place relations. Consider (8.69); here, the VP has to denote a three-place relation, and the subject NP, accordingly, a set of such relations:

(8.69)   No boy's mother's car allows her to transport all his gear.

          (a) $[\![\text{no boy's mother's car}]\!]^g = \lambda R^3 \in D_{\langle e, \langle e, et \rangle \rangle}$. there is no b such that b is a boy and there are m and c such that m is b's mother and c is m's car and $R^3(b)(m)(c)$

          (b) $[\![\text{allows her to transport all his gear}]\!]^g = \lambda x \lambda y \lambda z.z$ allows y to transport all x's gear

By the end of the day, a system capable of interpreting constructions like this will presumably generalize to the worst case, i.e. assume that QNPs, no matter how complex (or simple), generally quantify over *all* variables in their argument, i.e. over assignments. Such a system is developed in Chierchia (1995), although indirect binding by QNPs is not discussed there; see also Barker (2001a).

It should be noted that the e-type solution outlined in subsection 8.3.3 above doesn't face a problem with the subextraction syntax, since on that account it is always the container NP, and only it, that does the binding. The approach thus directly carries over to the subextraction analysis. For example, the LFs for (8.39a) and (8.69) are as in (8.70):

(8.70)   (a)   [[every city [μ_3 some person from t_3]] [β_8 likes [[the R_9 v_8]'s beaches]]]
                 (i)   let $g(R_9) = [\lambda x \lambda y.x$ is from y]; then ...
                 (ii) $[\![(8.70a)]\!]^g =$ for every city x, some person y from x likes the beaches of **the city y is from**

          (b)   [[no boy [μ_1[[t_1's mother] [μ_2 car]]]] [β_3 allows [the R_1 v_3][β_4 to transport all [[the R_2 v_4]'s gear]]]]
                 (i)   let $g(R_1) = [\lambda x \lambda y.y$ owns/drives x], and $R_2 = [\lambda x \lambda y.y$ is the son of y]; then ...
                 (ii) $[\![(8.70b)]\!]^g =$ there is no boy x such that the mother y of x has a car z and z allows **the owner u of** z to transport all of **u's son's** gear

I have indicated the necessary assignments to relational variables underneath the examples, and indicated the readings they produce. In each case, the important thing is that only the container NP itself gets to bind into the VP, which is compatible with the generalization that binding requires c-command from a non-derived position. How the container NP itself receives its meaning – via extraction, subextraction, or without QR at all – is irrelevant to the e-type analysis of indirect binding.

It should be mentioned, though, that the e-type analysis in its simplest version cannot be the whole story about these cases. For example, since the LF (8.70b) contains the definite NP *the R_2 v_4*, where R_2 is assigned the 'son of' relation, the whole LF should only be defined if each $g(v_4)$ has one unique son, i.e. if we only talk about mothers with just one son. But this is clearly not our intuition about this example: if we find two brothers, one of which can fit all his gear in his mom's car, we judge (8.69) to be false. And if neither brother can fit his gear, we judge the sentence to be true, not undefined. No such problem appears if we assume *no boy* to bind *his* directly, because then we effectively quantify over boy+mother+car triples, of which there are at least as many as there are boys.

This well-known *uniqueness problem* haunts most applications of e-type pronouns alike, including simple paycheck cases as in (8.71):

(8.71)   Every mother of a daughter wants her daughter to be successful, but no mother likes to hear that *she* is over-ambitious.

As the example illustrates, the question is not merely what *she* denotes, but even what its supposed antecedent *her daughter* does, if the pertinent mother has more than one daughter.

It seems, thus, that the proper analysis of e-type pronouns must be whatever the proper analysis of definite descriptions and possessive NPs is. What is clear is that neither *her daughter* nor *her* in (8.71) can denote just a function that maps an individual onto an individual. Many recent analyses using e-type pronouns thus assume that their meanings map individual+*situation* pairs onto individuals. For our example (8.69) that would mean that we are not simply quantifying over cars, but over car+situation pairs, where the situation contains the car, the mother who owns it, and a son of hers; for mothers with more than one son, there will be as many such situations as there are sons, and, accordingly, as many car+situation pairs (or more, if the woman has more than one car). The e-type pronouns then refer to 'her son in that situation,' which would make the analysis equivalent to one that quantifies over car+mother+son individual triples. Whether such an analysis can be devised for all cases of indirect binding is a controversial issue, and the reader is referred to the literature on this topic (Heim, 1990; Elbourne, 2001; Büring, 2001a, 2004; Barker, 2001a, a.o.).

We have seen in this section that indirect binding poses two problems for the system developed so far: first, since it involves binding from a position derived by quantifier raising (i.e. *wh*-movement), we need to formulate a new account

of weak crossover; second, if we want to avoid extracting the QNP from its
container, as seems preferable on theoretical and empirical grounds, we also
need an entirely new account of the semantics of binding, which doesn't require c-command. An alternative analysis using e-type pronouns was sketched,
which would circumvent both problems and allow us to maintain the Binder rule
in (8.25).

Exercise 8.5

In the context of donkey sentences, Neale (1990):ch. 6 suggests that
e-type pronouns can be interpreted as numberless descriptions, such that e.g. *the
R v* is interpreted as 'the sum of all elements in $g(R)(g(v))$', e.g. 'the son or
sons of $g(v)$.' Does this solution help for the e-type analysis of indirect binding?
Argue

Appendix: How to interpret the NP-adjoined structures

In discussing the subextraction analysis, we took it for granted that
an NP like *some person from every city*, after subextraction of *every city* will
denote the set of properties $[\lambda P.$ for every city x, there is at least one person y
from x who has $P]$ (i.e. such that $P[y]$). Let us now see how this meaning is
compositionally derived, starting with the lower NP segment (cf. the structure
in [8.66]):

(8.72) $[\![$some person from $t_8]\!]^g = \lambda P.$ there is a person x who is from $g(t_8)$ such
that $P(x) = 1$

Since *every city* has moved to the NP-adjoined position, it has a μ-prefix adjoined
next to it, so that as a next step we get:

(8.73) $[\![\mu_8 \, [\text{ some person from } t_8]]\!]^g = \lambda y\lambda P.$ there is a person x who is from
$g[t_8 \to y](t_8)$ (i.e. from y) such that $P(x) = 1$

This, unfortunately, cannot combine with *every city* by function application, because *every city* wants a property as its argument, which (8.73) isn't. What we
need is a way to 'skip' the λP argument in (8.73) for the purpose of composing it
with *every city*. The κ-operator introduced in chapter 4, section 4.5.3, to interpret
QNPs in object positions allows just that:[17]

(8.74)

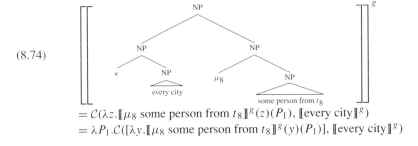

$= \mathcal{C}(\lambda z.[\![\mu_8 \text{ some person from } t_8]\!]^g(z)(P_1), [\![\text{every city}]\!]^g)$
$= \lambda P_1.\mathcal{C}([\lambda y.[\![\mu_8 \text{ some person from } t_8]\!]^g(y)(P_1)], [\![\text{every city}]\!]^g)$

---

[17] See Heim and Kratzer (1998):ch. 8 for more discussion about how to interpret structures like
these.

$$= \lambda P_1.[\![\text{every city}]\!]^g([\lambda y.[\![\mu_8 \text{ some person from } t_8]\!]^g(y)(P_1)])$$
$$= \lambda P_1.[\lambda P_2.\text{for every city } c, P_2(c) = 1]$$
$$([\lambda y.[\lambda z \lambda P_3. \text{ there is a person } x \text{ from } z \text{ s.t. } P_3(x) = 1](y)(P_1)])$$
$$= \lambda P_1.[\lambda P_2.\text{for every city } c, P_2(c) = 1]$$
$$([\lambda y.\text{there is a person } x \text{ from } y \text{ such that } P_1(x) = 1])$$
$$= \lambda P_1.\text{for every city } c,$$
$$[\lambda y. \text{ there is a person } x \text{ from } y \text{ such that } P_1(x) = 1](c)$$
$$= \lambda P_1.\text{for every city } c \text{ there is a person } x \text{ from } c \text{ such that } P_1(x) = 1$$

This NP, then, denotes the set of all properties P_1 such that for every city, some person from that city has P_1, which is an ordinary QNP meaning (of type $\langle et,e\rangle$).

Exercise 8.6

Using the lexical entries given in (8.48), and the model of (8.74), (i) calculate the interpretation for *every senator's portrait* using subextraction (i.e. adjunction of *every senator* to the container NP). (ii) Calculate the meaning again, leaving the QNP *in situ*. Do you find any difficulties or differences in interpretation? (iii) Give an LF for *every senator's portrait was on his desk* assuming the e-type analysis of indirect binding, and interpret that LF.

9 Plurals

9.1   The semantics of plural NPs

What is the denotation of a plural NP such as *we, they, yourselves, Heidi and Tor* or *the trombones*? We assume that these are referring expressions, and denote *pluralities*.[1] For example, [[the trombones]]^g is the plurality consisting of all (contextually salient) trombones, and [[Heidi and Tor]]^g denotes the plurality consisting of Heidi and Tor.

Technically, a plurality is an individual, just like the denotation of a singular NP like *he* or *Sidney* is; where we need to distinguish them, we call the latter *atoms* (as opposed to pluralities). So atoms and pluralities together make up the domain of individuals, D_e.

Being an individual, a plurality like [[Heidi and Tor]]^g is different from a QNP denotation like [[each of Heidi and Tor]]^g (which is a generalized quantifier, cf. chapter 4, sections 4.1 and 4.5.2); note, for example, that you can say *Heidi and Tor make a good couple*, but not **Each of Heidi and Tor make a good couple*. It is also different from the *set* containing Heidi and Tor (e.g. the denotation of the VP *is Heidi or Tor*). This is important to keep in mind, since thinking of plural NPs as denoting sets is probably the analytical option that comes to mind first (see e.g. Bennet [1994]). Though I won't argue against the plurals = sets view here (cf. again Link [1983], as well as Landman [2000]; Lasersohn [1995]; and Schwarzschild [1996] for overviews), note that this helps keep the semantics uniform: both *Heidi walks* and *Heidi and Tor walk* are true if the individual denoted by the subject is in the set denoted by the VP; if plurals denoted sets, we'd have to have a special rule to see whether that set is a subset of the VP-denotation. It also allows us to coordinate singular and plural NPs as in *Siouxsie and the Banshees*.

Of course, there *is* a relation between a plurality and the atoms (and smaller pluralities) that make it up, the (atomic) *part-of relation*, which we write as $\sqsubseteq$, read: 'is a part of.' For example, [[John]]$^g \sqsubseteq$ [[Mary and John]]^g, and [[Mary]]$^g \sqsubseteq$ [[Mary and John]]^g (but not [[John's liver]]$^g \sqsubseteq$ [[Mary and John]]^g).

---

[1] The more intuitive term *groups* has a special meaning in the relevant literature, which is different from that of *pluralities* there (Landman, 1989; Link, 1983, 1999, a.o.); though we won't deal with this distinction in this book, I use the term *pluralities* here to be consistent with the literature.

Table 9.1 *Boumaa Fijian cardinal pronouns (Dixon, 1988:54f.)*

	Singular	Plural	Dual	Paucal
1st exclusive	yau	'eimami	'eirau	'eitou
1st inclusive	–	'eta	'eetaru	'etatou
2nd	i'o	'emunuu	'emudrau	'emudou
3rd	'ea	(i)ra	(i)rau	(i)ratou

Since pluralities are members of the set of individuals D_e, assignment functions can assign pluralities to indices, which is what we want. The number information on pronouns can be treated as a presupposition in the familiar way:

(9.1)   (a) $[\![\text{she}_n]\!]^g = g(n)$ if $g(n)$ is a female, *atomic* individual, undefined otherwise

(b) $[\![\text{they}_n]\!]^g = g(n)$ if $g(n)$ is a plurality, undefined otherwise

If we were to index full NPs, this would work analogously, e.g. $[\![[\text{the trombones}]_n]\!]^g = g(n)$ if $g(n)$ is the plurality consisting of all (contextually salient) trombones, undefined otherwise. So if our semantics properly ensures that *the trombones* without an index denotes a plurality – and we assume that it does – this will carry over to indexed plural NPs.

Other than singulars and plurals, we find *duals, trials*, and *paucals* among the languages of the world (though not in English). A dual NP denotes a plurality with exactly two atoms, a trial one with exactly three, and a paucal one with more than two, but not many. Boumaa Fijian is an example of a language with a four-way articulated pronoun system, cf. table 9.1.[2] These can be handled by presuppositions similar to, but more differentiated than, those in (9.1) above. In fact, we can define the semantic counterparts of person, number, and gender features, and employ a general interpretation rule for pronouns (see Harley and Ritter [2002] for an elaborate morphosyntactic proposal):

(9.2)   (a) $[\![[\text{singular}]]\!]^{g,s,u} = \lambda x.x$ is an atomic individual

(b) $[\![[\text{dual}]]\!]^{g,s,u} = \lambda x.x$ has exactly two atomic parts

(c) $[\![[\text{feminine}]]\!]^{g,s,u} = \lambda x.$ all atomic parts of x are female individuals

(d) $[\![[\text{1st person}]]\!]^{g,s,u} = \lambda x.s \sqsubseteq x$

(e) $[\![[\text{2nd person}]]\!]^{g,s,u} = \lambda x.a \sqsubseteq x$, where a is the person or plurality s addresses in u

(9.3)   if P is a pronoun with features $F_1 \ldots F_n$, $[\![P_m]\!]^{g,s,u} = g(m)$ if for all i, $1 \leq i \leq n$, $F_i(g(m)) = 1$, undefined otherwise

---

[2] Harley and Ritter (2002):494 claim that there are no, or only extremely few, languages that have both a trial and a paucal. They suggest that both are instances of the same abstract feature *augmented*, which is interpreted slightly differently in different languages.

She can then be syntactically marked as [female, singular], *they* as [plural], *we* as [1st person, plural] etc.; Boumaa Fijian *'emudrau*, for example, will be [2nd person, dual].

Exercise 9.1

The *[1st person]* denotation in (9.2) doesn't specify the speaker, but the set of pluralities including the speaker. Give a feature representation for *me* and show how it nonetheless yields the speaker as its denotation.

Exercise 9.2

Table 9.1 lists first person inclusive and exclusive forms. An inclusive first person pronoun has the addressee as a subpart ('me and you'), an exclusive one mustn't ('me and him/her/them'). Find a representation for the Boumaa Fijian inclusive and exclusive first person plural and dual. Add (and semantically specify) new features, or operators on features, as necessary.

Some definitions

Introducing pluralities into our ontology requires us to make some adjustments to our formal theory. As mentioned above, we assume a relation $\sqsubseteq$, the part-of relation. In terms of this, we can define some other useful notions:[3]

(9.4)   Let $\sqsubseteq$ be a reflexive, antisymmetric, and transitive relation on the domain of individuals, D_e. Intuitively, $A \sqsubseteq B$ if A is identical to, or a proper part of, B. We can then define that . . .

(a)   The *sum of the individuals in a set A*, $\sqcup A$, is the smallest plurality that has all elements of A as parts, i.e. $\forall x \in D_e[x \in A \leftrightarrow x \sqsubseteq \sqcup A]$. For two-element sets we will sometimes write $A \sqcup B$ instead of $\sqcup\{A, B\}$. For example $[\![\text{Mary}]\!]^g \sqcup [\![\text{John}]\!]^g = [\![\text{Mary and John}]\!]^g$.

(b)   An individual A is an *atom*, ATOM(A) if it has no proper parts, i.e. if $\forall x \in D_e[x \sqsubseteq A \rightarrow x = A]$. For example ATOM($[\![\text{Heidi}]\!]^g$).

(c)   An individual B is an *atomic part* of an individual A if $B \sqsubseteq A$ and ATOM(B). For example, Joe Dalton is an atomic part of $[\![\text{the Daltons}]\!]^g$, but $[\![\text{Joe and Marty Dalton}]\!]^g$ or $[\![\text{the three youngest Daltons}]\!]^g$ are not.

(d)   Individuals A and B *overlap* iff there is an individual C such that C is a (possibly improper) part of both A and B, i.e. $\exists C \in D_e[C \sqsubseteq A \wedge C \sqsubseteq B]$; for example, $[\![\text{Astrid and Marion}]\!]^g$ and $[\![\text{Marion and Gunther}]\!]^g$ overlap, as does either of these and $[\![\text{Marion}]\!]^g$.

---

[3] For the formally inclined, we can furthermore state some basic requirements on the domain of individuals, which serve to ensure that our formal system of pluralities has all the properties we intuitively want:

(i)   (a)   for all $A, B \in D_e$, $\sqcup\{A, B\} \in D_e$; for any two individuals, there is their sum
           (b)   for all $A, B \in D_e$, if $A \sqsubseteq B$ and not $A = B$, then there is a $C \in D_e$ such that $\sqcup\{A, C\} = B$; each plurality is ultimately exclusively made up of atoms

Table 9.2 *Possible relations between NPs*

	Atomic parts of $[\![NP_1]\!]^g$	Atomic parts of $[\![NP_2]\!]^g$
Disjoint reference	Ana, Bo, Carl	Dale, Ernst, Flo
Coreference	Ana, Bo, Carl	Ana, Bo, Carl
Overlapping reference	Ana, Bo, Carl	Carl, Dale, Ernst

9.2   Anaphoric relations between plural NPs

Let us now turn to the behavior plural NPs display with respect to Binding Theory. As far as singular NPs went, there were only two options regarding their referential relations (setting aside semantic binding for the moment): they have the same referent (coreference) or they don't, in which case they are disjoint. With plurals, a further option arises in between: overlapping reference. This three-way distinction is summarized in table 9.2. Since we only have two representational options – coindexing and counter-indexing – two of the above cases must be represented by the same indexing.

Now, we can immediately dismiss the possibility that coindexing expresses anything but coreference, by noting that we never find a reflexive bound to an overlapping NP (in this chapter I will use italics to indicate either coreference or overlapping reference; where more fine-grained descriptive distinctions are needed, I will use upper case letter 'indices' to indicate reference):[4]

(9.5)   (a) *We like *myself.*
          (b) *I like *ourselves.*
          (c) *They like *himself.*
          (d) *He likes *themselves.*

If coindexing unequivocally represents coreference, counter-indexing must represent non-coreference, i.e. overlapping or disjoint reference. This predicts that overlap in reference should be irrelevant for BT, i.e. overlapping and disjoint NPs are predicted to behave alike. Is this prediction correct? The data in (9.6) and (9.7) suggest so for full NPs: a full NP may be c-commanded by an NP that includes its referent; that *inclusive NP*, as we will call it, may be a coordinate NP, or a plural:

(9.6)   (a) Mary and *Bill* were hoping that *Bill* would find a better job.
          (b) When they got married, *Sue/she* and her husband had no idea that *Sue* would be a famous writer.
          (c) Bill complained to his sister about his worn out clothes. So *they* went out to buy *Bill* a brand new outfit.

---

[4] Here and henceforth I use the term "overlapping" to mean "overlapping but not coreferential"; technically, coreferential NPs also overlap in reference, of course.

Likewise, NP_1 may c-command a full NP_2 if NP_1's referent is a part of NP_2's, in which case we call NP_1 a *partial NP*. This is, of course, not possible if the inclusive NP itself is a coordination containing a bound full NP, as with *Mary* in (9.7a), which is a plain Binding Condition C effect. But without this no effects obtain:

(9.7)   (a)   *Mary* was hoping that *she and Bill/they/*Mary and Bill* would find better jobs.
        (b)   *Keith* couldn't deny that pictures of *the band members* had been sold to the press
        (c)   *The lead actress* had stolen all the money for *the players*.
        (d)   *The captain* represents *the players on the team*.

The picture becomes a little murky if we consider pronouns. While some researchers (e.g. Lasnik [1981, 1989]; and Lasnik and Uriagereka [1988]) claim that overlapping reference with pronouns is generally bad (Lasnik stars, for example, *We like me*, which many speakers find acceptable, though pragmatically odd), most speakers find examples as in (9.8) perfectly fine:[5]

(9.8)   (a)   If we're captured, *I*'ll shoot/defend *us*!
        (b)   *John* said that *Mary* represented *them*.
        (c)   John and Mary often connive behind their colleagues' backs to advance the position of one or the other. This time *they* got *her* a job in the main office.
        (d)   *John* really resented *Mary*'s description of *them*.
        (e)   John and Mary were experiencing marital strife, so they called up Bill to discuss the situation. *They*$_{J\&M\&B}$ talked about *them*$_{J\&M}$ for the rest of the evening.

Reinhart and Reuland (1993) and Kiparsky (2002) claim that the acceptability of overlapping reference depends on whether the verb is read *collectively* or *distributively*. Thus, according to these papers, (9.9a) is fine only if Max and Lucie can be seen as discussing the issue (of Max) together. If understood as reporting two independent acts of talking, as facilitated by *both* in (9.9b), overlapping reference becomes impossible:[6]

(9.9)   (a)   *Max and Lucie* talked about *him*.
         (b)   (*) Both *Max and Lucie* talked about *him*.
(9.10)   (a)   (*)*We* voted for *me*.
         (b)   *We* elected *me*.

The contrast in (9.10) is explained along the same lines: *to elect* is a collective predicate, since no single individual elects but only the plurality does. *To vote*, on the other hand, even if applied to a plurality, consists of each individual voting,

---

[5] (9.8b)–(9.8e) from Berman and Hestvik (1997); see also Seely (1993).
[6] Examples are Reinhart and Reuland (1993)'s (36), (32a), and (35a).

thus the predicate is *reflexive* (cf. also chapter 11) and overlapping reference between the pronouns is blocked.

Some remarks are in order, though. First, by far not all speakers share these intuitions (e.g. about the contrast in [9.10]) – hence the parentheses around the asterisks. Second, it seems unclear in which sense e.g. *I'll shoot us*, or *I'll shoot the both of us* should be considered collective (what more is there to shooting us than shooting you and me?), yet the example is acceptable. Third, we must wonder what the limits on collective readings are. Take (9.7d). Clearly, if the captain represents the players on the team, the captain will represent himself as a matter of logical necessity (since he is a member of the team). Furthermore, while it might be argued that he represents 'the team' as a collective, he also represents the individual players (say if they feel they get less playing time than the others, which is certainly not a collective case), including, if need be, himself. Can we reasonably argue that this sentence has one particular *reading* on which it is purely collective and hence acceptable?

In sum, Reinhart and Reuland (1993)'s observations need – and deserve – further study. What is particularly interesting is that on their proposal, overlapping reference effects are strictly local, since they involve the readings of particular predicates. Thus, regardless of the type of NP involved, we don't expect long-distance effects as in (9.6) and (9.7).

We conclude, however, that the data about overlapping reference are inconclusive. Given the amount of acceptable examples, we could – and in fact will, in the remaining chapters of this book – stick to our assumption that overlapping reference need not be signalled by any special indexing, and thus that Binding Conditions are blind to it.

In the following sections I will nonetheless present a system that is capable of representing overlapping reference and the like in the grammar. The reason is that there are at least two phenomena that I think are rather solid and require a more complex indexing system. These will be discussed below. Furthermore, we will use that system to illustrate how some of the proposed, and tentatively dismissed, treatments of overlapping reference presented in this section could be implemented (this might also be useful given that overlapping reference effects seem stronger in languages other than English, e.g. French [Philippe Schlenker, p.c.]). In other words, it's good to have it, just in case . . . .

9.3   Set indexation

9.3.1   Basics

Lasnik (1986), elaborating on a proposal in Sportiche (1985), proposes to replace the single index of standard BT by an *index set*. Thus a plural pronoun could be represented as *they$_2$*, *they$_{2,6}$*, *they$_{2,6,7}$*, etc. Adopting the gist of Lasnik's proposal, we let the interpretation of such a pronoun be subject to the following constraint:[7]

(9.11)   Let S be a (possibly singleton) set of natural numbers, then for all NPs, $[\![NP_S]\!]^g$ is the smallest plurality G such that for all $n \in S$, $g(n)$ is a subplurality or a member of G (if that plurality meets the lexical presuppositions of NP, undefined otherwise).[8]

Note that in the case of $they_2$, $[\![they_2]\!]^g$ will be simply $g(2)$, given that the smallest plurality containing $g(2)$ *is* $g(2)$. The lexical plurality presupposition of *they* will then ensure that $g(2)$ is not a singular individual but a plurality. Similarly, we need not worry about explicitly excluding, say, $she_{2,3}$, because of the lexical presupposition of *she* as denoting a singular (female) individual (recall that by PACO, $g(2)$ cannot be equal to $g(3)$, blocking the only way for $she_{2,3}$ to denote an atom without violating [9.11]).

Now, as said earlier, we never want mere overlap in reference to allow for a reflexive. This follows directly if we assume, as we did in chapter 6, that a reflexive needs to be *semantically* bound by an NP within its domain; consider the configuration schematized in (9.12):

(9.12) $they_{1,2}$ [β_3 ... $themselves_3$ ...]

In this configuration (and only there), *they* semantically binds *themselves*. Note that it doesn't matter how many indices n the binder *they* carries, because an NP bound by *they* (via β_3) will always denote the sum of all $g(n)$ found on *they*. So if NP semantically binds NP', NP' can't just denote some *part* of the denotation of NP.

What, though, if *themselves* in (9.12) were indexed $themselves_{3,4}$? In this case, it would denote the sum of $g(1)$ and $g(2)$, i.e. the same as $they_{1,2}$, plus $g(4)$ (whoever that may be). But, intuitively, this is impossible (cf. also the ungrammaticality of *she likes themselves*). So we have to assume that an NP counts as semantically bound if there is a single NP* which binds *all* of NP's indices (which effectively means that NP must bear just one index). Such a definition will be given in (9.19) below.

In chapter 6, section 6.5.3 we concluded that the evidence in favor of reflexives having to be semantically – as opposed to semantically or syntactically – bound is not completely convincing. So let us close this subsection by formulating the prerequisite definition of *syntactically* bound as well. We define syntactic binding as in (9.13):

---

[7] Lasnik's original idea seems to be that there is one index for each atomic individual in the plurality (which might be problematic if, say, *they* refers to the natural numbers, or the stars in the galaxy); the modification here leads to a much simpler indexing procedure and arguably captures the same effects.

[8] Strictly speaking, this definition requires the representation to be $them_{\{2,6\}}$ rather than $them_{2,6}$. I will omit the set brackets for convenience.

(9.13)   NP$_1$ *syntactically binds* NP$_2$ iff
     (a)   NP$_1$ commands NP$_2$
     (b)   the (set) indices of NP$_1$ and NP$_2$ are identical.

From this, the familiar Binding Condition A facts will follow. To see this, consider the unacceptable *they like himself*: suppose Binding Condition A requires that a reflexive be syntactically bound in its domain; then by (9.13) that means its index set must be identical to that of a locally commanding NP. Thus we must have a representation like in (9.14):

(9.14)   (a) *they$_{1,2}$ like himself$_{1,2}$
     (b) *they$_3$ like himself$_3$

Either representation expresses coreference, as required by Binding Condition A, but the structure has no interpretation because of the opposing number presuppositions of the pronouns. A semantically feasible indexing such as (9.15), on the other hand, is excluded by Binding Condition A since overlapping index sets do not constitute a case of syntactic binding in the sense defined in (9.13):

(9.15)   *they$_{1,2}$ like himself$_1$

So far, then, the set indexing system derives the same anaphoric possibilities that the simple indexing system does, although its representations are very different. We will now turn to cases which tease the two systems apart.

9.3.2   Binding Condition B effects with split antecedents

Set indexing, unlike simple indexing, allows us to express a generalization argued for by Berman and Hestvik (1997), namely that a pronoun cannot refer to a plurality consisting of A and B if NPs referring to A and B, respectively, are both within the pronoun's binding domain. Thus the contrast in (9.16):

(9.16)   (a) *Bill* was pleased that *Mary* hadn't told John about *them*.
     (b) **Bill* told *Mary* about *them*.

Sentence (9.16a) must be represented as in (9.17a), while (9.17b) is the LF of (9.16b):

(9.17)   (a) Bill [β_4 was pleased that Mary [β_2 hadn't told John about them$_{2,4}$]]
     (b) *Bill [β_4 told Mary [β_2 about them$_{2,4}$]]

We assume here, in keeping with our conclusions in chapter 6, that names are not indexed, and that pronouns cannot corefer with c-commanding NPs because of the Coreference rule.[9]

---

[9] The same results could be achieved by indexing names and having the pronouns simply corefer with them. For that, the following syntactic definition of binding would have to be used:

(i)   Index *n* on NP$_2$ is bound by NP$_1$ iff
       (a)   NP$_1$ commands NP$_2$, and
       (b)   the set of indices on NP$_1$ contains *n*

The contrast between (9.16a)/(9.17a) and (9.16b)/(9.17b) can be accounted for if we assume that for a pronoun to be free in domain D, at least one of its indices must be free in D. Thus, it doesn't matter that $them_{2,4}$ in (9.17a) has one locally bound index, 2, nor that its other index is bound, but non-locally. The only thing that is impossible is for *all* of its indices to be locally bound, as in (9.17b).

Now, as is well known, reflexives don't take split antecedents; that is (9.18) is clearly bad:

(9.18)   * *Bill* told *Mary* about *themselves*.

What this means is that a reflexive is possible only if *all* of its indices are locally bound by the *same* NP. Its Binding Condition is thus not the reverse of Binding Condition B. Rather, we must formulate as follows:

(9.19)   Binding Conditions
    (A)   All indices of a reflexive must be bound to the same NP within the reflexive's domain.
    (B)   Some index of a non-reflexive pronoun must be free within its domain.

Before closing this section, we should make sure that the following LF for (9.16b) doesn't yield the incriminated reading:

(9.20)   Bill told Mary about $them_3$ (with $g(3) = $ Bill⊔Mary)

Obviously, the (non-)indexing in (9.20) doesn't violate the new Binding Condition B. But what stops $g(3)$ from being the plurality consisting of Bill and Mary? The answer should be: the Coreference Rule. Note that, pre-theoretically, (9.20) should be blocked by (9.17b) which employs semantic binding rather than coreference, in the same way that *Mary likes her_2* on a coreferential construal is blocked by *Mary β_2 likes her_2*. The structure the CR approves of, (9.17b), in turn violates Binding Condition B as given in (9.19) – the familiar 'either way you lose' scenario typical of the workings of the CR.

Unfortunately, since none of the NPs in (9.20) corefer, the CR doesn't apply here; we need to redefine it so as to block either coreference *or overlapping reference* if there is a binding alternative. Doing this is beyond the scope of this book, though.[10] We thus conclude our implementation of Berman and Hestvik

---

[10] Our refinement of the CR, Have Local Binding!, repeated here, almost derives this effect:

    (i)   Have Local Binding!
           For any two NPs α and β, if α could bind β (i.e. if it c-commands β and β is not bound in α's c-command domain already), α must bind β, unless that changes the interpretation.

The general idea can be illustrated as follows: Assume that $g(3)$ is Mary⊔Bill, and, for the sake of the argument, that $g(4)$ is Mary and $g(5)$ is Bill. Regarding *Bill* and *them*, (i) indistinguishable interpretation can be achieved via LF (iia):

    (ii)   (a)   Bill [β_1 told Mary about $them_{1,4}$]
           (b)   Bill told Mary [β_2 about $them_{2,5}$]

(1997)'s generalization at this point. In subsection 9.3.4, I will present a redefinition of PACO which derives the same generalization with full indexing and without appeal to the CR.

9.3.3   Partial binding

Let us now turn to a semantic argument for set indexing. Consider the following sentences (Philippe Schlenker, p.c.):

(9.21)   *Mary* is very popular in her class. At some point or other, *every boy* has asked *her* if *they* could go out on a date.

The reading we are interested in here is one where each boy asked Mary: 'Can the two of us go out on a date?' An LF that derives this reading is given in (9.22):

(9.22)   every boy [β_1 has asked her$_2$ β_2 [if they$_{1,2}$ could go out on a date]]

Here the index 1 on *they* is bound by *every boy*, while the index 2 is bound by *her* (if *her* was replaced by *Mary*, the index 2 could simply refer to Mary, yielding the same interpretation, and the same argument for partial binding). Hence, by (9.11), $[\![they_{1,2}]\!]^g$ must be the smallest plurality that contains $g(1)$ and $g(2)$; since $g(1)$ varies with boys, $[\![they_{1,2}]\!]^g$ will for each boy denote the plurality consisting of Mary and that boy. This is precisely the reading we want.

It should be evident that partial binding readings cannot be represented in a system using simple indices. We thus have a simple but compelling empirical argument for a more complex indexing system.[11]

9.3.4   A hypothetical case©

To close this section, suppose we believed, contrary to what was suggested in section 9.2, that overlapping reference generally incurs Binding Condition violations. That is, let us assume a language English′ in which all cases of overlapping reference are unacceptable, e.g.:

(9.23)   (a)   ᴱ′ *We* voted for *me*.

            (b)   ᴱ′ *The captain* represents *the team*.

Applied to *Mary* and *them*, again, binding should obtain, since (iib) too, yields the same interpretation as (9.20). Now, since (i) applies to all pairs of NPs, it follows that both bindings must obtain, which means that (9.17b) blocks all of (9.20), (iia) and (iib) as desired.

     This deduction, however, relies on a certain vagueness in the formulation of (i) regarding the point of comparison and variation. Clarifying these issues would take us far afield here. Note in general, though, that we presumably don't want partial binding to block coreference, unless *all* indices of the lower NP end up bound. Otherwise simple overlapping reference as in *The captain represents (the players on) the team* will be blocked in general (in favor of *the captain* β_1 *represents them*$_{1,2}$, where $g(2)$ is the rest of the team).

[11] A similar argument is made in Rullman (2004), discussion of which I could not include in this book.

So non-reflexive pronouns and full NPs in E' count as free only if *none* of their indices is bound, or could be bound (in its domain). To implement this, we will assume a theory in which all non-quantificational NPs, pronominal or not, are indexed. Then we can define the notion E'-*free* as in (9.24):

(9.24) NP_1 is E'-free in domain D iff for any NP_2 in D that commands NP_1, the index sets of NP_1 and NP_2 are disjoint.

Now we can assume the standard Binding Conditions B and C, according to which non-reflexive pronouns and full NPs must be free in their respective domains, while keeping a notion of *bound* for Binding Condition A which forces that the index set of NP_1 and NP_2 be identical. This will rule out LFs like $we_{1,2}$ *voted for* me_1 for (9.23a), in which *me* is not free in its domain; similarly for (9.23b).

Still, there are BT-compatible indexings for sentences like (9.23a), such as those in (9.25):

(9.25) $we_{2/1,3}$ like me_4

Assume that $g(2)$ (or the plurality consisting of $g(1)$ and $g(3)$, on the other indexing) contains the speaker, and that $g(4)$ *is* the speaker (any other assignment would violate the lexical presuppositions of *we* and *me*). We need to rule out such an assignment to derive that (9.23a) doesn't have *any* well-formed reading. To do this, we need to replace PACO from chapter 2 with the following:

(9.26)   Prohibition Against Accidental Overlapping Reference:
          For any matrix assignment g, any integers n and m, if $g(n)$ overlaps with $g(m)$, then $n = m$.

This new definition closes the loophole for (9.25): none of $g(1)$, $g(2)$ or $g(3)$ can overlap in reference with $g(4)$ without violating it. The only possible indexing then is one like $we_{1,2}$ *like* me_1, which violates Binding Condition B, with 'free' as defined in (9.24). (9.26) effectively prohibits plurality indices whenever parts of the plurality have their own index within the same LF. A language like E', then, disallows overlapping reference wherever it disallows coreference.

Exercise 9.3
Assume with Berman and Hestvik (1997) that if *they* in (9.27) refers to Bill and Mary, *them* can neither be Bill and Mary, nor Bill, Mary and Fred:

(9.27)   Bill and Mary said they told Fred about them.

Give at least three different indexings that would satisfy (9.19) above and show why they cannot yield either one of the two interpretations mentioned. Then show which indexings would, and why they are impossible.

9.4   More on overlapping reference ©

9.4.1   Asymmetrical overlapping reference

Overlapping reference facts aren't the same across languages. A particularly interesting pattern from Hungarian is discussed by den Dikken *et al.* (2001). Simplifying somewhat, transitive verbs in Hungarian show the following pattern of (im)possible overlapping reference:

(9.28)   (a)   we . . . me
                Mi engem képviselünk/választunk meg.
                we me   represent/ elect   PV
         (b)   *I . . . us
                * Én minket/bennünket választok meg.
                I   us/   us   elect   PV
         (c)   (s)he . . . us (with ⟦she⟧ᵍ part of ⟦us⟧ᵍ)
                Ő   minket/bennünket választ meg.
                (s)he us/   us   elect PV

If overlapping reference is generally ignored by the grammar, as we suggested it might be for English, (9.28a) and (9.28c) are expected to be good, but the unacceptability of (9.28b) comes as a surprise. If, on the other hand, overlapping reference was blocked, as in our hypothetical English′ in 9.3.4 above, the contrast between (9.28b) and (9.28c) comes as a surprise, given that in both cases the subject is a partial NP to the object, so they should be equally ungrammatical.

Note that this contrast is surprising even under our set indexing mechanism, since in (9.28b) and (9.28c) alike the index of the subject should be part of the index set of the object.

Den Dikken *et al.* (2001) propose therefore that the first person plural pronoun has a more complex representation, in which it is essentially identical to 'me with them/her/him/you.' Thus the contrast above ends up being parallel to the English (9.29):

(9.29)   (a)   I saw myself/*me with him/her/them/you.
         (b)   She saw me with him/her/them/you.

Such structures are called *comitative*. While it is not clear that the post-verbal material in the English examples forms a constituent, the example makes it clear that in a comitative structure, whatever its exact semantics, only the part before the *with* 'counts' as an immediate constituent of the clause in the sense of BT, which explains the contrast in (9.29). Now suppose that in Hungarian the first person pronoun is indeed a syntactically complex NP with a structure roughly as in (9.30), where *pro* is a number- and gender-less non-reflexive pronoun (the structure assumed in den Dikken *et al.* [2001] is more complex, for reasons of no concern here):

(9.30)   [$_{NP}$ I/me$_n$ ['with' [pro$_m$]]]

Obviously, neither I/me_n nor pro_m c-command anything outside of the NP, which explains why (9.28a) $(we \dots me)$ above is good. Now assume, crucially, that the binding domain for I/me_n equals that of the full NP (perhaps because it is in some sense the 'head' of NP), while the domain for pro_m is the NP itself. Then in a configuration like (9.28b) – abstractly: I_4 *elect* $[_{NP}$ *me_4* $[$*with pro_9*$]]$ – *me_4* is illicitly bound within its domain, while in (9.28c) – abstractly: *she_9 elects* $[_{NP}$ *me_4* $[$*with pro_9*$]]$ – both *me_4* and *pro_9* are free in their domains (S and NP, respectively; *pro_9* is bound in the root domain by *she_9*).

This is but a brief presentation of the data and analysis in den Dikken *et al.* (2001). The point it is meant to illustrate is that, first, there is cross-linguistic variation concerning the possibility of overlapping reference; and second, that at least first and second person plural pronouns appear to behave asymmetrically with respect to their 'ingredients' in Hungarian. In other words, there may be more structure to these cases than we discussed in the main part of this chapter (be it syntactically, as suggested by den Dikken *et al.* [2001], or semantically, in the form of more complex, potentially asymmetrical index tuples). The reader who intends to do research on Binding Theory should thus be aware of the range of possibilities, and carefully collect the relevant data in the language under discussion to help her or him make the correct analytical choices.

9.4.2   Counter-indexing

In this subsection I will briefly discuss yet a different system for representing plurals for the purposes of BT, that of Chomsky (1980), and following him Lasnik and Freidin (1981) and Lasnik (1981). Since these proposals all strive to block overlapping reference in general, we will present them from the perspective of our hypothetical language English$'$, in which all sentences marked by $^{E'*}$ are unacceptable.

We can render the proposal as follows: each NP now comes with a *referential index*, which is the same as the simple index on NPs in section 9.1, and what I will call here an *obviation set* of indices. The idea is that this set contains the referential indices of all NPs the pertinent NP must *not* overlap in reference with. Take a simple example:

(9.31)   George$_{2,\{\}}$ likes him$_{4,\{2\}}$

The complex index on *him* encodes that the referent of *him*, $g(4)$, must not overlap with $g(2)$, which here means: *him* must not refer to George. A slightly more complex example is (9.32):

(9.32)   George$_{1,\{\}}$ introduced him$_{2,\{1\}}$ to him$_{3,\{1,2\}}$

This representation expresses that the first *him* must not refer to George, and that the second *him* must not refer to either George or the referent of the first *him*. Note that in both examples the obviation set on the NP *George* is empty, meaning that there are no coreference restrictions on it. To be explicit about this interpretation we devise a new interpretation rule for NPs:

(9.33)   Constraint on NP-Denotations:
            $NP_{n,O}$ presupposes that for all $m \in O$, $g(n)$ and $g(m)$ do not overlap in reference.

The lexical entries for NPs remain essentially the same as in chapter 2, as exemplified in (9.34):

(9.34) $[\![\text{him(self)}_{n,O}]\!]^g = g(n)$ if $g(n)$ is an atomic male individual, undefined otherwise

We now redefine 'bound' and 'free' as follows:

(9.35)   (a) NP_1 *binds* NP_2 iff
                  (i) NP_1 commands NP_2, and
                  (ii)   the referential indices of NP_1 and NP_2 are identical.
            (b)   NP is *free* in domain D iff the obviation set of NP contains the referential indices of every NP' that commands NP in D.

It should be clear how these definitions force (9.31), repeated here from above, to have the kind of indexing it does:

(9.36) $George_{2,\{\}}$ likes $him_{4,\{2\}}$

Since *George* c-commands *him* within its domain, and since *him* is subject to Binding Condition B (i.e. it must be bound within its subject domain), the index of *George*, 2, must be in the obviation set of *him*. By the condition in (9.33) this implies that the referent of *him*, $g(4)$, must not be overlapping in reference with George, which boils down to saying that *him* must not refer to George; directly coindexing *George* and *him* is ruled out as a trivial case, given that $him_{4,\{4\}}$ cannot receive any interpretation conforming to (9.33).

   The important thing is that this treatment extends straightforwardly to our plural cases. Representations for some pertinent English cases are given in (9.37):

(9.37)   (a) ${}^{E'}*We_{1,\{\}}$ like $me_{2,\{1\}}$.
            (b) $We_{1,\{\}}$ think that $I_{2,\{\}}$ will win.
            (c) ${}^{E'}*We_{1,\{\}}$ like $myself_{1,\{\}}$.

Take (9.37a). The presence of the index 1 in *me*'s obviation set is required by Binding Condition B. By the lexical entry for *we*, $g(1)$ must be a plurality including the speaker. By the lexical entry for *me*, $g(2)$ must be the speaker. But by the constraint on NP denotations (9.33), it is presupposed that $g(1)$ and $g(2)$ do not overlap in reference. These demands are contradictory, so no interpretation for the sentence can be derived.

   No such problem arises in (9.37b), given that the obviation index of *I* is not required to have 1 as a member because we_1 is not in *I*'s GC. This is, of course, just the familiar observation that pronouns can be bound outside their GC. Finally for reflexives like in (9.37c) the obviation index is irrelevant, given that Binding Condition A imposes no restrictions on it (since 'bound' is defined with reference to the referential index only). Binding Condition A does, however, require the referential index of a reflexive to be locally bound. Given that coindexing is interpreted as coreference, it follows that *we* and *myself* should refer to the same individual, which will inevitably violate the presuppositions of at least one of them.

Exercise 9.4

The pronoun *ye* in Dogrib, an Athapaskan language spoken in Northwestern Canada, must co-occur with a commanding NP in its tense domain, *from which it must be disjoint in reference*. Formulate a 'Binding Condition D' which pertains to *ye* only and enforces this behavior, using the obviation set (data from Saxon [1984], as quoted in Enç [1989]):

(9.38)　　(a)　John ye -hk'è   ha.
　　　　　　　　J.   YE 3.shoot FUT
　　　　　　　　'John is going to shoot him$_{*John}$.'
　　　　　(b)　John ye -mǫ   eʔį.
　　　　　　　　J.   YE mother 3.saw
　　　　　　　　'John saw his$_{*John}$ mother.'
　　　　　(c)　∗ʔekàanì ye -enda.
　　　　　　　　thus   YE 3.survive
　　　　　　　　'He lives this way.'
　　　　　(d)　∗ Ye -zha shèetį.
　　　　　　　　YE son 3.ate
　　　　　　　　'His son has eaten.'
　　　　　(e)　John sìi   Joe ye -gha ʔelà whehtsį yek'èrèzhǫ.
　　　　　　　　J.   FOC J. YE for   boat 3.made 3.know
　　　　　　　　'John knows that Joe made a boat for him$_{John/5/*Joe}$.'

Exercise 9.5

Can you formulate Berman and Hestvik (1997)'s generalization that pronouns can overlap in reference with a c-commanding NP within their domain, as long as not all their partial binders are within their domain, within the obviation-indexing system? That is, can you model the contrast in (9.16), repeated here? Argue!

(9.39)　　(a)　*Bill* was pleased that *Mary* hadn't told John about *them*.
　　　　　(b)　∗*Bill* told *Mary* about *them*.

10 Reciprocals

A special case of a plural anaphoric relation is reciprocity. Reciprocity can be expressed by definite NPs, adverbials or verbal affixes, or be part of a lexical meaning:

(10.1)   (a)   *Each child* helped *the others.*

           (b)   *Die Kinder* halfen *sich* **gegenseitig**.   (German)
                the children helped self mutually
                'The children helped each other.'

           (c)   *Juma na Halima* wa- na-   pend- **ana**.   (Swahili)
                J.   with H.   3PL PRESENT *love* RECIPROCAL
                'Juma and Halima love each other.' (Vitale [1982]:147)

           (d)   *The children* differ.

In addition, many languages, among them English, have dedicated reciprocal pronouns, for short, reciprocals:

(10.2)   (a)   *John and Mary* saw *each other*.

           (b)   *Most calligraphers* know *one another*.

Standardly, it is said that reciprocals, like reflexives, must be bound by a local antecedent. Semantically, however, this can't be the whole story. If we interpreted an index, n, on a reciprocal in the usual way, namely as setting the denotation of the NP to $g(n)$, reciprocal sentences would be synonymous to the parallel reflexive sentences, which they obviously aren't: clearly, the object arguments in the examples above are neither semantically bound by, nor coreferent with, the subject. To see what the semantic relation between a reciprocal and its antecedent is, we need to look into the semantics of plural predication more in general.

Exercise 10.1

    Find more examples of inherently reciprocal verbs (or nouns) like *differ*. Do they *have* to be interpreted reciprocally, or are there other options (e.g. interpreting the 'missing' argument as a contextually given individual)? Give examples. Can you give paraphrases with overt reciprocal expressions?

10.1   Plural preliminaries

10.1.1   Distributivity

As discussed in detail in chapter 9, we assume that simple plural NPs such as *John and Mary* and *the parachuters* are terms, not quantifiers. They denote plural individuals, so-called *pluralities*, as opposed to singular NPs like *Mary* or *the parachuter*, which denote *atom(ic individual)s*.

But how do pluralities enter the semantic composition? To interpret a sentence like *Mary and John snore*, we introduce a *distributive operator D*. Loosely speaking, a property $[\![D]\!]^g(\alpha)$ will hold of a plurality P iff α holds of all atomic parts of P. We will use the notation $x \sqsubseteq_A X$ from chapter 9 (for perspicuity, I use upper case variables for pluralities and lower case variables for atoms, even though this is not part of the official semantics, given that both range over D_e; likewise I will often use the lower case letter to range over the (atomic) parts in the plurality denoted by the upper case letter):

(10.3)   For any α s.t. $[\![\alpha]\!]^g \in D_{et}$, 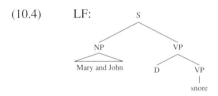 $=_{\mathrm{def}} \lambda X_e$. for all x s.t. $x \sqsubseteq_A X$, $[\![\alpha]\!]^g(x) = 1$

(Instead of 'for all x s.t. $x \sqsubseteq_A X, \ldots$' we will henceforth write '$\forall x \sqsubseteq_A X[\ldots]$.') D is the covert counterpart of *each*. At LF, D mediates between the plural subject term and the semantically singular verb, as in . . .

(10.4)   LF:

```
              S
         ┌────┴────┐
        NP         VP
      ┌──┴──┐    ┌──┴──┐
  Mary and John  D     VP
                       │
                     snore
```

(a) $[\![[D[\text{snore}]]]\!]^g = \lambda X_e. \forall x \sqsubseteq_A X [\![\text{snore}]\!]^g(x)]$
(b) $[\![[[\text{Mary and John}][D[\text{snore}]]]]\!]^g = 1$ iff
          $\ldots \lambda X_e. \forall x \sqsubseteq_A X [\![\text{snore}]\!]^g(x)]([\![\text{Mary and John}]\!]^g) = 1$
          $\ldots \forall x \sqsubseteq_A \text{Mary} \sqcup \text{John} [[\![\text{snore}]\!]^g(x)]] = 1$

. . . yielding 'each of John and Mary snores,' or 'Mary and John each snore'.

The operator D must be generalized to allow for the interpretation of plural non-subject NPs as in *Kuno kissed Lasser and Meyer*, which we want to mean 'Kuno kissed Lasser and Kuno kissed Meyer.' For our purposes, it will suffice to add a clause for transitive verbs as in (10.5) to (10.3) above:[1]

---

[1] A more general way is to introduce a semantic distributor $\mathcal{D}$, and then use the composition operation $\mathcal{C}$ from subsection 4.5.3 in chapter 4 to interpret the syntactic operator D:

(i)   (a) $\mathcal{D} =_{def} \lambda P_{et} \lambda X_e [\forall x \sqsubseteq_A X[P(x)]]$
        (b) $[\![D]\!]^g = \lambda \psi . \mathcal{C}(\psi, \mathcal{D})$

(10.5)   For any α, $[\![\alpha]\!]^g \in D_{e,et}$, $\left[\!\!\left[\begin{array}{c} \overset{\frown}{} \\ \text{D} \quad \alpha \end{array} \right]\!\!\right]^g =_{\text{def}} \lambda X_e \lambda y_e. \forall x \sqsubseteq_A X [[\![\alpha]\!]^g$

$(x)(y) = 1]$

Exercise 10.2

Give an LF, and calculate the denotation, for *Kuno kissed Lasser and Meyer.*

10.1.2   Dependent plurals

The *D* operator interacts with semantic binding in a systematic fashion. Consider (10.6):

(10.6)   Jorun and Smilla photographed their feet.

Sentence (10.6) is ambiguous between a reading where Jorun and Smilla each photographed her own feet (two feet per picture), and one where Jorun photographed their feet, and so did Smilla (four feet per picture). These two readings correspond to different relations between the distributive operator *D* and the binder prefix β at LF (throughout this chapter I use simple indices – rather than set indices – as introduced in chapter 9, section 9.2):

(10.7)   LF1 (four feet/picture):
                    [Jorun and Smilla] [β_1 [D [photographed [their$_1$ feet]]]]

   (a) $[\![\text{photographed their}_1 \text{ feet}]\!]^g = \lambda x.x$ photographed $g(1)$'s feet
   (b) $[\![\text{D [photographed their}_1 \text{ feet]}]\!]^g = \lambda X.\forall x \sqsubseteq_A X[x$ photographed $g(1)$'s feet]
   (c) $[\![\beta_1 \text{ [D [photographed their}_1 \text{ feet]]}]\!]^g = \lambda X.\forall x \sqsubseteq_A X[x$ photographed X's feet]
   (d) $[\![\text{[Jorun and Smilla] }[\beta_1 \text{ [D [photographed their}_1 \text{ feet]]]}]\!]^g$
           $= \lambda X.\forall x \sqsubseteq_A X[x$ photographed X's feet]$(\text{Jorun} \sqcup \text{Smilla})$
           $\equiv \forall x \sqsubseteq_A \text{Jorun} \sqcup \text{Smilla } [x$ photographed Jorun$\sqcup$Smilla's feet]

   'Each of Jorun and Smilla photographed Jorun and Smilla's feet.'[2]

(10.8)   LF2 (two feet/picture):
                    [Jorun and Smilla] [D [β_1 [photographed [their$_1$ feet]]]]

   (a) $[\![\text{photographed their}_1 \text{ feet}]\!]^g = \lambda x.x$ photographed $g(1)$'s feet (as above)
   (b) $[\![\beta_1 \text{ [photographed their}_1 \text{ feet]}]\!]^g = \lambda x.x$ photographed x's feet
   (c) $[\![\text{D }[\beta_1 \text{ [photographed their}_1 \text{ feet]]}]\!]^g = \lambda X.\forall x \sqsubseteq_A X[x$ photographed x's feet]
   (d) $[\![\text{[Jorun and Smilla][D }[\beta_1 \text{ [photographed their}_1 \text{ feet]]]}]\!]^g = \lambda X.\forall x \sqsubseteq_A X[x$ photographed x's feet]$(\text{Jorun} \sqcup \text{Smilla})$
           $\equiv \forall x \sqsubseteq_A \text{Jorun} \sqcup \text{Smilla}[x$ photographed x's feet]

   'Jorun photographed her feet and Smilla photographed her feet.'

---

[2] As indicated in the paraphrases, by 'x's feet' we mean the sum of all of x's feet, and by 'X's feet' we mean the sum of all feet that belong to some $x \sqsubseteq_A X$.

We may say that the pronoun *their* is bound to the *genuine plural* NP *Jorun and Smilla* in LF1, but to the *distributed plural* in LF2. Note that, semantically, the pronoun is interpreted as an atom in LF2; the morphology is thus vacuous and merely a syntactic agreement phenomenon. For this reason, plural pronouns that are bound to distributed plurals are commonly referred to as *dependent plurals*.

10.2   Strong reciprocity

We are now in a position to formalize our intuition about simple reciprocal sentences to a first approximation. We will start with cases in which the antecedent NP denotes a plurality of cardinality two ('dual reciprocity'), and then move on to pluralities of larger cardinalities.

10.2.1   Dual reciprocity

The bottom line is that *Jorun and Smilla like each other* is interpreted parallel to (10.9a), or more precisely though less perspicuously (10.9b):

(10.9)   (a)   Jorun and Smilla each like the other one of them.
           (b)   Jorun and Smilla each like the one other than herself among them.

The *each* in the paraphrase corresponds to the distributivity operator D introduced above. The *them* is bound to the genuine plural *Jorun and Smilla*, whereas the *other* part relates to the distributed plural. In other words, *each other* as a whole is doubly dependent on its antecedent, once bound to the genuine plural, once to the distributed plural. To express this, we have to give *each other* two indices, interpreted as follows:

(10.10) $[\![\text{each other}_{r,c}]\!]^g = $ the $x \sqsubseteq_A g(r)$ such that $x \neq g(c)$

I have used the letters r and c for the two indices on *each other*, to remind us of the words *range* and *contrast*. The range variable determines the plurality from which the denotation of *each other* must be taken, and the contrast variable requires that denotation to exclude a particular element. Relative to a particular choice of $g(r)$ and $g(c)$, $[\![\text{each other}_{r,c}]\!]^g$ will denote that atomic part of the plurality $g(r)$ which is distinct from $g(c)$.

Using this denotation we can analyze the sentence *Jorun and Smilla like each other* as in (10.11):

(10.11)   LF: [Jorun and Smilla] β_1 [D [β_2 [like [each other$_{1,2}$]]]]
           (a) $[\![\text{like [each other}_{1,2}]]\!]^g = \lambda y.y$ likes the $x \sqsubseteq_A g(1)$ such that $x \neq g(2)$
           (b) $[\![\beta_2 \text{ [like [each other}_{1,2}]]]\!]^g = \lambda y.y$ likes the $x \sqsubseteq_A g(1)$ such that $x \neq y$
           (c) $[\![\text{D }[\beta_2 \text{ [like [each other}_{1,2}]]]]\!]^g = \lambda Y.\forall y \sqsubseteq_A Y[y$ likes the $x \sqsubseteq_A g(1)$ such that $x \neq y]$

(d) $[\![\beta_1 [D [\beta_2 [like [each other_{1,2}]]]]]\!]^g = \lambda Y. \forall y \sqsubseteq_A Y[y$ likes the $x \sqsubseteq_A$ Y such that $x \neq y]$

(e) $\forall y \sqsubseteq_A Jorun \sqcup Smilla[y$ likes the $x \sqsubseteq_A Jorun \sqcup Smilla$ such that $x \neq y$

It is tempting to associate the semantic complexity of *each other* with its morphological complexity as e.g. in (10.12) (cf. Sauerland [1998]:190 and 196):

(10.12)

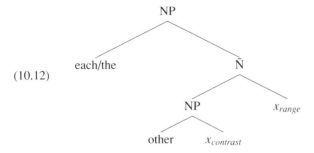

Assuming the standard interpretation for *the* and an interpretation of $[\![other]\!]^g(x)(y)$ as $[\lambda z.z \sqsubseteq y$ and neither $z \sqsubseteq x$ nor $x \sqsubseteq z]$ – again quite arguably the same as in *a book other than this* – we get the same interpretation as above. Such a move is proposed in Heim *et al.* (1991) and Roberts (1991) (who both assume the reciprocal to be a universal quantifier rather than a definite term, which squares well with the presence of the *each* morpheme) as well as Sauerland (1998) (who opts for the definite version), and criticized in Dalrymple *et al.* (1994). In the remainder of this chapter I will simply write *each other$_{r,c}$*, leaving open the possibility of a decomposition along these lines.

10.2.2   Reciprocity with pluralities bigger than two

Above we restricted our attention to antecedents of cardinality two. The question is what happens in examples with bigger pluralities:

(10.13)   (a)   Jorun, Smilla, and Erica like each other.
           (b)   The astronomers like each other.

The first thing to note is that *each other* as defined above would be undefined for range variables that denote pluralities bigger than two, given that it fixed the denotation of *each other* as '*the x* such that ...'. Given our plural semantics, however, this can easily be fixed:

(10.14) $[\![each\ other_{r,c}]\!]^g =$ the biggest $X \sqsubseteq g(r)$ such that neither $g(c) \sqsubseteq X$ nor $X \sqsubseteq g(c)$, for short $\sigma X[X \sqsubseteq g(r) - g(c)]$

This will give us the following denotations:

(10.15)   (a) $[\![each\ other_{1,2}]\!]^{g[1 \rightarrow Jorun \sqcup Smilla \sqcup Erica][2 \rightarrow Jorun]} = Smilla \sqcup Erica$
           (b) $[\![each\ other_{1,2}]\!]^{g[1 \rightarrow Jorun \sqcup Smilla \sqcup Erica][2 \rightarrow Smilla]} = Jorun \sqcup Erica$
           (c) $[\![each\ other_{1,2}]\!]^{g[1 \rightarrow Jorun \sqcup Smilla \sqcup Erica][2 \rightarrow Erica]} = Jorun \sqcup Smilla$

Given that *each other* can denote a plurality now, we have to distribute over the object argument, too. This will give us what is called *strong reciprocity*. The pertinent LF for *Jorun, Smilla, and Erica like each other* is given as $LF_{(10.16)}$ below, with the interpretation in (10.16):

$LF_{(10.16)}$

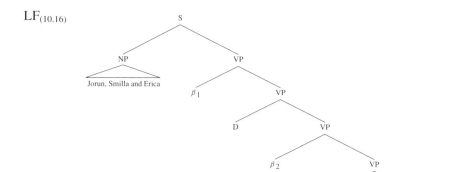

(10.16)   (a) $[\![like]\!]^g = \lambda x \lambda y . y$ likes x

(b) $[\![D[like]]\!]^g = \lambda X \lambda y . \forall x \sqsubseteq_A X[y$ likes $x]$

(c) $[\![D[like]][each\ other_{1,2}]\!]^g =$
$$\lambda X \lambda y . \forall x \sqsubseteq_A X[y \text{ likes } x](\sigma Z[Z \sqsubseteq_A g(1) - g(2)])$$
$$\equiv \lambda y . \forall x \sqsubseteq_A (\sigma Z[Z \sqsubseteq_A g(1) - g(2)])[y \text{ likes } x]$$

(d) $[\![\beta_2[D[like]][each\ other_{1,2}]\!]^g = \lambda y . \forall x \sqsubseteq_A (\sigma Z[Z \sqsubseteq_A g(1) - y])$
$[y$ likes $x]$

(e) $[\![D[\beta_2[D[like]][each\ other_{1,2}]]\!]^g =$
$$\lambda Y . \forall y \sqsubseteq_A Y[\forall x \sqsubseteq_A (\sigma Z[Z \sqsubseteq_A g(1) - y])[y \text{ likes } x]]$$

(f) $[\![\beta_1[D[\beta_2[D[like]][each\ other_{1,2}]]]\!]^g =$
$$\lambda Y . \forall y \sqsubseteq_A Y[\forall x \sqsubseteq_A (\sigma Z[Z \sqsubseteq_A Y - y])[y \text{ likes } x]]$$

(10.16e) holds of a plurality Y if every atomic part of Y likes all the other atomic parts of Y (more in detail: if for each $y \sqsubseteq_A Y$, the complement plurality $Y - y$ is such that each of its atomic parts is liked by y), which seems reasonable for this example. This reading is called *strong reciprocity* and can be schematized as:

(10.17)   strong reciprocity:
$[\![NP\ V\ each\ other]\!]^g = 1$ iff
$$\forall x \sqsubseteq_A [\![NP]\!]^g [\forall y \sqsubseteq [\![NP]\!]^g \ \& x \neq y[[\![V]\!]^g(x)(y) = 1]]$$

In section 10.4 we will return to the question of the lexical meaning of the reciprocal pronoun. First, though, we will look at some more syntax-related issues.

10.3   The syntax of reciprocal binding

10.3.1   Long-distance reciprocals

Above we saw that reciprocals are doubly anaphoric in that they have a range variable and a contrast variable. In all the examples discussed, range and contrast are bound by βs within the minimal clause containing the reciprocal, and indeed it seems that the tense-domain is universally the domain within which reciprocal expressions must be bound (see the references in chapter 3, section 3.3). We can note, secondly, that the two indices on the reciprocal are always (derivatively) bound by the same NP, once as a genuine plural and once as a distributed plural. A natural question to ask is whether these two variables can ever be bound by distinct NPs. At first glance, the answer is 'no,' cf. (10.18):

(10.18)   (a)   The members of the band regret that Charleen and Klaus sued each other.

(b) *LF: [the members of the band][β_1[D[regret [that [Charleen and Klaus][D [β_2 [sued [each other$_{1,2}$]]]]]]]]

Given the indexing in (10.18b), the sentence should mean something like 'each member of the band regrets that Charleen sued all band members except herself (Charleen) and that Klaus sued all band members except himself (Klaus).' If neither Charleen nor Klaus are band members, this boils down to each of them suing the entire band. But, more interestingly, if they are band members, they each sue the rest of the band. Clearly, neither of these readings is available. We can only understand the sentence to mean that the object of the band members' regret is that Charleen sued Klaus and Klaus sued Charleen. The LF that correctly represents that reading is (10.19):

(10.19)   [the members of the band][D[regret [that [Charleen and Klaus][β_3 [D [β_2 [sued [each other$_{3,2}$]]]]]]]]]

Given that, it is tempting to conclude that both the range index and the contrast index of the reciprocal must be bound within their domain. Before drawing that conclusion, however, we should consider sentences like (10.20):

(10.20)   Kamela and Saralee hope that they will beat each other.

A little inspection will reveal that the *they* in the embedded clause is (most naturally) interpreted as a dependent plural. Each woman has a hope about herself winning, not about them both winning. The respective hopes are (Kamela) 'I will beat Saralee,' and (Saralee) 'I will beat Kamela.' As far as the interpretation of *they* goes, there is no problem at all:

(10.21)   [Kamela and Saralee][D [β_7 [hope that they$_7$ will beat each other]]]

The index 7 ranges over atomic individuals, given that the binder index 7 is introduced *below* the distributor; accordingly, *they* is a dependent plural, as desired.

As such, 7, or a new binder index introduced by *they*, can act as the contrast argument for *each other*. But the only genuine plural available as the *range* argument is *Kamela and Saralee*, the subject of the matrix clause. A complete LF will thus have to look like (10.22) (note that 4 and 7 are semantically equivalent):

(10.22)   [Kamela and Saralee][β_2 [D [β_7 [hope that they$_7$ [β_4 will beat [each other$_{2,4}$]]]]]]]

While this LF is semantically perfectly well-formed, note that the range index 7 is bound from outside the domain of *each other* (the contrast index is bound locally). But such long-distance binding of the range index is precisely what we blamed for the ungrammaticality of (10.18) above.

The difference between (10.18) and (10.20)/(10.22) is that in the latter the range antecedent *they* is *in some sense* the same as the contrast antecedent, *Kamela and Saralee*. More precisely, the local subject of *each other* in (10.20), although not the semantic antecedent for *each other*'s range argument, is *dependent* on the semantic antecedent of the range argument: *they* in (10.20) is bound by *Kamela and Saralee* – though mediated by a distributive operator – while *Charleen and Klaus* in (10.18a) is not anaphorically related to *the members of the band*.

It seems thus that the Binding Conditions for reciprocals need to contain an extra clause that allows the range index to be non-locally bound if the long distance binder is 'related' to the local antecedent (the one binding the contrast variable) in the way found in (10.22). I will sketch such a stipulation here, leaving out the details.

Let us informally say that an index *i* *directly depends* on an NP iff the binder prefix β_i that binds *i* is separated from NP by at most Ds and βs. Thus *they$_7$* in (10.22) directly depends on *Kamela and Saralee* via the sequence 'β_2 D β_7,' as does *each other*'s range index 2, via the binder β_2. This is pretty much our derivative notion of semantic binding by an NP from chapter 4, factoring in the possibility of distributive operators.

In contrast to that, we say that an index *i* *indirectly depends* on NP$_j$ if either *i* directly depends on *j*, or both *i* and NP directly depend on some NP*. So *each other*'s contrast index 2 in (10.22) indirectly depends on its local subject *they$_7$* – since they both depend on *Kamela and Saralee* – though it doesn't directly.

Note that, in contradistinction, the range index of *each other* in (10.18), whose LF is repeated here, does not even indirectly depend on *Charleen and Klaus*:

(10.23)   *[the members of the band][β_1[D[regret [that [Charleen and Klaus][D [β_2 [sued [each other$_{1,2}$]]]]]]]]

We can thus state the Binding Conditions on reciprocals as in (10.24):

(10.24)   Binding Condition for reciprocals:
               (a)   the contrast index of a reciprocal must be bound in its domain
               (b)   the range argument of a reciprocal must indirectly depend on an argument within its domain

For discussion and various implementations of this idea see Heim *et al.* (1991); Higginbotham (1983); Sauerland (1998:194); and Dimitriadis (1999) among others.

10.3.2   Reciprocals as binders

For the sake of completeness, let us look at reciprocals that function as binders. The comforting conclusion will be that everything works just as expected. A classic example is sentence (10.25):

(10.25)   John and Mary told each other that they should leave.

John and Mary is the only available antecedent for the reciprocal, so that part of the indexing must be as in (10.26):

(10.26)   [John and Mary] [β_3 [D [β_9 [told [each other$_{3,9}$] [that they should leave]]]]]]

As far as the antecedent for *they* goes, there are three logical possibilities (apart from the one of leaving it free): it could go with 3, with 9 (as a dependent plural), or be bound by the reciprocal. All three indexings result in different meanings, as illustrated below, with the meanings paraphrased in parentheses. And, indeed, all three meanings seem intuitively available for this sentence:[3],[4]

(10.27)   (a)   [John and Mary] [β_3 [D [β_9 [told [each other$_{3,9}$] [that they$_3$ [D should leave]]]]]]]
                    (John and Mary (each) say: 'We should leave!')
             (b)   [John and Mary] [β_3 [D [β_9 [told [each other$_{3,9}$] [that they$_9$ should leave]]]]]]
                    (John and Mary (each) say: 'I should leave!')
             (c)   [John and Mary] [β_3 [D [β_9 [told [each other$_{3,9}$] [β_5 [that they$_5$ should leave]]]]]]
                    (John and Mary (each) say: 'You should leave!')

The interesting case here is (10.27c), where *they* is bound as a dependent plural to *each other*. Given the meaning of *each other* as 'the one(s) of them that is not him/herself,' $[\![$each other$_{3,9}]\!]^{g[3 \to John \sqcup Mary]}$ will refer to Mary if $g(9)$(the one telling) is John, and to John if $g(9) = Mary$, so that in effect $g(5)$ will always be the one being told (cf. Heim *et al.* [1991]; Higginbotham [1985]).

---

[3] (10.27a) contains an additional distributor in the embedded clause, given that $g(3)$ ranges over pluralities and that *leave* is a predicate that holds of atoms only.

[4] Note that in (10.27c) *each other* must command the embedded clause, cf. the discussion of binding in double object constructions in chapter 1, section 1.3 and chapter 4, section 4.5.4. If we want to use a syntactic binder β, as in (10.27a), it must be adjoined to a lower segment of VP as argued for by Larson (1988) in order to get binding from the indirect object NP into the direct object clause; similar effects will be obtained by wrapping mechanisms in categorial grammar or binding applied to argument-lists (again, see chapter 4, section 4.5.4), but the details are irrelevant here.

Exercise 10.3

Jackendoff and Culicover (1995) explore the syntactic and semantic behavior of expressions like *something else*, *everyone else*, etc. Their hypothesis 3 (p. 261) can be rendered in our current framework as in (10.28):

(10.28)   (a)

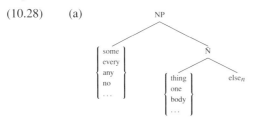

(b) $[\![\text{else}_n]\!]^g = \lambda x.g(n)$ does not overlap with x (i.e. $x \not\sqsubseteq g(n)$ and $g(n) \not\sqsubseteq x$)

The index n can be a free variable, or semantically bound, as in the most plausible readings for (10.29a) and (10.29b), respectively:

(10.29)   (a)   Stevie is not good at doing taxes. Most of us hire someone else to do it.

(b)   Very few people do their taxes themselves. Most of us hire someone else to do it.

(i) Give LFs for the prominent readings of (10.29a) and (10.29b) and calculate their interpretations (you can ignore the *to do it* part). (ii) Can you find any locality conditions on the relation between *else* and its antecedent?

Exercise 10.4

Explain the grammaticality patterns in the following crossover paradigm:

(10.30)   (a)   *Who* does $\begin{Bmatrix} *he \\ ?no\ one\ else \end{Bmatrix}$ think will win?

(b)   *Who* does $\begin{Bmatrix} ?his \\ ?someone\ else's \end{Bmatrix}$ mother love?

Exercise 10.5

Jackendoff and Culicover (1995) then go on to discuss more complex cases such as (10.31a), which has a reading according to which Bill had dinner with someone other than his (Bill's) kids; a similar case can be made for the quantificational variant in (10.31b):

(10.31)   (a)   John had dinner with his kids, but Bill had dinner with someone else.

(b)   Sally named her husband as her closest friend, but interestingly, most women named someone else.

They show that examples of these kinds pose a problem for their hypothesis 3 ($\approx$[10.28] above), and go on to present more arguments to the effect that BT cannot apply to syntactic structure at all.

Show that the pertinent readings of these examples are not derived by the analysis in (10.28). What is a correct paraphrase of these readings? Notwithstanding how to formulate the mapping from surface structure to LF systematically, can you give an LF that captures the reading (see Jackendoff and Culicover [1995] for discussion)?

10.4   Alternative meanings for reciprocal sentences

Above we have only concerned ourselves with strong reciprocity. But, as is well known since the works of Fiengo and Lasnik (1973) and in particular Langendoen (1978), this is merely one of many different ways of interpreting the reciprocal, some of which I will discuss in this section, starting with so-called...

10.4.1   Weak reciprocity

Consider sentence (10.32):

(10.32)   Gilles, Malu, Otto, and Jaqueline are touching each other.

Suppose Gilles, Malu, Otto, and Jaqueline form a circle by holding hands, so that Gilles touches Malu and Jaqueline, Malu touches Gilles and Otto, Otto touches Malu and Jaqueline, and Jaqueline touches Otto and Gilles. Intuitively the sentence is true in this scenario, but according to strong reciprocity it should be false. To see this, take Gilles: as an atomic part of the plurality, Gilles is required to touch every atomic part of the plurality except himself. But he doesn't touch Otto, just as Malu doesn't touch Jaqueline. Not all atomic parts touch all atomic parts. The weaker relation expressed is that every atomic part touches some other atomic part, and every atomic part is touched by some other atomic part. This is *weak reciprocity*:

(10.33)   weak reciprocity:
$[\![\text{NP V each other}]\!]^g = 1$ iff
$\forall x \sqsubseteq_A [\![\text{NP}]\!]^g \,[\exists y \sqsubseteq_A [\![\text{NP}]\!]^g \,[\, x \neq y \,\&\, [\![\text{V}]\!]^g(x)(y) = 1]\,]$ and
$\forall x \sqsubseteq_A [\![\text{NP}]\!]^g \,[\exists y \sqsubseteq_A [\![\text{NP}]\!]^g \,[x \neq y \,\&\, [\![\text{V}]\!]^g(y)(x) = 1]\,]$

Before we try to derive this reading compositionally, we should note with Langendoen (1978) that weak reciprocity has a counterpart in ordinary transitive plural sentences. For example (10.34a) will be understood as saying that Gilles and Malu *between them* ate the peanuts, i.e. Gilles and Malu each ate some peanuts, and each peanut was eaten by either Gilles or Malu (any other reading would be odd):

(10.34)   (a)   Gilles and Malu ate the peanuts.
           (b)   Jaqueline and Otto photographed Gilles and Malu.

Similarly (10.34b) is ambiguous between a strong reading (each of Jaqueline and Otto photographed each of Gilles and Malu) and a weak reading (each of

Jaqueline and Otto photographed one of Gilles and Malu and each of Gilles and Malu was photographed by one of Jaqueline and Otto). The latter reading, which is *weaker* in that it is true in a superset of the cases in which the former is, is called a *cumulative reading*. Acknowledging the existence of cumulative readings, weak reciprocity can be analyzed as a case of a reciprocal cumulative reading along the lines of (10.35) (Sternefeld, 1998):

(10.35)   Gilles, Malu, Otto, and Jaqueline are touching Gilles, Malu, Otto, and Jaqueline, and no one is touching themselves

As a first step towards a compositional analysis, we introduce a *cumulation* operator:

(10.36)   for any two-place predicate P, $[\![*^2 P]\!]^g$ denotes that function π in $D_{e,et}$ such that for any $x_1, y_1 \in D_e$, $\pi(x_1)(y_1) = 1$ iff
   (a)   either $[\![P]\!]^g(x_1)(y_1) = 1$, or
   (b)   there are $x_2, x_3, y_2, y_3 \in D_e$ such that $x_2 \sqcup x_3 = x_1$, $y_2 \sqcup y_3 = y_1$, $\pi(x_2)(y_2) = 1$ and $\pi(x_3)(y_3) = 1$

This operator $*2$ guarantees the validity of the following kind of inference:

(10.37)

| Knut brought potato salad. | $[\![\text{brought}]\!]^g([\![\text{potato salad}]\!]^g)([\![\text{Knut}]\!]^g) = 1$ |
| Bela brought falafel. | $[\![\text{brought}]\!]^g([\![\text{falafel}]\!]^g)([\![\text{Bela}]\!]^g) = 1$ |

therefore

Knut and Bela brought	$[\![*^2\text{brought}]\!]^g([\![\text{potato salad and falafel}]\!]^g)([\![\text{K. and B.}]\!]^g)$
potato salad and falafel.	$\equiv [\![*^2\text{brought}]\!]^g([\![\text{potato salad}]\!]^g \sqcup [\![\text{falafel}]\!]^g)$
	$([\![\text{Knut}]\!]^g \sqcup [\![\text{Bela}]\!]^g)$

(10.34a) now gets the LF representation in (10.38), which gives us the cumulative reading:

(10.38)   [Gilles and Malu][[$*^2$ate][the peanuts]]

Returning then to reciprocal sentences, we want to apply the cumulation operator $*^2$ to the transitive verb *after* excluding reflexive pairs from the base denotation. For example, for (10.32) to be true, we require that among the plurality Gilles⊔Malu⊔Otto⊔Jaqueline everyone touch someone other than him/herself, and everyone be touched by someone other than him/herself. To do this, we need to introduce another operator, which I call OTHER; OTHER simply excludes all reflexive pairs from the denotation of a transitive verb:

(10.39)   for any two-place predicate P, $[\![\text{OTHER } P]\!]^g$ denotes that function $\pi \in D_{e,et}$ such that $\pi(x)(y) = 1$ iff $[\![P]\!]^g(x)(y) = 1$ and $x \neq y$

The weak reciprocal reading can now be analyzed as the cumulated OTHER predicate applied to the antecedent and an identical anaphor:

(10.40)   [Gilles, Malu, Otto, and Jaqueline][β_8 [[$*^2$[OTHER touch]][them$_8$]]]

While this representation brings out the parallelism between weak reciprocity and cumulativity, it is somewhat at odds with the syntax of the reciprocal construction, splitting the reciprocal into a plain anaphor in argument position and a verbal affix. Furthermore, despite certain formal similarities – the pronominal part in (10.40) resembles the range variable in (10.14), and both contain a non-identity statement – it is far from obvious how strong and weak reciprocity can be compositionally derived using the same lexical element *each other* (the two attempts that I am aware of, Beck [1999] and Sternefeld [1998], both avail themselves of a fair bit of LF movement and/or semantic 'glue'). For further discussion I refer to the works just mentioned.

A different way to accommodate weak reciprocity is along the lines of the proposal in Schwarzschild (1996):ch. 5. Taking the semantics of strong reciprocity as a point of departure, let us make the following amendment to the meaning of *each other* in (10.14) from above:

(10.41)   (a) $[\![\text{each other}^f_{r,c}]\!]^g = g(f)(g(r))(g(c))$, where $g(f)$ must be an other function

   (b) f' is an other function iff it is a function in $D_{\langle e,\langle e,e\rangle\rangle}$, such that for any $r', c' \in D_e$, $f'(r')(c')$ is a part of r' that doesn't overlap with c'.

Given a range r and a contrast c, with $g(c) \sqsubseteq g(r)$ as usual, *each other*$^f_{r,c}$ no longer denotes the *maximal* complement of $g(r)$ minus $g(c)$, but some possibly proper subpart thereof, as determined by the function $g(f)$. By assumption, f cannot be bound, and $g(f)$ is thus always contextually given. In a context in which Gilles, Malu, Otto, and Jaqueline form a circle by joining hands, $g(f)$ might be that function which associates each $g(c)$ with the set of individual parts of $g(r)$ that are $g(c)$'s neighbors in the circle. Accordingly, $[\![\text{each other}^f_{1,2}]\!]^{g[1 \to Gilles \sqcup Malu \sqcup Otto \sqcup Jaqueline]}$ would associate with any choice of $g(2)$ the maximal plurality of $g(2)$'s neighbors, but not the person opposite to $g(2)$.

Obviously, such an approach relegates a lot of work to the pragmatics, in particular the task of making sure that any element of the antecedent will be the 'other' at least once. This is trivial for a symmetric relation like *touch*, but consider *hate*: while the distribution operator guarantees that each atomic part of the antecedent plurality hate at least one other atomic part, nothing guarantees that each atomic part is hated by at least one other. See Schwarzschild (1996) for further discussion.

10.4.2   Other reciprocities

Even weaker reciprocities

Dalrymple *et al.* (1998) point out that certain reciprocal sentences have truth conditions even weaker than weak reciprocity, for example (10.42):[5]

(10.42)   "The captain!" said the pirates, staring at each other in surprise.

---

[5] Examples (10.42) (from *Peter Pan*), (10.43c) and (10.43d), are Dalrymple *et al.*'s (6), (8), and (54).

Dalrymple *et al.* (1998) argue that for (10.42) to be true, not every pirate must be stared at (though every pirate must stare at some other pirate). Accordingly, weak reciprocity is not met. We could capture this using the revised denotation of *each other* in (10.41a) above, by letting f' choose one or more pirates c' happens to stare at. But such a treatment will not carry over to cases like (10.43):

(10.43)   (a)   The children followed each other into the room.
          (b)   The tables are piled atop each other.
          (c)   The third-grade students in Mrs. Smith's class gave each other measles.
          (d)   He and scores of other inmates slept on foot-wide wooden planks stacked atop each other...

Take (10.43a): we judge it as true if the children enter the room in one orderly procession. But not only is there a child that isn't followed by another child (the last) in this situation, there is even a child that doesn't follow any child (the first). Similarly in (10.43b–10.43d). That is, even the weakest kind of reciprocity considered so far isn't met here, and it won't be as long as we use a distributive operator or any of its kin to relate the plural antecedent to its argument slot.

According to Dalrymple *et al.* (1998) the use of reciprocals to describe such situations is not just a pragmatic weakening that allows us to ignore certain kids (tables, planks...) but a systematic effect in the semantics. The sentence is true because each child participates in the 'follow into the room' relation as *either the follower or the followee* to some other child. This idea is corroborated by our intuition that e.g. *the children are touching each other* is not judged true if one child is not included in the circle at all; similarly (10.43b) would seem false in a scenario in which five tables are piled up, while a sixth table is standing next to the pile.

But if this intuition reflects the semantics of these examples, we are forced into a considerable revision of our previous treatment of the reciprocal. A possible analysis runs like this: we treat *each other* as a function which takes a two-place function (a transitive verb meaning) and returns a one-place function (an intransitive verb/VP meaning) (generalization to n-place functions will be omitted here). The resulting function will hold true of an individual x if there is a y different from x in the range such that the two-place relation holds between y and x *or* x and y:

(10.44) $[\![\text{each other}_{r,c}]\!]^g$ is that function f in $\langle\langle e,et\rangle,et\rangle$ such that for any $R \in D_{\langle e,et\rangle}, x \in D_e, f(R)(x) = 1$ iff there is a $y \sqsubseteq g(r)$ such that neither $y \sqsubseteq g(c)$ nor $g(c) \sqsubseteq y$, and either $R(x)(y)$ or $R(y)(x)$

Example (10.43a) receives the usual LF (10.45a), but a new interpretation along the lines of (10.45b):[6]

---

[6] The reference to the index c of *each other* could be replaced by a direct reference to x in the above definition; similarly, the distributor and the genuine plural binder could have been built into this rule as well. I retained the familiar format for reasons of comparability.

(10.45)   (a)   [the children] $[\beta_1 [D [\beta_2 [$followed [each other$_{1,2}]$ into the room]]]]

         (b)   for each child x_2 among the plurality X_1 of children, there is at least one child y in X_1 which is not x_2 and either x_2 follows y into the room, or y follows x_2 into the room

We mentioned above that many languages use verbal affixes to express reciprocity; moreover, the sentences thus marked usually look like intransitive sentences (no transitive marking on the V, no ergative marking on the subject, etc; e.g. Nyulnyulan [McGregor, 1999], Halkomelem [Gerdts, 1999]). We could view this as corroborating morphosyntactic evidence that the reciprocal, also in English, is indeed a function on the verb meaning, as Dalrymple *et al.* (1998) suggest, rather than an argument to it, as assumed in sections 10.2 through 10.3.2.

It should be mentioned, though, that, as with reflexives, there are cases where the arguments 'reciprocalized' are not coarguments. These include possessive and other NP-internal reciprocals in English (*each other's bicycle, friends of each other*), but also, more strikingly, semantically analogous constructions with verbal reciprocal markers, as in the following example from Malagasy:[7]

(10.46)   (a)   m-   **if-**   aN-   sintona volo Ravao sy Ravelo
            PRESENT RECIP ACTIVE *pull*   *hair Ravao and Ravelo*
            'Ravao and Ravelo are pulling each other's hair.'

         (b)   M-   **if-**   aN-   fantatra toetra i Soa sy i Vao
            PRESENT RECIP ACTIVE *know*   *nature the Soa and the Vao*
            'Soa and Vao are getting to know each other's character.'

It would seem extremely tricky to formulate a meaning for the reciprocal affix which, when applied to the verb, yields the prerequisite meaning compositionally to interpret (10.46). Examples of this kind thus suggest that the relation between morphosyntax and semantics is more roundabout than we might have hoped for, and thus that conclusions about the semantics based on morphosyntactic properties have to be taken with a grain of salt in this case.

Intermediate reciprocities

Dalrymple *et al.* (1998) bring to attention a second set of cases that suggests treating *each other* as a function that takes transitive verb meanings as its argument. They note that certain reciprocal sentences receive a reading intermediate between strong and weak (or weakest) reciprocity:[8]

(10.47)   As the preposterous horde crowded around, waiting for the likes of Evans and Mike Greenwell, five Boston pitchers sat alongside each other: Larry Anderson, Jeff Reardon, Jeff Gray, Dennis Lamp, and Tom Bolton.

Clearly, not every pitcher can sit next to every other pitcher. One could argue that weak reciprocity is met (each pitcher sits next to some other pitcher), but

---

[7] Ed Keenan (p.c.); see also Keenan and Razafimamonjy (2001).
[8] (10.47) and (10.48) are Dalrymple *et al.*'s (5) and (41).

intuitively the sentence says something stronger than that, namely that no non-pitcher sits in between the pitchers, and that all pitchers sit on one row, rather than, say, on two separate benches. A similar case can be made for (10.48):

(10.48)   The telephone poles are spaced 500 feet from each other.

If the telephone poles are arranged in pairs of two within 500 feet, but each pair is separated from the next by 800 feet, we judge (10.48) to be false, even though each pole is within 500 feet from *some* other pole. Dalrymple *et al.* suggest that the truth conditions for these and similar sentences require that there be a linear sequence of pairs of poles, all of which are within 500 feet. To illustrate a little further, let us define the *transitive closure* of a two-place function:

(10.49)   for any $R \in D_{e,et}$, let TC(R) be that function $f \in D_{e,et}$ such that for any $x, y \in D_e$, $f(x)(y) = 1$ *iff*:
(a) $R(x)(y) = 1$, or
(b)   there is a $z \in D_e$ s.t. $f(x)(z) = 1$ and $f(z)(y) = 1$

If R is ⟦be spaced 500 feet from⟧^{g}, $TC(R)$, its transitive closure, will be a function that holds between any two poles (or other things) x and y if either x is 500 feet apart from y, or x is 500 feet away from a pole z which is 500 feet from y, or which is 500 feet from a pole r that is 500 feet from y, or ... and so on and so forth. It should be clear that in the scenario which makes (10.48) true, every pair of poles is (not in ⟦be 500 feet away from⟧^{g} but) in TC(⟦be 500 feet away from⟧^{g}), i.e. strong reciprocity holds for that derived relation. *Each other* can accordingly be assigned the following denotation:

(10.50)   ⟦each other$_{r,c}$⟧^{g} is that function f in ⟨⟨e,et⟩,et⟩ such that for any $R \in D_{\langle e,et \rangle}$, $x \in D_e$, $f(R)(x) = 1$ iff for all $y \sqsubseteq g(r)$ such that neither $y \sqsubseteq g(c)$ nor $g(c) \sqsubseteq y$, $TC(R)(y)(x) = 1$

The sequence of poles in (10.48), as well as that of kids in (10.43a), among others, are instances of what is called a *chaining situation* in the typological literature (Lichtenberk, 1985, 1999, a.o.). Many languages, just like English, use their reciprocal-marking device to describe chaining situations. A random example is the verbal prefix *kwai* in To'aba'ita (Oceanic; Austronesian), which can mark true reciprocity as well as chaining:[9]

(10.51)   (a)   Roo wane kero   kwai- kumu-i.
                   two man   2-DUAL-NONFUT RECIP *punch*
                   'The two men are punching each other.'   (strongly reciprocal)
           (b)   Wela kera   futa   kwai- suli.
                   child 3-PL-NONFUT *be-born* RECIP *follow*
                   'The children were born in quick succession.'   (chaining)

It bears mentioning that chaining does not necessarily require a treatment of *each other* as a function on transitive verb meanings. Using the definition in (10.41a)

---

[9] Data from Lichtenberk (1999):35.

above, the same effect can be achieved by letting the contextual function $g(f)$ assign to every pole the (two) poles directly connected to it. It seems that the cases of weakest reciprocity discussed in the previous subsection are the hardest nut to crack for an approach that tries to analyze *each other* uniformly as term-denoting.[10]

Exercise 10.6

At first glance, the examples in (10.43) also seem to involve interme-diate reciprocity. However, according to the definition in (10.50), these sentencs will not be true in the scenarios described. Show exactly why. Which property of the verb meaning sets the cases in (10.43) apart from those in (10.47) and (10.48)?

10.4.3   The strongest meaning hypothesis

In the previous subsections we have discussed a wealth of different readings for reciprocal sentences, and the denotations for *each other* required to derive these. A natural question to ask is if we shouldn't simply assume weak reciprocity (or an even weaker variant) as the only semantic meaning of recipro-cal sentences, given that any stronger reciprocity is just a special case of weak reciprocity. Dalrymple *et al.* (1998) vehemently reject this. They point out that, all else being equal, weak reciprocity alone would lead to counter-intuitive truth conditions. Take (10.52): in a situation where Arabella knows Bruno and Bruno knows Chris, but Arabella and Chris are complete strangers, we would clearly judge (10.52) as false; but according to weak reciprocity the sentence is predicted as true (each knows and is known by one of the others):

(10.52)   Arabella, Bruno, and Chris know each other.

Dalrymple *et al.* (1998)'s conjecture is that a reciprocal sentence will have the strongest truth conditions compatible with the contextual and lexical properties of the relations involved. They call this the *Strongest Meaning Hypothesis* (SMH) and give a formal implementation of this idea. Take (10.52) as an illustration: we know that there are no obstacles to complete mutual knowledge within a

---

[10] Whether or not they prove lethal for such a project (as Dalrymple *et al.* [1998] conclude) seems unclear to me, and I refer the reader to Dalrymple *et al.* (1998), Sauerland (1998), and the other works mentioned in this chapter for more discussion. It is perhaps fair to say that ultimate answers regarding the question of what the semantic (as opposed to the pragmatic) meaning of reciprocal statements is can be expected only in the context of a discussion of the analogous questions in the semantics of plurals *per se*, which is at this point inconclusive.

In a nutshell, the question is if there are ways to make a plural predication true which are neither distributive nor cumulative, nor truly collective, as, for example, in *80 million Germans bought 720,045 cars* or *The boys touched the ceiling (forming a pyramid)*. While most authors seem to take refuge in such readings every now and then, no accounts to block these in the general case have been given. Pending that, discussions about the exact nature of cumulation, including alleged cumulation in reciprocal sentences, are hampered by the possibility that what appears to be a cumulative reading is 'loosely collective' instead.

plurality, so we require there to be complete mutual knowledge (i.e. strong reciprocity) in order for (10.52) to be true. On the other hand, we know that not more than two people can all sit alongside each other, which is why we judge a sentence like (10.47) (*Five Boston pitchers sat alongside each other*) true as long as the weaker reciprocity is met.

The case of touching in (10.32) above must be similar to that of sitting alongside, even though details remain obscure (in other configurations than circles, complete mutual touching seems imaginable for a plurality of four, considerations of decency aside).

Note that the general idea behind the SMH is independent of what exactly the actual readings are, or how they are compositionally derived (Dalrymple *et al.* [1998] deny, for example, that weak reciprocity as discussed above is an actual reading, but argue for the existence of three more readings besides the ones mentioned so far).

A potential problem arises for the SMH with examples like in (10.53):[11]

(10.53)   (a) #John and Bill are taller than each other.
            (b) #My mother and I procreated each other.

Given the lexical semantics and pragmatics of *taller* and *procreate*, it should be obvious that no strong reciprocity can hold between the atomic parts of the plurality. However, weakest reciprocity as in (10.44) above can, and does, hold: for each atomic part of the plurality there is one other atomic part that stands in the relation 'taller than' or 'procreate' *or their reverse* to that atomic part. Accordingly the SMH predicts the sentences to be true if John and Bill are of different height and if my mother procreated me. This is, of course, not our intuition. How this problem can be circumvented is unclear (cf. the references in n. 11).

We thus end this section without a firm conclusion. While it seems clear that more readings than just strong reciprocity are required, the questions of just which and how many readings there are, as well as how the actual reading is selected for a particular example, remain somewhat open. Accordingly the question of whether a term-denoting treatment along the general lines developed in the first two sections of this chapter is sufficient hasn't received a definite answer, even though the examples brought forward by Dalrymple *et al.* (1998) would seem to put the burden of argument on those who try to defend a term denotation for reciprocals.

10.5   Reflexives and reciprocals

Let me close by pointing out some open questions regarding the relation between reflexives and reciprocals. In English, plural reflexive sentences

---

[11] From Dalrymple *et al.* (1998):196; and Sauerland (1998):201, respectively.

cannot be interpreted as reciprocal; for example, *they like themselves* cannot mean that they each like the other(s). While this may appear obvious, it should be noted that the system developed in this chapter allows at least two LFs for reflexive sentences – alongside the correct (10.54a), which encodes strict reflexivity – which involve reciprocal relations: (10.54b), which says that they each like all of them(selves); and (10.54c), which says that they each like, and are liked by, at least one of them(selves) (which is true in a situation where they like each other):

(10.54)   (a)   they D [β_1 [like themselves$_1$]]
           (b)   *they [β_1 [D [[D like] themselves$_1$]]]
           (c)   *they [β_1 [^{*2}like themselves$_1$]]

It seems unclear, and hasn't, to the best of my knowledge, been discussed in the literature, why neither (10.54b) nor (10.54c) appears to be available in English.

Interestingly, reflexives in many languages do allow for a reciprocal reading. The German (just as the French or Polish) translation of *they like themselves* with a reflexive can be interpreted to mean that they like each other (indeed, this is the preferred way to express this statement, although a true and unambiguous reciprocal, *einander*, is possible here, too):

(10.55)   Sie mögen sich.
           they like   self
           'They like each other.' or 'They like themselves.'

Even more striking, many languages of the world, among them virtually all Australian languages, have only one morpheme to express reciprocity *and* reflexivity, for example the circumfix *mar-nyj* in (10.56) from Nyulnyul:[12]

(10.56)   Ku- rr   irrjiwar arri ku- li-   rr- mi-   jal- inyj.
           2   AUG *three*   *no* 2-   IRREALIS AUG REF/REC *see* REF/REC
           'Don't you three look at each other!' or '. . . yourselves!'

Perhaps these cases just show ordinary cumulative reflexive meanings as represented in (10.54c), which just happen to be true in situations that English would describe using reciprocals. Or perhaps they involve true ambiguity or polysemy; there doesn't seem to be any discussion of this question in the formal semantic literature, but see Hole and Gast (2003).

---

[12] McGregor (1999):91; AUG = augmented.

11 Exempt anaphora and reflexivity

In chapter 3 we concluded that the subject domain is the one within which English reflexives need to be bound, while non-reflexives have to be free in their coargument domain. Accordingly, we noted that there are a number of environments in which we find reflexive and non-reflexive pronouns alike.

In the late 1980s and early 1990s, this line of analysis was seriously challenged. In a series of publications, Pollard and Sag (1992, 1994) (P&S) and Reinhart and Reuland (1992, 1993) (R&R) independently proposed that the relevant domain for proper reflexives (and, in P&S's case, reciprocals) is the coargument domain, too. Crucial to these analyses is the insight that not all reflexives in English are governed by the same conditions.

11.1   Introducing exempt anaphora

11.1.1   Complementary and non-complementary positions

If we look at the distribution of reflexive and non-reflexive pronouns, we can pre-theoretically distinguish two kinds of positions: those in which reflexives and non-reflexives are in complementary distribution, and those in which they are not. The former kind is illustrated in (11.1):

(11.1)   (a)   Max criticized himself/*him.
          (b)   Some people talk to themselves/*them.
          (c)   Lucie's pictures of herself/*her

Non-complementary positions include NP-internal positions ('picture NPs'), but also certain adjuncts, as well as coordinations:[1]

(11.2)   (a)   Lucie saw a picture of herself/her.
          (b)   Mary likes jokes about herself/her.
          (c)   They believe that each other's/their pictures are on sale.

(11.3)   (a)   Max keeps a gun near himself/him.
          (b)   Lucie counted five tourists in the room apart from herself/her.

(11.4)   Max boasted that the queen invited Lucie and himself/him for a drink.

---

[1] (11.2b) and (11.3b), as well as (11.4), from Reinhart and Reuland (1993):661 and 670, respectively; see also Hole (2002) for more corpus data.

A plausible, and indeed common, conclusion drawn from examples like (11.2)–(11.4) is that the domain in which non-reflexive pronouns must be free is, at least in some structures, smaller than that in which reflexives need to be bound. In that way, a particular position such as the subjects in (11.2)–(11.4) can be within the domain of a reflexive, but outside of the domain of a non-reflexive in the same position, accounting for the non-complementarity. In the remainder of this chapter, we will refer to this line of analysis – exemplified in Chomsky (1981, 1986) and Huang (1983), among many others – as *Standard Binding Theory*.

R&R's and P&S's proposals radically depart from this conclusion reached by Standard Binding Theory, in that they assume that reflexives in non-complementary positions are subject to entirely different conditions from those in complementary positions, and that crucially only the latter requirements are purely structural (phrase structural or argument structural) in nature. (11.5) and (11.6) paraphrase Pollard and Sag (1992)'s proposal:

(11.5) Binding Condition A:
        A reflexive/reciprocal must be bound by a less oblique coargument, if there is one.

(11.6) Exempt Anaphor Condition:
        A reflexive/reciprocal that doesn't have a less oblique coargument must denote a *designated participant*.

Let us call a position without a less oblique coargument an *exempt position*, and one with a less oblique coargument a *regular position*. As indicated in (11.6), reflexives that occur in the former kind of position will be called *exempt anaphors*; reflexives that occur in regular positions, on the other hand, will be referred to as *regular anaphors*. Assuming that Binding Condition B is the complement of Binding Condition A as given in (11.5), the hypothesis is thus that non-complementarity occurs with exempt anaphors in exempt positions, while complementary distribution is found with regular anaphors in regular positions.

Going back to our examples, it is evident that in the classical, complementary environment (11.1a), the pronoun is in a regular position as defined, since it is the lower argument to the transitive predicate *criticize*. As discussed in chapter 3, section 3.1.4, NPs within certain argument PPs count as arguments, too. Thus the complement of *to* in (11.1b) counts as coargument to the subject of *talk* (another way of thinking about this is that *talk to* is *one* predicate). This reasoning, finally, applies equally to arguments within NPs, so that in *Lucie's pictures of herself*, *Lucie* and *herself* count as coarguments to the (nominal) predicate *pictures* (*of*), making the P complement a complementary position (cf. section 11.3.2 below). (11.5) correctly predicts that in all these positions reflexives can occur only if bound by a higher coargument, and are thus in complementary distribution with non-reflexives, which must be free in their coargument domain.

In the examples in (11.2) through (11.4), on the other hand, the pronouns do not have higher coarguments, because the predicate doesn't realize the higher coargument (*pictures of, jokes about, pictures*), or because it doesn't have one (*near, apart from*), or because the pronoun itself isn't an argument but only a part of an argument (coordination). Thus (11.5) doesn't apply, and reflexives can freely occur, interchangeably with non-reflexives (we will come to the notion of a *designated participant* used in [11.6] in section 11.2 below).

What constitutes the radical departure from Standard Binding Theory is not the exact specification of a regular anaphor's binding domain in (11.5) but the essentially disjunctive character of the condition, or, put differently: the fact that (11.6) is a qualitatively different condition from (11.5), which cannot naturally be unified with it (e.g. by refining the definition of binding domain, as in Chomsky [1986] or Huang [1983]).

11.1.2   Exempt anaphors have no structural binding domain

Let us now come to the main argument in favor of the proper/exempt distinction among reflexives. Recall that, according to Standard Binding Theory, reflexives in non-complementary positions are bound in essentially the same way as true reflexives, except in a bigger domain. According to (11.5), and especially (11.6), they don't obey by *any* structural principles. This latter view gains strong empirical support from the following striking observation: wherever reflexives and non-reflexive pronouns are non-complementary, the reflexives don't have to have a local antecedent at all! That is, the reflexive's antecedent doesn't need to c-command it, nor does it even have to be in the same clause:[2]

(11.7)   (a)   'It angered him that she . . . tried to attract a man like himself.'
           (b)   John's campaign requires that pictures of himself be placed all over town.
           (c)   The agreement that Iran and Iraq reached guaranteed each other's trading rights in the disputed waters until the year 2010.
           (d)   John was furious. The picture of himself in the museum had been mutilated.

In (11.7a) *himself* within the embedded final clause is bound across the embedded subject *she* to the matrix object *him*. In (11.7b) and (11.7c) the antecedent doesn't c-command the reflexive/reciprocal at all, and finally in (11.7d) the antecedent is not even within the same sentence as the reflexive. The conclusion to be drawn is that these anaphors are simply not subject to a structural Binding Condition at all: they do not need a binder within any domain; the positions they are in are *not* necessarily bound (though, of course, they can be, as in [11.2] through [11.4]).

It is perhaps worth while to reiterate that point: reflexives in non-complementary position *can* be bound, but don't ever have to be.

---

[2] Examples from Zribi-Hertz (1989); Lebeaux (1985):358, (55b); P&S (1992):(7a), (24a).

11.2   Conditions on exempt anaphora

We have remarked in subsection 11.1.2 above that the ability of exempt anaphora to occur with non-local binders is merely a special case of their ability to occur without any binder (i.e. c-commanding antecedent) at all. On the other hand, exempt anaphors, too, impose requirements on their antecedent, which are stricter than, for example, non-reflexive pronouns, and which we only hinted at by the notion of *designated participant* in (11.6). To give an example, a sentence like (11.8) seems hardly acceptable as it stands, despite the fact that *himself* is in an uncontroversially exempt position, namely the only argument to an adjunct P:

(11.8)   ?*Mary tried to attract a man like himself.

To the best of my knowledge, there is no comprehensive theory of what it takes to antecede an exempt anaphor, i.e. to be a 'designated participant' in the sense of (11.6). Descriptively, the following seems accurate (cf. the summary of the literature on exempt anaphora in P&S [1992]):

(11.9)   (a)   First and second person exempt anaphors don't need linguistic antecedents at all (i.e. speaker and hearer are automatically designated participants).

(b)   Third person exempt anaphors need an antecedent (i.e. no one else is automatically a designated participant).

(11.10) provides some examples of first and second person exempt anaphors without a linguistic antecedent:[3]

(11.10)   (a)   There were five tourists in the room apart from myself.
            (b)   Er waren vijf toeristen in de kamer behalve mezelf.
            (c)   Physicists like yourself are a godsend.
            (d)   'She gave both Brenda and myself a dirty look.'

What makes (11.8) unacceptable, then, is the fact that it lacks an antecedent at all, in violation of (11.9b). As expected, it improves if an antecedent is provided:

(11.11)   'It angered him that she ... tried to attract a man like himself.'

Contrast this with reflexives in complementary positions, as in (11.12): the third person reflexive in (11.12a) has neither an antecedent nor a local binder, so it is unacceptable, just like (11.8). But adding a potential antecedent doesn't improve the case – (11.12b):[4]

(11.12)   (a)   *She tried to attract himself.
            (b)   *It angered him that she tried to attract himself.

---

[3] From R&R:669; (11.10c) due to Ross (1970); (11.10d) to Zribi-Hertz (1989); (11.10b) is the Dutch counterpart to (11.10a).
[4] R&R (1993):666.

That (11.12b) is ungrammatical, despite the fact that the prerequisites for an exempt anaphor are met, confirms that we are dealing with a regular anaphor here – unlike in (11.8) and (11.11). Put differently, if (and only if) we know enough about the sufficient conditions for exempt anaphors, we can employ the (im)possibility of locally free reflexives/reciprocals as a diagnostic into the nature of the position it is in:

(11.13)   Diagnostic for the exempt/complementary nature of a position:
            (a)   locally free reflexive/reciprocal is possible in α → α is an exempt po-
                  sition
            (b)   locally free reflexive/reciprocal is impossible in α, *and* conditions for
                  exempt anaphors are met → α is a complementary position (BUT:
            (c)   locally free reflexive/reciprocal is impossible in α, but conditions for
                  exempt anaphors are *not* met: no conclusion about α warranted)

As for third person exempt anaphors, P&S mention two other important conditions on their acceptability: *intervention* and *perspective*, which I will discuss in
turn.

   Though the antecedent for an exempt anaphor can be as far away as in a different sentence (11.14a), intervention of another potential antecedent usually blocks
the long-distance option (11.14b):

(11.14)   (a)   John was furious. The picture of himself in the museum had been mu-
                  tilated.
            (b)   Bill remembered that Tom saw a picture of himself$_{T/*?B}$ in the post
                  office.

At first glance, data like (11.14b) might bring one back to thinking that the reflexive inside the picture NP needs a local antecedent, since *himself* apparently
must be bound to its local subject (where there is one); but as the data in (11.15)
show, this is not the case. Exempt anaphors simply take the closest *plausible*
antecedent:[5]

(11.15)   (a)   Bill finally realized that if *The Times* was going to print that picture
                  of himself with Gorbachev in the Sunday edition, there might be some
                  backlash.

---

[5] P&S (1992)'s (46b), (40d), (41a), and (41d). It is important to avoid confusion here: lack of an
appropriate antecedent in terms of agreement doesn't make a position exempt; contrast (11.15)
with the following, in which the reflexives/reciprocals are in complementary positions. In that
case a semantically implausible antecedent cannot simply be skipped:

(i)   *Bill remembered that *The Times* had quoted himself in the Sunday edition.
(ii)   *Bill and Lili suspected that *the silence* would crack each other up.
(iii)   *Bill thought that *nothing* could make himself acceptable to Sandy.

Only lack of any higher indexed coargument does, as in (11.7) and (11.14) above. Agreement
mismatches merely allow exempt anaphors to skip a structurally closer NP as antecedent.

    (b)   Bill suspected that *the silence* meant that a picture of himself would soon be on the office wall.

    (c)   Bill thought that *nothing* could make a picture of himself in *The Times* acceptable to Sandy.

    (d)   Bill knew that *it* would take a picture of himself with Gorbachev to get Mary's attention.

In all of (11.15), binding of *himself* 'skips' a potential local antecedent (because it is inanimate), and binds the reflexive to the closest animate NP, the matrix subject. The locality effect in (11.14b) is thus an intervention effect, not the result of any structural condition on binding.

As a last condition, note that exempt anaphors preferably refer to the person whose *perspective* the text is currently taking. In this they resemble logophoric pronouns as discussed in chapter 3, section 3.2.2 (indeed, R&R call exempt anaphors logophors). While the notion 'perspective' is certainly hard to make precise, P&S's examples (47)–(49) aptly illustrate the point:

(11.16)   (a)   John was going to get even with Mary. That picture of himself in the paper would really annoy her, as would the other stunts he had planned.

              (b)   Mary was quite taken aback by the publicity John was receiving. That picture of him/∗himself in the paper really annoyed her, and there was not much she could do about it.

Note that *John* is present as a structurally close antecedent in (11.16b), but fails, in an intuitive (though undefined) sense, to provide the perspective of the following sentence, as it does in (11.16a).

In what follows we will assume that these factors taken together constitute sufficient conditions for exempt anaphora to occur. Put the other way around, whenever we want to construct an example to show that a particular position is an exempt position, we will make sure that all the conditions discussed above are met.

11.3   On the notion of higher coargument

Having established the existence of exempt anaphors, we can now go back and examine various syntactic configurations in English to see what the exact scope of the 'real' Binding Condition A is, i.e. what the correct notion of 'higher coargument,' and hence 'coargument domain,' should be. When we discussed the binding of non-reflexives in English in chapter 3, we defined the coargument domain as in (11.17):

(11.17)   NP's *coargument domain* is the smallest constituent X which contains (i) NP, (ii) NP's case assigner C, (iii) NP's Θ-role assigner T, and (iv) every XP whose case or Θ-role is assigned by C or T.

Binding Condition A as given in (11.5) can be rephrased as: a reflexive has to be bound in its coargument domain, if there is a c-commanding NP in its c-command domain ('... if it can be'). We will see that this, coupled with (11.17), delivers (for the most part) the correct results.

Our primary probe will be whether we can – under the right circumstances, cf. section 11.2 – get non-locally bound reflexives. If we can, the position hosting the reflexive is an exempt position, and of no relevance to Binding Condition A; if we can't, we are dealing with a true case of regular, obligatory reflexive binding that should be captured by Binding Condition A.

A second probe will be to test whether a reflexive can be replaced by a non-reflexive (preserving interpretation, that is); this is, in fact, the test most frequently used in the literature, and non-complementarity is often taken to be a sufficient condition to establish the exempt status of a position. Two caveats are in order, though: first, non-reflexives may be banned from exempt positions for extraneous reasons, to be discussed in 11.4.3. So non-complementarity is indicative of an exempt position, but not necessarily vice versa. Second, the complementarity between (true) reflexives and non-reflexives is itself an independent hypothesis (namely that Binding Conditions A and B both refer to the same domain, the coargument domain). It could, in principle, turn out that while there are exempt anaphora in English, some cases of non-complementarity still reflect that, in addition, the binding domain for reflexives is larger than for non-reflexives, as assumed in Standard Binding Theory; in other words, contrary to Pollard and Sag (1992) and Reinhart and Reuland (1993), it could turn out that some non-complementary positions are *not* exempt positions (this, as we will see in section 11.5, is clearly the case in some other languages).

In the light of these caveats, binding without a structural binder seems to be the clearest indicator of an exempt position. Unfortunately, the literature on the different NP positions doesn't always provide the relevant data, and it is not the purpose of the discussion in this section to make up for that omission; this is especially true of the discussion of NP- and PP-internal reflexives below. In subsection 11.3.3, I will provide a more detailed, exemplary discussion of one particular case that is discussed controversially in the literature, in order to give the reader a sense of how such an investigation is in principle to be conducted, including the presentation of a few more analytical probes.

11.3.1   Purely syntactic coarguments

When we first discussed the notion of binding domain or governing category for reflexives in chapter 3, we mentioned two reasons to resort to a complex notion of domain: NP-internal pronouns, and pronouns in various raising constructions. While the former are 'analyzed away' as exempt anaphors in the present setting, something has to be said about the latter.

As discussed in chapter 3, the object position of exceptional case marking (ECM) verbs behaves like a true argument position to both the matrix verb and the embedded verb. This generalization can be reconfirmed: while the object NP in (11.18a) can be bound to a higher local subject, it cannot corefer with a non-local antecedent in (11.18b).[6] Clearly, subjects in ECM constructions are regular positions, not exempt ones:

(11.18)   (a)   Mary believes herself to be superior.
          (b)   *Mary said that John believes herself to be superior (to herself).

This means that the relevant notion of coargument can't be a purely semantic one; more particularly, the object position in ECM constructions must count as an argument to *both* predicates, as schematized in (11.19):[7]

(11.19)

predicate	arguments
believe	Mary, herself
(be) superior	herself

In other words, though *herself* is not a *semantic* argument to *believe* (on the rather standard assumption that *believe* denotes a relation between an individual and some clausal meaning, say a proposition), it counts as a coargument in the sense relevant to Binding Condition A in (11.5).

The same is diagnosed for raising-to-subject constructions: the raised subject qualifies as a true (less-oblique) coargument of the matrix verb; the reflexive in the PP is not an exempt anaphor, as demonstrated by the ungrammaticality of (11.20c):

(11.20)   (a)   Lucie seems to herself *t* to be beyond suspicion.
          (b)   Max strikes himself *t* as clever.
          (c)   *John said that Lucie seems to himself *t* to be beyond suspicion.

Matrix verb and embedded verb do not, however, simply merge their argument domains:

(11.21)   Georgina wants O'Leary to introduce himself/*herself.

The reflexive must be bound to its subject coargument *O'Leary*, not to *Georgina*, a semantic argument of the matrix verb, given that the latter is not a coargument.

11.3.2   Prepositional phrases

Turning to prepositional phrases (PPs), we will, for the purpose of the discussion, distinguish three kinds of PPs: PP arguments with a semantically inert P, PPs functioning as a place or path argument, and adjunct PPs. This taxonomy merely serves to introduce some relevant distinctions that have emerged

---

[6] P&S's (104a); cf. also R&R:680; note that the embedded subject *John* in (11.18b) should not count as an intervener in the sense of section 11.2 above, given that it doesn't agree with the reflexive.
[7] R&R (1993): 678 define: "The *syntactic arguments* of P are the projections assigned Θ-role *or Case* by P" (emphasis added); the same result was achieved by the definition of coargument domain in chapter 3, section 3.1.4.

in the literature, but is not meant to be final or exhaustive; in section 11.3.3 we will discuss a class of PPs of unclear status, and in the process illustrate how the various properties of exempt and regular positions can be used in a linguistic analysis.

The prepositions in certain PP objects appear to behave as mere case assigners, with no semantic contribution of their own (these are typically prepositions selected specifically by the verb, or the default preposition *to*). The complement position to such Ps behaves like a regular argument to the verb, not like an exempt position:

(11.22)   (a) *Mary talked to myself.
           (b) The peasants had to rely on themselves.
           (c) *The peasants wanted to make it clear that the king could no longer rely on themselves.

Neither a first person pronoun (which is otherwise happy to function as an exempt anaphor even without antecedents) nor a long-distance bound reflexive in a perspective-taking context seems possible in these positions. This means that the proper characterization of coargument can't be *purely* syntactic, but must take certain aspects of thematic structure into consideration.

In contradistinction to these cases, there are PPs that serve as verbal path or place arguments. While clearly selected, the Ps in these cases contribute semantic content (they can, for example, be replaced by other Ps expressing path/place). In chapter 3 we saw that the complement position to these Ps is a non-complementary one, which is already an indicator that we are dealing with an exempt position:

(11.23)   (a) John looked around him/himself.
           (b) John pulled the blanket over him/himself.
           (c) Muhammad hid the book behind him/himself.

Cases of non-local binding can be found, suggesting that these are indeed exempt positions, though they are rare:[8]

(11.24)   (a) Her arms hugged around herself . . . and it seemed quite incomprehensible to her now that she hadn't contacted her mother before.
           (b) But mostly it was directed towards herself . . . despite what she'd been through in the past couple of years she appeared to have learned precisely nothing.
           (c) It was only towards herself that she'd ever seen him act meanly.
           (d) 'Infinity Within' is looking more towards yourself as an individual, starting to take a stand.

---

[8] From *A Stranger's Trust* by Emma Richmond (1991), *The Boat House* by Stephen Gallagher (1992), *Battle for Love* by Stephanie Howard (1991), and *The Face* by Nick Logan (1992) as found in the British National Corpus.

Let us finally turn to adverbial (adjunct) PPs. In chapter 3, section 3.1.4, we concluded that reflexives are generally possible within adjunct PPs (although the literature reports certain examples as degraded in acceptability):[9]

(11.25) (a) André whimpered and flung himself back to the double doors, never taking his eyes off the two facing panes of glass, and fumbled behind himself for the door knob.

(b) She heard a sound behind herself and felt a gun on her head.

(c) The only persons I can identify in the two photos below, is my Grandmother, Edith Kehl, later Edwards, who made an ink mark next to herself on the photos, and the teachers.

The question to ask now is whether the reflexives within these PPs are regular or exempt anaphors. I was not able to find examples of reflexives within adjunct PPs without a binder, or with one outside of their subject domain in the literature, nor through a cursory corpus search. It does seem, though, that the reflexives in (11.25) can be replaced by non-reflexives, suggesting exempt status.

It is much more common to find adjunct PPs as adnominal modifiers without a coargument binder:[10]

(11.26) (a) All a man's interests are limited to those near himself.

(b) Dana holds tightly to the branches near herself as the tree she is clinging to sways with the force of impact above.

(c) In many instances a person may be legally exposed, contrary to her own wishes, to radiofrequency radiation by a phone user standing or sitting immediately next to herself.

These examples make it clear that these reflexives do not need to be bound within their coargument domain, and it seems thus plausible to conclude more in general that NP-complements to adjunct Ps like *near, next to*, etc. are exempt positions. An alternative hypothesis, however, is possible: that reflexives in adjunct positions are *not* exempt, but need to be bound within their subject domain (which is why we found long-distance binding only within adnominal adjuncts). Lacking data of adjunct reflexives bound from outside the subject domain, we cannot discard this possibility, though we will assume for the time being that reflexives within adjuncts are exempt anaphors. Clearer examples are found with adjunct PPs like the following:[11]

---

[9] Examples from http://users.chariot.net.au/ amaranth/index.htm, *The Best Gift Ever* by Lara A (www.planetlara.com), and http://www.rootsweb.com/ ilmorgan/pa-bcs.htm.

[10] Examples found on the world wide web: (11.26a) attributed to Alexis de Tocqueville.

[11] (11.27a) and (11.27b) from Zribi-Hertz (1989); (11.27c) from Ross (1970); (11.27d) from Safir (1997). Safir includes in this list the elements *apart from, but, rather than, except, save, besides, other than, in addition to, including, excluding*; he notes that, curiously, some of the verbs from which these are derived behave like their complement positions and are exempt, too, for example (i) (his [31a]):

(i) ?Powell rejects any list of candidates which excludes/includes himself.

(11.27)   (a)   'Clara found time to check that apart from herself there was a man from the BBC.'
          (b)   'It angered him that she ... tried to attract a man like himself.'
          (c)   Physicists like yourself are a godsend.
          (d)   HAL hates everyone except/besides/other than himself.

Note, in particular, that the reflexives in (11.27b) and (11.27c) are not bound at all, showing clearly that these positions are exempt.

Summing up, then, reflexives within PPs are exempt anaphors in all cases except argument PPs headed by semantically inert Ps. The notion of higher coargument must thus be defined as including all arguments to heads that assign either case or a Θ-role to the reflexive.

11.3.3   A case study

A case that does happen to be discussed rather thoroughly in the literature is that of *with* and *about* PPs with verbs like *talk* or *speak*. Are these akin to the argument PPs with semantically inert Ps as in *talk to* and *rely on*, and hence regular positions; or more like PP complements headed by semantically contentful Ps such as *around, over* or *behind*, or plain adjuncts – in any case, exempt positions?

P&S (p. 266) claim that the former is the case in (11.28a), their (17): both the NP within the *to* PP and the one within the *about* PP are elements of the argument-list, with the former less oblique than the latter. Therefore, the NP within the *about* PP has a higher coargument and is thus a regular position, and a reflexive in it has to be bound locally. As evidence, they provide (11.28b), which arguably shows that it is obliqueness (i.e. order on the argument-list), rather than linear order and/or c-command, that determines anaphor-binding possibilities:

(11.28)   (a)   Mary talked to John about himself.
          (b)   *Mary talked about John to himself.
(11.29)   (a)   We talked with Lucie about herself.
          (b)   *We talked about Lucie with herself.

R&R provide a very similar minimal pair – (11.29), their (121) – but their explanation for it is different in essential respects. According to them, *about* PPs, unlike *with* PPs, form their own coargument domains. Hence, *herself* in *about herself* in (11.29a) is an exempt anaphor: the fact that it is locally bound doesn't do it any harm, but is not enforced by Binding Conditions. *Herself* in *with herself* in (11.29b), on the other hand, is a verbal argument, which accordingly must be bound locally; since *Lucie* is *not* a verbal argument, it can't be the binder for *herself* in (11.29b), so Binding Condition A is violated (note that this is independent of the question of whether the entire *about* PP is an argument or an adjunct). Although R&R don't discuss the case of *talk to*, the explanation they offer seems to carry over to cases like (11.28). If *to*'s sister NP is an argument of *talk*, but *about*'s isn't, the reflexive in (11.28b) is not bound; the reflexive in (11.28a), on the other hand, isn't a verbal argument, hence has no higher coarguments, so that *himself* is a (locally bound) exempt anaphor.

Let us now use the various properties of the two types of positions that we have discussed so far as diagnostic probes for this case. It will turn out that the '*about* is its own coargument domain' position is better supported, though the evidence is not crystal clear. First, note that the *about* PP in either case allows, though marginally for some speakers, for a locally bound non-reflexive pronoun, which suggests that PP forms a coargument domain, and its complement is an exempt position:[12]

(11.30)   We talked with/to Lucie about her.

Second, a reflexive in the same position doesn't need to be locally bound. It is, for example, possible to have an unbound first person reflexive there, cf. (11.31a), which, as the minimally contrasting (11.31b) shows, is impossible for clear complementary positions (R&R[1993]:715); unbound third person reflexives seem at least marginally possible, as in the internet posting in (11.31c):

(11.31)   (a)   Can you talk with Lucie about myself?
            (b)   *Can you talk with myself about Lucie?
            (c)   We get to hear her sexy voice talk about herself!

Third, it seems that a reflexive within an *about* PP can have split antecedents, cf. (11.32). Unlike regular anaphors, which disallow split antecedents as in (11.32a) (cf. chapter 9, section 9.3.2), exempt anaphors generally allow them, cf. (11.32b) (presumably since they don't need to be semantically bound and hence don't have to agree with their antecedent). Thus, (11.32) suggests that we are dealing with an exempt anaphor; it must be noted, though, that many speakers find (11.32) awkward (but still prefer it to a version with *them* instead of *themselves*).

(11.32)   Mary talked to John about themselves.
            (a)   *John told Mary about themselves.
            (b)   John told Mary that there were some pictures of themselves inside.

Fourth, and finally, as P&S themselves note as an unexplained fact, alongside the two examples in (11.28), repeated here as (11.33a) and (11.33b), there is the unacceptable (11.33c), which shows that it cannot just be the order on the argument-list that governs anaphoric binding:

(11.33)   (a)   Mary talked to John about himself.
            (b)   *Mary talked about John to himself.
            (c)   *Mary talked about himself to John.

---

[12] The data to follow are mostly from R&R (1993):715f.

But, as we saw in section 11.2 above, it is typical for (third person) exempt anaphors to require a *preceding* coindexed NP. If *(about) himself* in (11.33c) is in fact an exempt anaphor, as R&R claim, it unacceptability wouldn't be so unexpected.

If the arguments presented above are valid, then, we can conclude that *about* as in *talk/speak about* is semantically active and forms its own coargument domain, making its NP complement an exempt position.

11.3.4   NPs with and without subjects

Regarding the distribution of reflexives/reciprocals within noun phrases, the generalization expressed by (11.5) is the one in (11.34):

(11.34)   Generalization on reflexives/reciprocals within NPs:
            If NP has a subject, post-nominal reflexives must be locally bound; otherwise, they are exempt.

This generalization is illustrated in (11.35): *picture* in (11.35a) doesn't have a higher argument than the NP in the *of* PP, so the reflexive is in an exempt position and doesn't need to be bound.[13] On the other hand, there *is* a higher argument – the possessive – in (11.35b) and (11.35c), so the N counts as a predicate and the *of/to* NP winds up being a complementary position:[14]

(11.35)   (a)   The picture of himself that John saw in the post office was ugly.
            (b)*? Your picture of himself that John saw in the post office was ugly.
            (c)   *Mary's letters to Sarah about himself obsessed him.

In a nutshell, then, a reflexive inside an NP never *needs* to be bound from outside that NP. If it is a regular anaphor, it has to be bound NP-internally; if it is an exempt anaphor, it doesn't have to be bound at all.

The reader may recall from chapter 3, section 3.1.3, that the grammaticality judgments underlying this generalization are dubious; the approaches discussed in the present chapter and classical BT thus derive the same, presumably inadequate, grammaticality pattern. Speakers generally accept reflexive binding into possessive NPs, especially under gender mismatch; in addition, especially in British writing, antecedent-less reflexives in post-nominal positions, with and without a subject, are found regularly:[15]

---

[13] In Pollard and Sag's (1992) view, *picture* in (11.35a) actually does have a higher argument, namely *the*. But such non-referential arguments do not "count" for the definition of exempt position; only potentially referring argument such as NPs and PPs do. We can abstract away from this detail by assuming that articles and the like aren't actually arguments in the relevant sense.

[14] (11.35b) and (11.35c) are from R&R (1993):681f and P&S's (13).

[15] (11.36a) and (11.36b) repeated from chapter 3; (11.36c)–(11.36e) from Nick Logan's *The Face* (1992), Joanna Neil's *The Water of Eden* (1993), and Ronald Dworkin's *Law's Empire* (1986), respectively, as found in the British National Corpus.

(11.36)   (a)   Hanna found Peter's picture of herself.
           (b)   C.B.'s father…resented his wife for her low opinion of himself.
           (c)   Well, were they making any statement about herself, perhaps?
           (d)   Even so, his remarks about herself were uncalled for.
           (e)   Unfortunately, you have a tendency to allow your obviously muddled,
                 rather juvenile feelings about myself to cloud your judgment.

It is interesting to note that at least (11.36b)–(11.36e) clearly illustrate what we
called *perspective effect* in section 11.2 above.[16]

11.4   Reflexivity Theory

In this section I will briefly introduce the particular implementation
Reinhart and Reuland (1992, 1993) give to the data around the exempt/regular
anaphor distinction, and some further observations made in these papers.

11.4.1   Reflexive marking

Why should condition (11.5) (a reflexive must be bound by a less
oblique coargument, if there is one) be the way it is? As part of their answer to
this question, Reinhart and Reuland (1992, 1993) offer the following principle in
its stead:

(11.37)   Condition A
           A reflexive-marked syntactic predicate is reflexive.

This condition looks rather different from (11.5) above. Let us compare them
carefully. First, note that there is no reference to non-exempt positions in (11.37).
However, R&R define a predicate as having an external argument (subject);[17]
so, by definition, NPs that are complements to categories without higher coarguments, such as adjunct prepositions and nouns without a possessive phrase,
are exempted from (11.37). Second, a predicate is called *reflexive* if it has two
coindexed arguments; so in this respect, too, (11.37) is parallel to (11.5).

One thing that is essentially new about (11.37) is that it is not a condition on
reflexives at all, but a condition on predicates. It doesn't talk about the reflexive

---

[16] Note that in all the cases discussed in this subsection we have used the prepositions *to* and *of*,
which are semantically inert in the sense discussed in 11.3.2. Clearly, if the PP itself forms a
coargument domain, its complement position should be exempt, regardless of whether the NP
containing it has a subject or not. We have seen numerous examples of *near* and *next to* PPs with
locally free reflexives in (11.26) above.

[17] Cf. Reinhart and Reuland (1993):678:

    (i)   The *syntactic predicate* formed of (a head) P is P, all its syntactic arguments, and an
           external argument of P (subject).
    (ii)   The *syntactic arguments* of P are the projections assigned Θ-role or Case by P.

pronoun having to be bound; instead, it talks about what has to hold of a predicate if it is combined with a reflexive pronoun. In this sense it is indeed natural that no structural restrictions apply to exempt anaphors in exempt positions: there are no structural conditions on reflexive binding in the first place; where reflexives combine with anything other than a predicate, they are automatically exempt.

R&R's (11.37) is not equivalent to P&S's (11.5), though. The reason is that the former doesn't specify anything about the relation between the reflexive pronoun and its binder, or, more generally, the two arguments that make the predicate reflexive. Thus (11.38a) through (11.38d) all meet the letter of (11.37): a predicate occurs with a reflexive argument (is thus reflexive-marked) and has two coindexed arguments (is thus reflexive):

(11.38)   (a) *Heself/himself recommended him/Bob.
            (b) *Lola sold himself to the slave.
            (c) *Lola sold himself to himself.
            (d) *Lola sold her/Lola to himself.

What goes wrong here is that the reflexive is either the wrong (namely the higher) one of the two anaphorically related arguments, as in (11.38a) and (11.38b), and in a way (11.38c), or none of the two anaphorically related arguments at all. But (11.37) speaks to none of these factors. To predict the stars in (11.38), R&R invoke what they call the *Chain Condition*:

(11.39)   General Condition on A-chains
            A maximal A-chain $(\alpha_1, \ldots, \alpha_n)$ contains exactly one link – α_1 – that is both +R [fully referential, i.e. a non-reflexive: DB] and case marked. (R&R[1993]:696)

A maximal A-chain is a sequence of coindexed c-commanding A-positions within a certain local domain, roughly the domain that A-movement could target (R&R:692ff.), or, put more obviously: the coargument domain. If we disentangle this condition, we see that it actually makes two more or less independent demands:

(11.40)   (a) No A-chain must consist of reflexives/reciprocals only.
            (b) A non-reflexive can only occur as the head of an A-chain.

(11.40b) is just the (syntactic) Binding Condition B, and so unsurprisingly blocks (11.38a) and (11.38b). (11.40a), on the other hand, encodes the residue of the old Binding Condition A that is not captured by (11.37), namely that true reflexives need a local antecedent.

Overall, one could argue that the conceptual attractiveness of (11.37) is somewhat weakened by the resulting need to add the Chain Condition – in particular (11.40a) – which, despite its suggestive name, has no independent role in the grammar (as noted e.g. in Safir [1997]:346ff.).[18]

---

[18] R&R's theory also encounters a problem with examples like (11.18a) or (i):

11.4.2   Reflexive and reciprocal subjects

There is one specific configuration that is ruled out by the Chain Condition, in particular (11.40a), which isn't captured by Pollard and Sag (1992)'s (11.5), namely a reflexive as the highest argument of a predicate. According to (11.5), the highest argument position of a predicate is always an exempt position (since by definition it doesn't have a higher coargument) and should thus be able to host a reflexive/reciprocal as exempt anaphor; on Reinhart and Reuland (1993)'s account – more specifically given in (11.39)/(11.40a) – on the other hand, no reflexive can occur in such a position.

What are the facts? In favor of their formulation, P&S offer examples like (11.41) (their [7a]), in which a reciprocal is the highest argument within an NP:[19]

(11.41)   The agreement that Iran and Iraq reached guaranteed *each other*'s trading rights in the disputed waters until the year 2010.

On the other hand, R&R are clearly correct in predicting that there can be no subject reflexives (other than in ECM cases):

(11.42)   (a) *Himself/heself left him.
(b) *Himself left.
(c) *Himself left himself.

R&R predict each of these sentences as ungrammatical, though for different reasons. In (11.42a), the foot of an A-chain is non-reflexive, *contra* the Chain Condition (in particular [11.40b]), in (11.42b) a non-reflexive predicate is reflexive marked, *contra* (11.37), and in (11.42c) the extended A-chain consists of reflexives only, violating aspect (11.40a) of the Chain Condition.[20]

To rule out all these cases, P&S must assume that "As a matter of lexical idiosyncrasy, English only has accusative anaphors (i.e. no *sheself/*heself/ *usselves* etc.)" (P&S[1992]:290). Arguably, this move merely reifies the facts, rather than explaining them. It is interesting to note, though, that almost the same shortcoming – failure to rule out reflexives in subject position – haunted the BT of Huang (1983) and Chomsky (1986) (where, in a nutshell, the binding domain

(i)   Max heard himself criticize Lucie.

Since *himself* is an argument to both *heard* and *criticize*, it marks both predicates reflexive (by [11.37]), but only the higher predicate *is* reflexive; *criticize* does not have two coindexed arguments. R&R need to resort to the stipulation that *criticize* LF raises to adjoin to *heard*:

(ii)   LF: Max [heard criticize] himself $t_{criticize}$ Lucie.

Thereby, *himself* is no longer subject to *criticize*, hence not an argument. It is an argument of *heard-criticize*, which it marks as reflexive in accordance with Binding Condition A (R&R[1993]:707–708).

[19] R&R's papers do not mention reciprocals, so this is not a counter-example to their theory.

[20] For the same reason as the latter, reflexive possessives are correctly predicted to be impossible:

(i)   *himself/heself/hisself's pictures (of himself)

for a reflexive extends upwards until a subject that doesn't contain the reflexive is found; cf. chapter 3, subsection 3.1.3).

Addressing this shortcoming, Rizzi (1989) argues that, generally, reflexive pronouns cannot occur in *agreeing* positions; he calls this the *Anaphor-Agreement Effect* (AAE). English subject reflexives are blocked as one case of the AAE, because they trigger verbal agreement, *not* because they bear nominative case, nor because they are embedded in a tensed clause (as suggested in Chomsky [1980, 1986]). In the context of reflexivity theory, this observation – if correct – would square nicely with P&S's account, providing a more general reason for the lack of subject reflexives in English.

To substantiate the AAE, Rizzi (1989), and in particular Woolford (1999), provide broad cross-linguistic evidence, showing that: (i) non-agreeing subjects *can* be reflexive; and (ii) agreeing non-subjects cannot. As for the former, we find nominative reflexives in Khmer, Vietnamese, Chinese, Korean, and Thai, all of which lack (subject) agreement:[21]

(11.43)　(a)　*Mit   teǔŋ-pii neǒq*　kit　thaa kluən ciə kounsəh.　　　(Khmer)
　　　　　　　 friend both   person think that self   be student
　　　　　　　 'The two friends reasoned that they(self) are students.'

　　　　　(b)　*Anh-ấy* e　r`üang *mình* c　ung không khỏi tội.　　　(Vietnamese)
　　　　　　　 he   fear that   self also   not   avoid sin
　　　　　　　 'He is afraid that he(self) will not avoid punishment.'

　　　　　(c)　*Süommüaay* khít wâa *tuaʔeeŋ* ca　dây pay.　　　(Thai)
　　　　　　　 s.   think that self　FUT *get go*
　　　　　　　 'Somai thinks that he(self) will get to go.'

(Unfortunately, Woolford's data do not allow us to determine whether the subject reflexives in these languages behave like exempt anaphors, as predicted by P&S – a topic for further research.) Furthermore, as Woolford argues, languages with object agreement disallow reflexives in such agreeing object positions. They either use specific reflexive markers instead of the object agreement marker or they utilize a non-canonical case, as in the following example from Inuit, where instead of the canonical, agreeing absolutive theme as in (11.44a), a reflexive theme must occur in the non-agreeing dative, as in (11.44b):[22]

(11.44)　(a)　Angutip　　　 arnaq　　　　　 taku -vaa.　　　(Inuit)
　　　　　　　 man-ERGATIVE *woman*-ABSOLUTIVE *see* IND.3SG.3SG
　　　　　　　 'The man sees the woman.'

　　　　　(b)　Angut immi   -nut taku -vuq.
　　　　　　　 man   himself DAT *see* INDICATIVE.3SG
　　　　　　　 'The man sees himself.'

Rizzi (1989) and Woolford (1999) include discussion of possible rationales behind the AAE, to which the interested reader is referred. In the context of

---

[21] Data from Huffman (1970):231; Trúóng Văn Chình (1970):202; Grima (1978):102, collected in Fisher (1988), as quoted in Woolford (1999).

[22] Bok-Bennema (1991):51, after Woolford (1999).

reflexivity theory we note in conclusion that nominative reflexives might be banned in English for more general reasons, in which case they should not be ruled out by the same principles that force them to be locally bound when occurring as non-subjects.

11.4.3   Non-reflexives

Let us finally and briefly revisit non-reflexive pronouns in light of our new Binding Condition A. We have assumed throughout that non-reflexives must be free in their coargument domain, and are in complementary distribution with regular reflexives. We start by noting with R&R that with certain binding patterns, exempt positions allow reflexives only:[23]

(11.45)   (a)   Max rolled the carpet over him/himself/*it.
           (b)   Max directed Lucie towards him/himself/*her (in the mirror)

In other words, exempt anaphors and non-reflexives are not always interchangeable; exempt positions are not always non-complementary. Is this expected? *Over* and *towards* are semantically "active" Ps, and therefore form their own coargument domain. Accordingly, *it* and *her*, being free within that domain, should be fine here, contrary to fact. (More in general, since exempt positions are defined as having no higher coarguments, a pronoun in an exempt position should by necessity be free in its coargument domain.)

According to R&R, the correct generalization here is that a non-reflexive cannot be bound by a higher *semantic* coargument. (11.45a) and (11.45b) say that the carpet is, or ends up being, over itself, and Lucie ends up next to herself, respectively. Therefore, *the carpet/Lucie* and *it/her* are semantic coarguments to a semantically reflexive predicate. R&R propose that a semantically reflexive predicate must have a reflexive pronoun as its argument. Put in present terms:

(11.46)   Semantic Binding Condition B:
           A non-reflexive cannot be bound in its semantic coargument domain.
(11.47)   Semantic coargument domain:
           The semantic coargument domain of NP is the smallest category that contains NP's Θ-role assigner T, and all (other) XPs that correspond to semantic arguments of T.

The definition of semantic coargument domain is different from that in (11.17), even ignoring the part about case assigners, since it replaces "XP whose Θ-role is assigned by T" with "XPs that correspond to semantic arguments of T." To see what is meant by this somewhat vague formulation in (11.47), consider (11.45a): the Θ-role assigner for *him/himself/it* is the preposition *over*. Plausibly, $[\![over]\!]^g$ denotes a relation, something like $[\lambda x \lambda y . y$ is over $x]$. The assumption is that, semantically, y corresponds to the carpet in (11.45a), i.e. that (11.45a) is interpreted as 'Max pulled the carpet, and the carpet came to be over Max/the carpet.'

---

[23] Examples in this section are R&R's (63), (62), (30), and (34), with their judgments.

There are thus two semantic predicates, corresponding to *pull* and *over*, respectively. The carpet is semantically the lower argument of $[\![pull]\!]^g$ and the higher of $[\![over]\!]^g$. If the complement of *over* is *him(self)*, neither predicate is reflexive, i.e. *him(self)* is not bound to a semantic coargument; if the complement of *over* is *it*, however, the predicate is 'the carpet came to be over the carpet,' which is reflexive, i.e. the complement of *over* is bound by a semantic coargument, and hence can't be a non-reflexive pronoun.

Things are even more complicated in (11.45b), since we can't paraphrase it as 'Max directed Lucie, and Lucie came to be towards Max/Lucie,' but only more abstractly '...and Lucie came to be at/near Max/Lucie,' or 'moved towards Max/Lucie'; in either case, we have to assume that Lucie counts as a semantic argument of *towards*. Given that, *directed Lucie towards her* is a case of a pronoun bound to its semantic coargument, and thus prohibits a non-reflexive.

Crucially, in neither case does the preposition (*over/towards*) assign a Θ-role to any NP external to it (*the carpet/Lucie*), given the common assumption that one NP can only bear one Θ-role (though it is beyond doubt that the carpet is semantically an argument to both predicates). If it did, the relation between e.g. *Lucie* and *herself* would wrongly be analyzed as essentially the same as that between *John* and *him(self)* in (11.48), repeated from chapter 3, section 3.1.4:

(11.48)   John sent a letter to himself/*him.

In (11.48), *to* is semantically vacuous, so *send* is the semantic predicate *and Θ-role assigner* for *him/himself*; accordingly, all of *send*'s arguments are within *him(self)*'s syntactic coargument domain as defined in (11.17). In (11.45), on the other hand, the prepositions are clearly not semantically empty, but have themselves a higher semantic argument, though they don't assign a Θ-role to it; accordingly, the NP corresponding to that NP (but not all other arguments to the main V) is within the semantic coargument domain of the complement to P, schematically:

(11.49)   (a)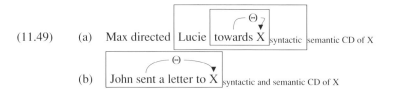

It is thus important to maintain the distinction between syntactic coargument domain (as relevant for reflexives), and semantic coargument domain (as relevant for non-reflexives).

Recall in this context that the NP in *sent to NP* is not an exempt position, whereas the complement of *towards* is:

(11.50)   (a)   (I noticed that) Max was directing Lucie towards myself.
            (b)   *(I noticed that) John had sent a letter to myself.

It is thus important to maintain the distinction between syntactic coargument domain (as relevant for reflexives), and semantic coargument domain (as relevant for non-reflexives).

Is (11.46) the only condition on non-reflexives? No, since non-reflexives also need to be free from purely syntactic coarguments, e.g. in ECM constructions like *John wants him*$_{*John}$ *to win*. Thus we continue to assume that non-reflexives are also subject to a syntactic Binding Condition as in (11.51), where syntactic coargument domain is defined as in (11.17):

(11.51)   Syntactic Binding Condition B:
           A non-reflexive pronoun cannot be bound in its syntactic coargument do-
           main.

The existence of these two independent conditions would receive independent support if we could find elements that are subject to one Binding Condition, but not the other. R&R suggest that the Dutch pronoun *zich* (as opposed to the full reflexive *zichzelf*) is an example of this kind. *Zich* cannot occur in regular object position, but it can occur as an ECM-subject:

(11.52)   (a)   Max hoorde zichzelf/*hem/*zich.
                  M.   heard   himself/   him/   ZICH
           (b)   Max hoorde zichzelf/*hem/ zich zingen.
                  M.   heard   himself/   him/   ZICH sing
           'Max heard himself/heard himself sing.'

This behavior follows assuming that *zich* is subject to the semantic Binding Condition B in (11.46) (hence cannot be bound as an ordinary object), but not the syntactic one in (11.51) (hence can be bound by a purely syntactic coargument).

We have seen pronouns similar to Dutch *zich* in Danish and Norwegian in chapter 3, section 3.5, there called *SE*-pronouns, and characterized them as pronouns that have to be bound (perhaps to a subject) in their tense domain, but free in their coargument domain (according to R&R, Dutch *zich* needs to be bound in its syntactic coargument domain).

Before closing this subsection, let me point to a few more observations from R&R that suggest that our definition of semantic coargument domain in (11.47) may yet be in need of refinement. Consider the following:

(11.53)   (a)   The queen invited both Max and herself/*her to our party.
           (b)   *Felix but not Lucie praised her.

Take (11.53a) first: the individual conjuncts *Max* and *her(self)* do *not* receive a Θ-role from *invited*; only the entire conjoined NP does. Yet, *the queen* and *her(self)* behave like semantic coarguments (blocking a non-reflexive); while not captured by the definition in (11.47) this may be because *invite* distributes over the conjuncts, entailing effectively that the queen invited Max and the queen invited her*self*.

According to R&R, even (11.53b) is bad on a reading where *her* is Lucie, because the sentence effectively says 'Max praised her but Lucie didn't praise *her.' Note that there is neither syntactic binding of *her* by *Lucie*, nor a distributive reading, as in (11.53a). If this example is to be ruled out, it would seem to have to be by reference to a structural representation which is highly remote from surface structure (and quite unlike LFs in transformationalist theories). We will not pursue this matter here, but simply note that there seems to be an additional, more semantic, disjointness requirement on non-reflexives, which prohibits them from being bound to a semantic coargument of their thematic predicate.[24]

11.5   Towards a cross-linguistic perspective

As mentioned at the outset, once exempt anaphors are factored out, the binding domain for regular reflexives (and hence the only structural binding domain for reflexives) in English is the coargument domain. All apparent instances of 'longer' binding, in particular NP-internal reflexives that are not bound within their NP, are re-analyzed as involving exempt anaphors.[25]

As we saw in this chapter, this view significantly improves the empirical accuracy of BT for English, and at the same time simplifies the formulation of the individual Binding Conditions. But how likely is it to be correct cross-linguistically? In many languages, exempt anaphors are simply unattested, judging by the criteria developed here. For example, typical instances of exempt anaphors are impossible with reflexives in Serbo-Croatian:[26]

(11.54)   *Niji bilo nikoga u sobi osim *sebe*
             not was nobody in room except from self
             'There was no one in the room apart from myself.'

(11.55)   *Ljutilo *ga* je da je ona pokusala napasti covjeka kao *sebe*.
             anger him did that did he try   attack man   like self
             'It angered him that she tried to attack a man like himself.'

(11.56)   *Ona slika   *sebe* u Glasu Slavonije je   mucila *Petra* cijeli dan.
             that picture self in Voice Slavonia did torture P.   whole day
             'That picture of himself in the Voice of Slavonia tortured Peter the whole day.'

Yet Serbo-Croatian has NP-internal (possessive) reflexives (which need to be bound within their tense domain):

(11.57)   Maja voli svoje   knjige.
             *M.   love self-*POSS* book*
             'Maja loves her books.'

It appears that *svoje* in (11.57) is just a regular anaphor that has to be bound within the tense domain (similar remarks apply to many other languages, among

---

[24] R&R, in fact, suggest that there is a level of 'semantic representation,' which includes indices; independent justification of such a level, as well as closer investigation of its properties, remains a topic of further research.

[25] Indeed, under Reinhart and Reuland (1993)'s conceptualization, things couldn't be otherwise: since it is at the very heart of reflexivity to mark reflexive predicates, obligatory reflexive marking in a domain bigger than the coargument domain would seem to make little sense.

[26] All data courtesy of Irena Polic (p.c.).

them German, which, too, lacks exempt anaphors, but allows for bound post-nominal reflexives such as *Geschichten über sich*, 'stories about self'). In other words, the Binding Condition for *svoje* (or *sich*) needs to require structural binding within a domain that is bigger than the coargument domain. It cannot be formulated as a condition on predicates in the way R&R's Binding Condition A in (11.37) is. Interestingly, (11.57) is also grammatical if the reflexive *svoji* is replaced by the non-reflexive possessive *njene*. In other words, even if we factor out the effect of exempt anaphors, reflexives and non-reflexives are not generally in complementary distribution.

Other languages show complementary distribution among possessives, e.g. the distinction between the possessive *hän-en* (3SG-GEN), which must be free within its clause, and the zero-possessive, which allows local binding in Finnish (van Steenbergen [1992]:234); or, for many speakers, between the reflexive (*svou knihu*, 'self's book') and the non-reflexive possessive (*jeji knihu*, 'his/her book') in Czech (Ann Sturgeon, p.c.). This only reminds us that negative conditions such as Binding Condition B, too, aren't restricted to the coargument domain in general; cf. chapter 3.

Summing up this section and this chapter: English has exempt anaphors which fall outside the classical Binding Theory, in particular Binding Condition A. It furthermore seems that, once the effects of exempt anaphors are factored out, true reflexives in English are most accurately described as obligatorily bound within their coargument domain, rendering various complications in the classical BT superfluous.

On the other hand, it appears unlikely that, cross-linguistically, all reflexives that don't require coargument binders can be analyzed as exempt anaphors. Clearly, there are regular reflexives whose binding domain is bigger than that for English reflexives.

12 Binding and movement

So far, we have touched upon the interaction of binding and syntactic movement in two places: we have seen that a *wh*-moved NP cannot bind anything it couldn't from its base position, the weak crossover effect (chapter 8); and we have seen that an NP that has raised to subject position can bind a reflexive it couldn't bind before (chapter 11, section 11.3.1):

(12.1)   (a) *$*Whom$ did *his* uncle phone t_{whom}?
          (b)   *Lucie* seems to *herself* t_{Lucie} to be beyond suspicion.

While these two findings may appear contradictory at first, they illustrate a fundamental distinction in binding behavior for two distinct movement types, which we can preliminarily describe as follows: *wh*-movement and its kin (including relativization, topicalization, covert quantifier raising, and perhaps long scrambling; the cover term for these in transformational theories is $\bar{A}$-*movement*) don't change binding options at all; for all intents and purposes, moved phrases behave as if *in situ*. Grammatical function changing movement, or as it's sometime called a(rgument)-movement, on the other hand (including raising to subject, raising to object, passivization, and perhaps clause-internal scrambling), *does* affect binding possibilities; the derived position seems to count for the purposes of binding and BT.

In what follows, we will substantiate these generalizations by looking at the relevant data, and point out certain exceptions or dubious cases.

12.1   Argument movement

Let us start with raising-to-subject constructions. First, we find that the derived subject position has all the properties of a *bona fide* binder position: it can bind reflexives and bound variables, and induce Binding Condition B and C violations:

(12.2)   (a)   Every boy seems to himself/his mother to be a genius.
          (b) *$*She$ seems to *her/Cassandra* to be a genius.

In both cases, the base-position of the matrix subject is in the subject position of the embedded infinitival clause, from which it doesn't c-command the

PP-internal NP. Thus, the binding must take place from the derived position:

(12.3)   every boy β_1 [μ_2 [seems [to himself$_1$/his$_1$ mother] [t_2 to be a genius]]]

Second, we note that coarguments in the lower clause can still be locally bound by the base position. This is particularly evident in raising which results from passivizing an ECM verb, (12.4b), which minimally contrasts with the active version, (12.4c), in which binding from the matrix subject position is impossible. The LF in (12.5) accounts for this, by making the trace within the embedded clause the binder:

(12.4)   (a)   *Cassandra* seems to contradict *herself*.
           (b)   *John* is believed to contradict *himself*.
           (c)   **Mary* believes John to contradict *herself*.

(12.5)   John μ_1 is believed [t_1 [β_2 to contradict himself$_2$]]

Third, we observe that it suffices for a reflexive or a reciprocal to be bound in its derived position, and that likewise a non-reflexive is impossible if locally bound in its derived position; this holds for passive subjects as well as for subjects raised from an embedded clause (though the latter cases get convoluted; note that the raised subject must itself be embedded under an ECM verb to make local binding possible):

(12.6)   (a)   *The students* expect *each other/themselves/*them* to be nominated for the prize.
           (b)   *John* wants *himself/*him* to seem to be innocent.

All these cases would follow, if Binding Conditions were to be checked after movement. We will return to this issue in detail in section 12.3 below.

   In (12.3) we had to let *every boy* bind the pronoun *himself/his* from a derived position, using the prefix sequence $\beta_1 \mu_2$. But we concluded in our discussion of weak crossover in chapter 8, section 8.2.2 that β can*not* be adjoined to a derived position. These appear to be contradictory demands, but our formulation of the Binder rule in chapter 8, repeated here, already anticipated this:

(12.7)   Binder rule with WCO, final version:

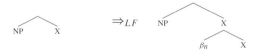

           (where NP has not undergone *wh*-movement)

(12.7) only prohibits adjunction of β to a position derived by *wh*-movement, not by argument movement. Thus, (12.3) is in fact a legitimate LF, although it resembles a(n illicit) crossover structure in certain respects.

   It is not surprising to find that in many theoretical frameworks, argument movement isn't analyzed as involving a trace, or, more generally, a binding dependency at all, but as an operation on argument structures. The different behavior of the two kinds of derived positions thus follows more naturally in such accounts.

Exercise 12.1

The sentence *John is believed to contradict him* does not have a reading where *him* is anaphorically related to *John*. What blocks the following LF, which would derive this interpretation and doesn't violate Binding Condition B?

(12.8)   John [β_6 [μ_4 is believed [t_4 to contradict him$_6$]]]

Exercise 12.2

A different way to conceptualize the *wh*/argument movement difference is to think of the traces of argument movement as pronouns, rather than traces. In other words, we assume that a trace t_2 is interpreted as $g(t_2)$ when left by *wh*-movement, but as $g(2)$ when left by argument movement. Let us notate a trace of the latter kind as t_n^A; then $[\![t_n^A]\!]^g = g(n)$. Let us furthermore assume that raising and passive verbs have a "vacuous" argument position for their subject, as in (12.9a); then (12.2a) can be interpreted via the LF in (12.9b), and we can prohibit $\beta\,\mu$ sequences in general:

(12.9)   (a) $[\![\text{seem}]\!]^g = \lambda p \lambda x \lambda y.$ it seems to x that p
          (b)   every boy β_1 [seems [to himself$_1$/his$_1$ mother] [t_1^A to be a genius]]

Calculate the interpretation for (12.9b). Discuss the relative merits of this proposal and the one endorsed in the main text.

12.2   *Wh*-movement

We already saw that the base position of argument movement remains active as a binder. The same evidently holds for *wh*-movement: reflexives or reciprocals remain acceptable even if their binder has been moved out of the local domain, while non-reflexives remain ungrammatical:

(12.10)   *Which guy* do you think would contradict *himself/*him* in such a blatant way?

This again suggests that the trace of *wh*-movement remains active as a binder, in the same way as seen with argument movement in (12.5); thus the moved element isn't a binder (which it can't be by [12.7]), but the trace is.

Let us then turn to the moved element as a bindee. We start by observing that binding options possible before movement remain so, even if the derived position is no longer (locally) bound; this holds for reflexives/reciprocals, as well as pronouns bound by QNPs:

(12.11)   (a)   Which pictures of *himself* did Mary say that *every boy* should burn?

         (b)   Proud of *himself* we found that *he* is.

         (c)   Disguise *himself* we found that *he* did.

         (d)   In *himself*, I think *he* can trust.

         (e)   *Herself*, we know *she* admires.

While the picture seems clear here, some comments are in order. First, we note that the reflexive in (12.11a) is in an exempt position (cf. chapter 11). It is thus not subject to Binding Condition A to begin with, and its acceptability after movement is not surprising (cf. section 12.4 below); consistent with this, a non-reflexive pronoun is possible in this sentence, too:

(12.12)   Which pictures of *him* did Mary say that *every boy* should burn?

The cases of topicalized AP and VP in (12.11b) and (12.11c), on the other hand, have been argued to involve topicalization of a trace in the specifier of AP/VP (Heycock [1995]; Huang [1993]), so that it is perhaps that trace that locally binds the reflexives. This still leaves us with the cases of topicalized reflexives in (12.11d) and (12.11e), as well as the fact that *himself/him* in (12.11a)/(12.12) can be interpreted as a variable bound to the QNP *every boy*. Since we know that QNPs can only bind from non-derived positions, and that semantic binding requires c-command, we can conclude that the base position of the *which*-phrase is crucial here.

  We can further substantiate that claim by looking at a language that doesn't have exempt anaphors, to vindicate our conclusions about (12.11a). In the German (12.13), a reflexive (and only a reflexive) within the moved *wh*-phrase is possible, although German doesn't have any exempt anaphors. We conclude that in this case, too, the pre-movement configuration must be crucial in rendering the reflexive locally bound:

(12.13)   Wieviele   Gedichte   über   *sich/*ihn* wird Schulze noch schreiben?!
          how many poems   about self/*him will S.   still   write
          'How many more poems about himself is Schulze going to write?!'

Note that the unclarity about the English cases resulted from the fact that it is hard or impossible to *wh*-move a phrase that contains a reflexive in complementary position, but not its antecedent as well. What should be easier to observe is whether a pronoun or full NP can "escape" a Binding Condition B/C violation by moving. And here, too, it seems as if movement doesn't change anything, i.e. the Binding Condition violations are not alleviated:[1]

(12.14)   (a)   *Her, I think that *she* likes.

         (b)   *To *him*, we thought that *John* talked.

         (c)   *How many claims that *Nixon* is a crook is *he* going to tolerate?

         (d)   *Which investigation of *Nixon* did *he* resent?

---

[1] (12.14b) from van Riemsdijk and Williams (1983):338; (12.14d) from Safir (1999):589.

12.3   Analytical options

12.3.1   NP-structure and connectivity

We will return to some examples of the type discussed in the previous section below. For the moment, let us ask what to make of the findings we have so far. In an obvious way, the facts reported would seem to follow, if we assumed that BT applied to a structure that includes the effects of argument movement, but not of *wh*-movement. Van Riemsdijk and Williams (1981) propose just that, and call that level *NP-structure*.[2] Similarly, in theories where Binding Conditions apply to argument structures or functional structures, a picture very much like this emerges: while argument movement changes argument structures (e.g. by sharing an element between two argument-lists, as in the case of raising, or rearranging the argument-list, as for passives), *wh*-movement does not, so only the effects of the former are visible.

In this book, we have assumed β-prefixation to apply at the level of Logical Form, and hence that the Binding Conditions, too, apply at that level. Note, however, that nothing excludes the possibility that β-prefixation applies to a structure akin to van Riemsdijk and Williams (1981)'s NP-structure, so that violations of Binding Conditions B and C, as well as the satisfaction of Binding Condition A, are registered before *wh*-movement takes place. To illustrate with a somewhat stilted example, the NP-structure for *about himself, every man can speak* (which in this case happens to be identical to its d-structure) is (12.15a) (the argument to follow could be made using more natural examples such as [12.12], which, however, introduce irrelevant complications). Here, the reflexive is properly locally bound by β_1, which I indicate with the little heart on the index. After movement, in (12.15b), *himself* is no longer bound, but the fact that it bears the heart is sufficient for it to be grammatical:

(12.15)   (a)   every man β_1 can speak about himself$_{1\heartsuit}$
            (b)   [$_{PP}$ about himself$_{1\heartsuit}$] μ_2 [every man β_1 can speak t_2]

An equivalent result can be achieved if we find some way of determining directly from the derived structure in (12.15b) (without the heart) whether the reflexive "once was" bound. Consider the following definitions, adopted from Barss (1988):

(12.16)   (a)   Node A *d-dominates* NP iff
            (i)   A dominates NP or
            (ii)   A dominates the *wh*-trace of a category that d-dominates NP
            (b)   NP$_1$ *d-commands* NP$_2$ iff NP$_1$ is sister to a node that d-dominates NP$_2$

Roughly, d-command would replace our notion of c-command. As a first step, note that β_1 in (12.15a) d-commands *himself* because it c-commands it (it is

---

[2] Argument movement is sometimes called "NP-movement," whence the name.

sister to a node dominating *himself*). But second, β_1 also d-commands *himself* in (12.15b), because it c-commands (is sister to a node that dominates) the trace of the PP *about himself*, which in turn d-dominates (here: simply dominates) *himself*. It is a little more tricky to define the various local domains in terms of d-command, for which I refer the reader to the seminal Barss (1986, 1988) and the references therein. In a nutshell, a notion like d-command serves to determine whether a certain c-command relation obtained at a previous stage of the derivation by looking at the traces in the final stage. Such approaches, as well as the effects they set out to describe, are often referred to as *connectivity* approaches/effects.

On either one of these treatments, NP-structure and connectivity, however, we fail to derive an actual bound *interpretation* for *himself* in (12.15b): the β_1 prefix doesn't bind anything, and, more severely, *himself₁* – heart or not – is semantically a free variable and will be interpreted to refer to $g(1)$. So how can we derive an interpretation on which *himself* is semantically bound by *every man*?

There are at least three options. The first is that *every man* in turn raises at LF to a position from which it c-commands, and hence can bind, *himself*, as shown in (12.17):

(12.17)   [every man] [$\beta_1 \mu_3$ [[PP about himself₁♡] μ_2 [t_3 β_1 can speak t_2]]]

This LF still has a vacuous lower β_1 prefix, but it receives the correct interpretation because the higher β_1 binds the reflexive. Note, though, that the higher β_1 is adjoined next to an NP in a position derived by *wh*-movement, contrary to what our Binder rule (12.7) allows. Adopting this line of analysis, then, forces us to come up with an entirely new analysis of the weak crossover effect (cf. chapter 8), which would, effectively, have to tie the availability of binding from an (LF-)derived position to the configuration between binder and bindee prior to that movement. More generally, this line of analysis would have to abandon the perspective on the c-command requirement on binding and the crossover effect we pursued in chapters 4 and 8, according to which these reflect essential properties of the way semantic interpretation (of binding dependencies in particular) works, rather than filters on representations. While this might very well turn out to be the correct move to make, we will not pursue the formulation of the prerequisite constraints any further here.

A second option is to devise a semantics that can, in fact, derive a bound variable reading for (12.15b). Such an analysis, often referred to as *semantic reconstruction*, will be sketched in section 12.3.3 below.

A third option is to assume that the LF for *about himself, every man can speak* is neither (12.15b) nor (12.17), but something much closer to (12.15a) where, in particular, *every man* does bind *himself* from a non-derived position. It is this option, which is known in the literature under the label of *syntactic reconstruction*, that I want to explore now.

12.3.2   Syntactic reconstruction

Assume that a *wh*-moved phrase, or at least relevant parts of it, are *reconstructed* to their base-position at LF, as in (12.18a). For a more complex case like (12.11a), the LF would look something like (12.18b) or even (12.18c):[3]

(12.18) (a) every man β_1 can speak about himself$_1$

(b) [which] μ_1 did Mary say that every boy β_2 should burn [t_1 pictures of him(self)$_2$]

(c) (did) Mary say that every boy β_2 should burn [which pictures of him(self)$_2$]

The term reconstruction here can be interpreted either literally, i.e. as saying that the same phrase is first moved up (in the visible syntax), and then down again (at LF); or metaphorically, in conjunction with the so-called *copy view of movement*. According to the latter, the *wh*-moved phrase leaves a full copy of itself in its base position, so that one of the two copies (the moved one) is pronounced (but is ignored at LF), while the other one (the one in base position) is interpreted (but "phonologically deleted").

It is far beyond the scope of this book to present and discuss what there is in the way of a theory of syntactic reconstruction, and in particular to explore in any detail how reconstructed structures should and could be compositionally interpreted. It is worth noting, though, that *if* there is reconstructed material at LF, Binding Conditions A–C can make reference to those, rather than to traces (connectivity) or by reference to pre-movement structures (NP-structure). In addition, and more importantly, as far as semantic binding is concerned, that same level of LF can be interpreted by our standard interpretation rules, respecting the built-in constraints on binding and β-insertion.

The alert reader may wonder how the reconstruction view is different from a view according to which checking of the Binding Conditions and interpretation *both* simply take place *before wh*-movement, say at NP-structure. To answer that question, note that assuming the latter amounts to claiming that *wh*-movement never influences semantic interpretation. This is obviously an inconsistent position for the case of semantically motivated LF-movements like quantifier raising. But, even ignoring that, it is very likely to be untenable for overt movements such as *wh*-movement, relativization, and certain instances of topicalization, which, among other things, serve to mark scope, abstract over certain argument positions, or mark clause types.

But if we find grounds to dismiss the "interpretation before (*wh*-)movement" idea, how can we get away with reconstruction, which essentially "undoes" movement before interpretation takes place? This question leads to a fascinating research area, which we can't do justice to here at all. Let me make just two remarks: first, I was deliberately vague above in saying that reconstruction might not apply to the entire moved phrase. Thus relevant parts, e.g. scope-taking

---

[3] I ignore the question of how exactly the chain *which* $\mu_1 \ldots t_1$ is to be interpreted.

elements, may remain in their derived positions, while others, in particular those relevant to BT, reconstruct, as, for example, in (12.18c). So, LF, even after reconstruction, *is* different from NP-structure. Second, we can observe cases in which a derived position does seem to be the one relevant for BT. So, for these cases, it would seem that NP-structure can't be the locus of application for Binding Conditions. On the reconstruction view, one can assume that LF is the single locus of interpretation and BT, but that reconstruction is, in some cases, optional or even impossible. We will discuss such cases in section 12.5 below.

12.3.3   Semantic reconstruction

Above we charged the NP-structure approach, as well as the connectivity approach, with failing to derive bound variable interpretations for moved bindees (unless additional means to derive LFs are employed, that is). Take again our case of *about himself every man can speak*, assuming the LF in (12.19):

(12.19)   [about himself$_1$] μ_2 every man β_1 can speak t_2

Let us be clear about what exactly goes wrong in interpreting this LF. We know that, given the interpretation of the μ-prefix and the trace t_2, $[\![\mu_n[_Y \ldots t_n \ldots]]\!]^g([\![X]\!]^g)$ will essentially be interpreted the same as $[\![[_Y \ldots X \ldots]]\!]^g$. So why wouldn't the interpretation of (12.19) come out *exactly* the same as that of *every man can speak about himself*? For concreteness' sake, let us assume that *about himself* is an (optional) property denoting argument to *speak*, i.e. that *speak* denotes the relation $[\lambda P_{et} \lambda y_e . y$ speaks, and $P(\text{what } y \text{ says}) = 1]$ (informally: '...and what y says is P'), and *about himself$_1$* simply denotes $[\lambda x \lambda y . y$ is about $g(1)]$ – the property of being about $g(1)$ (more realistically, the PP would be interpreted as a modifier, but nothing hinges on this in the present context).

The problem is that the two daughters of the root node are going to be interpreted as $[\![\text{about himself}_1]\!]^g$ and $[\![\mu_2 \text{ every man } \beta_1 \text{ can speak } t_2]\!]^g$ once and for all. The meaning of the topicalized PP, call it ϕ, is $[\lambda x . x$ is about $g(1)]$ – a property – and the meaning of its sister, call it γ, is the set of properties $[\lambda P.$ for every man y, y speaks, and $P(\text{what } y \text{ says}) = 1]$. Now, the denotation of *himself$_1$* has already been determined at this stage as $g(1)$, i.e. it is determined by what the matrix assignment happens to assign to it. The fact that ϕ will eventually end up as the semantic argument to γ, and within the semantic scope of β, in a manner of speaking, i.e. the fact that the meaning of the sentence will be $\gamma(\phi)$, is irrelevant. In a slogan, the problem is that all pronouns are assigned their denotation once the double brackets apply, and no semantic maneuver will ever be able to access them again.

The key to semantic reconstruction is to circumvent this dilemma by converting a free variable into an open argument slot *before the double brackets apply*, as it were. Suppose that instead of ϕ and γ as above, we could assign the following denotations:

(12.20) (a) $[\![\text{about himself}_1]\!]^g = \lambda x \lambda y. y \text{ is about } x$
         (b) $[\![\mu_2 \text{ every man } \beta_1 \text{ can speak } t_2]\!]^g = \lambda R.$ for every man y, y speaks, and $R(y)(\text{what } y \text{ says}) = 1$

Here, the PP denotes a relation, and the clause denotes a set of relations. *Himself₁* is no longer treated as a referring expression, but as inducing an additional argument position, the one corresponding to λx. The reader may convince herself that given the meanings assigned in (12.20), $[\![\mu_2 \text{ every man } \beta_1 \text{ can speak } t_2]\!]^g([\![\text{about himself}_1]\!]^g)$ will, in fact, come out meaning: 'for every man y, y speaks, and what y says is about y,' as desired.

It would go beyond the scope of this section to revise our entire formal system so as to utilize meanings as in (12.20) in general. For the sake of illustration, I will introduce an extra device to serve this purpose in the examples at hand. We will define an operator $\uparrow_n$ which turns a free variable indexed n into an argument position, and its dual $\downarrow_n$, which saturates such an extra argument:[4]

(12.21) (a) $[\![\uparrow_n \alpha]\!]^g = \lambda x_e.[\![\alpha]\!]^{g[n \to x]}$
         (b) $[\![\downarrow_n \alpha]\!]^g = [\![\alpha]\!]^g(g(n))$

The semantics of $\uparrow_n$ is almost the same as that of μ_n, except that $\uparrow$ affects the assignment of values to pronouns, rather than traces. To understand what these operators do, note first that the following structure will be interpreted the same as the same structure without the two arrows, i.e. they cancel each other out (compare [12.23b] and [12.23d]):

(12.22)

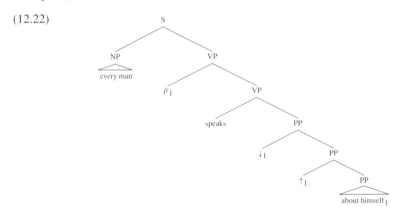

---

[4] These operators are, in fact, more naturally defined as turning *all* free variables into arguments by making the assignment function itself an argument, as in the definitions below; in the main text, we will stick with the specialized version, which should be easier to grasp, given its formal similarity to the familiar β and μ:

(i) $[\![\uparrow \alpha]\!]^g = \lambda g.[\![\alpha]\!]^g$
(ii) $[\![\downarrow \alpha]\!]^g = [\![\alpha]\!]^g(g)$

(12.23) (a) $[\![\text{himself}_1]\!]^g = g(1)$, if $g(1)$ is an atomic male individual, undefined
                otherwise (presupposition will be omitted henceforth)
          (b) $[\![\text{about himself}_1]\!]^g = \lambda y.y$ is about $g(1)$
          (c) $[\![\uparrow_1 \text{ about himself}_1]\!]^g = \lambda x.[\![\text{about himself}_1]\!]^{g[1 \to x]}$
                                $= \lambda x \lambda y.y$ is about $g[1 \to x](1) = \lambda x \lambda y.y$ is about x
          (d) $[\![\downarrow_1 \uparrow_1 \text{ about himself}_1]\!]^g = [\![\uparrow_1 \text{ about himself}_1]\!]^g(g(1))$
                                $= [\lambda x \lambda y.y$ is about $x](g(1)) = \lambda y.y$ is about $g(1)$
          (e) $[\![\text{speak} \downarrow_1 \uparrow_1 \text{ about himself}_1]\!]^g =$
                                $\lambda x.x$ speaks, and what x says is about $g(1)$
          (f) $[\![\beta_1 \text{ speak} \downarrow_1 \uparrow_1 \text{ about himself}_1]\!]^g =$
                                $\lambda x.x$ speaks, and what x says is about x

Crucially, using the arrows now gives us a way to get the bound variable interpretation for the moved structure as well:

(12.24)

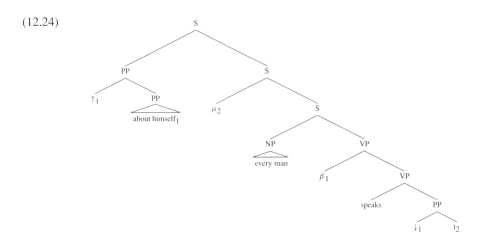

(12.25) (a) $[\![\uparrow_1 \text{ about himself}_1]\!]^g = \lambda x \lambda y.y$ is about x $[=(12.23c)]$
          (b) $[\![t_2]\!]^g = g(t_2)$, where $g(t_2) \in D_{e,et}$ (!)
          (c) $[\![\downarrow_1 t_2]\!]^g = g(t_2)(g(1))$
          (d) $[\![\text{speaks} \downarrow_1 t_2]\!]^g = \lambda x.x$ speaks, and what x says is $g(t_2)(g(1))$
          (e) $[\![\beta_1 \text{ speaks} \downarrow_1 t_2]\!]^g = \lambda x.x$ speaks, and what x says is $g[1 \to x](t_2)(g[1 \to x](1))$
                                $= \lambda x.x$ speaks, and what x says is $g[1 \to x](t_2)(x)$
          (f) $[\![\text{every man } \beta_1 \text{ speaks} \downarrow_1 t_2]\!]^g =$ for every man $x.x$ speaks, and what
                x says is $g[1 \to x](t_2)(x)$
          (g) $[\![\mu_2 \text{ every man } \beta_1 \text{ speaks} \downarrow_1 t_2]\!]^g = \lambda R_{e,et}.$ for every man $x.x$ speaks,
                and what x says is $g[1 \to x][t_2 \to R](t_2)(x)$
                                $= \lambda R_{e,et}.$ for every man $x.x$ speaks, and what x says is $R(x)$
          (h) $[\![(12.24)]\!]^g = [\lambda R_{e,et}.$ for every man $x.x$ speaks, and what x says is
                $R(x)](\lambda x \lambda y.y$ is about $x)$
                $=$ for every man $x.x$ speaks, and what x says is $[\lambda x \lambda y.y$ is about $x)](x)$
                                $=$ for every man $x.x$ speaks, and what x says is about x

Since $[\![\uparrow_1$ about himself$_1]\!]^g$ is a relation (rather than a property like $[\![$about himself$_1]\!]^g$), the trace it leaves is interpreted as a relational variable in (12.25b). This relation is "fed" a variable by $\downarrow_1$, which eventually gets bound by β_1. In this way, *himself$_1$* gets, in a manner of speaking, "bound in the semantics," because the trace of the PP containing it – though not the PP itself – is c-commanded by β_1 at LF.

Semantic reconstruction, then, delivers the correct truth conditions for movement structures in which the bindee has moved out of the c-command domain of the binder, without reconstructing it in the syntax. I do not intend to give a full account of when and how the arrow operators should be applicable. Suffice it to say that they won't do any harm as long as we make sure that they always occur "in pairs," i.e. $\downarrow_n$ minimally c-commanding $\uparrow_n$ before movement, as in (12.22) and (12.24) above.

What about the Binding Conditions? Obviously, since no syntactic reconstruction is assumed under the semantic reconstruction approach, no direct violations of Binding Conditions A–C at LF will be recorded for structures like (12.24). Now, given that we derive bound variable interpretations even in the cases without c-command, at least the Binding Condition C effects will follow from the Coreference rule, which simply excludes full NPs and unbound pronouns where semantic binding is possible. What is not accounted for, however, are Binding Condition A and B effects, and for this additional mechanisms are needed.

Summarizing this section, then, we have seen that a "check Binding Conditions before *wh*-movement" account (e.g. Van Riemsdijk and Williams [1981]'s NP-structure) as well as a connectivity account along the lines of (12.16) (Barss, 1986, 1988) can be utilized to derive Binding Condition effects, but not the semantics of variable binding. Semantic reconstruction, on the other hand, derives the correct semantics, although at the price of a more complicated semantic apparatus, but no Binding Condition A and B effects. Consequently, an account that combines these two can handle the full range of cases (see e.g. Sharvit [1996a,b, 1999] and the references therein). Syntactic reconstruction, on the other hand, can deliver both Binding Condition effects and bound variable interpretations, though at the price of a severely complicated, and only partially understood, syntactic machinery.

12.4   An apparent case of binding after *wh*-movement

It is often argued that sentences like (12.26a) show that Binding Condition A can apply *after wh*-movement (e.g. Chomsky [1995], his [36]). According to this story, *wh*-movement of *which picture of himself* has moved *himself* in (12.26a) into a position – SpecC – where its binding domain includes the matrix subject (we don't need to go into the prerequisite definition of binding domain here); consequentially, the same anaphoric pattern is unavailable in (12.26b), since the binding domain for *in situ himself* is the embedded clause, as expected:

(12.26)   (a)   John wondered [which picture of himself$_{J/B}$] Bill saw
           (b)   John wondered [who β_2 saw [which pictures of himself$_{2/*J}$]]

It should be clear that – even all technical details aside – this interpretation of the contrast between (12.26a) and (12.26b) crucially requires that Binding Condition A can apply *after wh*-movement. However, as Reinhart and Reuland (1993):684, as well as Pollard and Sag (1992):296, point out, the same contrast can be accommodated under the assumption that the reflexives in (12.26a) and (12.26b) are exempt anaphors (cf. chapter 11): *who* in (12.26b) is simply a closer antecedent to the reflexive, which therefore cannot take the more remote *John* as its antecedent, an intervention effect (cf. chapter 11, section 11.2). In (12.26a), no intervention takes place, so both subjects qualify as possible antecedents (where the term *antecedent* has to be taken with a grain of salt; it remains to clarify under what exact conditions backwards logophors, as found between *John* and *himself* in [12.26a], are allowed).

This alternative analysis is further supported by (12.27), which is structurally analogous to (12.26b), except that the intervention effect is ameliorated by making the intervenor inanimate. While the availability of long-distance coreference in (12.27) is predicted under the assumption that *himself* is an exempt anaphor, it would be entirely mysterious and unexpected under a purely phrase-structure based approach such as Chomsky (1995)'s (see also Safir [1999]:595, for more arguments in favor of an exempt anaphor treatment of these cases):

(12.27)   John wondered which newspaper would publish which picture of himself.

Additional, suggestive evidence for the exempt anaphor analysis of (12.26a) comes from the fact that a structurally analogous sentence in German, which doesn't have exempt anaphors, sounds hopeless with a reflexive:

(12.28)   *Hans* fragte [welche Bilder   von *ihm/*sich*] ich gesehen hatte.
           *Hans asked which   pictures of   him/*self   I   seen   had*

The exempt anaphor analysis also immediately provides an account for the contrasts in (12.29): while the AP-internal reflexives are in argument positions, and hence subject to Binding Condition A *relative to their base-positions*, the NP-internal reflexives are exempt and thus show flexibility in their choice of antecedent (cf. Reinhart and Reuland [1993]:684):

(12.29)   (a)   Which pictures of himself/herself does Max think that Lucie likes?
           (b)   How proud of herself/*himself does Max think that Lucie is?
           (c)   Max knows which pictures of himself/herself Lucie likes.
           (d)   Max knows how proud of herself/*himself Lucie is.

It thus seems that, in keeping with our earlier conclusion, there are no cases of reflexive binding *after wh*-movement in English, despite appearances. The discussion furthermore aptly illustrates how crucial it is to properly analyze BT facts in the light of recent research, before drawing far-reaching conclusions about other areas of grammatical theory.

12.5   A real case of interaction of Ā-movement and BT?

Let us now turn to a rather intriguing complication of the facts about binding and movement, which is not so easily explained. Above we suggested, on the basis of examples like (12.14c) and (12.14d), repeated here, that *wh*-movement cannot ameliorate Binding Condition violations: the name appears to incur a Binding Condition C violation because the coreferring pronoun c-commands it *before movement*:

(12.30)   (a) ∗How many claims that *Nixon* is a crook is *he* going to tolerate?
          (b) ∗Which investigation of *Nixon* did *he* resent?

It has been noted, however, that in other cases, violations do seem to be "repaired" by movement: thus in (12.31), coreference between *Nixon* and *he* is possible, even though the latter c-commands the trace of the moved phrase *which claims that offended Nixon/which investigation near Nixon's house*:[5]

(12.31)   (a) Which claim that offended *Nixon* did *he* repeat?
          (b) Which investigation near *Nixon*'s house did *he* resent?

Lebeaux (1990) suggests that the crucial difference between these cases is that *Nixon* in (12.30) is contained in an argument (the PP and the embedded clause are arguments to the Ns *claims* and *investigation*, respectively), while *Nixon* in (12.31) is contained in adjuncts (the relative clause to *claim* and the locative modifier to *investigation*, respectively).

Why would the adjunct/argument distinction be relevant here? Lebeaux (1990) proposes that adjuncts, but not arguments, can be "added" to the clause late in the derivation, to wit after BT has applied. In other words, Binding Condition C violations are detected at a stage when (12.30b) and (12.31b), for example, still have the forms in (12.32):

(12.32)   (a) ∗*he* did resent which investigation of *Nixon*
          (b) *he* did resent which investigation

As indicated, (12.32a) incurs a Binding Condition C violation at this stage in the derivation, while BT will find nothing wrong in (12.32b), since the adjunct *near Nixon's house* with the offending name in it simply isn't present. Later on, the adjunct will be inserted, but BT doesn't care about that.

Lebeaux (1990)'s proposal obviously adopts the "BT before *wh*-movement" perspective discussed in section 12.3 above. Fox (2000), following suggestions in

---

[5] Cf. Van Riemsdijk and Williams (1981); Freidin (1986); Lebeaux (1988); Chomsky (1995); Safir (1999), esp. n. 1; this is sometimes, though awkwardly, called an *anti-reconstruction effect*.

Chomsky (1995), provides a rendering of the same idea within the copy view of movement. Under the copy view, remember, *wh*-movement leaves full copies, not traces, behind. Those *in situ* copies incur Binding Condition violations, yielding the effect of reconstruction or pre-movement BT effects.

Now, if, as Lebeaux suggests, adjuncts are added later in the derivation, in particular after *wh*-movement, it is clear that the *in situ* copy will not contain a copy of the adjunct. Thus, the pertinent LFs for (12.30b) and (12.31b) look something like (12.33a) and (12.33b), with the copy underlined (ignoring the possibility that parts of the moved phrases will be deleted at LF):

(12.33)   (a) ∗ which investigation of *Nixon* did *he* resent <u>which investigation of Nixon</u>

    (b)   which investigation near *Nixon*'s house did he resent <u>which investigation</u>

This analysis receives subtle support from other areas of BT. As we saw earlier, a strong argument in favor of having moved phrases "back" *in situ* at LF comes from variable binding: a QNP can bind a pronoun inside a *wh*-phrase it doesn't c-command in the overt syntax:

(12.34)   Which pictures of *him* did Mary say that *every boy* should burn?

This, as suggested, could be fit into the theory by assuming that the *wh*-phrase, or at least its descriptive content, is reconstructed to, or leaves a full copy within, the embedded clause at LF.

Now, as a first step, we find that variable binding into a *wh*-phrase is possible if the bound pronoun is inside an adjunct:

(12.35)   Which claim *he* had made earlier did *every senator* deny?

How does this fit with the idea that adjuncts are only added *after wh*-movement? Clearly (12.35) forces the copy-theoretician to assume that there must be an LF in which *claim that he had made earlier* sits within the embedded VP, so that *he* can be bound by *every senator*. It must be concluded that adjuncts can, optionally, be inserted *before* movement (or, if one assumes that reconstruction involves real downward movement, that they can be reconstructed into a position that they never occupied before). In either case, elements within adjuncts *can* be in their derived positions at LF, but don't have to; unlike with all other phrases, reconstruction of these is not obligatory but optional.

If we accept this reasoning, it provides us with a neat probe to test our tacit assumption that variable binding and Binding Conditions apply to the same structural representation. We observe that *if* an adjunct reconstructs, it does so for *all* pertinent principles. Consider (12.36), where both a bindable pronoun and a name are embedded within the adjunct within the moved *wh*-phrase. If the phrase stays in its derived position, the name will be free with respect to all the pronouns in the sentence and can corefer with *she*; but the pronoun *he* can't be semantically bound by the lower QNP *every senator* and must be interpreted referentially. If, on the other hand, the *wh*-phrase reconstructs, the variable can be bound by the QNP, but the name must not corefer with *she*. According to judgments in the pertinent literature, the sentence can indeed have either interpretation, but crucially *not* one in which *he* is bound by *every senator* and *she* refers to Maggie:

(12.36)   Which claim that he had made about Maggie did she expect every senator to retract?

This result, if reliable, reenforces the conclusion drawn earlier that adjuncts may or may not reconstruct. It furthermore suggests rather strongly that variable binding, which is part of the interpretive procedure, and Binding Conditions, which could be in principle purely syntactic and hence apply at any stage of the derivation, do, in fact, apply to the very same structure.[6] At the end of section 12.3 we tentatively suggested that a combination of semantic reconstruction (to get the interpretation right) and a connectivity/NP-structure approach (to derive Binding Condition A–C effects) yields the same coverage as syntactic reconstruction. But it would seem unclear, under such a view, why Binding Condition effects are sometimes alleviated, and why, in particular, this would correlate with the interpretation of these phrases. The effects around binding into adjuncts, and in particular the parallelism between Binding Condition violations and semantic binding in examples like (12.36), thus provide an additional, strong argument in favor of the syntactic reconstruction view.

Before closing this section, though, a caveat must be made, namely that the adjunct/argument asymmetries, for which the "late insertion" analysis accounts, are not always very poignant. Safir (1999):609f. provides the following list of examples,[7] in all of which a name embedded in an argument nonetheless shows no Binding Condition C effects:

(12.37)   (a)   That *Ed* was under surveillance *he* never realized.
           (b)   Which witness's attack on *Lee* did *he* try to get expunged from the trial records?
           (c)   Whose criticism of *Lee* did *he* choose to ignore?
           (d)   Which claim that *Al* had defeated Lea was *he* unaware of?

The examples in (12.37) all bring out very clearly a factor discussed at great length in Kuno (1987):ch. 3, namely that *wh*-movement doesn't rescue those Binding Condition C violations in which the full NP refers to the individuals

---

[6] A counterpart argument to this one, which suggests that reconstruction even of non-adjuncts will sometimes *not* occur, if independent interpretive demands block it, is presented in Fox (2000):ch. 6. Since the argument is rather complex and involves a special kind of ellipsis, we can only refer the reader to that work here.

   A further argument, which involves BT and the interpretation of *how many* phrases, can be found in Heycock (1995); such effects are sometimes referred to as *freezing effects*.

[7] Which he attributes to Ross (1973):198 ([12.37a]), and an unpublished manuscript by Kuno ([12.37b]–[12.37d]), respectively.

whose actions or feelings as speakers or hearers are reported. To illustrate, observe the contrast between (12.37d) and (12.38) below:[8]

(12.38)   *Which claim that *Al* had defeated Mary did *he* later admit *he* made?

In (12.38), the statement '(I admit that) I made the claim that *I* defeated Mary' is attributed to Al. No such statement is attributed in (12.37d) (it's not that Al is unaware of: 'I defeated Lea'), or in any other of the examples in (12.37), which all involve predicates that don't express that the referent of the name said, thought, or experienced the prerequisite statement about himself.

Kuno (1987) provides more examples of this effect, e.g. the contrast in (12.39):

(12.39)   (a) ??The statement that *Churchill* was vain was often made to *him*.
          (b)   The statement that *Churchill* was vain has often been made about *him*.

Note first that, since these examples involve passives, rather than *wh*-movement, it is less obvious that there is a pre-movement structure in which *him* c-commands *Churchill*. Second, and more importantly, the contrast in acceptability cannot be due to any adjunct–argument asymmetry, given that the name in both examples is embedded in the same (argument) configuration. Instead, it can be seen to reflect the fact that (12.39a) reports that the statement 'You are vain' has been made, whereas the pertinent statement in (12.39b) is 'He/Churchill is vain.'

Kuno (1987)'s generalization is that only those NPs that can be replaced by first or second person pronouns in a direct speech rendering cannot be full NPs in these sentences. This bears a certain resemblance to the cases of logophoric pronouns discussed in chapter 3, section 3.2.2, and, indeed, Kuno captures these effects by what he calls the *logophoric pronoun rule*; the reader is referred to that work for further details.

Given that the relevance of the argument/adjunct distinction isn't obvious, we might ask whether anything in Kuno (1987)'s account explains the *appearance* of its relevance, which led Freidin (1986), Lebeaux (1988), and those following them to their approaches. While I am not aware of any systematic study of this, we can at least speculate that adjuncts generally don't have to be part of the content of a reported speech act. Consider again (12.31a) (*Which claim that offended* Nixon *did* he *repeat?*), an adjunct case. If the pertinent statement was *Only criminals use wire taps*, and if it offended Nixon, then what Nixon repeated is likely to be '... only criminals use wire taps,' not '... only criminals use wire taps, which offended me.'

Generally, the adjunct in these cases is easily interpreted as part of the speaker's *description* of what was said, rather than its *content*; hence, no logophoric pronoun effect will be observed. Arguments, in particular argument clauses as in *claim that, argument that*, etc., on the other hand, express the

---

[8] Again from Kuno, as quoted in Safir (1999).

content of the reported statement and, as such, are more likely to correspond to sentences containing first or second person pronouns.

This ends our caveat about the interactions between movement and binding theory discussed in this section. It seems clear that more than just structural factors influence the "reconstruction effects" discussed. Whether there is still a structural core, perhaps along the lines of Fox (2000); Freidin (1986); or Lebeaux (1988) to them, or the phenomenon is purely non-structural, as assumed in Kuno (1987), on the other hand, seems very much an open question.

12.6   Binding without binders

We will close this chapter with a brief discussion of *connectivity in copular sentences*. Though the phenomena to be discussed arguably don't involve any interaction between BT and movement, they are nonetheless relevant in the present context, as will be seen shortly. Consider the following sentences:

(12.40)   (a)   What *Mary* was was proud of *herself*.   (Binding Condition A)
            (b)   What *Mary* was was proud of *her*$_{*M}$.   (Binding Condition B)
            (c)   What *she*$_{*M}$ was was proud of *Mary*.   (Binding Condition C)

As indicated, these sentences appear to show Binding Condition A–C effects parallel to a simple sentence *Mary was proud of her*(self)/*Mary*. But clearly, *Mary*, which is embedded in a free relative clause, doesn't command the complement of *proud*, which leaves us with no explanation for the distribution of the elements in that position.

(12.40a)–(12.40c) are *identificational sentences*, i.e. sentences which express something roughly like 'X = Y.' We crucially need to distinguish them from ordinary subject–predicate sentences, even those with the verb *be*, which express something like 'X is a Y.' The latter class doesn't show the puzzling behavior of identificational sentences:

(12.41)   What *Mary* did was/became important to *her*/*herself*.

Intuitively, the reason why a reflexive is acceptable in (12.40a) but not in (12.41) is that the former can be paraphrased as 'Mary is proud of herself,' where the reflexive is bound in the regular fashion, while no such paraphrase exists for the latter. However, virtually all researchers agree that there is no level of syntactic representation at which the NP *Mary* actually is the subject of *(be) proud of herself* in (12.40a). The binding effects in (12.40) have thus been recognized as a puzzle for BT, and have become known under the heading of *connectivity effects*, expressing the intuition that the complement of *proud of* is, if not bound, then still in some other way *connected* to *Mary* in (12.40).

While connectivity effects are frequently discussed in the context of *pseudo-cleft* sentences such as (12.40), they are not restricted to them. Identificational sentences whose subject is not a free relative, but an ordinary NP, show parallel behavior:[9]

(12.42)   (a)   *His*₊_J_ claim was that *John* was innocent.
           (b)   *His* sole output for the day was a picture of *himself*.
           (c)   The woman *he* loves the most is *his/*John's* mother.
           (d)   That *he/*John* was crazy was just one of the things Mary said to *him*.
           (e)   That *he/*John* had a medical appointment that afternoon was one of the things *he* remembered.

Furthermore, connectivity effects are not restricted to Binding Conditions A–C but are also found with variable binding:

(12.43)   (a)   The woman *every Englishman* loves the most is *his* mother.
           (b)   What *nobody* seems to be is proud of *himself*.

One line of analysis for these sentences has been to assume that there *is* a local binder in the post-copular material, which has been deleted (den Dikken *et al.*, 2000):

(12.44)   (the answer to the question) what Mary is is : she is proud of herself

Clearly, if such an analysis can be motivated, and if it can be extended to *all* cases of identificational sentences, nothing further needs to be said: all bindings appear perfectly regular. It is, however, not obvious what the underlying structures for sentences like (12.42b), (12.42c), (12.42d), (12.42e), or (12.43a) should be.

Are there alternatives? We can replace c-command as the relevant notion with something like d-command, defined in (12.16) above, and add another clause that makes the post-copular material in identificational sentences d-dominated by the pre-copular material (a proposal along these lines is developed in Barrs [1986]). Without going into the details, our definition would ensure that, for example, everything that dominates the trace of *what* in (12.40a) (*What* Mary *was was proud of* herself.) d-dominates *proud of herself*.

But, apart from the fact that it is not clear how such an account generalizes to the entire range of identificational sentences illustrated above, it falls short of deriving the bound *interpretation* for pronouns, just as it did for the cases of syntactically dislocated phrases discussed in section 12.3. Whether or not *every Englishman* and *nobody* are defined to d-command – and eventually syntactically bind – the pronouns in (12.43), they cannot semantically bind them from where they are, nor raise to a position from which they do without violating fundamental constraints on LF-movement and pronoun binding.

---

[9] (12.42b) from Heycock and Kroch (1999):368; (12.42c) inspired by Jacobson (1994); (12.42d) and (12.42e) from Kuno (1987):110f.

What, if anything, can be done, then? It should be noted that the cases of bound reflexives such as in (12.40a), repeated here, can (almost) be accommodated within our present system:

(12.45)   (a)   What *Mary* was was proud of *herself*.
          (b)   what Mary was was [$_{AP}$ β_1 proud of herself$_1$]

The LF in (12.45b) expresses an idea similar to Heycock (1995)'s proposal that fronted APs contain a trace of the subject, which can bind a reflexive within the AP in examples like (12.11b) above. Crucially, since we assume that not an NP itself, but a binder prefix, binds pronouns, we don't have to assume a trace in the AP in (12.45b) (which we can't, given the fact that there never was an actual subject in the AP in these constructions), and still get the desired reflexive binding.

The post-copular constituent *β_1 proud of herself* will denote the property of being proud of oneself, or, briefly: self-pride. Though we can't get into the semantics of free relatives like *what Mary was* here, we will assume that the entire LF in (12.45b) will be interpreted to a first approximation as 'The property that Mary had was that of self-pride.' This seems intuitively satisfactory.

This kind of analysis carries over to a quantificational case such as *What every woman was was proud of herself*. The property ascribed to every woman here is, again, self-pride. Notice that, just like in the non-quantificational case, this sentence is not analyzed as directly stating that every woman is proud of herself. Rather, it equates two properties: that property which every woman had, and self-pride.

Can we derive Binding Condition C violations, as in **What she/Mary was was proud of Mary*, along these lines, too? Note that this sentence has the exact same interpretation as its reflexive counterpart in (12.45a). So, by the Coreference rule (cf. chapter 6), the version utilizing a bound pronoun blocks the coreferent version using a name. In a way, as long as we manage to get the bound-pronoun version to receive the correct interpretation even without c-command, the impossibility of coreferent full NPs or pronouns in the same position will automatically follow – without c-command – since it is merely identity of interpretations that determines the applicability of the Coreference rule (the same thing, unfortunately, isn't true for the Have Local Binding! rule introduced in chapter 6, an issue we can't address here).

Finally, a non-reflexive pronoun in the position of *herself* in (12.45a) will be ruled out, too: if it is not bound by a β adjoined to AP, the Coreference rule will kick in in the same way it does with a full NP. If it is bound by β, it violates Binding Condition B.

One minor and one major point need to be made, though. First, our Binder rule as defined in (8.25) in chapter 8 allows for adjunction of β only next to (immediately c-commanded by) an NP. There is no such NP within the AP in (12.45b). To accommodate this case, we have to reformulate the condition on β-adjunction so that it can adjoin to any constituent that *can license an NP position* – roughly a constituent with an unassigned Θ-role or unfilled argument position.

Second, an analysis along the lines of (12.45b) will only work in a case where the post-copular constituent itself denotes a reflexive property. But take (12.43a), repeated here:

(12.46)   The woman *every Englishman* loves the most is *his* mother.

Intuitively, an analogous analysis should interpret this sentence as something like (12.47):

(12.47)   The function which maps every Englishman to the woman he loves the most equals the function that maps every individual to his or her mother ($[\iota f_{\langle e, e\rangle}$.for every x, if x is an Englishman, then x loves $f(x)]=[\lambda y.\iota z.z$ is y's mother]).

Were we able to derive such an interpretation for sentence (12.46), the same reasonings as in the case of (12.45a) would apply to derive the pertinent facts. But can we assign such a meaning?

Again, we will not concern ourselves with how to derive the interpretation for the pre-copular NP. But what about *his mother*? According to (12.47), this NP should denote a function from individuals to individuals. But $[\![\text{his}_1 \text{ mother}]\!]^g$ will simply denote $g(1)$'s mother, not a function from individuals to their mothers. The desired meaning would be expressed by μ_1 *[his₁ mother]*, which, however, cannot be derived by our rules, or any minor modification thereof (remember that in general, μ cannot ever bind overt elements). Similar remarks apply to examples (12.42a)–(12.42e) above.

We can derive this meaning, though, using the $\uparrow_n$ operator defined in subsection 12.3.3 above; the pertinent representation will be *[↑₁ his₁ mother]*. This technique can indeed be successfully applied to all the examples of copular connectivity. What has to be made sure, though, is that both the pre- and the post-copular material always get the correct interpretation, too. For example, *his claim* in (12.42a) will have to be $\uparrow_1$ *his₁ claim*, interpreted as a function which maps people to the claim they made, so that *that John was innocent* is ruled out because of the availability of $\uparrow_1$ *that he₁ was innocent*. To devise a full treatment for these cases is beyond the scope of this book.

The most thorough discussion of these cases can be found in Pauline Jacobson's work (1994, 1996, 1999, 2000, a.o), which at the same time provides a strong plea for treating pronouns, in our terms, generally as open arguments rather than as free variables.

How does our discussion of copular connectivity bear on the central issue of this chapter, the interaction of (*wh*)-movement and binding? As should have become clear, the resources utilized to account for copular connectivity facts are very much the same as those used to account for "reconstruction" facts. However, syntactic reconstruction in terms of undoing overt movements, or alluding to copies left behind by movement, arguably cannot be used to account for the copular connectivity cases, which simply do not have a derivational source of the prerequisite sort. This is remarkable, since syntactic reconstruction promises a very successful and elegant account of the original movement and binding facts. Accordingly, syntactic reconstruction is often seen as part and parcel with the syntactic deletion approach to copular connectivity sketched around (12.44), primarily because in that combination (and, as far as I can see, only in that combination) could we avoid tapping any further resources such as semantic reconstruction, connectivity rules involving d-command, etc.

On the other hand, to the extent that the deletion approach to copular connectivity fails to derive the full range of facts, copular connectivity facts may provide independent evidence that some extra machinery is needed, which then, in turn, will also be available in cases involving *wh*-movement. So, when it comes to comparing the various approaches not just in terms of their empirical success but in terms of the overall parsimony of the resulting theory, it seems likely that both *wh*-movement facts and copular connectivity facts will have to be taken into consideration.

Bibliography

Almog, Joseph, John Perry, and Howard Wettstein, eds. (1989). *Themes from Kaplan*. Oxford University Press.

Ariel, Mira (1999). "Referring and Accessibility." *Journal of Linguistics* 24:65–87.

   (2001). "Accessibility Theory: an Overview." In T. Sandeler, J. Schliperoord, and W. Spooren, eds., *Text Representation*, 29–87. Amsterdam: Benjamins.

Asudeh, Ash, and Frank Keller (2002). "Experimental Evidence for a Predication-based Binding Theory." In Heidi Elston, Mary Andronis, Chris Ball, and Sylvain Neuvel, eds., *CLS 37: The Main Session. Papers from the 37th meeting of the Chicago Linguistic Society, Vol. 1*. Chicago, Ill.: Chicago Linguistic Society.

Avrutin, Sergey (1994). "The Structural Position of Bound Variables in Russian." *Linguistic Inquiry* 25(4):709–727.

Bach, Emmon (1970). "Problominalization." *Linguistic Inquiry* 1:121–122.

Bach, Emmon, and Barbara H. Partee (1980). "Anaphora and Semantic Structure." In J. Kreiman and A. Ojeda, eds., *Papers from the Parasession on Pronouns and Anaphora*, Chicago Linguistic Society, 1–28.

   (1984). "Quantification, Pronouns, and VP Anaphora." In Jereon Groenendijk, Theo M.V. Janssen, and Martin Stokhof, eds., *Truth, Interpretation and Information*, 99–130. Dordrecht: Foris.

Barbosa, Pilar, Danny Fox, Paul Hagstrom, Martha McGinnis, and David Pesetsky (1998). *Is the Best Good Enough? Optimality and Competition in Syntax …* Cambridge, Mass.: MIT Press.

Barker, Chris. (2001a). "Continuations and the Nature of Quantification." unpubl. ms. U.C. San Diego.

   (2001b). "Integrity: a Syntactic Constraint on Quantifier scoping." unpubl. MS. U.C. San Diego.

Barker, Chris., and Geoffrey K. Pullum (1990). "A Theory of Command Relations." *Linguistics and Philosophy* 13:1–34.

Barrs, Andrew (1986). "Chains and Anaphoric Dependencies." Ph.D. thesis, MIT.

   (1988). "Paths, Connectivity, and Featureless Empty Categories." In Anna Cardinaletti, Guglielmo Cinque, and Giuliana Giusti, eds., *Constituent Structure*, 9–34. Dordrecht: Foris.

Barrs, Andrew, and Howard Lasnik (1986). "A Note on Anaphora and Double Objects." *Linguistic Inquiry* 17:347–354.

Barwise, Jon, and Robin Cooper (1981). "Generalized Quantifiers and Natural Language." *Linguistics and Philosophy* 4(4):159–219.

Bäuerle, Rainer, Christoph Schwarze, and Armin von Stechow, eds. (1983). *Meaning, Use and Interpretation of Language*. Berlin: de Gruyter.

Beck, Sigrid (1999). "Reciprocals and Cumulation." In *Proceedings of SALT IX*, 16–33. Ithaca, NY: Cornell University.

Belletti, Adriana, and Luigi Rizzi (1988). "Psych-Verbs and Theta-Theory." *Linguistic Inquiry* 6(3):291–352.

Benedicto, Elena (1992). "Latin Long-distance Anaphora." In Koster and Reuland (1992a), 171–184.

Bennet, Michael (1994). "Some Extensions of a Montague Fragment of English." Ph.D. thesis, UCLA. Reprinted 1975, Indiana University Linguistics Club, Bloomington, Ind.

Bennis, Hans, Pierre Pica, and Johan Roryck, eds. (1997). *Atomism and Binding*. Dordrecht: Foris.

Berman, Steven, and Arild Hestvik, eds. (1992). *Proceedings of the Stuttgart Workshop on Ellipsis*, No. 29 in Arbeitspapiere des SFB 340, University of Stuttgart.

(1997). "Split Antecedents, Noncoreference, and DRT." In Bennis *et al.* (1997), 1–29.

Bhat, D. N. A. (1978). *Pronominalization*. Pune: Postgraduate and Research Institute, Deccan College.

Bok-Bennema, Reineke (1991). *Case and Agreement in Inuit*. Dordrecht: Foris.

Borer, Hagit, ed. (1986). *Syntax and Semantics: the Syntax of Pronominal Clitics*. New York: Academic Press.

Bouma, Gosse, Robert Malouf, and Ivan Sag (2001). "Satisfying Constraints on Extraction and Adjunction." *Natural Language and Linguistic Theory* 19:1–65.

Bresnan, Joan (2000). *Lexical Functional Syntax*. Oxford: Blackwell.

Büring, Daniel (2001a). "Binding out of DP and Weak Cross-Over." MS. UCLA.

(2001b). "A Situation Semantics for Binding out of DP." In Hastings *et al.* (2001), 56–75.

(2004). "Crossover Situations." *Natural Language Semantics* 12:23–62.

Burzio, Luigi (1996). "The Role of the Antecedent in Anaphoric Relations." In Freidin (1996), 1–45.

(1998). "Anaphora and Soft Constraints." In Barbosa *et al.* (1998), 93–113.

Carden, Guy, and Thomas Dieterich (1981). "Introspection, Observation, and Experiment: an Example where Experiments Pay Off." In *PSA 1980: Proceedings of the 1980 Biennial Meeting of the Philosophy of Science Association. Vol. 2: Symposia*, 583–597. East Lansing, Mich.: Philsophy of Science Association.

Chapin, Paul G. (1970). "Samoan Pronominalization." *Language* 46(2):366–378.

Chierchia, Gennaro (1992). "Anaphora and Dynamic Binding." *Linguistics and Philosophy* 15:111–183.

(1995). *Dynamics of Meaning*. Chicago: University of Chicago Press.

Chomsky, Noam (1976). "Conditions on Rules of Grammar." *Linguistic Analysis* 2:303–351.

(1980). "On Binding." *Linguistic Inquiry* 11:1–46.

(1981). *Lectures on Government and Binding*. Dordrecht: Foris Publications.

(1986). *Knowledge of Language*. New York: Praeger.

(1995). *The Minimalist Program*. Cambridge, Mass.: MIT Press.

Clements, George N. (1975). "The Logophoric Pronoun in Ewe: its Role in Discourse." *Journal of West African Languages* 10:141–177.

Cole, Peter, Gabriella Hermon, and C.-T. James Huang, eds. (2000). *Long-Distance Reflexives*. Syntax and Semantics. San Diego, Ca.: Academic Press.

Cole, Peter, Gabriella Hermon, and Li-May Sung (1990). "Principles and Parameters of Long-Distance Reflexives." *Linguistic Inquiry* 21(1):1–22.

Cole, Peter, and Li-May Sung (1994). "Head Movement and Long-Distance Reflexives." *Linguistic Inquiry* 25(3):355–406.

Cole, Peter, and Chengchi Wang (1996). "Antecedents and Blockers of Long-Distance Reflexives: the Case of Chinese *ziji*." *Linguistic Inquiry* 27(3):357–390.

Comrie, Bernard, ed. (1990). *The World's Major Languages*. New York and Oxford: Oxford University Press.

Cooper, Robin (1979). "The Interpretation of Pronouns." In *Syntax and Semantics*, Vol. 10, 61–92.

Dalrymple, Mary (1993). *The Syntax of Anaphoric Binding*. Stanford: Center for the Studies of Language and Information.

Dalrymple, Mary, Makoto Kanazawa, Yookyung Kim, Sam Machombo, and Stanley Peters (1998). "Reciprocal Expressions and the Concept of Reciprocity." *Linguistics and Philosophy* 21:159–210.

Dalrymple, Mary, Sam Mchombo, and Stanley Peters (1994). "Semantic Contrasts and Similarities between Chicheŵa and English Reciprocals." *Linguistic Inquiry* 25:145–163.

Dalrymple, Mary, Stuart M. Shieber, and Fernando C. N. Pereira (1991). "Ellipsis and Higher-Order Unification." *Linguistics and Philosophy* 14:399–452.

de Geest, Wim, and Yvan Putsey (1984). *Sentential Complementation*. Dordrecht: Foris.

Déchaine, Rose-Marie, and Martina Wilschko (2002). "Decomposing Pronouns." *Linguistic Inquiry* 33(3):409–442.

Demirdache, Hamida (1997). "Condition C." In Bennis *et al.* (1997), 51–87.

den Dikken, Marcel, Anikó Lipták, and Zsófia Zsvolensky (2001). "On Inclusive Reference Anaphora: New Perspectives from Hungarian." In Megerdoomian and Barel (2001), 137–149.

den Dikken, Marcel, André Meinunger, and Chris Wilder (2000). "Pseudoclefts and Ellipsis." *Studia Linguistica* 54:41–89.

Dimitriadis, Alexis (1999). "Reconciling Dependent Plurals with *Each Other*." In *Proceedings of SALT IX*, 52–69. Ithaca, NY: Cornell Linguistics Club Publications.

Dixon, Robert M. (1988). *A Grammar of Boumaa Fijian*. Chicago: University of Chicago Press.

Dowty, David (1980). "Comments on the Paper by Bach and Partee." In Jody Kreiman and Almerindo Ojeda, eds., *CLS Parasession on Pronouns and Anaphora*, 29–40. Chicago: Chicago Linguistic Society.

Eckardt, Regine (2002). "Reanalyzing *selbst*." *Natural Language Semantics* 9(4):371–412.

É. Kiss, Katalin (1992). "The Primacy Condition of Anaphora and Pronominal Variable Binding." In Koster and Reuland (1992a), 245–262.

Elbourne, Paul (2000). "E-Type Pronouns as Definite Articles." In *West Coast Conference in Formal Linguistics 2000 Proceedings*, 83–96.

———— (2001). "E-Type Anaphora as NP-Deletion." *Natural Language Semantics* 9:241–288.

Enç, Mürvet (1989). "Pronouns, Licensing, and Binding." *Natural Language and Linguistic Theory* 7(1):51–92.

———— (1991). "The Semantics of Specificity." *Linguistic Inquiry* 22(1):1–26.

Evans, Gareth (1977). "Pronouns, Quantifiers, and Relative Clauses." *The Canadian Journal of Philosophy* 7:467–536.

———— (1980). "Pronouns." *Linguistic Inquiry* 11:337–362.

Everaert, Martin (1986). *The Syntax of Reflexivization*. No. 22, Publications in Language Sciences. Dordrecht: Foris.

———— (1992). "Contextual Determination of the Anaphor/ Pronominal Distinction." In Koster and Reuland (1992a), 77–118.

Faltz, Leonard M. (1977). "Reflexivization: a Study in Universal Syntax." Ph.D. thesis, U. C. Berkeley.

Fanselow, Gisbert (1993). "Die Rückkehr der Basisgenerierer." *Groninger Arbeiten zur Germanistischen Linguistik* 36:1–74.

Farmer, Ann, and Robert M. Harnish (1987). "Communicative Reference with Pronouns." In M. Papi and E. J. Verschueren, eds., *The Pragmatic Perspective*. Amsterdam: Benjamins.

Fiengo, Robert, and Howard Lasnik (1973). "The Logical Structure of Reciprocal Sentences in English." *Foundations of Language* 9:447–468.

Fiengo, Robert, and Robert May (1994). *Indices and Identity*. Cambridge, Mass.: MIT Press.

Fisher, Karen (1988). "Agreement and the Distribution of Anaphors." In Michael Hammond and Edith Moravcsik, eds., *Studies in Syntactic Typology*, 25–36. Amsterdam: John Benjamins.

Fontana, Josep M., and John Moore (1992). "VP-Internal Subjects and *Se*-Reflexivization in Spanish." *Linguistic Inquiry* 23(3):501–510.

Fox, Danny (2000). *Economy and Semantic Interpretation*. Cambridge, Mass.: MIT Press.

Frajzyngier, Zygmunt, and Traci S. Curl, eds. (1999a). *Reciprocals – Forms and Functions*. No. 41 in Typological Studies in Language. Amsterdam/Philadelphia: John Benjamins.

    eds. (1999b). *Reflexives – Forms and Functions*. No. 40 in Typological Studies in Language. Amsterdam/Philadelphia: John Benjamins.

Freidin, Robert (1986). *Principles and Parameters in Comparative Grammar*. Cambridge, Mass.: MIT Press.

    (1996). *Current Issues in Comparative Grammar*. Dordrecht: Kluwer.

Geach, Paul (1962). *Reference and Generality*. Ithaca, NY: Cornell University Press.

Gerdts, Donna B. (1999). "Combinatory Restrictions on Halkomelem Reflexives and Reciprocals." In Frajzyngier and Curl (1999a), 133–160.

Gerken, LouAnn, and Thomas G. Bever (1986). "Linguistic Intuitions are the Result of Interactions between Perceptual Processes and Linguistic Universals." *Cognitive Science* 10:457–476.

Grewendorf, Günther (1988). *Aspekte der deutschen Syntax. Eine Rektions-Bindungs-Analyse*. No. 33, Studien zur deutschen Grammatik. Tübingen: Gunter Narr Verlag.

Grima, John (1978). "Categories of Zero Nominal Reference and Clausal Structure inThai." Ph.D. thesis, University of Michigan, Ann Arbor.

Grodzinsky, Yosef, and Tanya Reinhart (1993). "The Innateness of Binding and Coreference." *Linguistic Inquiry* 24(1):69–101.

Groenendijk, Jeroen, and Martin Stokhof (1991). "Dynamic Predicate Logic." *Linguistics and Philosophy* 14:39–100.

Grosz, Barbara J., Aravind K. Joshi, and Scott Weinstein (1995). "Centering: a Framework for Modelling the Local Coherence of Discourse." *Computational Linguistics* 21(2):203–226.

Guéron, Jacqueline, Hans-Georg Obenauer, and Jean-Yves Pollock, eds. (1984). *Grammatical Representation*. No. 22, Studies in Generative Grammar. Dordrecht: Foris.

Gundel, Jeanette, Nancy Hedberg, and Ron Zacharski (1993). "Cognitive Status and the Form of Referring Expressions in Discourse." *Language* 69(2):274–307.

Gunkel, Lutz, Gereon Müller, and Gisela Zifonun (2003). *Arbeiten zur Reflexivierung*. Tübingen: Niemeyer.

Hagège, C. (1974). "Les pronoms logophoriques." *Bulletin de la Société de Linguistique de Paris* 69:287–310.

Haïk, Isabelle (1984). "Indirect Binding." *Linguistic Inquiry* 15:185–223.

Haiman, John (1985). *Natural Syntax*. Cambridge and New York: Cambridge University Press.

    (1995). "Grammatical Signs of the Divided Self. A Study of Language and Culture." In Werner Abraham, ed., *Discourse Grammar and Typology*. Amsterdam: Benjamins.

Harbert, Wayne (1995). "Binding Theory, Control and PRO." In Webelhuth (1995), 177–240.

Hardt, Daniel (1993). "Verb Phrase Ellipsis: Form, Meaning and Processing." Ph.D. thesis, University of Pennsylvania.

Harley, Heidi, and Elisabeth Ritter (2002). "Person and Number in Pronouns: a Feature-Geometric Analysis."*Language* 78(3):482–526.

Hastings, Rachel, Brendan Jackson, and Zsofia Zvolenski, eds. (2001). *Proceedings from Semantics and Linguistic Theory XI*, Ithaca, Cornell Linguistics Club.

Hawkins, John A., ed. (1988). *Explaining Language Universals*. Oxford: Basil Blackwell.

Hegarty, Michael, Jeanette K. Gundel, and Kaja Borthen (2001). "Information Structure and the Accessibility of Clausally Introduced Referents." *Theoretical Linguistics* 27(2/3):163–186.

Heim, Irene (1982). "The Semantics of Definite and Indefinite Noun Phrases." Ph.D. thesis, University of Massachusetts, Amherst.

(1983). "File Change Semantics and the Familiarity Theory of Definiteness." In Rainer Bäurle, Christoph Schwartze, and Armin von Stechow, eds., *Meaning, Use, and Interpretation of Language*, 164–189. Berlin: de Gruyter.

(1990). "E-Type Pronouns and Donkey Anaphora." *Linguistics and Philosophy* 13:137–177.

(1993). "Anaphora and Semantic Interpretation: a Reinterpretation of Reinhart's Approach." 205–246. SfS Report 07-93, Universität Tübingen. Published in Sauerland and Percus (1998).

(1997). "Predicates or Formulas? Evidence from Ellipsis." In Aaron Lawson, ed., *Proceedings of Semantics and Linguistics Theory VII*, 197–221. Ithaca, NY: Cornell University.

Heim, Irene, and Angelika Kratzer (1998). *Semantics in Generative Grammar*. Oxford: Blackwell.

Heim, Irene, Howard Lasnik, and Robert May (1991). "Reciprocity and Plurality." *Linguistic Inquiry* 22:63–101.

Hellan, Lars (1988). *Reflexives in Norwegian and the Theory of Grammar*. Dordrecht: Foris.

(1992). "Containment and Connectedness Anaphors." In Koster and Reuland (1992a), 27–48.

Hestvik, Arild (1991). "Subjectless Binding Domains." *Natural Language and Linguistic Theory* 9(3):455–496.

(1992). "Strict Reflexives and the Subordination Effect." In Berman and Hestvik (1992), 1–50.

Heycock, Caroline (1995). "Asymmetries in Reconstruction." *Linguistic Inquiry* 26(4):547–570.

Heycock, Caroline, and Anthony Kroch (1999). "Pseudocleft Connectedness: Implications for the LF Interface Level." *Linguistic Inquiry* 30(3):365–397.

Higginbotham, James (1980a). "Anaphora and GB: Some Preliminary Remarks." In *Proceedings of North Eastern Linguistics Society X*, 223–235. University of Ottawa.

(1980b). "Pronouns and Bound Variables." *Linguistic Inquiry* 11(4):679–708.

(1983). "Logical Form, Binding, and Nominals." *Linguistic Inquiry* 14:395–420.

(1985). "On Semantics." *Linguistic Inquiry* 14:547–593.

(1987). "On the Varieties of Cross-Reference." In A. Cardinaletti, G. Cinque, and G. Giusti, eds., *Constituent Structure. Papers from the 1987 GLOW Conference*, Annali di ca' Foscari. Rivista della Facoltà di Lingue e Letterature Straniere Dell' Università di Venezia, 123–142.

Higginbotham, James, and Robert May (1981). "Questions, Quantifiers and Crossing." *The Linguistic Review* 1:41–80.

Hirschberg, Julia, and Gregory Ward (1991). "Accent and Bound Anaphora." *Cognitive Linguistics* 2(2):101–121.

Hole, Daniel (2002). "Spell-bound? Accounting for Unpredictable Self-forms in J.K. Rowling's Harry Potter Stories." *Zeitschrift für Anglistik und Amerikanistik* 50:285–300.

Hole, Daniel, and Volker Gast (2003). "On Paradigmatic (In)coherence in Romance and Germanic Reflexives." In Gunkel *et al.* (2003), 75–89.

Hornstein, Norbert (1995). *Logical Form – from GB to Minimalism*. Oxford: Blackwell.

Huang, C.-T. James (1982). "Logical Relations in Chinese and the Theory of Grammar." Ph.D. thesis, MIT.

(1983). "A Note on Binding Theory." *Linguistic Inquiry* 14(3):554–561.

(1993). "Reconstruction and the Structure of VP: Some Theoretical Consequences." *Linguistic Inquiry* 24:103–138.

Huang, C.-T. James, and C.-C. Jane Tang (1992). "The Local Nature of the Long-Distance Reflexive in Chinese." In Koster and Reuland (1992a), 263–282.

Huang, Yan (2000). *Anaphora – A Cross-Linguistic Study*. Oxford University Press.

Huffman, Franklin E. (1970). *Modern Spoken Cambodian*. New Haven, Conn.: Yale University Press.

Iatridou, Sabine (1986). "An Anaphor not Bound in its Governing Category." *Linguistic Inquiry* 17(4):766–772.

Iida, Masayo, Stephen Wechsler, and Draga Zec, eds. (1987). *Working Papers in Grammatical Theory and Discourse*. No. 11, CSLI Lecture Notes. Stanford: Center for the Studies of Languages and Information.

Jackendoff, Ray (1972). *Semantics in Generative Grammar*. Cambridge, Mass.: MIT Press.

(1990). *Semantic Structures*. Cambridge, Mass.: MIT Press.

Jackendoff, Ray, and Peter W. Culicover (1995). "*Something Else* for the Binding Theory." *Linguistic Inquiry* 26(2):249–275.

Jacobs, Joachim, Arnim von Stechow, Wolfgang Sternefeld, and Theo Vennemann, eds. (1993). *Handbuch Syntax – Ein internationales Handbuch zeitgenössischer Forschung*. Berlin: De Gruyter.

Jacobson, Pauline (1977). "The Syntax of Crossing Coreference Sentences." Ph.D. thesis, U.C. Berkeley. (Published 1980, Garland Press).

(1992). "Antecedent Contained Deletion in a Variable Free Semantics." In *Proceedings of Semantics and Linguistics Theory II*, 193–213.

(1994). "Binding Connectivity in Copular Sentences." In Mandy Harvey and Lynn Santelmann, eds., *Proceedings of SALT IV*, 161–178.

(1996). "The Syntax/Semantics Interface in Categorial Grammar." In Shalom Lappin, ed., *The Handbook of Contemporary Semantic Theory*, 89–116. Oxford: Blackwell.

(1999). "Towards a Variable Free Semantics." *Linguistics and Philosophy* 22:117–184.

(2000). "Paycheck Pronouns, Bach-Peters Sentences, and Variable Free Semantics." *Natural Language Semantics* 8(2):77–155.

Kameyama, M. (1984). "Subjective/Logophoric Bound Anaphor *Zibun*." In J. Drogo, V. Mishra, and D. Testen, eds., *Papers from the 12th Regional Meeting*. Chicago Linguistic Society.

Kamp, Hans (1981). "A Theory of Truth and Semantic Representation." In J. A. G. Groenendijk, T. M. V. Janssen, and M. B. J. Stokhof, eds., *Formal Methods in the Study of Language*, 277–322. Amsterdam: Mathematisch Centrum.

Kamp, Hans, and Uwe Reyle (1993). *From Discourse to Logic. Introduction to Modeltheoretic Semantics of Natural Language, Formal Logic and Discourse Representation Theory*. No. 42, Studies in Linguistics and Philosophy. Dordrecht: Kluwer Academic Publishers.

Kaplan, David (1977). "Demonstratives. An Essay on the Semantics, Logic, Metaphysics, and Epistemology of Demonstratives and Other Indexicals." MS, UCLA; reprinted in Almog *et al.* (1989).

Katada, Fusa (1991). "The LF Representation of Anaphors." *Linguistic Inquiry* 22(2):287–313.

Keenan, Edward L. (1972). "On Semantically Based Grammar." *Linguistic Inquiry* 3:413–461.

(1974). "The Functional Principle: Generalizing the Notion of 'Subject Of'." In *Chicago Linguistic Society*, No. 10, 298–309.

(1988). "On Semantics and the Binding Theory." In Hawkins (1988), 105–144.

(2002). "Explaining the Creation of Reflexive Pronouns in English." In Donka Minkova and Robert Stockwell, eds., *Studies in the History of English: A Millenial Perspective*, 325–355. Berlin: Mouton de Gruyter.

Keenan, Edward L., and Jean Paul Razafimamonjy (2001). "Reciprocals in Malagasy." MS. UCLA.

Keenan, Edward L., and Edward P. Stabler (1995). "There is More Than One Language." In Tsoulas and Nash (1995).

Kehler, Andrew (2002). *Coherence, Reference, and the Theory of Grammar*. Stanford: Center for the Studies of Language and Informations.

Keller, Frank, and Ash Asudeh (2001). "Constraints on Linguistic Coreference: Structural vs. Pragmatic Factors." In *Proceedings of the 23rd Annual Conference of the Cognitive Science Society*, 483–488. Mahwah, NJ: Lawrence Erlbaum Associates.

Kemmer, Suzanne (1993). *The Middle Voice*. No. 23, Typological Studies in Language. Amsterdam and Philadelphia: John Benjamins.

Kennedy, Christopher, and Jeffrey Lidz (2001). "A (Covert) Long Distance Anaphor in English." In Megerdoomian and Barel (2001).

Kiparsky, Paul (2002). "Disjoint Reference and the Typology of Pronouns." In Ingrid Kaufmann and Barbara Stiebels, eds., *More than Words*, Studia Grammatica 53. Berlin: Akademie Verlag.

Kitagawa, Yoshihisa (1991). "Copying Identity." *Natural Language and Linguistic Theory* 9:497–536.

Klein, Ewan H., and Ivan A. Sag (1985). "Type-Driven Translation." *Linguistics and Philosophy* 8:163–201.

König, Ekkehard, and Peter Siemund (2000). "Intensifiers and Reflexives: a Typological Perspective." In Frajzyngier and Curl (1999b), 41–74.

König, Ekkehard, and Letizia Vezzosi (2002). "Strategies of Reflexivization and the Meaning of Predicates." In W. Bisang and B. Wiener (eds.), *Grammaticalization and the Background*. Berlin: Mouton de Gruyter.

Koopman, Hilda, and Dominique Sportiche (1983). "Variables and the Bijection Principle." *The Linguistic Review* 2:139–160.

Koster, Jan (1984). "Reflexives in Dutch." In Guéron *et al.* (1984), 141–167.

Koster, Jan, and Eric Reuland, eds. (1992a). *Long-Distance Anaphora*. Cambridge University Press.

    (1992b). "Long-Distance Anaphora: an Overview." In Koster and Reuland (1992a).

Krifka, Manfred (2004). "Semantic and Pragmatic Conditions for the Dative Alternation." *Korean Journal of English Language and Linguistics* 4:1–32.

Kripke, Saul A. (1972). *Naming and Necessity*. Cambridge, Mass.: Harvard University Press.

Kuno, Susumo (1987). *Functional Syntax – Anaphora, Discourse and Empathy*. Chicago University Press.

Landau, Idan (2001a). "Control and Extraposition: the Case of Super-equi." *Natural Language and Linguistic Theory* 19:109–152.

    (2001b). *Elements of Control – Structure and Meaning in Infinitival Constructions*. Studies in Natural Language and Linguistic Theory 51. Dordrecht: Kluwer.

Landman, Fred (1989). "Groups 1 & 2." *Linguistics and Philosophy* 12:559–605, 723–744.

    (2000). *Events and Plurality*. Studies in Linguistics and Philosophy 76. Dordrecht: Kluwer.

Langendoen, D. Terence (1978). "The Logic of Plurality." *Linguistic Inquiry* 9:177–197.

Lappin, Shalom (1996). *The Handbook of Contemporary Semantic Theory*. Oxford: Blackwell.

Larson, Richard K. (1987). "Quantifying into NP." Unpubl. MS.

    (1988). "On the Double Object Construction." *Linguistic Inquiry* 19:335–391.

Lasersohn, Peter (1995). *Plurality, Conjunction and Events*. Dordrecht: Kluwer.

Lasnik, Howard (1981). "On Two Recent Treatments of Disjoint Reference." *Journal of Linguistic Research* 1:48–58.

(1986). "On the Necessity of Binding Conditions." In Freidin (1986), 7–28. MIT Press. Repr. as ch. 9 in Lasnik (1989).

(1989). *Essays on Anaphora*. Kluwer.

Lasnik, Howard, and Robert Freidin (1981). "Disjoint Reference and *Wh*-trace." *Linguistic Inquiry* 12:39–53. repr. as ch. 5 in Lasnik (1989).

Lasnik, Howard, and Tim Stowell (1991). "Weakest Crossover." *Linguistic Inquiry* 22(4):687–720.

Lasnik, Howard, and Juan Uriagereka (1988). *A Course in GB Syntax*. Cambridge, Mass.: MIT Press.

Lebeaux, David (1983). "A Distributional Difference between Reciprocals and Reflexives." *Linguistic Inquiry* 14(3):723–730.

(1985). "Locality and Anaphoric Binding." *The Linguistic Review* 4(4):343–363.

(1988). "Language Acquisition and the Form of the Grammar." Ph.D. thesis, University of Massachusetts, Amherst.

(1990). "Relative Clauses, Licensing, amd the Nature of the Derivation." In Juli Carter, Rose-Marie Déchaine, Bill Philip, and Tim Sherer, eds., *Proceedings of North Eastern Linguistics Society 20*, 318–332. Graduate Linguistics Student Association, University of Massachusetts, Amherst.

Levinson, Stephen C. (1987). "Pragmatics and the Grammar of Anaphora: a Partial Pragmatic Reduction of Binding and Control Phenomena." *Journal of Linguistics* 23:379–434.

(1991). "Pragmatic Reduction of the Binding Conditions Revisited." *Journal of Linguistics* 27:107–161.

(2000). *Presumptive Meanings*. Cambridge, Mass.: Bradford.

Lichtenberk, Frantisek (1985). "Multiple Uses of Reciprocal Constructions." *Australian Journal of Linguistics* 5:19–41.

(1999). "Reciprocals without Reflexives." In Frajzyngier and Curl (1999a), 31–62.

Lidz, Jeffrey (1995). "Morphological Reflexive Marking: Evidence from Kannada." *Linguistic Inquiry* 26(4):705–710.

(2001). "Condition R." *Linguistic Inquiry* 32(1):123–140.

Link, Godehard (1983). "The Logical Analysis of Plurals and Mass Terms: a Lattice-theoretic Approach." In Bäuerle et al. (1983), 302–323. Repr. as ch. 1 in Link (1999).

(1999). *Algebraic Structures in Language and Philosophy*. Stanford: Center for the Studies of Language and Information.

Mahajan, Anoop (1990). "The A/Ā-Distinction and Movement Theory." Ph.D. thesis, MIT.

Maling, Joan (1984). "Non-Clause-Bounded Reflexives in Modern Icelandic." *Linguistics and Philosophy* 7:211–241.

Manning, Christopher D., and Ivan A. Sag (1999). "Dissociations Between Argument Structure and Grammatical Relations." In Jean-Pierre Koenig, Gert Webelhuth, and Andreas Kathol, eds., *Lexical and Constructional Aspects of Linguistic Explanation*, 63–78. Center for the Studies of Language and Information Publications.

Manzini, Rita, and Kenneth Wexler (1987). "Parameters, Binding Theory and Learnability." *Linguistic Inquiry* 18(3):413–444.

Marantz, Alec, and Tim Stowell, eds. (1982). *MIT Working Papers in Linguistics 4*.

May, Robert (1977). "The Grammar of Quantification." Ph.D. thesis, MIT.

(1985). *Logical Form*. Cambridge, Mass.: MIT Press.

(1988). "Bound Variable Anaphora." In *Mental Representations*, 85–104. Cambridge University Press.

McGregor, William (1999). "Reflexive and Reciprocal Constructions in Nyulnyulan Languages." In Frajzyngier and Curl (1999a), 85–122.

Mchombo, Sam A. (1993a). "On the Binding of the Reflexive and the Reciprocal in Chicheŵa." In Mchombo (1993b), 181–207.

ed. (1993b). *Theoretical Aspects of Bantu Grammar*. Stanford: Center for the Studies of Languages and Information.

Megerdoomian, K., and L. A. Barel, eds. (2001). *Proceedings of West Coast Conference in Formal Linguistics 2001*, Somerville, Mass.: Cascadilla Press.

Mohanan, K. P. (1982). "Grammatical Relations and Anaphora in Malayalam." In Marantz and Stowell (1982).

Mohanan, Tara (1990). "Arguments in Hindi." Ph.D. thesis, Stanford University.

Müller, Gereon (1993). "On Deriving Movement Type Asymmetries." Ph.D. thesis, Tübingen. Published as Müller (1995).

(1995). *A-bar Syntax. A Study of Movement Types*. Studies in Generative Grammar. Vol. 42. Berlin: Mouton de Gruyter.

Neale, Stephen (1990). *Descriptions*. Cambridge, Mass.: MIT Press.

Pesetsky, David (1987). "Binding Problems With Experiencer Verbs." *Linguistic Inquiry* 18(1).

Pica, Pierre (1983). "On the Distinction Between Argumental and Non-Argumental Anaphors." In de Geest and Putsey (1984), 185–193.

(1984). "Subject, Tense and Truth: Towards a Modular Approach to Binding." In Guéron *et al.* (1984), 259–291.

(1987). "On the Nature of the Reflexivization Cycle." In *Proceedings of NELS 17*. Graduate Linguistic Student Association, Amherst.

Pollard, Carl, and Ivan Sag (1992). "Anaphors in English and the Scope of Binding Theory." *Linguistic Inquiry* 23:261–303.

(1994). *Head-Driven Phrase Structure Grammar*. University of Chicago Press.

Postal, Paul (1971). *Cross-Over Phenomena*. New York: Holt, Rinehart & Winston.

(1993). "Remarks on Weak Crossover Effects." *Linguistic Inquiry* 24(3):539–556.

Potts, Christopher (2001). "Three Types of Transderivational Constraint." In Séamas Mac Bhloscaidh, ed., *Syntax at Santa Cruz*, Vol. 3, 21–40. Linguistics Department, U.C. Santa Cruz.

Progovac, Ljiljana (1992). "Relativized SUBJECT: Long-distance Reflexives without Movement." *Linguistic Inquiry* 23(4):671–680.

Pulleyblank, Douglas (1986). "Clitics in Yoruba." In Borer (1986), 43–64.

(1990). "Yoruba." In Comrie (1990), 971–990.

Pullum, Geoffrey (1986). "On the Relations of IDV-Command and Government." In *Proceedings of the West Coast Conference on Formal Linguistics 5*, 192–206.

Rappaport, Gilbert C. (1986). "On Anaphor Binding in Russian." *Natural Language and Linguistic Theory* 4(1):97–120.

Reinders-Machowska, Ewa (1992). "Binding in Polish." In Koster and Reuland (1992a), 137–150.

Reinhart, Tanya (1976). "The Syntactic Domain of Anaphora." Ph.D. thesis, MIT.

(1982). "Pragmatics and Linguistics: an Analysis of Sentence Topics." *Philosophica* 27:53–94.

(1983a). *Anaphora and Semantic Interpretation*. University of Chicago Press.

(1983b). "Coreference and Anaphora: a Restatement of the Anaphora Question." *Linguistics and Philosophy* 6:47–88.

(1987). "Specifier and Operator Binding." In Eric J. Reuland and Alice G. B. ter Meulen, eds., *The Representation of (In)definiteness*, 130–167. Cambridge, Mass.: MIT Press.

Reinhart, Tanya, and Eric Reuland (1992). "Anaphors and Logophors: an Argument Structure Perspective." In Koster and Reuland (1992a), 283–334.

(1993). "Reflexivity." *Linguistic Inquiry* 24(4):657–720.

Reuland, Eric (2001). "Primitives of Binding." *Linguistic Inquiry* 32(3):439–492.

Rizzi, Luigi (1989). "On the Anaphor–Agreement Effect." *Rivista di Linguistica* 27–42.

Roberts, Craige (1987). "Modal Subordination, Anaphora and Distributivity." Ph.D. thesis, University of Massachusetts, Amherst (published 1990, NY): Garland.

(1989). "Modal Subordination and Pronominal Anaphora in Discourse." *Linguistics and Philosophy* 12:683–721.

(1991). "Distributivity and Reciprocal Distributivity." In *Proceedings of SALT I*, 209–229. Ithaca: Department of Modern Languages and Literatures Publications.

(1996). "Anaphora in Intensional Contexts." In Lappin (1996), 215–246.

Roeper, Tom, and Edwin Williams, eds. (1987). *Parameter Setting*. Dordrecht: Reidel.

Rooth, Mats (1985). *Association with Focus*. Ph.D. thesis, University of Massachusetts, Amherst.

(1992a). "Reduction Redundancy and Ellipsis Redundancy." In Berman and Hestvik (1992).

(1992b). "A Theory of Focus Interpretation." *Natural Language Semantics* 1:75–116.

Ross, John R. (1970). "On Declarative Sentences." In Roderick A. Jacobs and Peter S. Rosenbaum, eds., *Readings in English Transformational Grammar*. Waltham, Mass.: Ginn and Company.

(1973). "Nouniness." In Osamu Fujimura, ed., *Three Dimensions of Linguistic Theory*, 137–257. Tokyo: TEC Company.

Rullman, Hotze (2004). "First and Second Person Pronouns as Bound Variables." *Linguistic Inquiry* 35:159–168.

Runner, Jeffrey T., Rachel S. Sussman, and Michael K. Tanenhas (2002). "Logophors in Possessed Picture Noun Phrases." In Line Mikkelsen and Chris Potts, eds., *Proceedings of West Coast Conference in Formal Linguistics 21*, 401–414. Somerville, Mass.: Cascadilla Press.

Ruys, E. G. (2000). "Weak Crossover as a Scope Phenomenon." *Linguistic Inquiry* 31:513–539.

(2004). "A Note on Weakest Crossover." *Linguistic Inquiry* 35:124–140.

Safir, Ken (1984). "Multiple Variable Binding." *Linguistic Inquiry* 15:603–638.

(1997). "Symmetry and Unity in the Theory of Anaphora." In Bennis *et al.* (1997), 341–379.

(1999). "Vehicle Change and Reconstruction in A-Chains." *Linguistic Inquiry* 30(4):587–620.

Sag, Ivan A. (1976). "Deletion and Logical Form." Ph.D. thesis, MIT.

Sag, Ivan A., and Carl Pollard (1991). "An Integrated Theory of Argument Control." *Language* 67:63–113.

Sag, Ivan A., and Thomas Wasow (1999). *Syntactic Theory – A Formal Introduction*. CSLI Publications.

Sauerland, Uli (1998). "Plurals, Derived Predicates, and Reciprocals." In Sauerland and Percus (1998), 177–204. MIT Working Papers in Linguistics.

(2000). "The Content of Pronouns: Evidence from Focus." In Tanya Matthews and Brendan Jackson, eds., *The Proceedings of SALT 10*, 167–184. Ithaca, NY: Cornell Linguistics Club Publications.

Sauerland, Uli, and Orin Percus (1998). *The Interpretive Tract*. MIT Working Papers in Linguistics 25.

Saxon, Leslie (1984). "Disjoint Anaphora and the Binding Theory." In *Proceedings of the West Coast Conference on Formal Linguistics 3*, 242–251. Stanford University.

Schachter, Paul (1974). *Studies in the Structure of Toba Batak*. Technical Report 5, UCLA Occasional Papers in Linguistics.

Schlenker, Philippe (1999). "Propositional Attitudes and Indexicality." Ph.D. thesis, MIT.

Schwarzschild, Roger (1996). *Pluralities*. Kluwer.

(1999). "GIVENness, AvoidF and Other Constraints on the Placement of Accent." *Natural Language Semantics* 7(2):141–177.

Seely, Daniel T. (1993). "Binding Plural Pronominals." In Katherine Beals *et al.*, eds., *CLS 29: Papers from the 29th Regional Meeting, Vol. II*, 305–317. Chicago: University of Chicago.

Sells, Peter (1987). "Aspects of Logophoricity." *Linguistic Inquiry* 18:445–479.

Sells, Peter, Annie Zaenen, and Draga Zec (1987). "Reflexivization Variation: Relations between Syntax, Semantics, and Lexical Structure." In Iida *et al.* (1987), 169–238.

Sharvit, Yael (1996a). "Functional Dependencies and Indirect Binding." In Teresa Galloway and Justin Spence, eds., *Semantics and Linguistic Theory VI*, 227–244. Cornell University, Ithaca, NY: Cornell Linguistics Club Publications.

    (1996b). "The Syntax and Semantics of Functional Relative Clauses." Ph.D. thesis, Rutgers University, New Brunswick, NJ.

    (1999). "Functional Relative Clauses." *Linguistics and Philosophy* 22:447–478.

Sigurðsson, H. (1986). "Moods and (Long-Distance) Reflexives in Icelandic." In *Working Papers in Scandinavian Syntax 25*. Trondheim.

Sperber, Dan, and Deirdre Wilson (1995). *Relevance: Communication and Cognition*. Blackwell.

Sportiche, Dominique (1985). "Remarks on Cross-Over." *Linguistic Inquiry* 16:460–471.

    (1986). "*Zibun*." *Linguistic Inquiry* 17(2):369–374.

Steinbach, Markus (2002). *Middle Voice. A Comparative Study of the Syntax–Semantics Interface of German*. Linguistik Aktuell/Linguistics Today 50. Amsterdam: Benjamins.

Sternefeld, Wolfgang (1992). *Voice Phrases and Their Specifiers*. Technical Report 2, Arbeitspapiere des SFB 340, Tübingen University.

    (1993). "Anaphoric Reference." In Jacobs *et al.* (1993), 953–963.

    (1998). "Reciprocity and Cumulative Predication." *Natural Language Semantics* 6:303–337.

Tang, Chih-Chen Jane (1989). "Chinese Reflexives." *Natural Language and Linguistic Theory* 7(1):93–121.

Thráinsson, Höskuldur (1992). "Long-Distance Reflexives and the Typology of NPs." In Koster and Reuland (1992a), 49–75.

Toman, Jindřich (1992). "Anaphors in Binary Trees: an Analysis of Czech Reflexives." In Koster and Reuland (1992a), 151–170.

Tomioka, Satoshi (1997). "Focusing Effects and NP Interpretation in VP Ellipsis." Ph.D. thesis, University of Massachusetts, Amherst.

    (1999). "A Sloppy Identity Puzzle." *Natural Language Semantics* 7:217–241.

Trúóng Văn Chình (1970). *Structure de la Langue Vietnamienne*. Paris: Imprimerie Nationale.

Tsoulas, George, and Lea Nash, eds. (1995). *Proceedings of Langues et Grammaire I*. Paris: University of Paris VIII.

van Gelderen, Elly (2000). *A History of English Reflexive Pronouns*. Linguistik Aktuell 39. Amsterdam and Philadelphia: John Benjamins.

van Riemsdijk, Henk, and Edwin Williams (1981). "NP Structure." *The Linguistic Review* 1:171–217.

    (1983). *Introduction to the Theory of Grammar*. Cambridge, Mass.: MIT Press.

van Rooy, Robert (1997). *Attitudes and Changing Contexts*. Ph.D. thesis, IMS Stuttgart.

    (2001). "Exhaustiveness in Dynamic Semantics: Referential and Descriptive Pronouns." *Linguistics and Philosophy* 24:621–657.

van Steenbergen, Marlies (1992). "Long-distance Binding in Finnish." In Koster and Reuland (1992a), 231–244.

Vanden Wyngaerd, Guido (1989). "Object Shift as an A-Movement Rule." In *MIT Working Papers in Linguistics*, Vol. 11. MIT.

Vikner, Sten (1985). "Parameters of Binder and of Binding Category in Danish." *Working Papers in Scandinavian Syntax* 23:1–61.

Vitale, Anthony J. (1982). *Swahili Syntax*. Dordrecht: Foris.

von Heusinger, Klaus (1997). *Salienz und Referenz – Der Epsilonoperator in der Semantik der Nominalphrase und anaphorischer Pronomen*. Studia Grammatica 43. Berlin: Akademie Verlag.

Walker, Marilyn A., Aravind K. Joshi, and Ellen F. Prince (1998). *Centering Theory in Discourse*. Oxford University Press.

Webelhuth, Gert (1995). *Government and Binding Theory and the Minimalist Program*. Oxford: Blackwell.

Wechsler, Stephen, and I Wayan Arka (1998). "Syntactic Ergativity in Balinese: an Argument Structure Based Theory." *Natural Language and Linguistic Theory* 16:387–441.

Wexler, Kenneth, and Rita Manzini (1987). "Parameters and Learnability in Binding Theory." In Roeper and Williams (1987), 41–76.

Wilkins, Wendy (1988a). *Thematic Relations, Syntax and Semantics*. Vol. 21. New York: Elsevier.

(1988b). "Thematic Structure and Reflexivization." In Wilkins (1988a), 191–213.

Williams, Kemp (1988). "Exceptional Behavior of Anaphors in Albanian." *Linguistic Inquiry* 19(1):161–168.

Woolford, Ellen (1999). "More on the Anaphor Agreement Effect." *Linguistic Inquiry* 30(2):257–287.

Yang, Dong-Whee (1983). "The Extended Binding Theory of Anaphors." *Language Research* 19(2):169–192.

Zribi-Hertz, Anne (1989). "Anaphor Binding and Narrative Point of View: English Reflexive Pronouns in Sentence and Discourse." *Language* 65(4):695–727.

Index